Rethinking Black German Studies

Studies in Modern German and Austrian Literature

Series Editors

Professor Robert Vilain, University of Bristol
Dr Benedict Schofield, King's College London
Dr Alexandra Lloyd, University of Oxford

Volume 7

PETER LANG
Oxford • Bern • Berlin • Bruxelles • New York • Wien

Rethinking Black German Studies

Approaches, Interventions and Histories

Edited by Tiffany N. Florvil
and Vanessa D. Plumly

PETER LANG

Oxford • Bern • Berlin • Bruxelles • New York • Wien

Bibliographic information published by Die Deutsche Nationalbibliothek
Die Deutsche Nationalbibliothek lists this publication in the Deutsche Nationalbibliografie;
detailed bibliographic data is available on the Internet at http://dnb.d-nb.de.

A catalogue record for this book is available from The British Library,
Great Britain, and from The Library of Congress, USA
Library of Congress Cataloging-in-Publication Data:

Names: Florvil, Tiffany Nicole, editor.
Title: Rethinking Black German studies : Approaches, Interventions and
    Histories / Tiffany N. Florvil and Vanessa D. Plumly (eds).
Description: New York : Peter Lang, 2018. | Series: Studies in Modern German
    and Austrian Literature ; 7 | Includes bibliographical references and
    index.
Identifiers: LCCN 2017029893 | ISBN 9783034322256 (alk. paper)
Subjects: LCSH: German literature--Black authors--History and criticism. |
    Austrian literature--Black authors--History and criticism. |
    Africans--Germany--Study and teaching. | Africans--Austria--Study and
    teaching. | Africans--Germany--Music--History and criticism. |
    Africans--Austria--Music--History and criticism.
Classification: LCC PT170.A37 R48 2017 | DDC 830.9/896--dc23 LC record available at
    https://lccn.loc.gov/2017029893
Cover Art by patricia vester | spotaday.blog

ISSN 2235-3488
ISBN 978-3-0343-2225-6 (print) • ISBN 978-1-78707-851-2 (ePDF)
ISBN 978-1-78707-852-9 (ePub) • ISBN 978-1-78707-853-6 (mobi)

© Peter Lang AG 2018

Published by Peter Lang Ltd, International Academic Publishers,
52 St Giles, Oxford, OX1 3LU, United Kingdom
oxford@peterlang.com, www.peterlang.com

This publication has been peer reviewed.

Printed in Germany

Contents

vi

Illustrations

Permission to reprint all images in Chapter 7 obtained from
Gisela Sorge and Management Samy Deluxe.

Acknowledgments

It seems only fitting that this book evolved out of our very first meeting in Berlin on 29 August 2011, when Silke Hackenesch, a member of the research network Black Diaspora and Germany, introduced us at the ceremonial unveiling of the May Ayim memorial plaque at the May-Ayim-Ufer, two years after its official renaming. Without Silke bringing the two of us together, this collaborative volume and many of our other academic and activist endeavors, including the seminars that we co-organized and co-facilitated at the German Studies Association (GSA) conferences in 2014 and 2015 and the establishment of the Black Diasporic Studies Network at the GSA, with the assistance of professor emeritus at the University of Massachusetts Amherst, Sara Lennox, would never have come to fruition. Our co-operation as scholars has been seamless and easy, and we complement each other quite well. In many ways, it seems as if we have always been destined to work together. We are an excellent team and value each other's scholarship and friendship, as well as the impact that we have had on one another's lives; indeed, we are in this together. Our efforts to engage race publicly within German Studies serve as an intervention, and the volume is a source of optimism for us, given the current nativist climate in the United States and across Europe. While this is our first collaboratively published work, it certainly will not be the last one you will see from us. We will continue to foreground the importance of Black German Studies (BGS), as well as the broader scholarship on race, racialization, racial difference and the Black/African Diaspora in the field of German Studies.

Yet, this volume owes a considerable debt to the cultural contributions, activist work and intellectual interventions of Black Germans such as Fatima El-Tayeb, Philipp Khabo Koepsell, Alexander Weheliye, Peggy Piesche, Katharina Oguntoye, Ricky Reiser, Lara-Sophie Milagro and Maisha Auma, to name a few. Without their consistent and incisive work on both sides of the Atlantic, this volume would not exist. To them, we owe our sincere appreciation. We would also like to thank scholars like

Michelle M. Wright, Tina Campt, Sara Lennox and others, who have helped to push the field of BGS in exciting new directions throughout the years. This volume also owes its existence to them.

We want to express our gratitude to the participants in both of our GSA seminars. They helped to make the seminars meaningful and energizing. Many of the participants are contributing to the field of Black German Studies and have been supportive of our work throughout the years. Sadly, there are far too many of them to name. To Rosemarie Peña, we owe our thanks, especially for her establishment of the Black German Heritage and Research Association and her countless efforts to forge a space for Black German Studies that includes the voices of Black Germans. Her dedication to the field has allowed us to build on the network's conferences and scholarly production and help increase its reach.

We must also thank the amazing contributors to this volume. We certainly appreciated their patience and willingness to work with us. They integrated all of our feedback, producing astute and critical pieces that we are thrilled to include in the volume.

We also want to express our appreciation of Patrica Vester, a Black German graphic artist who designed the beautiful and inspiring cover art for this book, as well as the chapter break images. We are grateful that the book's exterior reflects the internal content. We are also happy that we can share the beauty of her work with others.

Finally, we want to thank everyone at Peter Lang, especially Laurel Plapp for supporting our project. Laurel's confidence and her initial suggestion that we co-edit a volume as two junior academics is what empowered us to pursue our work on this volume. Her understanding and encouragement (digitally and face-to-face at the GSA) has made the process of publishing this volume enjoyable.

I, Vanessa, would also like to thank Dr. Tanja Nusser for her unending academic and personal support, as well as Mercedes Rooney, Dr. Anne R. Roschelle, and Dr. Sunita Bose for their guidance, mentorship, friendship and boundless support and concern for my academic career. You have helped sustain me. My family has always encouraged me to pursue my career and become the person I am. Last, but certainly not least, I thank my friend and colleague Tiffany for her unending passion, which continually inspires me and others, for her intellectual commitment to the field, and for her trust in me. You have made this process seamless.

I, Tiffany, would also like to thank my mom, who has made so many sacrifices that have enabled me to take this academic path. She has continued to support all of my academic endeavors by offering prayers, encouragement, love, and support each step of the way. My husband and best friend, Dave, has been so supportive, especially when I became discouraged with the process. He has continued to lend his ear and assisted me in so many ways. For that, I am truly grateful. I want to thank my son, Isaac, who came into my life halfway through this project. His arrival has transformed my life and made me a better person. I am grateful that I am his mother and enjoy life so much more because of him. Finally, I want to thank my colleague and friend Vanessa, for being such a fabulous collaborator, advocate and scholar. Her dedication and critical editorial eye has only helped to make this process fun and rewarding. I am confident this volume would not be as dynamic without you!

Tiffany N. Florvil and Vanessa D. Plumly
Albuquerque, New Mexico and Kingston, New York
30 June 2018

TIFFANY N. FLORVIL AND VANESSA D. PLUMLY

Introduction: Rethinking Black German Studies

Integrating Theory and Praxis

In the autumn of 2014 and 2015, as the German Studies Association (GSA) met to convene for its annual conferences, something seemingly radical appeared on the program. At the 2014 conference in Kansas City, Missouri, a three-day seminar titled 'Black German Studies: Then and Now' was held.[1] Focusing our seminar on the themes of 'Practices, Productions and Progressions', we sought to examine the field as a critical, hermeneutic point of inquiry and to thematically trace its evolution over the last three decades. During the course of the seminar, questioning the title's implicit delineation of a past distinct from the present made it clear that it is impossible to separate the intertwining of the two temporalities or to discuss the Black/African[2] Diaspora in Germany from a strictly teleological and,

---

1   'Black German Studies Then and Now' Seminar, German Studies Association Conference, 18–21 September 2014, Kansas City, Missouri.

2   We are fully aware that Black or African Diaspora evokes different meanings in current studies on both sides of the Atlantic. For some, the Black Diaspora offers a more inclusive discussion that can be but is not necessarily bounded up with the continent or narratives of slavery and colonialism. In this way, the Black Diaspora allows for a

indeed, Western perspective with one origin point.[3] Above all, we hoped that our first seminar would initiate exchanges and encourage creative and collaborative work by academics and non-academics alike that would not only underscore the experiences of Black Germans, but also continue to complicate the notions of Blackness, politics, racialized and gendered discourses, as well as diasporic identity across many affective, temporal and spatial borders. In addition, we envisioned that this seminar would help to create an inclusive intellectual community and space and to give this type of critical work on race, racialization and intersectionality a more visible presence at the GSA. Little did the seminar participants or the attendees of the GSA conference know at the time, but activist and writer Sharon Dodua Otoo, who became the first Black British female author to win the prestigious Ingeborg Bachmann Prize for literature in 2016, was also in attendance.[4]

The following year, the GSA conference took place in Arlington, Virginia, and delivered yet another opportunity for a follow-up seminar. This time the seminar's theme revolved around 'Political Activism in the Black European Diaspora: From Theory to Praxis', and it included different approaches to social, political and cultural activism that engaged a variety

---

more holistic approach. The usage of African Diaspora, for some, certainly reveals an explicit connection to the continent as well as the other 'routes and roots' (Gilroy) of the Diaspora. In our volume, some of the contributors use 'Black' while others use 'African'. We allowed this diverse usage to exist in order to further complicate our understandings of narratives on the Diaspora and to open up more possibilities for theorizing these terms.

3   See, for example, Michelle M. Wright, 'Middle Passage Blackness and Its Diasporic Discontents: The Case for a Post-war Epistemology', in Eve Rosenhaft, and Robbie Aitken, eds, *Africa in Europe: Studies in Transnational Practice in the Long Twentieth Century* (Liverpool: Liverpool University Press, 2013), 217–33.

4   'Britin Sharon Dodua Otoo gewinnt den Bachmann-Preis', *Spiegel Online* (3 July 2016) <http://www.spiegel.de/kultur/literatur/bachmann-preis-2016-fuer-sharon-dodua-otoo-publikumspreis-fuer-stefanie-sargnagel-a-1101073.html> accessed 19 July 2017 and Philip Oltermann, 'Black British Writer Wins Major German Language Fiction Award', *The Guardian* (12 July 2016) <https://www.theguardian.com/books/2016/jul/12/black-british-writer-wins-major-german-language-fiction-sharon-dodue-otoo-ingeborg-bachmann-prize> accessed 19 July 2017.

of chronologies, theories and geographies.[5] Here, questions of the trajectory of theory into praxis and praxis into theory were critically examined, as both became understood as simultaneously necessary interventions, especially in institutions that structure racism and continue to normalize whiteness. These seminars offered a step forward in enhancing the visibility of Black Germans and the scholarship on the Black Diaspora in Germany and Europe institutionally.[6] In fact, both of these seminars can be considered an articulation and enactment of theory and praxis.

Privileging English and African Diaspora Studies scholar Michelle M. Wright's concept of *spacetimes*, we recognized that Black/African narratives in Europe challenge linear teleological histories and that Blackness was not a fixed trait, but constantly evolving.[7] Our first seminar affirmed the critical role that Black German Studies (BGS) has had on both sides of the Atlantic, albeit in distinctive ways. It also grappled with questions of how the field is structured and might be framed outside of existing hegemonies, for example, through the lens of Queer Studies. The work of Black German critical theorist Fatima El-Tayeb has paved the way through her charge for more inclusive work that 'queers' the dimensions of diasporic memory and moves beyond strictly confined, delineated and marked boundaries and genealogies.[8] Additionally, our seminar assessed Black German cultural practices (art, literature, theater, music) by examining the range of genres that Black Germans employ and that enable their subjectivity to be

5   'Political Activism in the Black European Diaspora: From Theory to Praxis' Seminar, German Studies Association Conference, 1–4 October 2015, Washington, DC.

6   In our introduction, we use Black German exclusively, which is considered a more inclusive designation than Afro-German, though some within the larger community use them interchangeably.

7   Michelle M. Wright, *The Physics of Blackness* (Minneapolis: University of Minnesota Press, 2015), 14–26.

8   See, Fatima El-Tayeb, *European Others: Queering Ethnicity in Postnational Europe* (Minneapolis: University of Minnesota Press, 2011) and Fatima El-Tayeb, *Undeutsch: die Konstruktion des Anderen in der postmigrantischen Gesellschaft* (Bielefeld: Transcript, 2016).

polyphonically performed, represented and affirmed.[9] Many of the papers presented in the first seminar that broke new ground for the second one had already evinced how contemporary Black German cultural productions serve as acts of emplacement, in which Black Germans assert themselves as citizens of the German nation. These productions are also forms of social activism, reflecting how political engagement and positioning impacts aesthetic expression and reception.

Using this latter point, the second seminar re-imagined politics and activism across Europe. In it, we stressed the need for decolonizing processes at the academic level through grassroots activist practices that help to engender direct social change. Intercultural and comparative analyses provided a fruitful means to explore the Black European Diaspora – an area rife for future research, and, as a burgeoning field, it offers productive points for articulating nuance across Black/African diasporic landscapes. Thus, our second seminar expressed the idea that activism must not only take place within the realm of knowledge production and dissemination (i.e. the ivory tower, itself a colonizing concept), but just as importantly in the realm of implementation and application through critical intervention and constant rethinking and reworking (i.e. intellectual activism, grassroots activism and public engagement). Here, we believe that social activism, much like the production of history, occurs inside and outside of academia.[10] Indeed, this understanding of social activism proves particularly compelling given that every day brings news of yet another Black life taken too soon through unjust actions and institutional violence across Europe and the United States. While the Black Lives Matter (BLM) movement originated in the United States as a form of digital activism in 2013 after the murder of Trayvon Martin in 2012, the last few years have produced sustained movements, with BLM groups and marches in Britain, France

9   See Stuart Hall, 'Cultural Identity and Diaspora', in Jonathan Rutherford, ed., *Identity: Community, Culture, and Difference* (London: Lawrence & Wishart, 1990), 222–37. For more on the concept of polyphony, see Mikhail Bahktin, *Problems of Dostoyevsky's Poetics*, tr. Caryl Emerson (Minneapolis: University of Minnesota Press, 1984), 21–23.

10   See Michel-Rolph Trouillot, *Silencing the Past: Power and the Production of History* (Boston, MA: Beacon, 1995).

and the Netherlands.[11] Last June intersectional and multicultural feminist organizers held their first month-long series of events that culminated with a BLM March in Berlin, which built from the 2016 summer marches.[12] Likewise, protests took place in Paris, France, in February 2017 after police sodomized a Black French man named 'Theo'.[13] In addition to these developments, activists practicing intersectional feminism have pursued digital activism with hashtag campaigns in Europe such as #CampusRassismus, #Schauhin and #Rhodesmustfall.[14] Each of these campaigns not only reveal

11   See Tracy McVeigh, 'Why activists brought the Black Lives Matter movement to the UK', *The Guardian* (6 August 2016) <https://www.theguardian.com/uk-news/2016/aug/06/black-lives-matter-uk-found-vital-social-justice> accessed 12 June 2018; Nabeela Zahir, 'In France, Black Lives Matter has become a rallying cry', *Al Jazeera* (2 September 2016) <https://www.aljazeera.com/indepth/features/2016/08/france-black-lives-matter-rallying-cry-160818103854211.html> accessed 12 June 2018 and Mandy Hendriks, 'Black Lives Matter Movement Goes Dutch', *NWSNET* (2 December 2016) <http://journalistiekzwolle.nl/nwsnet/black-lives-matter-goes-dutch/> accessed 12 June 2018.

12   For more on this see, Josephine Apraku, among others, 'Wenn ich sage, Black Lives Matter', dann sage ich auch, dass mein eigenes Leben zählt', *Missy Magazine* (20 June 2017) <http://missy-magazine.de/blog/2017/06/20/wenn-ich-sage-black-lives-matter-dann-sage-ich-auch-dass-mein-eigenes-leben-zaehlt/> accessed 12 June 2018 and Tiffany Florvil, 'From ADEFRA to Black Lives Matter: Black Women's Activism in Germany', *Black Perspectives* (5 July 2017) <https://www.aaihs.org/from-adefra-to-black-lives-matter-black-womens-activism-in-germany/> accessed 12 June 2018.

13   Angelique Chrisafis, 'Protests spread across Paris estates as anger grows over alleged police rape', *The Guardian* (8 February 2017) <https://www.theguardian.com/world/2017/feb/08/12-arrested-as-french-youths-clash-with-police-on-estates-near-paris> accessed 30 August 2017.

14   Students of Color at the Hochschule in Mainz and in Frankfurt am Main initiated #CampusRassismus. This campaign is seen as an effort to raise awareness and visibility of instances of racism and microaggressions that Students of Color encounter and experience on school grounds and in the classroom. #Schauhin is also a hashtag that People of Color employ to raise awareness of everyday racism in Germany. #Rhodesmustfall began as an online initiative to decolonize the University of Cape Town. In particular, the focus was on a statue of Cecil Rhodes that students demanded be removed from campus. The statue's removal occurred on 9 April 2015. See Frauke Lüpke-Narberhaus, 'Ich erkenne schon am Nachnamen, ob jemand durchfällt', *bento* (13 December 2015) <http://www.bento.de/today/

the persistence of everyday racism, including anti-Black, anti-Semitic and Islamophobic hate, but also the global structures and routes of racism in diverse contexts.

Political platforms on social media may be new outlets due to the advent of modern technology, but campaigns like these are anything but novel. Individuals from across the Black/African Diaspora, who have studied, lived, performed and struggled in Germany and its colonies, have often made claims for social justice and recognition. Advocacy in Communities of Color in Germany has a long-standing history. Black Germans and African colonials in the colonies and the metropole, for instance, agitated for racial equality and basic rights from German colonial authorities.[15] Other diasporic individuals, such as Mary Church Terrell and George Padmore, used Germany as a space to draw attention to sexism, racism and class oppression. As one of the founding members of the National Association for the Advancement of Colored People (NAACP), Terrell delivered a speech in both German and French at the 1904 International Congress of Women held in Berlin. In 1930, Padmore organized an international conference in Hamburg. He was active in the International Trade Union Committee of Negro Workers (ITUCNW) and edited its journal *The Negro Worker*.[16] Padmore also spent time in Vienna, Austria. Furthermore,

---

campus-rassismus-studenten-erzaehlen-von-alltagsrassismus-194006/> accessed 2 July 2018; Steffi Hentschke, 'Der Aufschrei gegen Alltagsrassismus', *Stern* (9 September 2013) <https://www.stern.de/digital/online/-schauhin-der-aufsch rei-gegen-alltagsrassismus-3913892.html> accessed 2 July 2018 and '"Rhodes Must Fall" – Decolonization Symbolism – What is happening at UCT, South Africa?' *The Postcolonialist* (29 March 2015) <http://postcolonialist.com/civil-discourse/rhodes-must-fall-decolonisation-symbolism-happening-uct-south-africa/> accessed 2 July 2018.

15 Katharina Oguntoye, *Eine afro-deutsche Geschichte: Zur Lebenssituation von Afrikanern und Afro-Deutschen in Deutschland von 1884 bis 1950* (Berlin: Hoho Verlag Christine Hoffmann, 1997) and Robbie Aitken, and Eve Rosenhaft, *Black Germany: The Making and Unmaking of a Diaspora Community, 1890–1960* (Cambridge: Cambridge University Press, 2013).

16 Paulette Reed-Anderson, *Rewriting the Footnotes: Berlin und die afrikanische Diaspora* (Berlin: Die Ausländerbeauftragte des Senats, 2000), 30–32; Clarence Lusane, *Hitler's Black Victims: The Historical Experiences of Afro-Germans, European Blacks, Africans,*

in the 1950s and 1960s, Civil Rights and Black Power activists, such as Dr. Martin Luther King, Jr., Paul Robeson and Angela Davis, traveled to (East and West) Germany, advocating across geographic boundaries and garnering more attention for the civil rights struggle in the United States. African American GIs stationed in the country, oftentimes together with West German students, rallied against American imperialism, especially the war in Vietnam.[17] Foreign students from the Congo protested the Prime Minister Moise Tshombe's visit to West Berlin in 1964, particularly given his involvement in the overthrow of and eventual murder of the first democratically elected Prime Minister of the Democratic Republic of the Congo, Patrice Lumumba.[18] This transnational activism demonstrates the necessity of diasporic connections and activist work that extends beyond national and cultural contexts. All of these actions had common goals: the challenging of corrupt political systems and leaders as well as the international liberation of People of Color from oppressive governments

and *African Americans in the Nazi Era* (New York and London: Routledge, 2003), 86–87 and Noaquia N. Callahan, 'A Rare Colored Bird: Mary Church Terrell, *Die Fortschritte der farbigen Frauen*, and the International Council of Women's Congress in Berlin, Germany 1904', in Britta Waldschmidt-Nelson, and Anja Schüler, eds, *Forging Bonds Across Borders: Mobilizing for Women's Rights and Social Justice in the 19th Century Transatlantic World*, German Historical Institute Bulletin Supplement 13 (2017): 93–110.

17   Maria Höhn, and Martin Klimke, *A Breath of Freedom: The Civil Rights Struggle, African American GIs, and Germany* (New York: Palgrave MacMillian, 2010); Maria Höhn, 'The Black Panther Solidarity Committee and the Trial of the Ramstein 2', in Belinda Davis, among others, eds, *Changing the World, Changing Oneself: Political Protest and Collective Identities in the 1960s/70s West Germany and U.S.* (New York: Berghahn, 2010), 215–40; Martin Klimke, *The Other Alliance: Student Protest in West Germany and the United States in the Global Sixties* (Princeton, NJ: Princeton University Press, 2010), esp. Chapter 4; Katharina Gerund, *Transatlantic Cultural Exchange: African American Women's Art and Activism in West Germany* (Bielefeld: Transcript Verlag, 2013), 101–56 and Katrina Hagen, 'Ambivalence and Desire in the East German "Free Angela Davis" Campaign', in Quinn Slobodian, ed., *Comrades of Color: East Germany in the Cold War World* (New York: Berghahn Books, 2015), 157–87.

18   Quinn Slobodian, *Foreign Front: Third World Politics in Sixties West Germany* (Durham, NC: Duke University Press, 2012), esp. Chapter 2.

and regimes throughout the world. As these few examples reveal, Black/
African diasporic consciousness has always operated in a queer fashion,
one that navigates outside of prescribed filial bonds from a rigid Western
framework that adheres to normative identities, behaviors and practices.
Black German Studies encompasses these histories, movements and lived
experiences, among many others.

Learning and adapting to their particular nation-specific and socio-
historical conditions, Black Germans have continually expressed dissent
about a variety of topics that have impacted and continue to affect their
lives. For instance, Black German activist and singer Fasia Jansen was politically active in left-wing circles in the post-World War II period, in which
she pushed issues of equality and peace.[19] Black German author and artist
Ika Hügel-Marshall was active in the West German feminist and lesbian
movements of the late 1960s and 1970s.[20] U.S.-based Black German journalist Hans Massaquoi also became a figure for civil rights through his
career at *Jet* and then *Ebony* magazines.[21] Activists and intellectuals such
as May Ayim, Katharina Oguntoye, John Kantara, Mike Reichel, Jasmin
Eding, Helga Emde, Katja Kinder, Eleonore Wiedenroth-Coulilaby, Ricky
Reiser and others catalyzed and supported the modern Black German
movement of the 1980s and 1990s. This movement began with the establishment of the organizations *Initiative Schwarze Deutsche* [Initiative of
Black Germans, ISD] and *Afrodeutsche Frauen* [Afro-German Women,
ADEFRA].[22] Its members have always been attentive to transnational issues

---

19   Bundeszentrale für politische Bildung and Initiative Schwarze Menschen in
     Deutschland, eds, *Homestory Deutschland. Schwarze Biografien in Geschichte und
     Gegenwart* (Berlin: bpb, 2009), 62–65.
20   Ika Hügel-Marshall, *Daheim unterwegs. Ein deutsches Leben* (Frankfurt: Fischer,
     2001).
21   Hans J. Massaquoi, *Destined to Witness: Growing Up Black in Nazi Germany*
     (New York: William Morrow Paperbacks, 1999) and Hans J. Massaquoi, *Neger,
     Neger Schornsteinfeger. Meine Kindheit in Deutschland* (Munich: Droemersche
     Verlagsanstalt, 2001).
22   ISD is now known as *Initiative Schwarze Menschen in Deutschland* (n.d.) <http://
     isdonline.de> accessed 12 June 2018. ADEFRA is now known as *Schwarze Frauen
     in Deutschland* <http://www.adefra.com/> accessed 12 June 2018.

of the Black/African Diaspora and to the need to draw attention to and practice Caribbean American poet Audre Lorde's idea of 'connected differences' with Blacks and Communities of Color in Germany and across the globe.[23] Thus, while both of the GSA seminars that convened over the past few years provided the foundation for this edited volume, they are not, by any means, the sole impetuses for its genesis, and it would be a colonizing act for the authors to claim as much. Black German Studies is an academic field of inquiry because of the actions, initiatives, efforts and labor that Black Germans have performed to increase their visibility, advocate for their rights and articulate their positionality as *both* Black and German.

Though we used the seminars to bring junior and senior scholars as well as activists together to interrogate and inform our own understandings of the concepts of Blackness, Black German, Black Europe and the Black/African Diaspora, the seminars were not devoid of tensions and uncomfortable moments during which several white participants failed to listen and fully understand their own positionalities, privilege and power. Regardless, the seminars were useful, particularly as certain questions arose, such as: who and what do we engage with when we use the category of

---

23   The phrase 'connected differences' is taken from Audre Lorde. See Audre Lorde, 'Foreword,' in Dagmar Schultz, May Ayim and Katharina Oguntoye, eds, *Showing Our Colors: Afro-German Women Speak Out* (Amherst: University of Massachusetts Press, 1991), vii-xiv. There have been many works that have helped to describe some of the dynamics of the Black German Movement. See, for example, Denise Bergold-Caldwell, among others, eds, *Spiegelblicke: Perspektiven Schwarzer Bewegung in Deutschland* (Berlin: Orlanda Frauenverlag, 2015); Peggy Piesche, ed., *Euer Schweigen schützt euch nicht: Audre Lorde und die Schwarze Frauenbewegung in Deutschland* (Berlin: Orlanda Frauenverlag, 2012); Fatima El-Tayeb, 'Dimensions of Diaspora: Women of Color Feminism, Black Europe, and Queer Memory Discourses', in *European Others*, 43–80; Philipp Khabo Koepsell, 'Literature and Activism', in Asoka Esuruoso, and Philipp Khabo Koepsell, eds, *Arriving in the Future: Stories of Home and Exile: An Anthology of Poetry and Creative Writing by Black Writers in Germany* (Berlin: epubli, 2014), 36–47 and Tiffany N. Florvil, 'Black German Feminists and their Transnational Connections of the 1980s and 1990s', in Friederike Bruehoefener, Karen Hagemann and Donna Harsch, eds, *Gendering Post-1945 German History: Entanglements* (New York: Berghahn Books, forthcoming 2018). See also Audre Lorde, *A Burst of Light and Other Essays* (New York: Ixia Press, 2017), esp. 48.

Black German Studies? Do non-critical white subjects producing culture on Black Germans constitute a part of Black German Studies and, if not, why? Which scholarly voices get privileged over others and why? Finally, how do we imagine and conceptualize Black Europe? In many ways, our discussions engaged the pressing themes of scholars' power, voice and public engagement, Black German Studies scholar Tina Campt's notion of 'diasporic asymmetries' and decolonizing German Studies more generally.[24] Understanding decolonization in the way in which scholar of Diversity Studies Maisha-Maureen Auma (formerly Maureen Maisha Eggers) explores it is one of the best existing ways to frame the field and its agents.[25] She writes in relation to Black women activists that their decolonizing work serves 'as an interruption of an (exclusive and canonized) focus on texts authored and authorized by the West', and 'is a substantial shift of focus away from the imperial center'.[26] At the bare minimum, then, we must be attentive to and acknowledge the white hegemonic center that often dominates German Studies, particularly when undertaking work in the field of Black German Studies. Even more so, white scholars must be attentive to and acknowledge their privileged positionality and potential for blind spots. While it is possible for white Germans, white Americans and any other number of white people to critique culturally constructed and historically embedded notions of race and ethnicity, which is what some of the chapters in this volume accomplish, the criticism often remains incomplete. Moreover, it can and often does serve to reify these categories in the process of an attempted deconstruction. Since sexism also intersects with the historical trajectory of race, Auma points to 'Black women' as the example of decolonizers par excellence. Some of the chapters in

24   Tina Campt, 'The Crowded Space of Diaspora: Intercultural Address and the Tensions of Diasporic Relation', in Ian Christopher Fletcher, ed., 'Citizenship, National Identity, Race, and Diaspora in Contemporary Europe', Special issue, *Radical History Review* 83 (Spring 2002): 94–113.

25   In 2017, she publicly changed her name to Auma.

26   Maureen Maisha Eggers, 'Knowledges of (Un-)Belonging: Epistemic Change as a Defining Mode for Black Women's Activism in Germany', in Sara Lennox, ed., *Remapping Black Germany: New Perspectives on Afro-German History, Politics, and Culture* (Amherst: University of Massachusetts Press, 2016), 42.

this volume therefore also emphasize the role of sexism as a transgressive act that intersects with racism, homophobia and classism. In fact, several of the contributions employ intersectional approaches that recognize the interplay of race, gender, class and sexuality.

As scholars, one positioned as a Woman of Color and the other a white woman, and both from the United States, we are aware that our own statuses offer us certain privileges when studying Black Germany's Diaspora. We also recognize that whiteness is normalized and affords an extreme privilege that operates within diverse institutional settings. This is particularly important given that in Germany there are very few Black, African or People of Color professors, and that there are no Black German or Black European Studies institutes established there.[27] While American Studies scholar Sabine Broeck and other white scholars in Bremen made some efforts to create Black Bremen Studies and a Black Knowledges Research Group in 2015, these individuals failed to include Black German or People of Color scholars, and organizations and members of Black communities in Germany and Austria responded to this significant omission.[28] With all this being said, in no way, do we claim to speak for or represent Black Germans throughout this volume. Rather, it is our goal to make visible their experiences as well as the variegated power structures that exist and to engage them critically, and at times, perhaps failing to fully do so. For instance, as a white woman, I (Vanessa) am cognizant that I have more privilege than (Tiffany) my co-editor and that my voice likely generates more resonance among white audiences. I (Tiffany), also acknowledge my privilege as an Afro-Caribbean tenure-track scholar working at a research university in the United States. Verbalizing and citing these 'asymmetrical powers' is one step; actively seeking to shift them is, of course, another. This,

---

27   See Karim Fereidooni, 'Rassismus an der Uni: Warum es in Deutschland kaum schwarze Professor gibt', *Huffpost Voices Blog* (30 June 2017) <http://www.huffing tonpost.de/karim-fereidooni/rassismus-uni-deutschland_b_17332910.html> accessed 23 August 2017.

28   'Community Statement: "Black" Studies at the University of Bremen', *Present Tense Scholars Network: Black Perspectives and Studies Germany* (January 2015) <https:// blackstudiesgermany.wordpress.com/statementbremen/> accessed 31 August 2017.

we believe, is why a constant 'rethinking' is what Black German Studies should strive for. Rethinking what might be missing from the narrative, from the analysis, from the discourse and from one's own perspective is the necessary and critical work that scholars in this field must continually seek to address. Likewise, we must always rethink our own power to simultaneously reaffirm the diverse Black German actors, perspectives and experiences that we want to illuminate through our work and reject categories that often exclude, silence and haunt them. It will never be a complete process, but rather remains an ongoing interrogational and introspective one that is much more productive than laying claim to any intellectual territory and alleging to have mastered it. Herein lies the promise and the potential of the field for the present and the future.

Understanding Black German Studies

Unofficially, Black German Studies began at what Peggy Piesche calls the kitchen table conversations that were had within the modern Black German community – a common practice among other diasporic groups across the globe.[29] Likely the very first of such conversations will never be officially documented in textual form because it was something spontaneous that arose out of necessity. The collective origin narrative of BGS thus lies in unmappable territory; it is fugitive and refuses to be bound to a single *spacetime*. At the level of the individual, the Black German Diaspora and its European counterpart also have a long history that predates any theorizing solely in the academic realm. Indeed, Black male intellectuals

---

29   Peggy Piesche made this comment at the second Black German Studies Seminar, 'Political Activism in the Black European Diaspora: From Theory to Praxis' Seminar, German Studies Association Conference, 1–4 October 2015, Washington, DC. See also Barbara Smith, 'A Press of Our Own Kitchen Table: Women of Color Press', *Frontiers: A Journal of Women Studies*, 10/3 (1989): 11–13, where she discusses similar dynamics for African American women.

analyzed the societies in which they lived, including Anton Wilhelm Amo, C. R. L. James, Frantz Fanon and Stuart Hall, to name a few well-known examples.[30] But we should also not forget the contributions that women such as Jeanne and Paulette Nardal, Una Marson, Claudia Jones and Olive Morris – often outside of the academy – made to Black European intellectualism and internationalism through their activism and literary productions.[31] Still, many Black German scholars, writers and activists have contributed to the evolution of the field in just the last thirty years, and their archive includes *Farbe bekennen: Afrodeutsche Frauen auf den Spuren ihrer Geschichte, Mythen, Masken und Subjekte: Kritische Weißseinforschung in Deutschland, The BlackBook: Deutschlands Häutungen, re/visionen: Postkoloniale Perspektiven von People of Color auf Rassismus, Kulturpolitik und Widerstand in Deutschland, Euer Schweigen schützt Euch nicht: Audre Lorde und die Schwarze Frauenbewegung in Deutschland, Arriving in the Future: Stories of Home and Exile, Spiegelblicke: Perspektiven Schwarzer Bewegung in Deutschland* and *Souls and Sisters: Inspirationen von May Ayim.*[32] These examples, along with countless others, deftly illustrate that

---

30 Peter Martin, 'Der schwarze Philosoph', in Peter Martin, *Schwarze Teufel, Edle Mohren* (Hamburg: Junius, 1993); Minkah Makalani, *In the Cause of Freedom: Radical Black Internationalism from Harlem to London, 1917–1939* (Chapel Hill, University of North Carolina Press, 2011); Lewis Gordon, *Fanon and the Crisis of European Man: An Essay on Philosophy and the Human Sciences* (New York: Routledge, 1995) and Stuart Hall, and Bill Schwarz, *Familiar Stranger: A Life Between Two Islands* (Durham, NC: Duke University Press, 2017).

31 T. Denean Sharpley-Whiting, *Negritude Women* (Minneapolis: University of Minnesota Press, 2002); Imaobong Umoren, *Race Women Internationalists: Activist-Intellectuals and Global Freedom Struggles* (Oakland: University of California Press, 2018); Carol Boyce Davies, *Left of Karl Marx: The Political Life of Black Communist Claudia Jones* (Durham, NC: Duke University Press, 2008) and Tanisha Ford, 'We Were the People of Soul', in *Liberated Threads: Black Women, Style, and The Global Politics of Soul* (Chapel Hill: University of North Carolina Press, 2015), 123–57.

32 Katharina Oguntoye, May Opitz/Ayim and Dagmar Schultz, eds, *Farbe bekennen: Afro-deutsche Frauen auf den Spuren ihrer Geschichte* (1986; repr., Berlin: Orlanda Frauenverlag, 2006); Maureen Maisha Eggers, Grada Kilomba, Peggy Piesche and Susan Arndt, eds, *Mythen, Masken und Subjekte: Kritische Weißseinforschung in Deutschand* (Munster: Unrast, 2006); AntiDiskriminierungsBüro (ADB) Köln and

Black German scholars, writers and activists have been critically engaged
in promoting their own narratives, developing their own theoretical frameworks for analyzing institutionalized racism and the power of whiteness
and producing knowledge for future generations to expand upon and
deepen.[33] Of course this volume builds on this rich and important legacy.

Representing Black/African intellectualism and internationalism,
Black Germans have frequently utilized non-academic initiatives and ave-
nues to highlight their presence, culture and history. Some of these col-
lective, institutional and individual projects include ISD's Black History
Month celebrations and the *Homestory Deutschland* exhibition; Katharina
Oguntoye's association Joliba, Natasha Kelly's *Edewa*; the Each One Teach
One e.V. (EOTO)'s Black/African Diaspora library and archive and the
Black German theater ensemble Label Noir's production, *Heimat, bittersüße
Heimat,* among others. Each of these projects organizes programming that

---

cyberNomads, eds, *The BlackBook: Deutschlands Häutungen* (Frankfurt am Main
and London: IKO-Verlag für Interkulturelle Kommunikation, 2004); Kien Nghi
Ha, Nicola Lauré al-Samarai, and Sheila Mysorekar, eds, *Re/visonen: Postkoloniale
Perspektiven von People of Color auf Rassismus, Kulturpolitik und Widerstand in
Deutschland* (Munster: Unrast, 2007); Peggy Piesche, ed., *Euer Schweigen schützt
Euch nicht: Audre Lorde und die Schwarze Frauenbewegung in Deutschland* (Berlin:
Orlanda Frauenverlag, 2012); Asoka Esuruoso, and Philipp Khabo Koepsell, eds,
*Arriving in the Future: Stories of Home and Exile. An Anthology of Poetry and Creative
Writing by Black Writers in Germany* (Berlin: epubli, 2014); Denise Bergold-Caldwell,
and others, *Spiegelblicke: Perspektiven Schwarzer Bewegung in Deutschland* (Berlin:
Orlanda Frauenverlag, 2015) and Natasha A. Kelly, ed., *Souls and Sisters: Inspirationen
von May Ayim* (Berlin: Orlanda Frauenverlag, 2015).

33 See some other works on Black German experiences: Tina Campt, *Other Germans:
Black Germans and the Politics of Race, Gender, and Memory in the Third Reich*
(Ann Arbor: University of Michigan Press, 2004); Yara-Colette Lemke Muñiz
de Faria, *Zwischen Fürsorge und Ausgrenzung: Afrodeutsche "Besatzungskinder"
im Nachkriegsdeutschland* (Berlin: Mertopol Verlag, 2002); Patricia Mazón, and
Reinhild Steingröver, eds, *Not So Plain as Black and White: Afro-German Culture
and History, 1890–2000* (Rochester: University of Rochester Press, 2005); Marion
Kraft, ed., *Kinder der Befreiung: Transatlantische Erfahrungen und Perspektiven
Schwarzer Deutscher der Nachkriegsgeneration* (Münster: Unrast, 2015) and Sara
Lennox, ed., *Remapping Black Germany New Perspectives on Afro-German History,
Politics, and Culture* (Amherst: University of Massachusetts Press, 2016).

foregrounds topics on Black Germanness, the Black/African Diaspora, multiculturalism and racial discrimination. They also represent Black Germans' ability to consistently produce spaces for themselves in a majority white German society.

Influenced by African Americans in Germany and modeled after the African American annual observances that historian Carter G. Woodson established in 1926, Black History Month (BHM) began in 1990 in West Berlin. With regional ISD and ADEFRA groups' assistance, these BHM events helped to signal the importance of the Black/African Diaspora both within and beyond the borders of the German nation. The BHM eventually emerged in cities such as Frankfurt and Hamburg.[34] The BHMs certainly became a cultural and political institution that Black Germans looked forward to for a sense of community and empowerment. Moreover, ISD's traveling exhibition *Homestory Deutschland*, which began as a collective project in 2006, has featured the narratives of individuals of the Black/African Diaspora across different *spacetimes* in Germany. These narratives include those of African American, African and Black German individuals, and there is also an accompanying book published in conjunction with the exhibition.[35] *Homestory Deutschland* has traveled and been displayed throughout Germany, the United States and Africa since 2006, albeit in a slightly altered format.[36]

Katharina Oguntoye, who helped to co-found ISD-Berlin and ADEFRA-Berlin, eventually established Joliba in 1997. Joliba, a non-profit organization, sponsors intercultural projects that engage the themes of migration, war, discrimination and racism. Under Oguntoye's guidance, Joliba has also helped to promote and advance the knowledge of Black

---

34 Eleonore Wiedenroth-Coulibaly, and Sascha Zinflou, '20 Jahre Schwarze Organisierung in Deutschland – Ein Abriss', in AntiDiskriminierungsBüro (ADB) Köln and cyberNomads, eds, *The BlackBook: Deutschlands Häutungen* (Frankfurt am Main and London: IKO-Verlag für Interkulturelle Kommunikation, 2004), 133–44.

35 Bundeszentrale für politische Bildung and Initiative Schwarze Menschen in Deutschland, *Homestory Deutschland*.

36 See Initiative Schwarze Menschen in Deutschland, e.V., 'Ausstellungsorte/Programm', *Homestory Deutschland: Schwarze Biografien in Geschichte und Gegenwart* (n.d.) <http://www.homestory-deutschland.de/> accessed 28 March 2018.

German youth and other People of Color in Germany; it has become a critical space for youth empowerment as well as the dissemination of materials
on youth, parenting and the experiences of People of Color. In addition,
Joliba offers integration assistance, encourages mutual understanding and
uses cultural events to inform the public. Some of its events include film
screenings, workshops, exhibitions and more.[37]

EOTO, formed on 21 March 2014, has provided both a space of visibility and an archive of Black/African diasporic knowledge for future
generations of Black Germans and People of Color in Germany. Their
goal, as the title of the initiative makes clear, is to educate themselves and
others about their own history, in a similar vein to the women of the first
generation of the Black German women's movement. Consisting of the
ISD member Vera Heyer's personal library and other donated literature and
films, EOTO serves as a community-based education and empowerment
project that includes over 2,500 works related to individuals of the Black/
African Diaspora.[38] There is also archival material that Heyer collected on
the Black German movement that is currently being processed at EOTO.
Housed in Wedding, their location is close to the African quarter, which
itself is part of the initiative's program of educating others on the history
of the presence of Black people in Germany and Germany's colonial past.[39]
Workshops and networking events are also held at the location.

37   See Katharina Oguntoye, 'Joliba: Interkulturelles Netzwerk in Berlin e.V.', *Joliba*
     (2017) <http://www.joliba.de> accessed 1 August 2017.
38   Vera Heyer collected books, both fiction and non-fiction, at local flea markets and
     during her travels on topics relevant to the Black diaspora. She left her collection to
     Nouria Asfaha, whose efforts to obtain the funding for this project and whose vol-
     untary time of archiving this material, in conjunction with the efforts of Tina Bach
     made the project a reality. For more on this see, Nouria Asfaha, 'Each One Teach One
     (EOTO e.V.) und das 'Vera Heyer Archiv' als Meilenstein der Schwarzen Deutschen
     Bewegung', in Natasha A. Kelly, ed., *Souls and Sisters: Inspirationen von May Ayim*
     (Berlin: Orlanda Frauenverlag, 2015), 94–104. Each One Teach One (EOTO e.V.)
     (2016) <http://eoto-archiv.de/> accessed 28 March 2018.
39   In April 2018, the municipal authorities representing Wedding, a district in Berlin
     where the African Quarter is located, finally agreed to rename these streets. Much
     like the fight for the renaming of the former Gröbenufer to May-Ayim-Ufer in

Furthermore, Black Germans have used diverse artistic mediums as creative tools for engaging the often-ignored histories of colonialism, migration, the Black/African Diaspora and identity. Employing art, Natasha Kelly's 'Edewa' or *Einkaufsgenossenschaft antirassistischen Widerstandes* [Wholesale Co-operative of Antiracist Resistance] was an interactive installation that addressed the colonial history of Germany as well as its connection to capitalism and consumerism. The title is a play on Edeka or *Einkauf sgenossenschaft der KoloniAlwarenhändler im Halleschen Torbezirk zu Berlin* [Purchasing Co-operative of Colonial Goods Retailers in the Hallesches Tor district of Berlin], the largest German supermarket chain. The installation was on display at the Rathaus Schöneberg's Goldener Saal from 7–14 December 2013 and then later in Munich in March of 2016.[40] Theater has

---

Kreuzberg, this was a decade-long community effort. The streets will be renamed after African heroes. M. S. Mboro and Joshua Kwesi Aikins have been two of the main advocates pursuing this renaming. Femi Awoniyi, 'Berlin Streets to be renamed after African Heroes', *African Courier* (16 April 2018) <http://www.theafricancourier.de/europe/berlin-streets-to-be-renamed-after-african-heroes/> accessed 30 June 2018; Christian Kopp, and Marius Krohn, 'Blues in Schwarzweiss. Die Black Community im Widerstand gegen kolonialrassistische Straßennamen in Berlin Mitte', *Berlin- Postkolonial* (n.d.) <http://www.berlin-postkolonial.de/cms/index.php/orte/78-afrikanisches-viertel> accessed 25 June 2018 and Daniel Gyamerah, and Saraya Gomis, 'Each One Teach One, e.V.: Ein Ort der Begegnung', *Each One Teach One (EOTO) e.V.* (2016) <https://eoto-archiv.de> accessed 1 September 2017. Yonas Endrias also founded the initiative *Lern- und Erinnerungsort Afrikanisches Viertel* [*Learning and Remembrance Space African Quarter*]. For more on this see, Bezirksamt Mitte von Berlin, *Lern- und Erinnerungsort Afrikanisches Viertel* (n.d.) <https://www.leo-afrika.de> accessed 30 June 2018.

40 Natasha Kelly, 'EDEWA – Einkaufsgenossenschaft antirassistischen Widerstandes eröffnet eigene "Filiale" in Berlin-Neukölln', *Natasha A. Kelly: Academic Activist* (8 November 2015) <http://www.natashaakelly.com/edewa-einkaufsgenossenschaft-antirassistischen-widerstandes-eroffnet-eigene-filiale-in-berlin-neukolln/> accessed 20 June 2016. In 2018, Kelly also directed a film, *Millis Erwachen* [Milli's Awakening], taken from a Ludwig Kirchner painting entitled *Schlafende Milli* [*Sleeping Milli*] (1911), and it brings together the voices of eight Black German women of different generations. The film was screened at the 10th Annual Berlin Biennale for Contemporary Art. 'Natasha A. Kelly', *Berlin Biennial for Contemporary Art* (2018) <http:bb10.berlinbiennal.de/artists/n/natasha-a-kelly> accessed 12 June 2018.

also become an important cultural and political space that enables Black Germans to share their narratives, experiences and messages on stages throughout the country. Black German theater ensemble Label Noir serves as an example of this. The troupe has integrated intersectional perspectives in their performances, especially with their play *Heimat, bittersüße Heimat*.[41] Both the *Ballhaus Naunynstraße* and *Maxim Gorki Theater* have illuminated the experiences of social exclusion of individuals of the Black/African Diaspora and People of Color in Germany.[42]

Furthermore, Black German adoptees in the United States like Rosemarie Peña and Shirley Gindler-Price have also established organizations, such as the Black German Heritage & Research Association (BGHRA) and the Black German Cultural Society (BGCS), that blend the public, cultural, political and academic by hosting conferences and exhibitions, offering knowledge about Black German history and facilitating transnational exchanges that include Black Germans in the conversation.[43] Together, all of these projects represent Black Germans' efforts to not only engender crucial spaces for themselves, but also to promote recognition and produce critical knowledge about Black German history and culture within the German national polity, as well as transnationally. In Austria, for instance, Black Austrians also are increasingly active, campaigning against racial violence and racist policies, creating and advancing their literature and curating their individual and collective experiences.[44]

41   'Label Noir', *Label Noir* (n.d.) <https://www.labelnoir.net> accessed 5 May 2016, Vanessa D. Plumly, 'BLACK-Red-Gold in "der bunten Republik": Constructions and Performances of Heimat/en in Afro-/Black German Cultural Productions', Dissertation, University of Cincinnati, 2015 and Jamele Watkins, 'Rearticulating Black Feminist Thought in Heimat, bittersüße Heimat', *Women in German Yearbook* 32 (2016), 138–51.

42   Maxim Gorki Theater, 'Das Maxim Gorki Theater', GORKI (n.d.) <https://gorki.de> accessed 11 June 2018 and 'Haus', Ballhaus Naunynstrasse (n.d.) <http://www.ballhausnaunynstrasse.de> accessed 11 June 2018.

43   Black German Heritage and Research Association (BGHRA) (2018) <http://bghra.org/> accessed 28 March 2018 and Black German Cultural Society (BGCS) (2018) <http://afrogermans.us/> accessed 28 March 2018.

44   See also Nancy P. Nenno, '*Here to Stay*: Black Austrian Studies' in Tiffany N. Florvil and Vanessa D. Plumly, eds, *Rethinking Black German Studies: Approaches, Interventions and Histories* (Oxford; Peter Lang, 2018), Chapter 2. See also, *Fresh*

Moreover, in Switzerland, the organization Afrolitt is a bilingual platform that uses Black/African diasporic literature to organize a variety of events that provide a forum for collaboration, community building and knowledge production and dissemination.[45]

As a field, then, BGS has evolved over time and space in multiple contexts. It has no single point of origin and, in fact, one could argue that this is one of its most valuable assets. As an evolving and expanding field, its inherent interdisciplinarity opens it up to endless possibilities. Black German Studies also has initiated and pioneered the discourse on white scholars and researchers' culpability in the field itself and within the larger context of German Studies as a whole. Offering a critique of existing epistemological frameworks predominantly defined and framed through Eurocentric perspectives and paradigms within which knowledge has been produced, amassed and disseminated without scrutiny, Black German Studies intervenes and poses questions that decenter the categories of analysis often perpetuated through a hegemonically structured (white) German Studies. In the same vein, Black German Studies also extends who constitutes a part of the Black/African Diaspora by complicating Black experiences and no longer centering them within the dominant Middle Passage paradigm.[46] Tina Campt has advocated for 'an alternative model of diaspora, albeit in a specifically German manifestation' and found an incisive response in Michelle M. Wright's articulation of a postwar epistemology of Blackness in Germany.[47] In countering the theorized homogeneity of the Black/African

---

Magazin (2018) <http://freshzine.at/> accessed 12 June 2018 and Araba Evelyn Johnston-Arthur, 'Es ist Zeit der Geschichte selbst eine Gestalt zu geben ... Strategien der Entkolonialisierung und Ermächtigung im Kontext der afrikanischen Diaspora in Österreich', in Kien Nghi Ha, and others, *re/visionen Postkoloniale Perspektiven von People of Color auf Rassismus, Kulturpolitik und Widerstand in Deutschland* (Berlin: Unrast Verlag, 2007), 423–44.

45   *Afrolitt. Réflexions et Partages sur la Littérature Noire* (2018) <http://www.afrolitt. com/en/home/> accessed 2 July 2018.

46   See Wright, *The Physics of Blackness*, esp. 14–26.

47   Tina Campt, 'Diaspora Space, Ethnographic Space: Writing History Between the Lines', in Kamari Maxine Clarke and Deborah A. Thomas, eds, *Globalization and Race: Transformations in the Cultural Production of Blackness Durham* (Durham, NC: Duke University Press, 2006), 96.

Diaspora, what she cites as the über Trope of the Middle Passage, referencing Paul Gilroy's *The Black Atlantic: Modernity and Double Consciousness* and Tommie Shelby's *We Who are Dark: The Philosophical Foundations of Black Solidarity*,[48] Wright takes issue with a singular reading of the Black/African Diaspora in global history (in the case of U.S. Blackness and the Middle Passage). Instead, she promotes a complex rendering of the many distinct arrivals of Blackness throughout the *spacetime* continuum that complicate collective and standard narratives. She explains, '[w]e are not all arriving on the same boat, either metaphorically or literally'.[49] Wright comprehends that Black/African diasporic experiences are extremely diverse, and recognizes this complexity rather than elides the differences. Our contributors in this volume certainly reflect this necessary shift.

Rethinking Black German Studies, however, does not mean that other areas cannot and should not be drawing on the research presented in this volume. In fact, rethinking as a critical practice should be an endeavor that all scholars in German Studies undertake, since as a field, it has often occluded Blackness and has been articulated through white, Western frameworks. Scholars in Black/African Diaspora Studies, too, can enrich their studies by seeing Germany, much like France and Britain, as a Black/African diasporic space that warrants further attention and inclusion in diasporic narratives. Thus, rethinking is fruitful beyond our disciplinary and constructed geographic boundaries. It is a constant reminder that research does (and should) not exist in a vacuum, that we are writing from a specific positionality and that about whom and on what we write, as well as how we write, is always already political. With our volume, we encourage scholars to see how Black German Studies helps to not only transform both German and Black/African Diaspora Studies, but also other disciplines in profound ways.

48 Wright, 'Middle Passage Blackness', 217–33, Michelle M. Wright, 'Pale by Comparison: Black Liberal Humanism and the Postwar Era in the African Diaspora', in Darlene Clark Hine, Trica Danielle Keaton and Stephen Small, eds, *Black Europe and the African Diaspora* (Urbana: University of Illinois Press, 2009), 260–76; Paul Gilroy *The Black Atlantic: Modernity and Double Consciousness* (Cambridge, MA: Harvard University Press, 1993) and Tommie Shelby, *We Who are Dark: The Philosophical Foundations of Black Solidarity* (Cambridge, MA: Belknap Press, 2005).

49 Wright, 'Pale by Comparison', 268.

We truly hope that this volume will continue to contribute to Black German Studies by showing its potential to produce rigorous and innovative scholarship that emphasizes the breadth of the field. Employing interdisciplinary methods, diverse sources and original analyses, the contributors challenge epistemologies of racial difference, racialization and Blackness by advancing novel understandings of Germany's Black/African Diaspora. Indeed, these developments can have profound implications in our classrooms, in our scholarship and in our activism. Moreover, one of our main goals for this volume was to showcase the insightful scholarship of another generation of scholars who are pushing the fields of Black German and Black Austrian Studies in new directions. This volume is by no means comprehensive, as there are scholars and activists on both sides of the Atlantic doing amazing work, including Philipp Khabo Koepsell, Joshua Kwesi Aikins, Eddie Bruce Jones, Priscilla Layne, Karina Griffith, Michelle Eley, Heidi Lewis, Ella Achola, Sonya Donaldson, Rosemarie Peña, Josephine Apakru, Natasha Kelly, Daniele Daude and Victoria Robinson. Recognizing this promising generation, we invited some Black Germans and other Afro-Europeans to contribute to the volume, but sadly, several of these individuals had to withdraw for both professional and personal reasons. Thus, we are fully cognizant of the lack of Black German and Afro-European scholarly voices featured in this volume, though Kevina King's work is included. Regardless of this, we do feel that the works presented in our volume showcase the critical work that these emerging scholars have produced and are demonstrative of where they are taking the field of Black German Studies often in collaboration and conjunction with the Black German community.

Overview

The volume is divided into three sections that focus on 'German and Austrian Literature and History', 'Theory and Praxis' and 'Art and Performance' and that speak to and across the three topics presented in the subtitle of the volume: Approaches, Interventions and Histories. Accordingly, each chapter and section is not entirely bound, as the themes and topics taken up in them recur throughout our volume. Indeed, these studies offer us new approaches to understanding Black Germany by showing the complexity of issues of race, Blackness, space, gender and activism within Central Europe and pushing beyond narratives on W. E. B. Du Bois's experiences in Germany or the aftermath of World War II and African American soldiers. The volume also demonstrates the contours of the Black/African Diaspora in Europe by not centering African American perspectives per se, but instead critically examining the influence and impact of African American positionalities, lived experiences and narratives on Black German and German realities of both the past and present. Further, some of our contributors' citational practices utilize and engage with diasporic sources, representing significant interventions in the field of German Studies and noting how Black/African diasporic or People of Color theorists' ideas are critical and necessary in these dialogues and offer points of intersection. All of this is accomplished by illuminating different *spacetimes* in the eighteenth, nineteenth, twentieth and twenty-first centuries.

The volume begins with historical accounts that investigate the need for socio-historical specificity and culturally contextual readings of Blackness, Otherness, Black activism and Black/African diasporic belonging. The first three contributions deal with exposed Black subjects and the reading of their bodies at the intersection of imagined and real histories. In Chapter 1, Silke Hackenesch analyzes nineteenth- and early twentieth-century images in imperial Germany and the commodity fetishization of Otherness through visual regimes that historically constructed and undergirded white German racist notions of Blackness that persist in advertisements today. The figurative photographic and the literal bodily exposure of Black Africans in the German colonies are framed in the postcards that circulated throughout the German empire. Signifiers representing consumable products, such as chocolate and cocoa, became the sticky substances that (ad)dressed these bodies and left their mark.[50] Hackenesch also reveals the profound visual and discursive power that these mass-produced colonial advertisements had in helping to engender German racial, social and gendered norms in Wilhelmine society. In this way, these images helped to inculcate ideas about

---

50 Sara Ahmed, *The Cultural Politics of Emotions* (2nd edn, New York: Routledge, 2015), 13.

Germanness/Europeanness and foreignness/Otherness. But in so doing, the Black subjects in the images are used, silenced and disempowered, and are always considered to be outside of (never inside of) the German nation. Hackenesch's astute analysis propels us to rethink white German relationships to consumption as well as efforts to modernize and re-imagine the nation throughout history.

Attending to an all too often neglected Black/African Diaspora, Nancy P. Nenno uses her chapter to probe Black German Studies as strictly limited to the confines of Germany's national borders. In her piece, she brings the oft-overlooked Black Austrian Diaspora into the broader picture and reinserts Black Austrian individuals, their bodies and voices into historical narratives in the process. Nenno traces the lineage of Black Austrians in the Habsburg Empire to the present day, providing a cohesive introduction to their activism that has intently sought to bring Blackness in the Austrian context to light and to counter existing historical narratives that have all but erased their presence. She articulates that while the predominance of source texts on and the visibility of Black Germans has been positive, there remains a dearth of scholarship and a silence surrounding Black Austrians. In connecting two temporally disjointed moments, Nenno signifies the overlapping layers of what it means to be Black in Austria in the past and present. She also helps to restore Black Austrians' agential voice, demonstrating their significant legacy, presence and political engagement in this predominantly white country. In this way, Black Austrians are actively (re)writing their own history.

Closing out this section and illuminating the experiences of Black subjects and their claims to Black/African diasporic belonging, Meghan O'Dea's chapter takes up the topic of kinship that manifests itself in Namibian women's autobiographies about their lives in East Germany. Given that scholarship on Blackness in the GDR remains limited, her contribution is a timely intervention.[51] O'Dea unmasks the government's

---

51   See, for example, Peggy Piesche, 'Making African Diasporic Pasts Possible: A Retrospective View of the GDR and Its Black (Step-) Children', in Sara Lennox, ed., *Remapping Black Germany: New Perspectives on Afro-German History, Politics, and Culture* (Amherst: University of Massachusetts Press, 2016) and Quinn Slobodian,

political call for solidarity in East Germany through the autobiographical narratives of former so-called 'GDR-kids' from Namibia that expose the latent racism pervasive in East Germany and manifest in the post-Wall era. Each of these autobiographies disclose the inherent ambivalences embedded in the government's own use of the term 'solidarity' in contrast to its understanding on a personal or individual level. Stressing the ties that both Lucia Engombe and Stefanie-Lahya Aukongo cultivated not only with fellow Namibians, but also with white East Germans, she conveys how each account of migration reveals that East Germany's politics of solidarity were multivalent and contradictory at best. The conflict that manifested itself in these women's uprooting also revealed itself in their inability to establish solid biological familial bonds across diverging contexts and experiences. Thus, O'Dea demonstrates how government intervention can change the course of both individual and collective historical narratives. Taken together, Hackenesch, Nenno and O'Dea's chapters explore unaccounted-for historical intersections that represent the intricacies and complexities of Black/African diasporic histories shaped by Germans and Austrians at home and abroad.

Part II once again explores the theme of corporeality by showing how the presence of haunting enables the Black (German) subject's body to become a metaphor for power and powerlessness. Such composite approaches and intricate interventions as those made in this section demand attention to the ways in which corporeality can be simultaneously a form of recognition and denial and a site of agency and victimization. Haunting further conjures ideas of 'black fugitivity' that both scholars Barnor Hesse and Tina Campt have theorized in relation to Afro-Europeans.[52] Kimberly Alecia Singletary's chapter explicitly focuses on the idea of haunting, in which she argues that Blackness haunts the German national imaginary

---

Comrades of Color: East Germany in the Cold War World (New York: Berghahn Books, 2015), esp. Chapters 5–8.

52   Barnor Hesse, 'Escaping Liberty: Western Hegemony, Black Fugitivity', *Political Theory* 42/3 (2014): 288–313 and Tina Campt, *Image Matters: Archive, Photography, and the African Diaspora in Europe* (Durham, NC: Duke University Press, 2012).

and undermines the use of whiteness as an organizing concept for German national identity and belonging. Through her sharp interpretation, she reveals how the imagery of Black Americanness in Germany often overshadows the Black German community, rendering them simultaneously invisible and foreign in the eyes of white Germans. In interrogating whiteness and representing haunting, Singletary encourages us to recognize how race continues to be a social construct that still has material impacts on People of Color across the globe. Yet her piece also illustrates how Black Germans could racially haunt other diasporic groups in German-speaking regions such as Austria and Switzerland – as Nenno's chapter reminds us.

Another form of haunting is present in Kevina King's contribution. The haunting here is one that Black Germans and Black Americans experience through institutionalized racism that is anchored in every level of society and is a specter of whiteness. Nevertheless, such a haunting is not limited to the geographically marked territories of Germany or the United States. Taking the last years' police shootings of innocent Black lives as a point of departure, King assesses the role of the Black (German) subject in transit or on the move. This fugitivity is precisely what becomes an element of state-sanctioned institutional racism, as the Black subject must be surveilled, contained and controlled at all costs. Black bodies, thus, haunt what whites have socially constructed as seemingly safe spaces devoid of danger or threat before a 'deviant' Black subject's entrance into them. In turn, white subjects h(a)unt People of Color, which certainly proves to be life threatening. The body becomes a signifier, allowing, as these chapters suggest, diverse Black/African diasporic individuals to gain visibility or invisibility or to be an active agent or subjected to harm within and beyond the hegemonic white German nation. Comparative approaches, such as those adopted by Singletary and King, intervene by bringing multiple points of 'connected differences' (Lorde) to the forefront of their work. Their research and theorizations provide an opportunity to shift power asymmetries through Black consciousness and cognitive awareness of the potential haunting properties that some forms of Blackness acquire in the white racial imaginary, while at the same time, the avowal of common, albeit distinct experiences, reasserts a space for activist alliances to materialize transnationally.

Each of the pieces in the final part on 'Art and Performance' emphasizes the role of Black embodiment through performativity and the act of undoing and redoing. These approaches eliminate the boundaries of the quotidian experiences of People of Color that relegate racial encounters and racist perceptions to a space outside of performance and instead examine them from within that space. As such, they offer necessary interventions. The contributions in this section underscore the importance of a stage presence for African American musicians, for Black German hip-hop singer Samy Deluxe and for Black German autodidact youth performers. Each articulates the ambivalent nature of performing race and gender for oneself and others and provides nuanced readings of music and theater in historical and contemporary contexts.

In Chapter 6, Kira Thurman turns to the role of sound and the active mode of listening in the register of high versus low art. However, sound does not remain the only factor in delineating what is ascribed to the categorization of high art, as the visual performance is also explored in her chapter. Thurman's study of African American musicians represents the performance of undoing and redoing. Differing from their 1920s counterparts, nineteenth-century African American performers sought to 'undo' or change Central Europeans' opinion of them as primitive, and they 'redo' by using their acts of performativity to complicate notions of race, culture and modernity. Examining Central European debates about African American spirituals draws attention to their ability to create or not create high art musically. Performances of African American spirituals in Europe, as Thurman lays them out, become located somewhere in the interstices of high and low art, bridging the constructed false dichotomy of the 'civilized' and 'uncivilized' world. Her archival unveiling of the mechanisms through which music is categorized, labeled and consumed points to the ever-shifting boundaries of identity as it was constituted in the nineteenth and early twentieth centuries in Central Europe. Sound, it seems, may have the power to change racial perception and character, transgressing bodily and cultural boundaries.

Stage dress and costume enhance the perception of musical art forms, and it is the art of self-fashioning on the covers of Samy Deluxe's hip-hop albums that Vanessa D. Plumly's chapter interrogates. Here, too, Plumly's contribution proves how Samy Deluxe's oeuvre unsettles normative notions of Germanness and masculinity – in essence engaging in a performance of undoing and redoing. Through Samy Deluxe's staging on his album covers and lyrics, she shows us how he self-styled in an effort to carve out spaces for himself within the nation and hip-hop culture at large. Bringing postwar German masculinity to the fore, Plumly shifts the focus away from Black German women (who often feature prominently in Black German Studies) to underscore the contributions that Black German men have made. Plumly argues that Samy Deluxe performs a Black German masculinity that must be considered separately from white German postwar masculinity, given its specific socio-historical conditioning and its constantly shifting contemporary *spacetime*. She provides an illustration of Black German agency. Samy Deluxe's acts of 'undoing and redoing' unsettle and, at times, transform normative understandings of race, gender and sexuality, in turn further delimiting the potential of whiteness and white heterosexual masculinity as organizing tools for the German nation.

Finally, in Chapter 8, Jamele Watkins points to the body as a site for transforming negative experiences into a source of empowerment and agency through the interaction of performative Black subjects who process and reflect on their lived realities on the stage. Watkins also shows the performance of redoing as Black German youth enact their childhood experiences on stage as a way of reflecting on, sharing with and educating their audience about instances of everyday racism and sexism in Germany. In the production and employment of strategies of resistance to racism in the Black German theater project *real life Deutschland*, Watkins addresses the transfer of hegemony in context from one that is class-based to one that is race-based. Assessing the implementation of Augusto Boal's *Theater of the Oppressed* and Paulo Freire's *Pedagogy of the Oppressed* that intersect on-stage through the production and performance of the Young Stars' collaborative theater project, she encourages us to recognize the realm of theater as an improvisational and empowering space for activism. It equally serves as a means through which to register Black German youth's involvement in the genre by enacting, affirming and representing the Black Diaspora on stages across Germany. Even though the act of performing produces self-empowerment in the Black German community and was the impetus behind the project, it also has a pedagogical impact on audience members. 'Redoing' responses to racism and microaggressions on stage furthers the 'undoing' of its structural embeddedness and allows the youth to reimagine their future. In this way, Watkins illustrates the significance of Black German youth's agency, creativity and performativity in calling for social and cultural change and for shifting the norms of theater in Germany by bringing Black actors to the stage.

All of the contributions to this volume force us to rethink Black German Studies from diverse and often contradictory perspectives, through novel theoretical approaches, performative interventions and historical nuance. To do so is not to *call* into question the scholarly work that has come before this volume. Rather, it is to add nuance and complexity to the layered histories of the Black German Diaspora and to intervene, where certain realities are overlooked or neglected. It is to continue to reflect critically on that which is missing from the narration and to seek out what has been made invisible in the context of hegemonic power structures both within the boundaries of Central Europe and beyond. Presenting the history and culture of Black Germany – and to a lesser extent Black Austria – in this volume brings scholars together to share and produce critical knowledge on the Black/African Diaspora. This is a task – creating community – that has been the intention of Black German Studies from its outset. To rethink also means to reconsider one's own place within this community, to examine one's own gaze, positioning and perspective and to reflect on them.

We believe that now is as urgent a time as any to consider the ways in which we as scholars can serve as activists in the academy, especially following the police brutality that the past year's events have brought into the public spotlight in the United States and that have also revealed university police to be part of the structural problem – as in the case of the murder of African American Samuel Dubose at the University of Cincinnati. More recently, the Supreme Court's decision to uphold President Donald Trump's Muslim ban and the march of white nationalist supremacists at the 'Unite the Right' rally in Charlottesville, Virginia, have made even more tangible the overt racism, anti-Semitism and Islamophobia pervasive in our nation. The academy can and should serve as a site for the disruption of its own *spacetime*, through protest, discourse and a *call* to action/reform.

Beyond U.S. borders, the current discussions and political actions taken within the European Union regarding Syrian refugees have taken center stage. These discussions have not been without controversy and indeed often evoke the haunting elements of Islamophobia, racism, xenophobia and more – evidenced by the debates surrounding the events of New Year's Eve 2015 and 2016 in Cologne (and other cities). They have attracted international attention to the intersections of race, gender, sexuality and economic/political crises, albeit belatedly, as political activism was already occurring on microlevels in cities across Germany and Europe. They also prove critical in light of the current scandal over the treatment of members of the Windrush generation in Britain; these older individuals, who have lived in the country since the late 1940s and 1950s, have been denied services, lost their jobs and even risk deportation. With all of this in mind, we convene in the *spacetime* of the *here* and *now* in our book to ask what our double role can be as both academics and activists. We hope the volume will contribute to the destabilization of entrenched scholarly categories and practices that often silence or ignore certain *minority* voices, narratives, methods and perspectives and that it will lend itself to the furthering of coalitional politics and the cultivation of intercultural alliances. Acknowledging our different positionalities is a key part of that endeavor. U.S.-based scholars of Color must be aware of their ability to haunt and silence, and white scholars must be open to critiques from scholars of Color whose experiences undoubtedly enable them to think differently in the context of Black German Studies.

Bibliography

Ahmed, Sara, *The Cultural Politics of Emotions*, 2nd edn (New York: Routledge, 2015).
Aitken, Robbie, and Eve Rosenhaft, *Black Germany: The Making and Unmaking of a Diaspora Community, 1890–1960* (Cambridge: Cambridge University Press, 2013).
AntiDiskrimierungs Büro (ADB) Köln and cyberNomads, eds, *The BlackBook: Deutschlands Häutungen* (Frankfurt am Main and London: IKO-Verlag für Interkulturelle Kommunikation, 2004).

Apraku, Josephine, Shaheen Wacker, Nela Biedermann, Kristin Lein, Jacqueline Mayen, Mic Oala, 'Wenn ich sage, Black Lives Matter', dann sage ich auch, dass mein eigenes Leben zählt', *Missy Magazine* (20 June 2017).

Asfaha, Nouria, 'Each one Teach one (EOTO e.V.) und das "Vera Heyer Archiv" als Meilenstein der Schwarzen Deutschen Bewegung', *Souls and Sisters: Inspirationen von May Ayim*, ed. Natasha A. Kelly (Berlin: Orlanda, 2015), 94–104.

Bahktin, Mikhail, *Problems of Dostoyevsky's Poetics*, tr. Caryl Emerson (Minneapolis: University of Minnesota Press, 1984).

Bergold-Caldwell, Denise, Laura Digoh, Hadija Haruna-Oekler, Christelle Nkwendja-Ngnoubamdjum, Camilla Ridha and Elenore Wiedenroth-Colibaly, eds, *Spiegelblicke: Perspektiven Schwarzer Bewegung in Deutschland* (Berlin: Orlanda Frauenverlag, 2015).

Bezirksamt Mitte von Berlin, *Lern- und Erinnerungsort Afrikanisches Viertel* (n.d.) <https://www.leo-afrika.de> accessed 30 June 2018.

Black German Cultural Society (BGCS) (2018) <http://afrogermans.us/> accessed 28 March 2018.

Black German Heritage and Research Association (BGHRA) (2018) <http://bghra.org/> accessed 28 March 2018.

'Black German Studies Then and Now', German Studies Association Conference, 18–21 September 2014, Kansas City, Missouri.

'Britin Sharon Dodua Otoo gewinnt den Bachmann-Preis', *Spiegel Online* (3 July 2016) <http://www.spiegel.de/kultur/literatur/bachmann-preis-2016-fuer-sharon-dodua-otoo-publikumspreis-fuer-stefanie-sargnagel-a-1101073.html> accessed 19 July 2017.

Bundeszentrale für politische Bildung and Initiative Schwarze Menschen in Deutschland, eds, *Homestory Deutschland. Schwarze Biografien in Geschichte und Gegenwart* (Berlin: bpb, 2009), 62–65.

Campt, Tina, 'The Crowded Space of Diaspora: Intercultural Address and the Tensions of Diasporic Relation', in Ian Christopher Fletcher, ed. 'Citizenship, National Identity, Race, and Diaspora in Contemporary Europe', Special issue, *Radical History Review* 83 (Spring 2002): 94–113.

——, 'Diaspora Space, Ethnographic Space: Writing History Between the Lines', in Kamari Maxine Clarke and Deborah A. Thomas, eds, *Globalization and Race: Transformations in the Cultural Production of Blackness* (Durham, NC: Duke University Press, 2006), 93–111.

——, *Image Matters: Archive, Photography, and the African Diaspora in Europe* (Durham, NC: Duke University Press, 2012).

——, *Other Germans: Black Germans and the Politics of Race, Gender, and Memory in the Third Reich* (Ann Arbor: University of Michigan Press, 2004).

Callahan, Noaquia N., 'A Rare Colored Bird: Mary Church Terrell, *Die Fortschritte der farbigen Frauen*, and the International Council of Women's Congress in Berlin, Germany 1904', in Britta Waldschmidt-Nelson and Anja Schüler, eds, *Forging Bonds Across Borders: Mobilizing for Women's Rights and Social Justice in the 19th Century Transatlantic World*, German Historical Institute Bulletin Supplement 13 (2017), 93–110.

Chrisafis, Angelique, 'Protests spread across Paris estates as anger grows over alleged police rape', *The Guardian* (8 February 2017) <https://www.theguardian.com/world/2017/feb/08/12-arrested-as-french-youths-clash-with-police-on-estates-near-paris> accessed 30 August 2017.

'Community Statement: 'Black' Studies at the University of Bremen', *Present_Tense Scholars Network: Black Perspectives and Studies Germany* (January 2015) <https://blackstudiesgermany.wordpress.com/statementbremen/> accessed 31 August 2017.

Davies, Carol Boyce, *Left of Karl Marx: The Political Life of Black Communist Claudia Jones* (Durham, NC: Duke University Press, 2008).

Eggers, Maureen Maisha, 'Knowledges of (Un-)Belonging: Epistemic Change as a Defining Mode for Black Women's Activism in Germany', in Sara Lennox, ed., *Remapping Black Germany: New Perspectives on Afro-German History, Politics, and Culture* (Amherst: University of Massachusetts Press, 2016), 33–45.

——, Grada Kilomba, Peggy Piesche, and Susan Arndt, eds, *Mythen, Masken und Subjekte: Kritische Weißseinforschung in Deutschand* (Munster: Unrast, 2006).

El-Tayeb, Fatima, *European Others: Queering Ethnicity in Postnational Europe* (Minneapolis: University of Minnesota Press, 2011).

——, *Undeutsch: die Konstruktion des Anderen in der postmigrantischen Gesellschaft* (Bielefeld: Transcript, 2016).

Esuruoso, Asoka, and Philipp Khabo Koepsell, eds, *Arriving in the Future: Stories of Home and Exile: An Anthology of Poetry and Creative Writing by Black Writers in Germany* (Berlin: epubli, 2014).

Fereidooni, Karim, 'Rassismus an der Uni: Warum es in Deutschland kaum schwarze Professor gibt', *Huffpost Voices Blog* (30 June 2017) <http://www.huffingtonpost.de/karim-fereidooni/rassismus-uni-deutschland_b_17332910.html> accessed 23 August 2017.

Florvil, Tiffany N., 'Black German Feminists and their Transnational Connections of the 1980s and 1990s', in Friederike Bruehoefener, Karen Hagemann and Donna Harsch, eds, *Gendering Post-1945 German History: Entanglements* (New York: Berghahn Books, forthcoming 2018).

——, 'From ADEFRA to Black Lives Matter: Black Women's Activism in Germany', *Black Perspectives* (5 July 2017) <https://www.aaihs.org/from-adefra-to-black-lives-matter-black-womens-activism-in-germany/> accessed 12 June 2018.

Ford, Tanisha, 'We Were the People of Soul', in *Liberated Threads: Black Women, Style, and The Global Politics of Soul* (Chapel Hill: University of North Carolina Press, 2015), 123–57.

Fresh Magazin (2018) <http://freshzine.at/> 12 June 2018.

Gerund, Katharina, *Transatlantic Cultural Exchange: African American Women's Art and Activism in West Germany* (Bielefeld: Transcript Verlag, 2013), 101–56.

Gilroy, Paul, *The Black Atlantic: Modernity and Double Consciousness* (Cambridge, MA: Harvard University Press, 1993).

Gordon, Lewis, *Fanon and the Crisis of European Man: An Essay on Philosophy and the Human Sciences* (New York: Routledge, 1995).

Gyamerah, Daniel, and Saraya Gomis, 'Each One Teach One, e.V.: Ein Ort der Begegnung', *Each One Teach One (EOTO) e.V.* (2016) <http://eoto-archiv.de> accessed 1 September 2017.

Hagen, Katrina, 'Ambivalence and Desire in the East German "Free Angela Davis" Campaign', Quinn Slobodian, ed., *Comrades of Color: East Germany in the Cold War World* (New York: Berghahn Books, 2015), 157–87.

Hall, Stuart, 'Cultural Identity and Diaspora', in Jonathan Rutherford, ed., *Identity: Community, Culture, and Difference* (London: Lawrence & Wishart, 1990), 222–37.

Hall, Stuart, and Bill Schwarz, *Familiar Stranger: A Life Between Two Islands* (Durham, NC: Duke University Press, 2017).

'Haus', Ballhaus Naunynstrasse (n.d.) <http://www.ballhausnaunynstrasse.de> accessed 11 June 2018.

Hendriks, Mandy, 'Black Lives Matter Movement Goes Dutch', *NWSNET* (2 December 2016) <http://journalistiekzwolle.nl/nwsnet/black-lives-matter-goes-dutch/> accessed 12 June 2018.

Hentschke, Steffi, 'Der Aufschrei gegen Alltagsrassismus', *Stern* (9 September 2013) <https://www.stern.de/digital/online/-schauhin-der-aufschrei-gegen-alltagsrassismus-3913892.html> accessed 2 July 2018.

Hesse, Barnor, 'Escaping Liberty: Western Hegemony, Black Fugitivity', *Political Theory* 42/3 (2014): 288–313.

Höhn, Maria, and Martin Klimke, *A Breath of Freedom: The Civil Rights Struggle, African American GIs, and Germany* (New York: Palgrave MacMillian, 2010).

——, 'The Black Panther Solidarity Committee and the Trial of the Ramstein 2', in Belinda Davis, Wilfried Mausbach, Martin Klimke and Carla MacDougall, eds, *Changing the World, Changing Oneself: Political Protest and Collective Identities in the 1960s/70s West Germany and U.S.* (New York: Berghahn, 2010), 215–40.

Hügel-Marshall, Ika, *Daheim unterwegs. Ein deutsches Leben* (Frankfurt: Fischer, 2001).

Johnston-Arthur, Araba Evelyn, 'Es ist Zeit der Geschichte selbst eine Gestalt zu geben ... Strategien der Entkolonialisierung und Ermächtigung im Kontext der afrikanischen Diaspora in Österreich', in Kien Nghi Ha, and others, *re/visionen Postkoloniale Perspektiven von People of Color auf Rassismus, Kulturpolitik und Widerstand in Deutschland* (Berlin: Unrast Verlag, 2007), 423–44.

Kelly, Natasha A., 'EDEWA – Einkaufsgenossenschaft antirassistischen Widerstandes eröffnet eigene "Filiale" in Berlin-Neukölln', *Natasha A. Kelly: Academic Activist* (8 November 2015) <http://www.natashaakelly.com/edewa-einkaufsgenossen schaft-antirassistischen-widerstandes-eroffnet-eigene-filiale-in-berlin-neukolln/> accessed 20 June 2016.

——, ed., *Souls and Sisters: Inspirationen von May Ayim* (Berlin: Orlanda Frauen- verlag, 2015).

——, *Berlin Biennial for Contemporary Art* (2018) <http:bb10.berlinbiennal.de/ artists/n/natasha-a-kelly> accessed 12 June 2018.

Klimke, Martin, *The Other Alliance: Student Protest in West Germany and the United States in the Global Sixties* (Princeton, NJ: Princeton University Press, 2010).

Koepsell, Philipp Khabo, 'Literature and Activism', in Asoka Esuruoso and Philipp Khabo Koepsell, eds, *Arriving in the Future: Stories of Home and Exile: An Anthology of Poetry and Creative Writing by Black Writers in Germany* (Berlin: epubli, 2014), 36–47.

Kopp, Christian, and Marius Krohn, 'Blues in Schwarzweiss. Die Black Commu- nity im Widerstand gegen kolonialrassistische Straßennamen in Berlin Mitte', *Berlin-Postkolonial* (n.d.) <http://www.berlin-postkolonial.de/cms/index.php/ orte/78-afrikanisches-viertel> accessed 12 December 2013.

'Label Noir', *Label Noir* (n.d.) <https://www.labelnoir.net> accessed 5 May 2016.

Lennox, Sara, *Remapping Black Germany: New Perspectives on Afro-German History, Politics, and Culture* (Amherst: University of Massachusetts Press, 2016).

Lorde, Audre, *A Burst of Light and Other Essays* (New York: Ixia Press, 2017).

——, 'Foreword', in Dagmar Schultz, May Ayim and Katharina Oguntoye, eds, *Show- ing Our Colors: Afro-German Women Speak Out* (Amherst: University of Mas- sachusetts Press, 1991), vii–xiv.

Lüpke-Narberhaus, Frauke, 'Ich erkenne schon am Nachnamen, ob jemand durchfällt', *bento* (13 December 2015) <http://www.bento.de/today/campus-rassismus- studenten-erzaehlen-von-alltagsrassismus-194006/> accessed 2 July 2018.

Lusane, Clarence, *Hitler's Black Victims: The Historical Experiences of Afro-Germans, European Blacks, Africans, and African Americans in the Nazi Era* (New York and London: Routledge, 2003).

Makalani, Minkah, *In the Cause of Freedom: Radical Black Internationalism from Harlem to London, 1917–1939* (Chapel Hill: University of North Carolina Press, 2011).

Martin, Peter, 'Der schwarze Philosoph', in Peter Martin, *Schwarze Teufel, Edle Mohren* (Hamburg: Junius, 1993).

Massaquoi, Hans J., *Destined to Witness: Growing Up Black in Nazi Germany* (New York: William Morrow Paperbacks, 1999)

——, *Neger, Neger Schornsteinfeger. Meine Kindheit in Deutschland* (Munich: Droemersche Verlagsanstalt, 2001).

Mazón, Patricia, and Reinheld Steingröver, eds, *Not So Plain as Black and White: Afro-German Culture and History, 1890–2000* (Rochester: University of Rochester Press, 2015).

McVeigh, Tracy, 'Why activists brought the Black Lives Matter movement to the UK', *The Guardian* (6 August 2016) <https://www.theguardian.com/uk-news/2016/aug/06/black-lives-matter-uk-found-vital-social-justice> accessed 12 June 2018.

Muñiz de Faria, Yara-Colette Lemke, *Zwischen Fürsorge und Ausgrenzung: Afrodeutsche 'Besatzungskinder' im Nachkriegsdeutschland* (Berlin: Mertopol Verlag, 2002).

Nghi Ha, Kien, Nicola Lauré al-Samarai and Sheila Mysorekar, eds, *Re/visionen: Postkoloniale Perspektiven von People of Color auf Rassismus, Kulturpolitik und Widerstand in Deutschland* (Munster: Unrast, 2007).

Oguntoye, Katharina, *Eine afro-deutsche Geschichte: Zur Lebenssituation von Afrikanern und Afro-Deutschen in Deutschland von 1884 bis 1950* (Berlin: Hoho Verlag Christine Hoffmann, 1997).

Oguntoye, Katharina, May Opitz/Ayim and Dagmar Schultz, eds, *Farbe bekennen: Afro-deutsche Frauen auf den Spuren ihrer Geschichte* (1986; repr., Berlin: Orlanda Frauenverlag, 2006).

——, 'Joliba: Interkulturelles Netzwerk in Berlin e.V.', *Joliba* (2017) <http://www.joliba.de> accessed 1 August 2017.

Oltermann, Philip, 'Black British Writer Wins Major German Language Fiction Award', *The Guardian* (12 July 2016) <https://www.theguardian.com/books/2016/jul/12/black-british-writer-wins-major-german-language-fiction-sharon-dodue-otoo-ingeborg-bachmann-prize> accessed 19 July 2017.

Piesche, Peggy, ed. *Euer Schweigen schützt euch nicht: Audre Lorde und die Schwarze Frauenbewegung in Deutschland* (Berlin: Orlanda Frauenverlag, 2012).

——, 'Making African Diasporic Pasts Possible: A Retrospective View of the GDR and Its Black (Step-) Children', in Sara Lennox, ed., *Remapping Black Germany: New Perspectives on Afro-German History, Politics, and Culture* (Amherst: University of Massachusetts Press, 2016).

Plumly, Vanessa D., 'BLACK-Red-Gold in "der bunten Republik": Constructions and Performances of Heimat/en in Afro-/Black German Cultural Productions', Dissertation, University of Cincinnati, 2015.

'Political Activism in the Black European Diaspora: From Theory to Praxis', German Studies Association Conference, 1–4 October 2015, Washington, DC.

Reed-Anderson, Paulette, *Rewriting the Footnotes: Berlin und die afrikanische Diaspora* (Berlin: Die Ausländerbeauftragte des Senats, 2000), 30–32.

'"Rhodes Must Fall" – Decolonization Symbolism – What is happening at UCT, South Africa?' *The Postcolonialist* (29 March 2015) <http://postcolonialist. com/civil-discourse/rhodes-must-fall-decolonisation-symbolism-happening-uct-south-africa/> accessed 2 July 2018.

Sharpley-Whiting, T. Denean, *Negritude Women* (Minneapolis: University of Minnesota Press, 2002).

Shelby, Tommie, *We Who are Dark: The Philosophical Foundations of Black Solidarity* (Cambridge, MA: Belknap Press, 2005).

Slobodian, Quinn, *Comrades of Color: East Germany in the Cold War World* (New York: Berghahn, 2015).

——, *Foreign Front: Third World Politics in Sixties West Germany* (Durham, NC: Duke University Press, 2012).

Smith, Barbara, 'A Press of Our Own Kitchen Table: Women of Color Press', *Frontiers: A Journal of Women Studies*, 10/3 (1989), 11–13.

Trouillot, Michel-Rolph, *Silence the Past: Power and the Production of History* (Boston, MA: Beacon, 1995).

Umoren, Imaobong, *Race Women Internationalists: Activist-Intellectuals and Global Freedom Struggles* (Oakland: University of California Press, 2018).

Watkins, Jamele, 'Rearticulating Black Feminist Thought in *Heimat, bittersüße Heimat*', *Women in German Yearbook* 32 (2016), 138–51.

Wiedenroth-Coulibaly, Eleonore and Sascha Zinflou, '20 Jahre Schwarze Organisierung in Deutschland – Ein Abriss', in AntiDiskrimierungs Büro (ADB) Köln and cyberNomads, eds, *The BlackBook: Deutschlands Häutungen* (Frankfurt am Main and London: IKO-Verlag für Interkulturelle Kommunikation, 2004), 133–44.

Wright, Michelle M., 'Middle Passage Blackness and Its Diasporic Discontents: The Case for a Post-war Epistemology', in Eve Rosenhaft and Robbie Aitken, eds, *Africa in Europe: Studies in Transnational Practice in the Long Twentieth Century* (Liverpool: Liverpool University Press, 2013), 217–33.

——, 'Pale by Comparison: Black Liberal Humanism and the Postwar Era in the African Diaspora', in Darlene Clark Hine, Trica Danielle Keaton and Stephen Small, eds, *Black Europe and the African Diaspora* (Urbana: University of Illinois Press, 2009), 260–76.

——, *The Physics of Blackness* (Minneapolis: University of Minnesota Press, 2015).

Zahir, Nabila, 'In France, Black Lives Matter has become a rallying cry', *Al Jazeera* (2 September 2016) <https://www.aljazeera.com/indepth/features/2016/08/france-black-lives-matter-rallying-cry-160818103854211.html> accessed 12 June 2018.

PART I

German and Austrian Literature and History

SILKE HACKENESCH

1 'Hergestellt unter ausschließlicher Verwendung von Kakaobohnen deutscher Kolonien': On Representations of Chocolate Consumption as a Colonial Endeavor

ABSTRACT

This chapter explores the entanglements of the history of cocoa as a colonial commodity with constructions of Blackness in early twentieth-century Germany. Examining various visual and textual sources illustrates how cocoa and chocolate became firmly linked to images of laboring Black bodies as well as stereotypical imagery of Africans that informed the discourses on colonialism and empire. At a time that also witnessed the emergence of a professional advertising industry, commodities such as cocoa were not only construed as colonial, but also exotic. The knowledge of brown-skinned people toiling on cocoa farms for the pleasurable consumption of chocolate by German consumers, in fact, enhanced the exotic appeal. Through endless repetitions, both visually and linguistically, Europeans 'learned' this association because it was normalized and made to appear 'natural'.

How seldom do we think when we drink a cup of cocoa or eat some morsels of chocolate, that our liking of these delicacies has set minds and bodies at work all the world over! Many types of humanity have contributed to their production. Picture in the mind's eye the graceful coolie in the sun-saturated tropics, moving in the shade, cutting the pods from the cacao tree; the deep-chested sailor helping to load from lighters or surf-boats the precious bags of cacao into the hold of the ocean liner; the skillful workman roasting the beans until they fill the room with a fine aroma; and the girl with dexterous fingers packing the cocoa or fashioning the chocolate in curious and delicate forms. To the black and the brown races, the negroes and the East

Indians, we owe a debt for their work on tropical plantations, for the harder manual
work would be too arduous for Europeans unused to the heat of those regions.[1]

Arthur Knapp, an employer of the British chocolate company Cadbury
Brothers who published a book on chocolate in 1920, wrote those words
about the global entanglements of chocolate.[2] The quotation offers a distorted narrative of how chocolate reaches its consumers. By naming the
subjects involved in the making of chocolate, Knapp described the various
stages of production from bean (cocoa farm) to bar (factory). Without
irony, he stated that the (allegedly white) consumers of chocolate were
indebted to People of Color for their hard plantation work. Echoing
sentiments in tune with scientific racism, the author claimed that white
Europeans were poorly equipped for working on cocoa farms. His account,
while mentioning hard manual labor, struck a tone of adventure, excite-
ment and exoticism. It thereby mitigated the inequalities that colonialism,
imperialism and global capitalism have produced.[3]

Tropical edibles, such as chocolate, however, cannot be analyzed
without taking into account the contexts of colonialism and imperialism.
Consuming chocolate while silencing the modes of producing cocoa beans
has been a key characteristic in the advertisement of chocolate and also serves
as a form of internalized imperialism.[4] The rise of cocoa as a global commodity would have been unthinkable without the influence of colonialism.

1   Arthur Knapp, *Cocoa and Chocolate: Their History from Plantation to Consumer*
     (London: Chapman and Hall, 1920), 17. The British Cadbury Brothers supported
     Knapp's study, and he was a research chemist for the company. His book contains an
     extensive bibliography, comprising of titles in English, Spanish, French and German
     from 1643 to 1919.
2   The book was published after the Cadbury Company had been at the center of a scan-
     dal in which it was accused of knowingly buying slave-grown cocoa from Portuguese
     West Africa. Knapp's account is an attempt to restore the company's reputation.
3   Due to the historical experience of European colonialism, exoticism is an inherently
     Eurocentric concept, as Michael Mayer has pointed out. See Michael Mayer, *'Tropen
     gibt es nicht'. Dekonstruktionen des Exotismus* (Bielefeld: Aisthesis Verlag, 2010).
4   See Angelika Epple, *Das Unternehmen Stollwerck: Eine Mikrogeschichte der
     Globalisierung* (Frankfurt am Main: Campus, 2010), 409.

It shaped not only politics and economies on a global scale, but also the migration and transfer of cultural goods and ideas. Through chocolate and other colonial commodities, Africans and Europeans were inextricably linked with the former largely at the point of production and the latter mostly at the point of consumption. This linkage of cocoa and colonialism, of chocolate and Blackness also found its way into advertisements. Trade cards from the early twentieth century solidly anchored chocolate within a German colonial context and reiterated a trope that conflated chocolate with (African) Blackness, connecting it with stereotypical images. As a result of this constant repetition, many consumers considered this false equation to be 'natural' and 'self-evident'. Yet, there was nothing natural about it. This conflation was learned and evolved into a 'natural' state, and it was created within a colonial (revisionist) culture.

In this chapter, I shed light on the history of the entanglements of chocolate and Blackness in Germany in the early twentieth century, a time that witnessed not only the consequences of Germany's complicity in the 'Scramble for Africa', but also the emergence of a modern mass advertising industry and an increased emphasis on the visual as a way of bolstering the modern nation. Analyzing visual sources, including picture postcards, that helped to promote cocoa products, reveals how these images establish a visual connection between chocolate and Blackness in different ways. The first example reprinted and analyzed in detail later is a postcard with a photograph that features a colonial scene in Cameroon, where African laborers, controlled by a white overseer, harvested cocoa beans. The postcard falsely suggests an image of colonial abundance and links the commodity and its consumption to the physical labor of Black men. Another example is a colored drawing on a historical trade card that shows a white woman feeding hot chocolate to a Black man. The image alludes to the idea that chocolate was considered an aphrodisiac with this tabooed and illicit interaction across the color line. Here, chocolate is not a colonial commodity (made of cocoa) anymore; rather it is hot chocolate and presented in its fluid and drinkable and thus more transgressive form. It becomes a product that a 'civilized' white German woman offers to a Black man, who was depicted as the stereotypical African savage. Both images represent how chocolate became a signifier with multiple meanings and messages.

Furthermore, I examine several issues of the monthly magazine called *Der Tropenpflanzer. Zeitschrift für tropische Landwirtschaft* [*The Tropical Planter. Magazine for Tropical Agriculture*] from the first decade of the twentieth century, which regularly documented the cultivation of cocoa in the German colonies and featured advertisements for cocoa and chocolate products. The magazine targeted colonial enthusiasts and those with a professional, economic interest in the colonies. Taken together these sources illustrate that the linkage of chocolate with Blackness was a construction that emerged within a specific historical moment. With the advent of the advertising industry, cocoa and chocolate were marketed as colonial, exotic products. The knowledge of brown-skinned people toiling on cocoa farms for the pleasurable consumption of chocolate by Germans enhanced their exotic appeal. Indeed, the equation of chocolate with Black people found in many historical trade cards and its continuity in today's popular parlance had nothing to do with any perceived similarities of skin color and the color of certain products. As my chapter demonstrates, there was nothing inherently 'natural' about the connection of brown and black products with the pigmentation of human beings. Instead, Europeans learned this association through endless repetition, which in turn normalized and naturalized these images.

Cocoa and Neoslavery

In the early twentieth century, cocoa increasingly became an in-demand commodity in many Western European countries and in the United States. Theodor Reichardt's cocoa company in Wandsbek, Hamburg, for instance, developed into Germany's biggest chocolate producer and processed three percent of the world's cocoa.[5] Reichardt had initially bought his cocoa

---

5   Heiko Möhle, 'Bittere Schokolade: Die Früchte der Plantagenwirtschaft', in Heiko Möhle, ed., *Branntwein, Bibeln und Bananen: Der deutsche Kolonialismus in Afrika – eine Spurensuche [in Hamburg]* (Hamburg: Verlag Libertäre Assoziation, 1999), 55.

from South America and the Portuguese West African colonies of São Tomé and Príncipe. The latter two islands were about the size of Berlin and literally turned into cocoa factories around 1900, producing most of the cocoa consumed worldwide.[6] While cocoa is usually a peasant crop in West Africa – as in Ghana, for example – these islands became infamous for the existence of coerced labor on privately owned plantations during a brief yet intense boom in the cocoa industry.[7] This sharp increase in the demand for cocoa could only be satisfied with a re-introduction of a coerced labor system akin to slavery. White Europeans bought the laborers on these islands from Angola and then forced them to march to the coast. The British investigative journalist Henry Nevinson called those laborers 'modern slaves'. *Harper's Magazine* in the United States hired Nevinson to verify rumors about the re-introduction of slavery in West Africa.[8] After travelling along the 'slave route' through Angola and observing the practice of slavery for the production of cocoa, he wrote several articles in 1905 and 1906, which were subsequently published as a book entitled *A Modern Slavery*.[9]

Once the enslaved arrived at the coast, they were shipped off to the cocoa farms. Between the years of 1880 and 1908, 70,000 of these workers came to São Tomé and Príncipe.[10] They were exploited on these islands,

---

In 1928, the Reichardt Werke closed its doors in Hamburg, and then the Stollwerck Company in Cologne purchased it.

6   William Gervase Clarence-Smith, 'Struggles over Labour Conditions in the Plantations of São Tomé and Príncipe', *Slavery and Abolition* 14/1 (1993), 149.

7   William Gervase Clarence-Smith, 'Cocoa Plantations and Coerced Labor in the Gulf of Guinea, 1870–1914', in Martin A. Klein, ed., *Breaking the Chains: Slavery, Bondage, and Emancipation in Modern Africa and Asia* (Madison: University of Wisconsin Press, 1993), 150.

8   H. N. Brailsford, revised by Sinead Agnew, 'Nevinson, Henry Woodd', in H. C. G. Matthew, and Brian Harrison, eds, *Oxford Dictionary of National Biography: From the Earliest Times to the Year 2000*, 40 (Oxford: Oxford University Press, 2004), 551–52.

9   Henry Woodd Nevinson, *A Modern Slavery. With an Introduction by Basil Davidson* (1906; New York: Schocken Books, 1968).

10   Kevin Grant, *A Civilised Savagery: Britain and the New Slaveries in Africa, 1884–1926* (New York: Routledge, 2005), 115.

while the nascent European advertising industry propagated colonial fantasies of consuming tropical riches. Both developments happened simultaneously in the early twentieth century because the consumer demand for cocoa and chocolate rapidly increased and could only be satisfied by a cheap and controllable labor force. The case of these two islands under Portuguese colonial control highlights the close interrelatedness of commodity consumption with capitalism and slavery. The slave trade had been abolished in 1836, and slavery in Portuguese West Africa was officially outlawed in 1875. Yet it was exactly because of the notorious slave trade from Angola and a rigid slavery system on Portuguese West African cocoa plantations, secured by strict labor laws in 1899, that the appetite for cocoa products could be satisfied.[11]

German businessmen, too, wanted to participate in the growing cocoa trade and reap a profit by importing cocoa beans from Cameroon, a German colony at that time. The Reichardt Company declared the import of cocoa a 'patriotic deed' and produced a whole series of photographs printed on

11   Catherine Higgs, *Chocolate Islands: Cocoa, Slavery, and Colonial Africa* (Athens, OH: Ohio University Press, 2012), 73–74. Wolf Mueller notes that '[e]in wesentlicher Faktor bei der Entwicklung der Kakaowirtschaft beider Inseln [São Tomé and Príncipe] war, dass ihr reichliche und billige Arbeitskräfte zur Verfügung standen, vom afrikanischen Festland, zumeist aus Angola eingeführte Sklaven. Zwar wurde die Sklaverei im Jahre 1878 [sic!] offiziell verboten, sie bestand jedoch in versteckter Form weiter. Der Erfolg, der der Kakaowirtschaft auf den beiden Inseln beschieden war, machte sie bald zu einem wesentlichen Faktor auf dem Kakao-Weltmarkt. Von 1000 Tonnen im Jahre 1886 hatte sich die Kakaoausfuhr der Inseln innerhalb von 10 Jahren versiebenfacht, um sich im Jahre 1900 nochmals auf 14000 Tonnen zu verdoppeln' ['One crucial factor in the development of a cocoa economy on both islands [São Tomé and Príncipe] was the abundant availability of a cheap labor force from the African mainland, mostly enslaved Africans from Angola. Even though slavery had been officially abolished in 1878 [sic!], it continued in disguise. The success of the cocoa economy on both islands made them a crucial player in the global cocoa trade. While the islands exported 1,000 tons of cocoa in 1886, that amount was sevenfold in the following ten years, only to double again to 14.000 tons in 1900']. All translations are my own, unless otherwise cited. Wolf Mueller, *Seltsame Frucht Kakao: Geschichte des Kakaos und der Schokolade* (Hamburg: Verlag Gordian-Max Rieck, 1957), 100.

postcards in 1910, which illustrated the voyage and transformation from raw cocoa beans to refined chocolate products and from the African cocoa farm to an industrialized manufactured product in Wandsbek, Hamburg. These cards circulated in Wilhelmine Germany not only to document and advertise Reichardt's endeavor into the cocoa business, but also to popularize the colonial enterprise as a whole. Through the cards, set in the colony, consumers were inculcated with notions of German effectiveness and superiority. For instance, it is the white German overseer in these cards that is not working and getting dirty but, rather, supervising the labor of Black bodies and illustrating the power dynamics at play.

Representations of German Colonialism

German media representations of colonialism actively shaped consumer tastes, while pretending to convey 'objective' knowledge of the 'Other'.[12] Analyzing the postcards that Reichardt and other chocolate companies distributed proves productive because they were not merely reflective of a widespread infusion of colonial ideology and German culture at the time, but actively produced and influenced such discourses. German colonial imagery in the form of advertisements, panoramas, exhibitions and more was extremely pervasive and bore little relation to the actual significance (or lack thereof) of Germany's colonial economy.[13] Its ubiquity did not correspond with a widespread vision of colonial expansion or enthusiasm for the colonies. And still, even though Great Britain, France, the Netherlands and Japan were much more influential colonial powers, Germany's colonial

12   Volker Langbehn, 'Introduction: Picturing Race: Visuality and German Colonialism', in Volker Langbehn, ed., *German Colonialism, Visual Culture, and Modern Memory* (New York: Routledge, 2010), 5.

13   David Ciarlo, 'Advertising and the Optics of Colonial Power at the Fin de Siècle', in Volker Langbehn, ed., *German Colonialism, Visual Culture, and Modern Memory* (New York: Routledge, 2010), 38.

ideas, aspirations and legacy did find expression in cultural artifacts such
as picture postcards. These postcards promoted colonial culture and scenes
that promised adventure, representing a small glimpse into a foreign world
and offering knowledge of an exotic product and images of Africans that
consumers could easily have found gratifying without being ardent sup-
porters of German colonialism.[14] Historian and cultural theorist Fatima
El-Tayeb has observed:

> Germany engaged in formal colonialism only for a short period [...] It is still a wide-
> spread belief, therefore, in Germany and beyond, that the possession of African and
> Pacific territories had no lasting impact on either the colonizing or the colonized
> societies; an assumption that was long supported by colonialism scholars' negligence
> of the German Empire.[15]

Similarly, the works of Jeff Bowersox, Andreas Eckert, Albert Wirz and
John Phillip Short have shown that the actual possession and occupancy
of colonies is not the same as colonialism as a culture. This means that the
colonial imagery existed independently of Germany's possession of colonies and their importance for the economy.[16] Even though those posses-
sions were modest compared to other colonial empires, colonial tropes in

14   Jeff Bowersox, *Raising Germans in the Age of Empire: Youth and Colonial Culture,
      1871–1914* (Oxford: Oxford University Press, 2013).

15   Fatima El-Tayeb, 'Colored Germans there will never be', in Dawne Y. Curry, Eric D.
      Duke and Marshanda A. Smith, eds, *Extending the Diaspora: New Histories of Black
      People* (Urbana: University of Illinois Press, 2009), 225.

16   Andreas Eckert and Albert Wirz thus note: '[d]er deutsche Kolonialbesitz war in der
      Tat wenig bedeutend und insgesamt von nur kurzer Dauer. Aus der Kürze der for-
      malen Kolonialherrschaft lässt sich jedoch keineswegs folgern, dass der Kolonialismus
      deswegen ohne Relevanz für die deutsche Geschichte gewesen wäre. Kolonialbesitz
      ist das eine, Kolonialismus und koloniales Denken etwas anderes' ['The German
      colonial possession was indeed insignificant and short-lived. This brevity, however,
      does not result in an irrelevance of colonialism for the course of German history.
      Colonial possessions are not to be conflated with colonialism and colonial thinking'].
      Andreas Eckert, and Albert Wirz, 'Wir nicht, die anderen auch: Deutschland und der
      Kolonialismus', in Sebastian Conrad, ed., *Jenseits des Eurozentrismus: Postkoloniale
      Perspektiven in den Geschichts- und Kulturwissenschaften* (Frankfurt/Main: Campus,
      2002), 374.

literature, games, toys and advertising, among others, permeated German culture and, in turn, influenced the nation.[17]

Visual representations of German colonialism have received increased scholarly attention.[18] These representations serve as valuable historical artifacts, for they influenced consumer taste, pretended to convey 'objective' knowledge of the 'Other' and functioned as 'a window onto the world'.[19] Volker Langbehn has argued that postcards played a central identity-forming role within German culture and society during the Wilhelmine era. Viewed as part of a wider pattern of cultural expression, postcards such as these provide an important understanding of the pervasive and persistent set of Eurocentric attitudes that informed Germany's position on the rest of the world, especially toward its colonies.[20] Granting visual material more agency further contributes to an understanding of why colonial imagery was so prevalent, particularly since it did not correspond with any actual economic significance.[21]

Postcards are especially noteworthy because according to postal statistics, a billion postcards were sent from the German Empire in 1900 alone.[22]

17 John Phillip Short, *Magic Lantern Empire: Colonialism and Society in Germany* (Ithaca, NY: Cornell University Press, 2012). See also, Sara Friedrichsmeyer, Sara Lennox and Susanne Zantop, eds, *The Imperialist Imagination: German Colonialism and its Legacy* (Ann Arbor: University of Michigan Press, 1999), 18.

18 See, for example, Jens Jäger, 'Bilder aus Afrika vor 1918: Zur visuellen Konstruktion Afrikas im europäischen Kolonialismus', in Paul Gerhard, ed., *Visual History: Ein Studienbuch* (Göttingen: Vandenhoeck & Ruprecht, 2006), 134–48.

19 Langbehn, 'Introduction', 5.

20 Volker Langbehn, 'The Visual Representation of Blackness during German Imperialism around 1900', in Michael Perraudin, and Jürgen Zimmerer, eds, *German Colonialism and National Identity* (London: Routledge, 2011), 90–100.

21 Ciarlo, 'Advertising and the Optics of Colonial Power', 38.

22 Felix Axster, '"... will try to send you the best views from here": Postcards from the Colonial War in Namibia (1904–1908)', in Volker Langbehn, ed., *German Colonialism, Visual Culture, and Modern Memory* (New York: Routledge, 2010), 55. See also Christraud M. Geary, and Virginia-Lee Webb, 'Introduction: Views on Postcards', in Christraud M. Geary, and Virginia-Lee Webb, eds, *Delivering Views: Distant Cultures in Early Postcards* (Washington, DC: Smithsonian Institution Press, 1998), 9.

They helped to popularize and disseminate distorted images and stereotypes of non-white people to large parts of the national populace and beyond.[23] Their popularity also illustrates the importance of postcards as a medium for communication, rendering an analysis of the visual imagery on the front of these cards even more relevant. These postcards could be distributed en masse so that colonialism's reach was not limited to any specific geographic locale. An article in the *Centralblatt für Ansichtskarten-Sammler* [*Central Journal for Postcard Collectors*], a journal devoted to private collectors of postcards, attributed the immense popularity of the picture postcard in Germany to 'the peculiarly German cosmopolitanism, its fondness for the foreign and exotic and its interest for all things foreign.'[24] Yet, what many of these cards disseminated were fantasies and imaginations of tropical places, exotic commodities and brown-skinned peoples. These images were empty signifiers, constructing a colonial world that had little, if anything, to do with real contexts. As far as photographs are concerned, they, in contrast to drawings, convey objective observations and reflections of reality. However, these photos were staged, taken from a distinctive perspective, made with a certain motivation and produced for a clearly defined purpose. Moreover, a photograph is a framed setting that leaves everything beyond the frame outside of it. This undermines the stability of the photograph as a reflection of reality, and by imagining the transgression of boundaries, the photo is open to interpretation and recontextualization.

The Reichardt Company's Picture Postcards

Figure 1.1 is the second one in a series from the Reichardt Company and depicts a scene of Black workers loading cocoa beans onto wagons while a white overseer stands in the back and returns the gaze of the photographer.

23   See Anne McClintock, *Imperial Leather: Race, Gender and Sexuality in the Colonial Contest* (New York: Routledge, 1995), 209.
24   Quoted in Axster, "'… will try to send you the best views from here'", 55.

The image speaks to the complex entanglements of the political and the visual, illustrating that images are indeed created in relation to power dynamics and powerful discourses.[25] The caption below the card on the left reads 'West African Plantation Company "Viktoria", Cameroon'. On the bottom left, it describes the scene as the 'transportation of the cocoa beans to the dry hall'.

2. Westafrikanische Pflanzungs-Gesellschaft „Viktoria", Kamerun.   Transport der Kakaobohnen zur Trockenhalle.

Figure 1.1. '2. Westafrikanische Pflanzungs-Gesellschaft "Viktoria," Kamerun. Transport der Kakaobohnen zur Trockenhalle', 1910 [2 West African Plantation Company 'Victoria', Cameroon. Transportion of cocoa beans to the drying hall, 1910]. Source: Stiftung Historische Museen Hamburg, Altonaer Museum, Inv.-Nr. 1988–475, 2.

The *Westafrikanische Pflanzungsgesellschaft Viktoria* [West African Plantation Company Victoria, WAPV] in Cameroon was the largest plantation company in the German colony, and though it mainly focused on the cultivation of cocoa, it also produced rubber, cola and bananas.[26] Max

25   W. T. J. Mitchell, 'What Do Pictures Really Want?' *October* 77 (1996), 71–82.
26   Walter Stollwerck, *Der Kakao und die Schokoladenindustrie: Eine wirtschafts-statistische Untersuchung* (Jena: Fischer Verlag, 1907), 28–29; Patrice Mandeng,

Esser, who executed the land expropriation and eviction of the local Bakweri people from the land of what eventually became his plantation, founded the company in 1895.[27] After Esser and others forcefully expropriated the land for these plantations from the indigenous population, the locals were only allocated two hectares of land per family.[28]

In the postcard, the Black workers become a visual metaphor for labor itself. In fact, the equation of dark-skinned peoples with hard manual labor is a visual trope found in many historical trade cards across the globe. The postcard depicts several Black male workers and a white overseer. The white man is the only person in the picture who returns the gaze of the camera, establishing an alliance with the (presumably white) photographer. The Black men are sweating and are simply dressed; some are undressed from the waist upwards. In contrast, the white man wears the insignia of colonial power, including a colonial hat, a white shirt and black shiny boots. The overseer looks quite short and lanky, possibly easy to overpower. His small figure stands in contrast to the physical strength of the Black workers. They are muscular; at least two of them are dripping in sweat, and their skin is glistening. In this way, the postcard plays with the (sub)conscious exotic attraction of the viewer to the Black (laboring) body. But it is not only Black bodies that are attractive to the consumers. The appeal also stems from the knowledge that these bodies are toiling for their consumers' pleasurable consumption. The postcard visually echoes what Arthur Knapp states in the quote that opened this chapter, '[t]o the black and the brown races ... we owe a debt for their work on tropical plantations, for the harder manual work would be too arduous for Europeans unused to the heat of those regions.'[29] Evinced in the image, masculine Blackness

Auswirkungen der deutschen Kolonialherrschaft in Kamerun (Hamburg: Buske, 1973), 71–72.

27 See Ute Röschenthaler, 'Der Kölner Jurist und Kaufmann Max Esser', *Kopfwelten* (29 October 2008) <http://www.kopfwelten.org/kp/personen/esser/> accessed 28 May 2018.

28 Horst Gründer, *Geschichte der deutschen Kolonien* (Paderborn: Schöningh, 2004), 146–47.

29 Knapp, *Cocoa and Chocolate*, 17.

is equated with physical labor and masculine whiteness with control and power, while the advertised commodity – the cocoa beans – are invisible.

The postcard succinctly expresses the hierarchical structure of colonial rule: the white body commands and disciplines, whereas Black bodies toil and sweat. It also communicates notions of efficiency that Germany allegedly brought to Cameroon: orderliness and technological improvements, such as railroad tracks and wagons. The image therefore underscores elements of the German 'civilizing mission' and presents Germans in the metropole with a fantasy in which everything 'foreign' and 'native' is subdued and controlled. The picture postcard is an illustrative example of how photographs were staged to convey an image of Germans as successful colonizers. The white gaze penetrates the Black workers and frames the whole setting. Moreover, the white overseer appears immobile and does not have to move to supervise. Some of the Black workers are bending forward in a clear position of servitude with all of them doing physical work. With the help of this postcard, Reichardt becomes a productive colonizer, and German consumers can absorb the (distorted) knowledge that sweating Black bodies in the African colony helped to produce their chocolate products. The palm trees in the background of the photograph further underscore the exotic appeal of the colony as a tropical place.[30] It also exemplifies the fact that Germany not only exploits the human resources of the African continent, but also its natural resources.

Equally striking are the contrasting colors in which the laborers and the overseer are dressed. The African laborers appear to be a part of the wagon or an extension of the earth due to the matching tones of the depicted objects and subjects conveyed through the lighting. The dark colors of their clothes – in part tattered and informal or improvised – resemble not only the color of their skin, but also the colors of their surroundings and thus firmly fix them in the African environment. In contrast, the white man in his white hat resembles the modern white house in the background, presumably an addition to the landscape and not a part of it. The image represents his transplantation into this new environment and his existence outside of this

---

30   See also, Joachim Zeller, *Weiße Blicke – schwarze Körper: Afrikaner im Spiegel westlicher Alltagskultur, Bilder aus der Sammlung Peter Weiss* (Erfurt: Sutton, 2010), 10.

'uncivilized' landscape that he now commands. Apart from that, the wagon and the tracks in the fore of the picture emphasize the advantages that the expanding cocoa industry brought to Cameroon, thereby implicitly arguing that customers who buy Reichardt's chocolate support the economic development and modernization of the colony.

Reichardt's series of postcards references what the introductory quotation from Arthur Knapp described. Indeed, it visually follows the journey of cocoa from beans harvested on cocoa farms in Cameroon to chocolate bars manufactured in German factories. While I only analyze one of these images here, looking at them in chronological order reveals a common strategy: with each card, the product becomes more and more industrial and thus 'civilized'. It is constructed as inherently modern, 'purified' and separated from its colonial context. Other postcards visually document the work life of German chocolate manufacturing by featuring technological equipment and machines along with white women and men working in clean white lab coats and caps. The emphasis on hygiene and the purity that their white clothing represent, removes them from the dust and dirt of the Black workers' labor. These images of cleanliness and orderliness communicate progress, control, hygiene and efficiency.[31] Moreover, they speak to the appropriation of originally 'tropical' riches such as cocoa beans, transformed into quality chocolate through modern technology and science.[32] Despite other advertisements that visually suggest otherwise, the series of postcards convey that chocolate is indeed an industrial product, bearing little resemblance to the cocoa bean harvested on the farm.

31   See also McClintock, *Imperial Leather*, 214–15.
32   See also Epple, *Das Unternehmen Stollwerck*, 66.

What Was 'German Colonial Chocolate'?

The quality of the cocoa from the German colony was not unanimously praised. Some celebrated it because to do otherwise would have contradicted the colonial success story. Others frequently pointed to its substantially lower quality and the impossibility of using it in its 'pure' form without adding cocoa varieties from other regions. An article in the monthly magazine *Der Tropenpflanzer* [*The Tropical Planter*] from 1906 vehemently attacked those who questioned the quality of the cocoa beans. Nevertheless, the text hints at the fact that this was an ongoing debate, suggesting that the quality issue remained a critical one.[33]

Despite these reservations, the Stollwerck Company, for instance, whose owners – the Stollwerck brothers – were not only members of the *Deutsche Kolonialgesellschaft* [German Colonial Society], but also shareholders of the WAPV, had imported cocoa beans from Cameroon since the 1880s.[34] Stollwerck produced a bar of chocolate and cocoa powder made purely of, at least according to the advertisements, cocoa beans that they imported from Cameroon and Samoa, respectively. Sold from 1908 onward and consequently called *Deutsche Kolonial-Schokolade* [German Colonial Chocolate] and *Deutscher Kolonial-Kakao* [German Colonial Cocoa], the caption on the packages informed the consumers that the chocolate was 'hergestellt unter ausschließlicher Verwendung von Kakaobohnen deutscher Kolonien' ['only made of cocoa beans from German colonies'].[35] By advertising chocolate with a reference to the origin of the cocoa beans,

---

33   See, for instance, *Der Tropenpflanzer. Zeitschrift für tropische Landwirtschaft* 10/5 (1906), 316–17.

34   Angelika Epple, 'Schwarz auf Weiß: Das Kölner Unternehmen Stollwerck im kolonialen Kontext', in Marianne Bechhaus-Gerst, and Anne-Kathrin Horstmann, eds, *Köln und der deutsche Kolonialismus: Eine Spurensuche* (Köln: Böhlau Verlag, 2013, 73–78), 76–77 and Bruno Kuske, *100 Jahre Stollwerck-Geschichte, 1839–1939* (Leipzig: Seemann, 1939), 50. Founded in 1887 and headquartered in Berlin, the German Colonial Society was established to promote German colonialism.

35   The historical packaging is on display at the general exhibition of the *Imhoff Schokoladenmuseum* [*Imhoff Chocolate Museum*] in Cologne, Germany.

businessmen sought to assure consumers that the sweets were made from raw commodities taken from the German colonies. These products speak to the close linkage between colonialism and consumption, and the commodification of colonialist culture respectively. It is impossible to determine if these products tasted any different than those which were made from cocoa beans from São Tomé, for instance. The reference was not necessarily about enhancing the quality of the product, but about relating chocolate to a specific geographic location, and thus to German colonial endeavors. By buying this particular chocolate, consumers could then express their support for or satisfy their fascination with colonialism.

The sheer amount of cocoa beans that arrived from Cameroon was so minimal though that it was hardly possible to have a range of chocolate products made from Cameroonian cocoa. The actual output, the low productivity, that is, was diametrically opposed to the efforts with which the German empire advertised the colony of Cameroon and the West African Plantation Company Victoria. Yet Cameroon eventually became an important colony economically, developing into the biggest plantation colony in West Africa with cocoa as its most profitable crop under German rule. Still, its profits remained low and imports from the colonies never played a major role in the German economy as a whole. As a matter of fact, none of the German colonies in Africa became economically profitable.[36] A limited number of entrepreneurs back in Germany, such as Reichardt and Stollwerck, were the only ones to reap a considerable profit. So while Cameroon was certainly ill-equipped to fully satisfy the insatiable appetite for cocoa in the metropole, it nevertheless cultivated and exported much more cocoa than the other German colonies, including Togo, German East Africa or Samoa.[37]

The German colonial enterprise certainly was not as smooth and efficient as the aforementioned postcard wanted the consuming populace to believe. Cocoa trees were threatened by decay and putridity, and the beans remained of a questionable quality. In addition, colonial entrepreneurs were

36 Friedrichsmeyer, and others, *The Imperialist Imagination*, 11 and Sebastian Conrad, *Deutsche Kolonialgeschichte* (München: Beck, 2008), 30.
37 Gründer, *Geschichte der deutschen Kolonien*, 144.

also trapped in competition with other companies as well as local farmers and entrepreneurs. These entrepreneurs also faced constant labor shortages and massive resistance from local populations, whom they tried to force to work on their plantations.[38] Commenting on the practice of coerced labor in Cameroon, historian William Gervase Clarence-Smith has attributed the 'numerous human tragedies of cocoa planting' to the exceptionally fertile soil in an exceptionally unhealthy environment.[39] According to estimates, 'death rates among laborers from south central Cameroon sent to the cocoa plantations in the German period averaged around 10 per cent a year, while the number of workers off sick at any given time often stood as high as 30 per cent.'[40] All these factors resulted in a colonial cocoa business that was not only exploitative and inhumane, but also far from effortless and economically profitable.

Moreover, as historian Andreas Eckert has shown, the German colonial period in Cameroon existed alongside and competed with the relative success of African entrepreneurship. The case of the Duala cocoa farming exemplifies that this local group of people, who organized as a socio-economic oligarchy, cultivated cocoa quite successfully through a workforce primarily made up of women and men the Duala had enslaved.[41] For Eckert, the success of the Duala elite was a mixture of reacting flexibly and innovatively to the new situation caused by German domination and in relation to cocoa specifically:

> Cocoa planting played a significant social and psychological role in the reproduction of symbolic resources of social power and status. The adoption of cocoa planting by the Duala elite indicated an ambition to appropriate more of the attributes of

---

38   Möhle, 'Bittere Schokolade', 57; see also, Chapter 5, 'Die Arbeitskräftebeschaffung für die Plantagenbetriebe', in Patrice Mandeng, *Auswirkungen der deutschen Kolonialherrschaft in Kamerun* (Hamburg: Buske, 1973), 67–99.

39   Clarence-Smith, 'Cocoa Plantations and Coerced Labor', 153.

40   Clarence-Smith, 'Cocoa Plantations and Coerced Labor', 166–67. This was equally true for the WAPV, which curiously was often cited as a model for health care. The most notorious sickness was malaria.

41   Andreas Eckert, 'African Rural Entrepreneurs and Labor in the Cameroon Littoral', *The Journal of African History* 40/1 (1999), 111–12.

Western civilization. The growing of a foreign plant like cocoa conferred on plant-ers an image of individuals who had access to spheres of technical agricultural and to a wider though unspecific cultural knowledge that was extraordinary. A number of Duala planters even portrayed their adoption of a foreign crop as proof of their superiority over fellow Africans.[42]

Thus, the agency of the colonized, their superior knowledge of the regions, the native populations and their access to labor put them in an advantageous position that remained unattainable for the German colonists. Indeed, a report in *Der Tropenpflanzer* complains about the slow progress that German entrepreneurs were making in cocoa cultivation in Cameroon compared to developments in the Gold Coast and Portuguese West Africa.[43] Figures published in the same journal two years later suggest that German cocoa imports from Cameroon continued to be insignificant in comparison to the amount of cocoa from other countries such as São Tomé.[44]

Nonetheless, a tremendous amount of advertising postcards and trade cards circulated in Wilhelmine Germany, and these cards not only pro-moted cocoa or chocolate but also featured many colonial scenes populated with images of People of Color. What these sources reveal is that choco-late, 'tropical' places and brown-skinned people were part of an imperialist imagination, which was reproduced and distributed again and again. The advertisement of chocolate was linked to a colonizing mission and played with constructions of inferior Otherness. As these visual images make clear, the material conditions – cocoa plantations, slave labor, imperialism and colonialism – reified and normalized the discursive and cultural connection between chocolate and Blackness that has been cited in so many chocolate advertisements both past and present.

42   Andreas Eckert, 'African Rural Entrepreneurs and Labor in the Cameroon Littoral', *The Journal of African History* 40/1 (1999), 114.

43   See *Der Tropenpflanzer. Zeitschrift für tropische Landwirtschaft* 8/1 (1904), 17–18.

44   'Deutschlands Ein- und Ausfuhr an Kakao und dessen Fabrikaten und an Vanille in den Jahren 1903 bis 1905' *Der Tropenpflanzer. Zeitschrift für tropische Landwirtschaft* 10/3 (1906), 185.

Print Ads in *Der Tropenpflanzer*

Already throughout 1904 and 1905, the *Deutsches Kolonial-Haus Bruno Antelmann* [German Colonial House Bruno Antelmann] in Berlin, a shop selling colonial wares, had placed ads for cocoa from Cameroon and Samoa in every monthly issue of *Der Tropenpflanzer*. One of them, a black-and-white ad, featured a silhouette of an 'African', whose 'Africanness' was established through stereotypical physical features such as a prominent forehead, coiled hair, broad nose and large lips, referencing the common visual features of racialization. The man appears to be naked from the waist upward and dressed only in what seems to be a white piece of cloth. The man carries, as if on a tray, a miniature house of the Antelmann shop. Behind the miniature store, two palm trees can be seen, underscoring the exoticism and the tropical appeal of the advertised commodities. Next to cocoa, the ad also promotes coffee, cola, coconut grease and peanut oil.

Antelmann also distributed a colorful poster to advertise cocoa. This brightly colored image, in which red, green and brownish shades dominate, depicts a long-haired, bare-breasted brown-skinned woman with a flowered necklace and flowers in her hair, and a cloth around her waist. Holding a huge umbrella, she walks arm in arm with a bare-chested Black man wearing only a hat and a cloth around his waist. The fact that both figures are partly naked does not come as a surprise, as such imagery not only evoked primitivism and exoticism, but also spoke to (tabooed and subconscious) sexuality and sexual attraction to brown-skinned peoples. The native woman, a light-skinned *'Südsee-Schönheit'* ['South Seas beauty'], is literally meant to embody Samoa, and she carries a box full of cocoa, which has *'Samoa-Edel-Kakao'* ['Samoa noble cocoa'] written on it. The dark-skinned man next to her is meant to personify Cameroon, likewise holding a box filled with cocoa that has *'Kamerun-Kakao'* ['Cameroon Cocoa'] printed on it. The picture evokes the impression that the two have not only cultivated and harvested these colonial commodities, hence toiled for white pleasurable consumption, but they are also bringing their riches to the white reader – and potential consumer.[45] One could also argue

---

45   The poster is reprinted in Zeller, *Weiße Blicke – schwarze Körper*, 169.

that the image suggests that the half-naked woman and man are offering themselves, too, to the female and male consumers. By locating cocoa in the colonial territories of Samoa and Cameroon, the image represents not only German colonialism, but also reflects the knowledge and labor of the 'natives' on how to cultivate and harvest the cocoa beans, thereby enabling the consumption of chocolate in Germany. The depiction of the colonized also renders them a commodity, ready to be sexually exploited on a visual level. While both are barely dressed, the depiction of the light-skinned woman embodying Samoa, with her jewelry, flowers and protruding breasts is highly sexualized.[46]

Analyzing other advertisements for the Colonial House Antelmann reveals, however, that images of Blackness were not always equated with physical labor, exoticism or a tropical landscape. An earlier ad from 1901, for instance, consists of a photograph of a group of young African boys. They are dressed in suits and stand in file. They are neither eating chocolate, nor are cocoa or any other colonial products strategically placed in the picture. Their sole function in this photograph is to attract possible consumers via their embodied Blackness. The boys and their dark skin color serve as a direct visual link to the commodities Antelmann sold – commodities that came from the colonies.[47] Since apparently both the goods and the young boys came from colonial Africa, they too are foreign and exotic and thus seem appropriate to represent the absent commodities. And yet, the fact that they are dressed in European style clothing (and are not partly naked) suggests that they have been 'civilized'. One of the boys in the photograph was Kwassi Bruce, the son of Nayo Bruce, a member of the political elite in Togo who later worked as a carney in Europe. Kwassi Bruce

46   On the colonial discourse in Germany concerning Samoa, see Gabriele Förderer, *Koloniale Grüße aus Samoa: Eine Diskursanalyse von deutschen, englischen und U.S.-amerikanischen Reisebeschreibungen aus Samoa von 1860–1916* (Bielefeld: Transcript, 2017).

47   The image is reprinted in Joachim Zeller, 'Dunkle Existenzen in Berlin: Die Präsenz Schwarzer Menschen im Spiegel weißer Ikonographien' in Marianne Bechhaus-Gerst, and Sunna Gieseke, eds, *Koloniale und postkoloniale Konstruktionen von Afrika und Menschen afrikanischer Herkunft in der deutschen Alltagskultur* (Frankfurt am Main: Peter Lang, 2006), 419–20.

came to Germany in 1896 for the colonial exhibition in Berlin Treptow. The *Deutsche Kolonial-Ausstellung* [the German Colonial Exhibit] was part of an industrial exhibition and featured an 'African village' in which stereo-typically dressed Africans were literally on display and could be observed by visitors while performing 'traditional' tasks.[48] Although Nayo Bruce and his wife left Berlin sometime after the exhibition, their son stayed. He was adopted by Bruno Antelmann and his wife and eventually made a career as a pianist.[49] The boys demonstrate that the German colonial project is not only able to 'civilize' people from Africa, but it also makes them subservient to the colonial effort. The image tries to convey the 'positive' impacts of colonization on the colonized through a civilizing mission that continues to educate and indoctrinate children in the European metropole.

The colored poster and the black-and-white photograph featuring the Black children dressed in suits contrast starkly in their representation of Blackness, and so does Reichardt's postcard discussed previously. The images chosen here illustrate the different notions of Blackness simul-taneously circulating in German culture. Blackness becomes an empty signifier, appropriated and manipulated in order to define whiteness and to secure white superiority. In these examples, Africans either need to be supervised and controlled, exploited for their labor and knowledge of native plants or are civilized through the benevolent effects of German colonialism. Moreover, the commodity that is advertised does not play a major role in any of these ads. For instance, we do not see the cocoa beans in the Reichardt postcard, though we might assume that they are in the wagons. Likewise, we do not see cocoa pods in the colorful poster or in the photograph of the young boys; the protagonists in these ads embody the cocoa and the colonies as such. These ads create a semiotic web of the German colony, Blackness and cocoa.

48   Conrad, *Deutsche Kolonialgeschichte*, 88–89.
49   See Rea Brändle, *Nayo Bruce: Geschichte einer afrikanischen Familie in Europa* (Zürich: Chronos, 2007).

Chocolate as a Civilizing Project

Another visual trope in the colonial representations of cocoa and Blackness often revolved around the negotiation of primitivism through the imperial project. A picture postcard for '*Schreiber's Cacao und Schokoladen*' ['Schreiber's chocolate and cocoa'] illustrates that the discourse of a 'civilizing mission' remains ever present, especially as the card argues that the metropole – that is, the (very modest) German Empire – helps to advance the 'backward' African colony and its inhabitants.[50] In this image, it is not a 'traditional courtly moor' who serves chocolate, but a white woman who offers chocolate to an African 'savage'. She personifies the German Empire that is bringing civilization to the African. This African appears to be naked for the viewer sees no clothing, and since there are no visible limbs, he needs to be spoon-fed. The card thus construes him as an 'uncivilized', childlike, 'primitive savage' bereft of history, culture, literacy and technology. The hierarchy of power in this image probably proved alluring to white consumers, regardless of their actual enthusiasm for the German colonial project as a whole. It affirmed their whiteness, German identity and German culture as superior to an inferior Otherness located in the colonies and outside the nation. The image visually reverses the actual production process of cocoa and chocolate. The card suggests that although cocoa beans come from the African colonies, fine hot chocolate is an accomplishment of European civilization. An industrially manufactured product is thus reimported to the country that grew its raw materials, and this re-import is signified by way of a white woman offering a cup of hot chocolate to a Black man.[51]

50   The postcard, of which this author has a scan, was supposed to be included in the
        chapter. Unfortunately, though, it was impossible to secure the permission and the
        rights to reproduce the analyzed postcard. In agreement with the editors of this
        volume, it was decided to nonetheless describe and interpret this visual source. The
        postcard is part of an extensive collection of colonial picture postcards by collector
        Peter Weiss. Parts of his visual material (though not the postcard in question) have
        been featured in the publication by Zeller, *Weiße Blicke – Schwarze Körper*.
51   See also Angelika Epple, 'Das Auge schmeckt Stollwerck', *Werkstatt Geschichte* 16/45
        (2007), 27.

The white woman in this postcard represents middle-class respectability with her fine apparel and delicate features. A white porcelain cup filled with hot chocolate is placed in front of her on a globe. The relatively huge globe also separates her from the caricatured African male. He is almost hidden behind it, whereas the woman is in the foreground. In one hand, she holds a spoon with hot cocoa, which she is offering to the 'savage', and in the other a laurel wreath. The laurel wreath serves to underscore both the high quality of the product and – on a larger scale – the 'superiority' of German civilization and culture.[52] In contrast to that, the alleged inferiority of the African and his complete Otherness is achieved through his nakedness, and the stereotypical big red lips stand in stark contrast to his otherwise pitch-black skin. The accentuation of his lips and their exaggerated coloring remained a common and essentialist trope in the process of visual racialization during this period. In addition to a skin color that lacks contours, nuances and light-reflections, the depiction references the popular iconography of blackface and minstrelsy. Minstrelsy was not a cultural phenomenon confined to the United States; it was also popular in Germany in the nineteenth and early twentieth centuries.[53] Apart from that, he wears a single bone in his hair, and the bone can be read as a reference to cannibalism, hence, further indication of his assumed savagery.

Yet despite the uneven hierarchical order of the two, there is also an erotic dimension at play here. The Black figure's red lips correspond visually to the red blouse of the woman and can be read as a reference to a sexual liaison between the two. Although it may seem unlikely for an advertisement that is intended to encourage people to buy a product to cite such a social taboo, an erotic dimension is nonetheless present. In this scene, the woman tries to allure the man by offering him Schreiber's hot chocolate. The card alludes to and recycles the myth of hot chocolate as an aphrodisiac par excellence. Chocolate is used to transgress racial boundaries, since the woman might not only offer hot chocolate to the man, but possibly

52   On the use of the laurel wreath in advertising, see Birgit Bergmann, *Der Kranz des Kaisers* (Berlin: de Gruyter, 2010).

53   Tobias Nagl, *Die unheimliche Maschine: Rasse und Repräsentation im Weimarer Kino* (München: edition text + kritik, 2009), 704–14. See also, Johnathan Wipplinger, 'The Racial Ruse: On Blackness and Blackface Comedy in *fin-de-siècle* Germany', *The German Quarterly* 84/4 (2011), 457–76.

herself, too. The fact that the man leans toward her suggests a reciprocal desire, one that is limited and contained by the globe between them. The globe provides the necessary distance between a Black man and a white woman; and, in terms of civilization, they are literally worlds apart. The man is not (yet) a 'domesticated', subdued servant, but a barbarous hyper-sexual African. It is through the juxtaposition of the dark-skinned Other with the light-skinned woman that she appears to be 'civilized', refined and European (meaning white).[54] Since the woman offers hot chocolate to the man, the image implies a 'giving back' as a way of assuaging those Germans who are critical of colonialism. Apart from that, the image also engages the gendered notion of women as caretakers and nurturers. The white female personifies German culture, values and attitudes that are not only offered to but also imposed on the colonized African. Moreover, the woman represents the colonial mission and German women's support of colonialism in which they played an active role.[55] Despite the fact that only the enforced labor and expert knowledge of indigenous peoples enabled the Western world to consume cocoa and chocolate in the first place, this woman generously feeds the African and thus allows him to participate in the civilized accomplishment of enjoying a cup of hot chocolate. Still, the interaction of the woman and the man in this image remains extremely contradictory; on the one hand, it demonstrates this woman's role in his 'domestication', but on the other hand, it also illustrates the inherent threat in allowing this (close) interaction within the colonial project.

This postcard establishes the origins of chocolate as occurring within the German metropole rather than in the colonies. A small drawing of the factory, including smoking chimneys, is inserted next to the dominant image and emphasizes Germany as the site where chocolate is produced. Moreover, this postcard illustrates Germany's need for a clearly defined, racialized Other in order to construct a white national identity. This Black Other had to be created in order to gain a sense of one's white self. The

---

54   David M. Ciarlo, 'Rasse konsumieren', in Birthe Kundrus, ed., *Phantasiereiche. Zur Kulturgeschichte des deutschen Kolonialismus* (Frankfurt am Main: Campus, 2003), 136.

55   On the involvement of German women in colonialism, see Lora Wildenthal, *German Women for Empire, 1884–1945* (Durham, NC: Duke University Press, 2001).

Other helped define German as well as European identity by corroborating what it was not. The depictions of colonized Others also helped Germans define the boundaries of the nation and citizenship more broadly.

Although the actual date of this card remains unknown, it is probably a postcard from the first decade of the twentieth century when images of Africans became a common visual motif. This period also includes the genocide of the Herero and Nama in Namibia at the hands of German colonialists from 1904 to 1908. Historian David Ciarlo has argued that during this period, images of Black people with grotesque facial features increased abruptly. These images corresponded visually with reports from the colony and helped to legitimize the Germans' horrendous actions.[56] Furthermore, such imagery helped German society to come to terms with the fact that the uprising of the Herero and Nama could not be suppressed for several years. The sustained resistance of the colonized severely unsettled the German belief in its racial superiority and the paternalistic colonial mission discourse.[57] At the same time, it also showed the power and agency that these indigenous communities maintained, in which they refused to be passive beings and fought for their lands and freedom. Although they were unable to defeat the colonial aggressors in the end, they still managed to resist European colonialism.[58]

56 See also Jürgen Zimmerer, 'Deutschlands erster Genozid: Der Völkermord an den Herero und Nama', *Der Überblick* 40 (2004), 83–86; Melber Henning, ed., *Genozid und Gedenken: Namibisch-deutsche Geschichte und Gegenwart* (Frankfurt am Main: Brandes und Apsel, 2005) and Ciarlo, 'Rasse konsumieren', 146. On the uprising, see also, Conrad, *Deutsche Kolonialgeschichte*, 52–54.

57 El-Tayeb, 'Colored Germans there will never be', 229; On representations of the Herero war in German consumer culture see David Ciarlo, 'Picturing Genocide in German Consumer Culture, 1904–10', in Michael Perraudin, and Jürgen Zimmerer, eds, *German Colonialism and National Identity* (London: Routledge, 2011), 69–89.

58 The genocide of the Herero and Nama as well as their imprisonment in concentration camps has been linked to the concentration camps under the National Socialist regime, and, in turn, this linkage has been contested. For a current overview of the scholarly debate, see Jonas Kreienbaum, *'Ein trauriges Fiasko': Koloniale Konzentrationslager im südlichen Afrika 1900–1908* (Hamburg: Hamburger Edition, 2015), 293–309.

Conclusion

The prevalence of lithographed trade cards and other chocolate advertisements, along with their portrayal of People of Color, reveals that diverse fantasies of colonialism pervaded German mass culture around the turn of the twentieth century. They resonated with various forms of circulated and racialized ideas of the African colonies and Black people. The wide dissemination of this iconography of Blackness, in Germany and various other sites across the Black Atlantic, as well as its persistence through several decades – often common today – suggests a cultural hegemony that these visual sources confirm. Employing images of Black people to advertise a colonial commodity has been a significant visual trope. In the case of cocoa and chocolate advertisements, the product itself and its mythical dimensions are racialized and sexualized by featuring colonial fantasies and barely dressed Black people. This association between certain black- and brown-colored products such as cocoa or coffee with the depiction of People of Color is a historical construction. It did not evolve from the 'nature of things'. Indeed, given the historical foundation on which this sort of imagery flourished, the connection of chocolate and Blackness in advertisements speaks to a colonization of white Germans' imagination that bears no real resemblance to Black people actually living in Germany and the German colonies.[59] This usage of chocolate as a racial signifier also for brown-skinned Germans is not based on supposed, vague similarities of colors. It has been learned through endless socio-historical and cultural repetitions, many of them depicted in visual colonial advertisements. Such a racist naming practice is thus far from being an 'obvious' given. It is a

---

59   See, for example, Robbie Aitken, and Eve Rosenhaft, eds, *Black Germany: The Making and Unmaking of a Diaspora Community, 1884–1960* (Cambridge: Cambridge University Press, 2013); Theodor Michael, *Deutsch sein und schwarz dazu: Erinnerungen eines Afro-Deutschen* (München: dtv, 2013) and Katharina Oguntoye, *Eine afro-deutsche Geschichte: Zur Lebenssituation von Afrikanern und Afro-Deutschen in Deutschland von 1884 bis 1950* (Berlin: Hoho Verlag Christine Hoffmann, 1997).

historical construction that has been repeatedly captured and (re)imagined in images that were disseminated for centuries.

Examining the history of chocolate advertisements not only in Germany, but also in other European countries, such as Britain, France, Italy and the Netherlands, reveals a tradition of linking chocolate to Blackness.[60] Particularly in Germany, the most well-known 'personification' of that connection is the *Sarotti Mohr*, a Black figure that was created in 1918 and rose to great popularity during the 1920s, and again in the post-World War II era.[61] Apart from a visual connection that conflates chocolate with People of Color, 'chocolate expressions' emerged and were used as racial signifiers for brown-skinned people. Terms such as '*Schokobaby*' ['Chocolate Baby'] and '*Mohrenkopf*' ['Moor Head'] remain common in Germany's popular parlance today. In fact, they are not 'cute' references, but racial slurs that many Afro-Germans have vehemently criticized. Such terminology is derogatory and offensive, especially as it exoticizes and objectifies Afro-Germans

60   For works on racialized imagery in British advertising as well as a discussion of chocolate in Britain see Emma Robertson, *Chocolate, Women and Empire: A Social and Cultural History* (Manchester: Manchester University Press, 2009) and Anandi Ramamurthy, *Imperial Persuaders: Images of Africa and Asia in British Advertising* (Manchester: Manchester University Press, 2003). For the history of chocolate in France, including a brief discussion of advertisements, see Susan Jane Terrio, *Crafting the Culture and History of French Chocolate* (Berkeley: University of California Press, 2000). For the German context, see also Silke Hackenesch, 'Advertising Chocolate, Consuming Race? On the Peculiar Relationship of Chocolate, German Colonialism, and Blackness', *Food & History* 12/1 (2015) 97–112, and Hackenesch, 'Der Sarotti-M*** (1918/1922), oder: Was hat Konsum mit Rassismus zu tun?', in Jürgen Martschukart, and Olaf Stieglitz, eds, *Race & Sex: Eine Geschichte der Neuzeit* (Berlin: Neofelis Verlag, 2016), 217–25.

61   One should note that the term '*Mohr*' ['Moor'] is quite ambivalent in European discourse since it is historically linked to racist assumptions of the biological inferiority of dark-skinned people. In the United States, however, the term has a more neutral connotation and can positively refer to the occupation of Spain by the Moorish Empire, for example. For a critical discussion of the *Sarotti Mohr* and the historical context of its emergence, see Silke Hackenesch, 'Advertising Chocolate', 217–25.

and other Germans of Color.[62] These racialized terms seem to suggest that
Blackness is something unnatural and that one's skin color is linked to
what one consumes. They are built on the assumption that brown-skinned
people's skin color was due to their consumption of cocoa, chocolate or
coffee, and this directly links their skin color to an edible product.

Moreover, expressions such as 'Schokobaby' are not only racist and sexist,
but also infantilize Black subjects. They turn dark-skinned adults into children and Black women into desirable commodities. And yet the racist connection of chocolate and Blackness is not limited to popular parlance and
historical trade cards long gone out of circulation but can unfortunately still
be found in contemporary chocolate advertisements. These contemporary
examples include the print ad *Yes I'm Magnum* Chocolate Ice Cream from
2006 that features a nude Black woman 'barred' behind a web of chocolate
drops as well as a television spot for the *Chocolat du Planteur* in the same
year. The latter example featured Ivorian soccer star Didier Drogba promoting Ivorian chocolate. The nude athlete plays with a football that, after
coming into contact with Drogba's body, turns into chocolate. In the spot,
Drogba literally sweats chocolate, so he comes to embody the product he
advertised.[63] This popular linkage, as I have argued, has its material basis
in Germany's colonial history. It is not an innocent reference but one connected to the exploitation and oppression of African peoples.

62   For an Afro-German critique of linking Blackness to chocolate see May Ayim,
      Grenzenlos und unverschämt (Frankfurt am Main: Fischer-Taschenbuch-Verlag,
      2002), 49; Katharina Oguntoye, and others, eds, *Farbe bekennen: Afro-deutsche Frauen
      auf den Spuren ihrer Geschichte* (Berlin: Orlanda-Frauenverlag, 1991), 105, 164, 179
      and Noah Sow, *Deutschland Schwarz Weiß: Der alltägliche Rassismus* (München:
      Bertelsmann, 2008), 222.

63   The Afro-German media watch organization *der braune mob, e.V.* likewise took issue
      with the ad. Their criticism is mainly directed at the portrayal of Drogba, though
      they do not take into account his agency in the making of the ad; see Julius B.
      Franklin, Mona El Omari Tsepo Bollwinkel, 'Koloniale Schokolade' *DER BRAUNE
      MOB* (21 December 2013) <http://www.derbraunemob.de/koloniale-schokolade/>
      27 December 2016. For an analysis of the ad, see Silke Hackenesch, *Chocolate and
      Blackness. A Cultural History* (Frankfurt: Campus, 2017), 100–104.

Bibliography

Aitken, Robbie, and Eve Rosenhaft, *Black Germany: The Making and Unmaking of a Diaspora Community, 1884–1960* (Cambridge: Cambridge University Press, 2013).

Axster, Felix, "'... will try to send you the best views from here": Postcards from the Colonial War in Namibia (1904–1908)', in Volker Langbehn, ed., *German Colonialism, Visual Culture, and Modern Memory* (New York: Routledge, 2010), 55–70.

Ayim, May, *Grenzenlos und unverschämt* (Frankfurt am Main: Fischer-Taschenbuch-Verlag, 2002).

Bergmann, Birgit, *Der Kranz des Kaisers* (Berlin: de Gruyter, 2010).

Bowersox, Jeff, *Raising Germans in the Age of Empire: Youth and Colonial Culture, 1871–1914* (Oxford: Oxford University Press, 2013).

Brailsford, H. N., revised by Sinead Agnew, 'Nevinson, Henry Woodd', in H. C. G. Matthew, and Brian Harrison, ed., *Oxford Dictionary of National Biography. From the Earliest Times to the Year 2000* (Oxford University Press, Vol. 40, 2004), 551–52.

Brändle, Rea, *Nayo Bruce: Geschichte einer afrikanischen Familie in Europa* (Zürich: Chronos, 2007).

Ciarlo, David, 'Advertising and the Optics of Colonial Power at the Fin de Siècle', in Volker Langbehn, ed., *German Colonialism, Visual Culture, and Modern Memory* (New York: Routledge 2010), 37–54.

——, 'Picturing Genocide in German Consumer Culture, 1904–10', in Michael Perraudin, and Jürgen Zimmerer, eds, *German Colonialism and National Identity* (London: Routledge, 2011), 69–89.

——, 'Rasse konsumieren' in Birthe Kundrus, ed., *Phantasiereiche: Zur Kulturgeschichte des deutschen Kolonialismus* (Frankfurt am Main: Campus, 2003), 135–79.

Clarence-Smith, William Gervase, 'Cocoa Plantations and Coerced Labor in the Gulf of Guinea, 1870–1914', in Martin A. Klein, ed., *Breaking the Chains: Slavery, Bondage, and Emancipation in Modern Africa and Asia* (Madison: University of Wisconsin Press, 1993), 150–70.

——, 'Struggles over Labour Conditions in the Plantations of São Tomé and Príncipe' *Slavery and Abolition* 14/1 (1993), 149–67.

Conrad, Sebastian, *Deutsche Kolonialgeschichte* (München: Beck, 2008).

Der Tropenpflanzer. Zeitschrift für tropische Landwirtschaft 8/1 (1904), 17–18.

Der Tropenpflanzer. Zeitschrift für tropische Landwirtschaft 10/3 (1906), 185.

Der Tropenpflanzer. Zeitschrift für tropische Landwirtschaft 10/5 (1906), 316–17.

Eckert, Andreas, and Albert Wirz, 'Wir nicht, die anderen auch: Deutschland und der Kolonialismus', in Sebastian Conrad, ed., *Jenseits des Eurozentrismus:*

Postkoloniale Perspektiven in den Geschichts- und Kulturwissenschaften (Frankfurt/Main: Campus, 2002), 372–92.

Eckert, Andreas, 'African Rural Entrepreneurs and Labor in the Cameroon Littoral' *The Journal of African History* 40/1 (1999), 109–26.

El-Tayeb, Fatima, 'Colored Germans there will never be', in Dawne Y. Curry, Eric D. Duke and Marshanda A. Smith, eds, *Extending the Diaspora: New Histories of Black People* (Urbana: University of Illinois Press, 2009), 225–44.

Epple, Angelika, 'Das Auge schmeckt Stollwerck', *Werkstatt Geschichte* 16/45 (2007), 13–31.

——, *Das Unternehmen Stollwerck: Eine Mikrogeschichte der Globalisierung* (Frankfurt am Main: Campus, 2010).

——, 'Schwarz auf Weiß: Das Kölner Unternehmen Stollwerck im kolonialen Kontext', in Marianne Bechhaus-Gerst, and Anne-Kathrin Horstmann, eds, *Köln und der deutsche Kolonialismus: Eine Spurensuche* (Köln: Böhlau Verlag, 2013, 73–78).

Förderer, Gabriele, *Koloniale Grüße aus Samoa. Eine Diskursanalyse von deutschen, englischen und U.S.-amerikanischen Reisebeschreibungen aus Samoa von 1860–1916* (Bielefeld: Transcript, 2017).

Franklin, Julius B., and Mona El Omari Tsepo Bollwinkel, 'Koloniale Schokolade' *DER BRAUNE MOB* (21 December 2013) <http://www.derbraunemob.de/koloniale-schokolade/> 27 December 2016.

Friedrichsmeyer, Sara, Sara Lennox and Susanne Zantop, *The Imperialist Imagination: German Colonialism and its Legacy* (Ann Arbor: University of Michigan Press, 1999).

Geary, Christraud M., and Virginia-Lee Webb, 'Introduction: Views on Postcards', in Christraud M. Geary, and Virginia-Lee Webb, eds, *Delivering Views: Distant Cultures in Early Postcards* (Washington, DC: Smithsonian Institution Press, 1998), 1–12.

Grant, Kevin, *A Civilised Savagery: Britain and the New Slaveries in Africa, 1884–1926* (New York: Routledge, 2005).

Gründer, Horst, *Geschichte der deutschen Kolonien* (Paderborn: Schöningh, 2004).

Hackenesch, Silke, 'Advertising Chocolate, Consuming Race?: On the Peculiar Relationship of Chocolate, German Colonialism, and Blackness', *Food & History* 12/1 (2015) 97–112.

——, *Chocolate and Blackness: A Cultural History* (Frankfurt: Campus, 2017).

——, 'Der Sarotti-M*** (1918/1922), oder: Was hat Konsum mit Rassismus zu tun?' in Jürgen Martschukart, and Olaf Stieglitz, eds, *Race & Sex: Eine Geschichte der Neuzeit* (Berlin: Neofelis Verlag, 2016), 217–25.

Higgs, Catherine, *Chocolate Islands: Cocoa, Slavery, and Colonial Africa* (Athens: Ohio University Press, 2012).

Jäger, Jens, 'Bilder aus Afrika vor 1918: Zur visuellen Konstruktion Afrikas im europäischen Kolonialismus', in Paul Gerhard, ed., *Visual History: Ein Studienbuch* (Göttingen: Vandenhoeck & Ruprecht, 2006), 134–48.

Knapp, Arthur, *Cocoa and Chocolate: Their History from Plantation to Consumer* (London: Chapman and Hall, 1920).

Kreienbaum, Jonas, *'Ein trauriges Fiasko': Koloniale Konzentrationslager im südlichen Afrika 1900–1908* (Hamburg: Hamburger Edition, 2015).

Kuske, Bruno, *100 Jahre Stollwerck-Geschichte, 1839–1939* (Leipzig: Seemann, 1939).

Langbehn, Volker, 'Introduction: Picturing Race: Visuality and German Colonialism', in Volker Langbehn, ed., *German Colonialism, Visual Culture, and Modern Memory* (New York: Routledge, 2010), 1–33.

——, 'The Visual Representation of Blackness During German Imperialism Around 1900' in Michael Perraudin, and Jürgen Zimmerer, eds, *German Colonialism and National Identity* (London: Routledge, 2011), 90–100.

McClintock, Anne, *Imperial Leather: Race, Gender and Sexuality in the Colonial Contest* (New York: Routledge, 1995).

Mandeng, Patrice, *Auswirkungen der deutschen Kolonialherrschaft in Kamerun* (Hamburg: Buske, 1973).

Mayer, Michael, *"Tropen gibt es nicht." Dekonstruktionen des Exotismus* (Bielefeld: Aisthesis Verlag, 2010).

Melber, Henning, ed., *Genozid und Gedenken Namibisch-deutsche Geschichte und Gegenwart* (Frankfurt am Main: Brandes und Apsel, 2005).

Michael, Theodor, *Deutsch sein und schwarz dazu: Erinnerungen eines Afro-Deutschen* (München: dtv, 2013).

Mitchell, W. T. J., 'What Do Pictures Really Want?' *October* 77 (1996), 71–82.

Möhle, Heiko, 'Bittere Schokolade: Die Früchte der Plantagenwirtschaft', in Heiko Möhle, ed., *Branntwein, Bibeln und Bananen. Der deutsche Kolonialismus in Afrika – eine Spurensuche [in Hamburg]* (Hamburg: Verlag Libertäre Assoziation, 1999).

Mueller, Wolf, *Seltsame Frucht Kakao: Geschichte des Kakaos und der Schokolade* (Hamburg: Verlag Gordian - Max Rieck, 1957).

Nagl, Tobias, *Die unheimliche Maschine: Rasse und Repräsentation im Weimarer Kino* (München: edition text + kritik, 2009).

Nevinson, Henry W., *A Modern Slavery. With an Introduction by Basil Davidson* (1906; Sourcebooks in Negro History. New York: Schocken Books, 1968).

Oguntoye, Katharina, *Eine afro-deutsche Geschichte. Zur Lebenssituation von Afrikanern und Afro-Deutschen in Deutschland von 1884 bis 1950* (Berlin: Hoho Verlag Christine Hoffmann, 1997).

Oguntoye, Katharina, and others, eds, *Farbe bekennen. Afro-deutsche Frauen auf den Spuren ihrer Geschichte* (Berlin: Orlanda-Frauenverlag, 1991).

Ramamurthy, Anandi, *Imperial Persuaders: Images of Africa and Asia in British Advertising* (Manchester: Manchester University Press, 2003).

Robertson, Emma, *Chocolate, Women and Empire: A Social and Cultural History* (Manchester: Manchester University Press, 2009).

Röschenthaler, Ute, 'Der Kölner Jurist und Kaufmann Max Esser', *Kopfwelten* (29 October 2008) <http://www.kopfwelten.org/kp/personen/esser/> accessed 28 May 2018.

Short, John Phillip, *Magic Lantern Empire: Colonialism and Society in Germany* (Ithaca, NY: Cornell University Press, 2012).

Sow, Noah, *Deutschland Schwarz Weiß: Der alltägliche Rassismus* (München: Bertelsmann, 2008).

Stollwerck, Walter, *Der Kakao und die Schokoladenindustrie: Eine wirtschafts-statistische Untersuchung* (Jena: Fischer Verlag, 1907).

Terrio, Susan Jane, *Crafting the Culture and History of French Chocolate* (Berkeley: University of California Press, 2000).

Wildenthal, Lora, *German Women for Empire, 1884–1945* (Durham, NC: Duke University Press, 2001).

Wipplinger, Johnathan, 'The Racial Ruse: On Blackness and Blackface Comedy in *fin-de-siècle* Germany', *The German Quarterly* 84/4 (2011), 457–76.

Zeller, Joachim, 'Dunkle Existenzen in Berlin: Die Präsenz Schwarzer Menschen im Spiegel weißer Ikonographien', in Marianne Bechhaus-Gerst, and Sunna Gieseke, eds, *Koloniale und postkoloniale Konstruktionen von Afrika und Menschen afrikanischer Herkunft in der deutschen Alltagskultur* (Frankfurt am Main: Peter Lang, 2006), 413–42.

——, *Weiße Blicke – schwarze Körper: Afrikaner im Spiegel westlicher Alltagskultur*, Bilder aus der Sammlung Peter Weiss (Erfurt: Sutton, 2010).

Zimmerer, Jürgen, 'Deutschlands erster Genozid: Der Völkermord an den Herero und Nama', *Der Überblick* 40 (2004), 83–86.

NANCY P. NENNO

2 *Here to Stay*:[1] Black Austrian Studies

ABSTRACT

As was true of Black *German* Studies, the historical context of the diverse 'roots and routes' of the African diaspora helps to define the field of Black *Austrian* Studies. However, burgeoning interest in historical individuals, such as Angelo Soliman, as well as reactions to the recent influx of asylum-seekers, often elides the voices of Black Austrians. This essay seeks to redress this erasure by examining two recent events in which Black Austrians intervened in the public discourse. Poet Chibo Oneiji and author Charles Ofoedu recorded the reactions of the Black Community to the brutal death of asylum-seeker Marcus Omofuma during his deportation in 1999. Seven years later, the counter-historical project 'Verborgene Geschichte/n – Remapping Mozart' mounted public installations depicting repressed Austrian histories. By undermining the 'white-washing' of Austrian identity, these events demonstrate how Black Austrians are claiming their status as agents of their own history.

In the summer of 2016, the *Volkskundemuseum* [Austrian Museum of Folk Life and Folk Art] in Vienna hosted an exhibition entitled 'SchwarzÖsterreich. Die Kinder afroamerikanischer Besatzungssoldaten' ['Black Austria. The Children of African American Occupation Soldiers']. A collaborative effort

---

1   This title is a reference to the documentary film, *Here to Stay. Rassismus in Wien*, Markus Wailand, dir. (pooldocs, 2008), that 'shows notable people with African roots who view Austria as their new homeland'. 'Here to Stay. Rassismus in Wien' *Filmfonds Wien* (2018) <http://www.filmfonds-wien.at/filme/here-to-stay-rassismus-in-wien> accessed 6 May 2018.

between the creators of the exhibition and members of the oral history project 'Lost in Administration' at the University of Salzburg,[2] the aim was twofold: 'to be able to present an additional group from Austrian society' and 'to participate in writing the life stories of the first generation of Black Austrians into the collective memory of the Republic of Austria'.[3] But is it accurate to claim the children of African American GIs and Austrian women in the ten years of occupation following World War II (1946–1955) as the *first* generation of Black Austrians? Although the description of the exhibition on the museum's website narrows the focus to 'der ersten Generation Schwarzer ÖsterreichInnen *in der Zweiten Republik*' [the first generation of Black Austrians *in the Second Republic*] (my italics), the impression nevertheless remains that, prior to 1946, there were no Black Austrians.[4] Furthermore, this nationality-centered tunnel vision elides the experiences of other so-called 'occupation children' of Color – for example, those born to Austrian women and French colonial soldiers from North Africa during this same period. And while Black Germans began to connect and to mobilize during

2   Albert Lichtblau, 'Lost in Administration. Afro-Austrian GI Children – A Research Project' (n.d.) <http://www.lostinadministration.at/> accessed 22 April 2017. The first international conference to address 'Besatzungskinder in Österreich und Deutschland' [Occupation children in Austria and Germany'] after World War II took place on 27 September 2012. It was held at the Diplomatic Academy in Vienna and supported by the Ludwig Boltzmann-Institut für Kriegsfolgen-Forschung. Barbara Stelzl-Marx, 'Tagungsbericht: "Besatzungskinder in Österreich und Deutschland"', *H-Soz-u-Kult* (9 April 2013) <http://www.hsozkult.de/conferencereport/id/tagungs-berichte-4749> accessed 6 May 2018.

3   Matthias Beitl, 'Vorwort', in Niko Wahl, Phillipp Rohrbach and Tal Adler, eds, *SchwarzÖsterreich: Die Kinder afroamerikanischer Besatzungssoldaten*, exhibition catalogue (Vienna: Löcker, 2016), 7. The catalogue was subsequently named one of three winners of the competition 'Austria's Most Beautiful Books 2016'. 'Drei Staatspreise für die schönsten Bücher verliehen', *Hauptverband des Österreichischen Buchhandels* (2016) <http://www.buecher.at/drei-staatspreise-fuer-die-schoensten-buecher-verliehen/> accessed 6 May 2018.

4   Curiously, the much shorter English description of the exhibition on the same page describes these children simply as 'a forgotten generation born between 1946 and 1956 to Austrian women and African-American [*sic*] GIs'. 'SchwarzÖsterreich. Die Kinder afroamerikanischer Besatzungssoldaten' *Volkskundemuseum Wien* (n.d.) <http://www.volkskundemuseum.at/schwarzoesterreich_die_kinder_afroameri kanischer_besatzungssoldaten> accessed 6 May 2018.

the 1980s and 1990s, the situation of Black Austrians appears, on the surface, to have been rather different. In her review of 'SchwarzÖsterreich', U.S.-historian Kira Thurman remarks that 'what is striking about the Austrian case is how little Black Austrians knew about each other in their adult and senior years. Isolation defined their experiences as mixed-race people in Austria.'[5] Thurman concludes her discussion by reflecting on what might be considered both the essence – and the failure – of the exhibition, namely that it 'implies that no such effort to establish a shared identity appears to have taken place in Austria.'[6]

In the years since the publication of Paul Gilroy's influential *The Black Atlantic*, activists and scholars have turned to focus on what Gilroy calls the 'rhizomorphic, fractal structure of the transcultural, international formation [that is] the Black Atlantic' in order to call attention to supranational communities and collective identities.[7] However, where a coherent history – let alone acknowledgment – of a nation's Black citizens is absent, and where the perception persists that no such collective even exists, is there not perhaps still a place for investigations into national contexts? Austrian historian Walter Sauer has argued that, despite the trend towards viewing the African diaspora through a transcultural lens, there is nonetheless a hidden potential in the national approach, namely '[d]ie Kontextualisierung afrikanischer Diaspora vor dem Hintergrund der spezifischen gesellschaftlichen (und nicht zuletzt politisch-rechtlichen) Strukturen der Habsburgermonarchie beziehungsweise der Republik Österreich' [the contextualization of the African diaspora against the background of the specific societal (and if nothing else political-legal) structures of the Habsburg monarchy as well as the Republic of Austria].[8] Following Sauer's lead, I shall use the term 'Austrian' in its broadest sense: as a national identity constructed by the

5   Kira Thurman, 'Museum Exhibit Review: "Black Austria: The Children of African American Occupation Soldiers"', *H-Black-Europe* 20 July 2016 <https://networks.h-net.org/node/19384/discussions/135747/cross-post-exhibit-review-thurman-black-austria-children-african> accessed 6 May 2018.

6   Thurman, 'Museum Exhibit Review'.

7   Paul Gilroy, *The Black Atlantic: Modernity and Double Consciousness* (Cambridge, MA: Harvard University Press, 1993), 4.

8   Walter Sauer, 'Reflexion zur afrikanischen Diaspora in Österreich', *Österreichische Zeitschrift zur Geisteswissenschaften* 17/4 (2006), 150. Unless otherwise specified, all

historical memory of a nation that has changed size and constitution over
several centuries.

This chapter consciously adopts this nation-focused approach in order
to draw attention to the specificity of the Black Austrian experience precisely because it has heretofore not been a part of Black German Studies.
As a white U.S.-American scholar, I am not attempting to speak for Black
Austrians; rather, my goal is to foreground Black Austrian experiences as
described by Black Austrians, thereby bringing their voices into English-
speaking academic dialogue. Following a brief overview of the history
of people of African descent in Austria, I will analyze two events that
argue for the importance of recognizing the specific historical context of
Black identity in Austria, in this case, where the Black Austrian community became visible within the public sphere. The first of these addressed
immanent political and social issues facing Black people in Austria at the
turn of the millennium. The highly publicized events surrounding the
death of twenty-six-year-old Nigerian asylum-seeker Marcus Omofuma
during his deportation in 1999 conclusively demonstrated that the Black
Community in Austria, and particularly in Vienna, is organized, politically
active and vocal. In addition to making themselves visible in contemporary Austria, Black Austrians are also working to redress the absence of
Black Austrians in the national historical narrative. In 2006, the counter-
history project 'Verborgene Geschichte/n – Remapping Mozart' ['Hidden
History/ies: Remapping Mozart'] – the brain-child of the *Recherchegruppe
zu Schwarzer österreichischer Geschichte und Gegenwart* [Research Group
on Black Austrian History and Presence] – confronted the historical and
historicized racism underlying the year-long Mozart jubilee. These two
interventions by Black Austrians into public discourse ask us to consider
the following questions: how does the Black Austrian experience differ
from that of the Black German one? Who produces narratives about Black
Austrians – and who hears them? How might the inclusion of specifically Austrian narratives expand the archive of Black German Studies, that
is, what might be (re)captured and redeemed in the process of allowing

----

translations from the German are my own. In order to provide access to Black Austrian
voices, all texts by Black Austrians are provided in both English and German.

national and transnational histories of the African diaspora in Austria to intersect?

Black Austrians Today and Yesterday

As the exhibition 'SchwarzÖsterreich' seemed to confirm, the misguided perception still persists that Black Austrians first 'came into being' only after World War II.[9] In an interview, Niko Wahl, one of the leaders of the project 'Lost in Administration', maintained that there was one primary difference between the history of Black children in Austria in the postwar period and that of Black Germans, namely, that, unlike Germany, which had experienced the occupation of the Rhineland by French African colonial troops in the early 1920s, in Austria, 'war dunkelhäutiger Nachwuchs für Österreich ein vollkommen neues Phänomen' ['dark-skinned progeny was a completely new phenomenon'].[10] It is certainly true that at the end of World War II, U.S. troops – including African American soldiers – were deployed to the former '*Ostmark*' (the name the National Socialists gave Austria), just as they were in defeated Germany. Of the 70,000 soldiers in the U.S.-occupied states of Salzburg and Upper Austria (as well as parts of divided Vienna), approximately 5,000 (5–6 per cent) were African American

9 This misconception was further reinforced by a made-for-TV movie that premiered on 8 December 2015 on ORF, Austria's public broadcast station. A German-Austrian co-production, *Kleine, Grosse Stimme* [*Small, Grand Voice*] is set in 1955 – the year that Allied occupation of Austria ended. It tells the story of Benedikt Thaler (played by Wainde Wane), the ten-year-old son of a (deceased) Austrian mother and an African American GI. Eerily reminiscent of the 1952 German film *Toxi, Kleine, grosse Stimme* calls attention to the presence of Black Austrians at the same time as it imagines their ultimate removal from Austria. *Kleine, grosse Stimme*, Wolfgang Murnberger, dir. (ORF, BR and ARD Degeto, 2015); *Toxi*, Robert A. Stemmle, dir. (Fono Film, 1952).

10 Niko Wahl, 'Heim ins Land der Väter', *Die Zeit* 52 (23 December 2010) <http://www.zeit.de/2010/52/A-Mischlingskinder> accessed 6 May 2018.

GIs,[11] while French African troops, primarily from Morocco and Senegal, were stationed in the French zone, which included Vorarlberg and Tirol.[12]

It should come as no surprise that fewer children were born in Austria during the occupation than in West Germany as the Allied occupation of Austria (1945–55) was considerably shorter than that of the Federal Republic. U.S. historian Heide Fehrenbach estimates that, of the approximately 94,000 so-called 'occupation children' born in West Germany, between 1945 and 1949, around 3,000 had Black fathers.[13] Austrian historian Ingrid Bauer projects that circa 5,000 children were born to American GIs and Austrian women.[14] Further, by the mid-1950s, there were between 500 and 600 children born to Austrian women and Allied soldiers of African descent. However, the curators of 'SchwarzÖsterreich' estimate the number as being somewhat smaller – between 350 and 400.[15] Nevertheless, as

---

11 Ingrid Bauer, '"Leiblicher Vater: Amerikaner (Neger)": Besatzungskinder afroamerikanischer Herkunft', in Helmuth Niederle, ed., *Früchte der Zeit: Afrika, Diaspora, Literatur und Migration* (Vienna: Vienna University Press, 2001), 49–51.

12 The Second Moroccan Infantry Division and the Fourth Mountain Division were the primary liberators of the area of Vorarlberg at the start of May 1945. Walter Sauer, *Expeditionen ins afrikanische Österreich: Ein Reisekaleidoskop* (Vienna: Mandelbaum, 2014), 371–72. See also, Hamid Lechhab, 'Marokkanische Besatzungskinder in Vorarlberg nach 1945', in Walter Sauer, ed., *Von Soliman zu Omofuma: afrikanische Diaspora in Österreich 17. bis 20. Jahrhundert* (Innsbruck: Studien Verlag, 2007), 177–86. According to Duygu Özkan writing in the Vienna daily paper *Die Presse*, 'A public discussion has recently begun about the occupation children of Moroccan colonial soldiers who were born in Vorarlberg – Vorarlberg was occupied by the French'. Duygu Özkan, 'Österreichs vergessene Kinder', *Die Presse* (27 April 2016) <http://diepresse.com/home/leben/4974018/Oesterreichs-vergessene-Kinder> accessed 18 April 2017.

13 Heide Fehrenbach, 'Black Occupation Children and the Devolution of the Nazi Racial State', in Rita Chin, Heide Fehrenbach and Geoff Eley, eds, *After the Nazi Racial State: Difference and Democracy in Germany and Europe* (Ann Arbor: University of Michigan Press, 2009), 31.

14 Stelzl-Marx, 'Tagungsbericht: "Besatzungskinder in Österreich und Deutschland"'.

15 Ingrid Bauer, '*Schwarzer Peter*: A Historical Perspective. Henisch and the Postwar Austrian Occupation', paper given at the 24th Annual Conference of the German Studies Association, Houston, Texas, 5–8 October 2000, 4. Cited with permission of the author. Wahl, Rohrbach and Adler, *SchwarzÖsterreich*, 46.

Walter Sauer has noted with more than a touch of irony, 'nie war Österreich "weißer" als nach 1945' ['Austria was never "whiter" than after 1945'].[16]

Although the Habsburg Empire never officially held overseas colonies nor joined in the 'Scramble for Africa',[17] historians have amply documented a continuous history of Africans and people of African descent in the Habsburg Empire dating back to the late Early Modern period.[18] One such early encounter records the visit of seven Ethiopian monks to the Benedictine monastery at Melk (a city west of Vienna) in 1517. In the sixteenth and seventeenth centuries, many of the Africans in Austria were captives – either slaves or soldiers – who were forced to serve in noble houses. And although the Empire may not have actively engaged in the slave trade, many Habsburg aristocrats nevertheless prized their '*Hofmohren*' ['court moors'], the most famous of whom is undoubtedly Angelo Soliman (1721–1796).[19] Less well known, however, is the mid-nineteenth-century practice of smuggling formerly enslaved girls from Ethiopia and the Sudan into Austrian cloisters where they were trained to return to Africa as Christian missionaries.[20] Even as late as the end of the nineteenth century, Marie Valérie, the favorite daughter of Empress Elisabeth (Sisi), had an African playmate named Rustimo, who had been 'gifted' to the Empress as a child.[21] Around the same time, Peter Altenberg's

16   Sauer, *Expeditionen*, 67.

17   Recent scholarship interrogates the long-standing myth of Austria-Hungary's 'clean hands' position vis-à-vis the slave trade, as well as the imbrication of various members of the Habsburg Empire in colonial politics and imperial ventures. Walter Sauer, ed., *k. u. k. Kolonial: Habsburgermonarchie und europäische Herrschaft in Afrika* (Vienna: Böhlau, 2002); 'Colonial Austria: Austria and the Overseas', special issue of *Austrian Studies* 20 (2012); Franz Kotrba, *k. u. k. in Ostafrika: Die Habsburgermonarchie im 'Scramble for East Africa'* (Vienna: SADOCC, 2015). Sauer has called this denial of Austrian involvement in colonialism 'eine weitere Lebenslüge der Zweiten Republik' [a further grand delusion of the Second Republic] – the first being that Austria was the first victim of the National Socialists. Sauer, *Expeditionen*, 65.

18   The following overview is informed by Sauer, *Expeditionen*, 11–68.

19   I will address Soliman more extensively later in this chapter.

20   Sauer, 'Reflexion', 151.

21   See the photo of Marie Valérie and Rustimo in Martha and Horst Schad, eds, *Marie Valérie: Das Tagebuch der Lieblingstochter von Kaiserin Elisabeth 1878–1899* (Munich: Langen Müller, 1998), n.p. See also, Sauer, *Expeditionen*, 232–33.

prose text about the 1896 'Völkerschau' [ethnographic exhibition] of Ashanti people in the Vienna *Tiergarten* [zoo], *Ashantee* (1897), captured the mixture of fascination and desire in the Empire vis-à-vis Africans at the turn of the twentieth century.

It would be misleading, however, to assume that all visitors and migrants to the Empire from Africa – or to the two Republics, for that matter – were servants and subalterns. The Habsburg Empire's political and economic interests outside Europe focused primarily on the Near East, and on Egypt in particular. As a result of these ties, around 1830, the reform-minded Ottoman governor Muhammad Ali began sending university students to Austria for technical training.[22] In addition, African American performers started including Austria on their travel itineraries – and continued to do so throughout the First and into the Second Republics.[23] The twentieth century witnessed both the incarceration of Black African freedom fighters from the Spanish Civil War in the concentration camp at Mauthausen and the occupation of Austria by African American and North African soldiers.[24] After World War II, due in large

22   Marcel Chahrour, '"Vom Morgenhauch aufstrebender Cultur durchweht": Ägyptische Studenten in Österreich 1830–1945', in Walter Sauer ed., *Von Soliman zu Omofuma: afrikanische Diaspora in Österreich 17. bis 20 Jahrhundert* (Innsbruck: Studien Verlag, 2007), 131–49.

23   See Kira Thurman, 'Africa in European Evening Attire': Defining African American Spirituals and Western Art Music in Central Europe, 1870s–1930s', in Tiffany N. Florvil and Vanessa D. Plumly, eds, *Rethinking Black German Studies: Approaches, Interventions and Histories* (Oxford: Peter Lang, 2018), Chapter 6.

24   The internment and deaths of African soldiers and civilians at Mauthausen is, as Walter Sauer writes, the most forgotten aspect of the camp's history. Sauer, *Expeditionen*, 274. See Herwig Czech, '"Vorwiegend negerische Rassenmerkmale": AfrikanerInnen und farbige "Mischlinge" im Nationalsozialismus', in Walter Sauer ed., *Von Soliman zu Omofuma: afrikanische Diaspora in Österreich 17. bis 20 Jahrhundert* (Innsbruck: Studien Verlag, 2007), 165–70; Barbara Fuchlehner, and Karin Röhling, 'Afrikanerinnen und Afrikaner im KZ Mauthausen: Teilauswertung der Datenblätter im Archiv der KZ-Gedenkstätte Mauthausen (Wien, Innenministerium)', Project Report (University of Vienna, 2016).

part to its self-proclaimed 'clean colonial past',[25] neutral Austria attracted students from nations in the process of decolonization,[26] while also developing diplomatic relations with these new countries, beginning with the city of Lagos in Nigeria in 1962.[27]

Schwarze or *Afro-Österreicher/Innen* [Black or Afro-Austrians][28] continue to be a diverse population whose biographies illustrate the heterogeneity of the 'roots and routes' in Black Austrian history.[29] The names of some of the most prominent among them are, however, likely unfamiliar to

25   Walter Sauer, 'Habsburg Colonial: Austria-Hungary's Role in European Overseas Expansion Reconsidered', *Austrian Studies* 20 (2012), 6.

26   The first African students at Austrian universities in the postwar period were primarily Egyptian. By the academic year 1961/62, the number had increased to 639, with students representing sixteen nations or colonies. Walter Sauer, 'Afro-österreichische Diaspora heute: Migration und Integration in der 2. Republik', Walter Sauer ed., *Von Soliman zu Omofuma: afrikanische Diaspora in Österreich 17. bis 20 Jahrhundert* (Innsbruck: Studien Verlag, 2007), 193.

27   Sauer, *Expeditionen*, 64.

28   Unlike in West Germany, where Caribbean-American poet Audre Lorde helped the women in her seminar at the Free University of Berlin in 1984 coin the term *Afro-Deutsche* [Afro-German], there does not appear to be a single originary moment for the term *Afro-ÖsterreicherIn*. In both cases, however, the act of self-naming serves to counteract and replace previous derogatory names based on skin color. In its narrowest meaning, the term Afro-ÖsterreicherIn encompasses People of Color born and raised in Austria. However, it is also used in a broader sense, namely as a designation encompassing all people of African descent living in Austria. Irene Gröpel, 'Eigen- und Fremdwahrnehemung: Afro-EuropäerInnen und Afro-ÖsterreicherInnen – Grenzen der Schwarz-Weiß-Konstruktion', MA thesis, University of Vienna, 2010, 110. The *Recherchegruppe zu Schwarzer österreichischer Geschichte* (established in 2005) prefers the term *Schwarze ÖsterreicherIn* [Black Austrian]. Claudia Unterweger, '*Talking Back*: Strategien der Vergangenheitserzählung am Beispiel der *Recherchegruppe zu Schwarzer österreichischer Geschichte*', MA thesis, University of Vienna, 2013, 1, 10–13.

29   The term 'roots and routes' was first used by Gilroy, *The Black Atlantic*, 19, 193. In 2010, there were 40,744 people of African descent living in Austria, and of this number, a little over half (22,083) held African citizenship. Clara Akinyosoye, 'Menschen afrikanischer Herkunft in Österreich', in simon INOU, and Beatrice Achaleke, eds, *Schwarze Menschen in Österreich 2010: Lagebericht* (Vienna: Black Publishers, 2010), 6 <http://www.m-media.or.at/gesellschaft/schwarze-menschen-in-osterreich-jahres-bericht-2010-die-zusammenfassung/2011/06/16/index.html> accessed 6 May 2018.

English-speaking audiences: Béatrice Achaleke (author and co-founder of
AFRA – the International Center for Black Women's Perspectives), Clara
Akinyosoye (editor-in-chief of *Fresh! Black Austrian Lifestyle*, the first
magazine for Black Austrians, and co-founder, with Simon Inou, of the
BlackAustria campaign),[30] David Alaba (star player for the soccer franchise
Bayern-München), Marie Edwige Hartig (Green Party member and the
first Black Austrian Councillor in Linz), Simon Inou (activist, journalist,
and founder of the website afrikanet.info), Araba Evelyn Johnston-Arthur
(scholar and activist), Arabella Kiesbauer (host of the German talk show
'Arabella' from 1994–2004), Helmut 'Heli' Köglberger (Austrian soccer
star in the 1960s and 1970s), Tyron Ricketts (actor/singer/songwriter) and
Claudia Unterweger (the first Black presenter at the Austrian Broadcasting
Company, ORF).[31] The heterogeneity of their roots in countries as diverse
as Ghana, Jamaica, Nigeria and the Philippines – as well as Austria – simply
underscores the diversity of the Black Austrian community.

30   'BlackAustria' was a media campaign launched by M-Media – Verein für Interkulturelle
     Medienarbeit and AFRA between 2006–2009 to confront racist imagery in advertis-
     ing. 'Black Austria Projektbeschreibung', *SozialMarie Prize for Social Innovation* 2007
     (n.d.) <https://www.sozialmarie.org/de-AT/projects/696> accessed 6 May 2018;
     'Kreative Gegenvorurteile', *Südwind Magazin* 2 (2007) <http://www.suedwind-
     magazin.at/kreativ-gegen-vorurteile> accessed 6 May 2018; Alice Drössler, and others,
     'Die Kampagne BLACKAUSTRIA in den Augen der BLACK COMMUNITY
     in Wien', Seminar project (University of Vienna, 2007) <http://www.blackaustria.
     at/downloads/studien/studie_black_community.pdf> accessed 20 April 2017.
31   The publicly funded broadcast channels ORF eins and ORF2 earned 32.9 per cent of
     the market share in 2016. APA, 'TV-Quoten 2016: ORF verliert leicht, Servus TV
     legt zu', *Salzburger Nachrichten* (2 January 2017) <https://www.sn.at/panorama/
     medien/tv-quoten-2016-orf-verliert-leicht-servus-tv-legt-zu-564109> accessed 18
     April 2017.

'ÖsterREICH für alle GLEICH'[32] [Austria for all equally]

Three short years after thousands of Hungarians fled across the border into Austria following their failed revolution against the government and its Soviet-friendly policies, Austria re-affirmed its commitment to aiding refugees. 'The granting of asylum has always been a holy duty for us, which we have honestly fulfilled in spite of all sacrifices', declared Chancellor Julius Raab of the *Österreichische Volkspartei* [ÖVP – Austrian People's Party] in 1959. Fewer than ten years later, in the spring of 1968, another revolution in yet another Soviet-dominated country – this time Czechoslovakia – prompted thousands to cross into neutral Austria. However, with the end of the Cold War, the relaxation of border controls, the onset of the Balkan Wars, and the entrance of Austria into the European Union, the Second Republic became less willing to accept refugees. Much like Germany and other Western European nations, Austria adopted the position of 'Fortress Europe'. Still, between 1988 and 2000, more than 400,000 immigrants from Eastern Europe and Africa entered the nation of 8 million – increasing the population by 5 per cent.[33] Anti-immigrant sentiment in the Second Republic steadily increased over the final decade of the twentieth century, finally coming to a head in the spring of 1999 during the national elections. The conservative ÖVP – which forty years earlier had embraced the 'holy duty' of aiding refugees – joined the xenophobic rightwing *Freiheitliche Partei Österreichs* [FPÖ – Austrian Freedom Party] to form a Black/Blue coalition government.

32   This slogan first appeared on 5 June 2001 at a demonstration where protesters demanded that Article 7 of the Federal Constitution be altered from 'All citizens of the state are equal before the law' to '[a]ll people are equal before the law and are entitled to equal protection before the law without discrimination'. Michael Genner, 'ÖsterREICH–für alle GLEICH!', *asyl-in-not.org* (2001) <http://www.asyl-in-not.org/php/oesterreich fuer_alle_gleich_,12311,4874.html> accessed 6 May 2018.

33   Jacob Heilbrunn, 'A Disdain for the Past: Jörg Haider's Austria', *World Policy Journal* 17/1 (2000), 75.

For People of Color in Austria, this new government represented a
double-edged sword. As activist and academic Araba Evelyn Johnston-
Arthur recalls:

> Als Wendepunkt in der 'schwarzen' österreichischen Geschichte betrachte ich
> die Nationalratswahl 1999, wo schwarze Menschen zum ersten Mal in Österreich
> instrumentalisiert worden sind – die Kriminalisierung schwarzer Menschen als
> Wahlkampfthema. Dieser Wendepunkt markiert unsere Wahrnehmung als
> Marginalisierte. Das ist ironisch, weil es gleichzeitig den Wendepunkt markiert, daß
> [sic] wir überhaupt als eine in Österreich lebende Gruppe wahrgenommen worden
> sind. Zuvor waren schwarze Menschen einfach nur exotische Ausnahmeerscheinungen,
> nicht wirklich existent – quasi von 'legal aliens' zu einer marginalisierten, krimina-
> lisierten Gruppe.

> [I consider the 1999 general election to be the turning point in 'black' Austrian his-
> tory, when black people were first instrumentalized in Austria, with the criminaliza-
> tion of black people as an election issue. This turning point marks our awareness as
> marginalized people. That's ironic since it simultaneously marks the point at which
> we were even recognized as a group living in Austria. Previously, black people were
> simply exotic exceptions, not actually real – in effect, [we went] from 'legal aliens'
> to a marginalized, criminalized group].[34]

Johnston-Arthur regards the final year of the millennium as a turning point
not only in Austrian history, but also in the history of Black Austrians. In
particular, the rightwing press and nativist politicians demonized migrants
from sub-Saharan Africa as drug-dealers who were putatively undermining white Austrian society. As a result, the Austrian police increasingly
subjected Black Austrians, migrants from Africa and asylum-seekers to
arbitrary treatment and racial profiling.[35]

---

34   Hakan Gürses, 'Schwarz ist eine politische Identität: Interview mit Araba Evelyn
      Johnston-Arthur', in *Stimmen von und für Minderheiten* 39 (2001) <http://minder
      heiten.at/stat/stimme/stimme39c.htm> accessed 6 May 2018.
35   Simon Kravagna, 'Schwarze Stereotype und weiße Behörden: Afrikaner,
      Drogenkriminalität und Strafverfolgung durch Polizei und Justiz', *SWS-Rundschau*
      45/2 (2005), 266–88 <http://www.ssoar.info/ssoar/handle/document/16490>
      accessed 6 May 2018.

The increasingly xenophobic atmosphere in Austria reached a watershed moment with the death of one such sanctuary-seeker whose application for asylum had been rejected. On 1 May 1999, after he had spent several months in pre-deportation custody, the Austrian government deported Marcus Omofuma to Nigeria by way of Sofia. The three immigration authorities who accompanied him to Bulgaria maintained that Omofuma's refusal to board the airplane peaceably required them to subdue him forcibly – despite protests by other passengers on the Balkan Air flight. Upon arrival in Sofia, Marcus Omofuma was found dead. The official cause of death, as determined first by a Bulgarian autopsy and later confirmed by German forensic scientists, was asphyxiation as a result of the deportee having been tied down and silenced with adhesive tape that partially covered his nostrils.[36]

The shock, grief and anger that shook the Black community, as well as many *MehrheitsösterreicherInnen* [majority, i.e. white Austrians], at the news of Omofuma's brutal death are the subject of texts by two Nigerian-born long-time residents of Vienna. Chibo Onyeji is an author and academic who has taught Economic Development at the University of Vienna. His 2006 collection of poetry and prose, *Flowers, Bread, and Gold*, chronicles the years 1999–2003, that is, from the death of Marcus Omofuma to the conclusion of the trial against the three officers in whose care he died.[37] Obiora Ci-K 'Charles' Ofoedu, a student of Communications and Political Science and a co-founder of the *Plattform für eine Welt ohne Rassismus* [Platform for a World Without Racism], provides an insider's view of

---

36 Bulgarian officials were the first to draw a connection between Ofomua's restraints and his death. The coroner in Vienna disputed this claim two years later, countering that Omofuma died of an embolism resulting from the deportee's own resistance. In the end, German forensic scientist Dr. Bernd Brinkmann definitively confirmed the Bulgarian ruling. 'Marcus Omofuma: "Klassischer Erstickungstod"' (6 February 2001) <http://no-racism.net/article/485/> accessed 6 May 2018; Stefan Müller, '"Das ist schrecklich"', *Zeit Online* (9 November 2015) <http://www.zeit.de/2015/45/interview-bernd-brinkmann-graz-fehlgutachten-forensik-gerichtsmedizin> accessed 6 May 2018.

37 Chibo Onyeji, *Flowers, Bread, and Gold* (Ranshofen/Osternberg: edition innsalz, 2006).

the Austrian legal system. In his book from 2000, *Morgengrauen: Ein literarischer Bericht* [*Dawn: A literary Report*] – translated from his *The Framed Boss* – Ofoedu describes the intensification of reprisals against Black protesters in the wake of Omofuma's death – actions that included wire-tapping and surveillance.[38] These tactics of intimidation ultimately culminated in 'Operation Spring', a nationwide drug raid. In this autobiographical text, Ofoedu details the dragnet targeting not only members of organized crime, but also critics of the government and its immigration policies. Both Onyeji and Ofoedu write in English, but Ofoedu's 'literary report' of his arrest and incarceration, the destruction of his reputation in the media and his ultimate release was translated and published in German. Whereas Onyeji's poems appeal to a broader international readership, Ofoedu clearly directs his work to a German-speaking audience.[39]

With *Flowers, Bread, and Gold*, Chibo Onyeji registers the horror and frustration that gripped the Black community after Marcus Omofuma's death, as well as the sense of being at the mercy of something irrational, uncontrolled and ultimately uncontrollable. In the poem 'City', the poet's voice eventually comes into dialogue with that of the city (presumably Vienna), which ventriloquizes the anti-Black rhetoric of the populist rightwing media and politicians:

> *They're foreigners, black, Africans*
> *for the most part Nigerians!* fumes city.[40]

Even as the poet attempts to contextualize the city's diatribe, nothing seems to de-escalate its growing fears, nor bring a sense of balance into the conversation.

---

38   Obiora Ci-K Ofoedu, *Morgengrauen: Ein literarischer Bericht*, tr. Ric Maréchal (Vienna: Mandelbaum, 2000). Because I did not have access to Ofoedu's papers at the Austrian National Library, the translations to English are my own and should not be confused with his original manuscript.

39   Ernst Grabovsky, 'Österreich als literarischer Erfahrungsraum zugewanderter Autorinnen und Autoren', in Helmut Schmitz, ed., *Von der nationalen zur internationalen Literatur. Transkulturelle deutschsprachige Literatur und Kultur im Zeitalter globaler Migration* (Amsterdam: Rodopi, 2009), 279–81.

40   Onyeji, 'City', in *Flowers*, 26. All italics are Onyeji's.

Their trade is ruinous to youth, our future!! cries city.
Youth already prone already failed by family

long before
they arrived, I suggest.

Told these truths city is bitter.[41]

The dominant metaphor of the collection – the figure of the storm – embodies the anti-immigrant hysteria of the spring of 1999 as something primal and base, not governed by rationality. Assuming the guise of Marcus Omofuma, the poetic voice of 'In the Eye of the Storm' increases the intensity – as well as the danger – of the wind at each of the narrator's stopping points. In Germany, he 'strolls the streets of Hamburg / in the company of a calm wind' while in Moscow, the wind is 'a leisurely, westerly wind'. Continuing to follow the path that led to Marcus Omofuma's death, the poetic voice arrives in Austria, a country located between the 'calm' wind of Germany and the 'leisurely' one of Russia. It is in Austria that he finds himself 'in the eye of the storm' – a storm that was '[s]eeded in the heart of Vienna', breaking only on its journey outward, namely, in the air, on the flight to Sofia.[42]

More than simply recounting the events surrounding Marcus Omofuma's death, *Flowers, Bread, and Gold* comments on and indicts the realities of life for African migrants in Austria. To this end, Onyeji repeatedly mobilizes the image of the shadow, his metaphor for refugees who, although physically present in Austria, remain unseen and unacknowledged, and thus without substance.

Having come for refuge and
in search of a living, and
receiving not the one and

finding not the other,
the shadows
not wanting to be shadows

41   Onyeji, 'City', in *Flowers*, 27.
42   Onyeji, 'In the Eye of the Storm', in *Flowers*, 43–44.

ply their trade round the clock to escape
shadowness; in time, hypnotized
by the allure of gold.

Told this truth city is bitter.[43]

Onyeji directs his most pointed criticism at those who see not people, but
shades – something less than human, insubstantial and abject. In 'Crystal
Nights' – clearly an allusion to *Kristallnacht* [Night of Broken Glass] –
the poet describes the men and women in prison and refugee camps as
shattered, fragmented beings: 'How broken they are / These black lives
smithereens of crystal glass'.[44] The melancholy tone of this poem contrasts
sharply with the accusatory stance in poems such as 'Heights and Circles'
and 'I Walked Past Parliament', where the poet chastises Austria for disre-
garding, and thus senselessly wasting, the potential contributions of these
immigrants.

The poet's general sense of the situation as monstrously unjust narrows to focus on a specific set of events: namely the media frenzy following Marcus Omofuma's death, the demonization of the victim and
the trial three years later of the officials who had restrained Omofuma
on the flight. 'A Memorable Day in Court' records the lack of emotion
displayed by the three defendants at their indictment, while the poem
'The Trial of Marcus Omofuma' captures the poet's feelings of powerlessness. On the one hand, he mistrusts a legal system that appears to be
inherently corrupt and racist. On the other hand, he expresses dismay at
the way that the conservative press blames the victim: 'In this perverse
alchemy of justice / victim transposes into virtual defendant'.[45] The cycle
of poems closes on a resigned tone with 'End of a Season', a poem that
records the final verdict in April 2002 – a suspended sentence of eight
months for the defendants with the charge: *fahrlässige Tötung* [involuntary
manslaughter].

---

43   Onyeji, 'City', in *Flowers*, 25.
44   Onyeji, 'Crystal Nights', in *Flowers*, 34.
45   Onyeji, 'The Trial of Marcus Omofuma', in *Flowers*, 59.

A closure
by no means a closure;

raising many more questions
than it answers;

plugging many more exits
than it opens –

The deceptive logic of its tone
italicizing the malice of its voice

whose timbre conjures
the levity of a traffic offence
out of the gravity of a felony,
transposing levity from gravity![46]

In *Flowers, Bread, and Gold*, the poet gives voice to the frustration of those who had believed that justice would prevail if enough public pressure were brought to bear. Initially, at least, this had not been a misplaced hope. Within hours of the public announcement of Omofuma's death, antiracist groups from human rights organizations to NGOs to members of Vienna's Black community had formed the *Plattform für eine Welt ohne Rassismus* [Platform for a World Without Racism]. On 8 May 1999, the first anti-government demonstration initiated a 100-day *Mahnwache* [vigil]. Held in front of the Ministry of the Interior, the vigil both commemorated Marcus Omofuma and assured that attention remained focused on the injustices committed. Ten years later, Nigerian-Austrian journalist Simon Inou recalled, '[d]as war das erste Mal, dass so viele Selbstorganisationen von Schwarzen in Österreich auf die Straße gingen' [[t]hat was the first time that so many grassroots groups organized by Blacks in Austria took to the streets'].[47] At the same time, the enormously popular right-wing

---

46   Onyeji, 'End of a Season', in *Flowers*, 60–61.
47   Simon Inou, 'Liebe Mama Felicia Omofuma', *DerStandard.at* (29 April 2009) <http://derstandard.at/1240550183494/Liebe-Mama-Felicia-Omofuma-> accessed 6 May 2018.

tabloid, *Die Neue Kronen Zeitung*, sided with the authorities and dismissed the protesters as 'drug bosses or their accomplices'.[48]

Despite calls to investigate Austrian policing strategies in the wake of Omofuma's death, authorities nevertheless mounted the largest police action in the Second Republic. In a massive drug raid on the cities of Vienna, Graz, Linz and St Pölten on 27 May 1999, more than 850 police stormed private residences and centers housing asylum-seekers. Police arrested more than 120 people, the majority from sub-Saharan Africa, during 'Operation Spring', although over a third of them had to be freed almost immediately for lack of evidence of wrongdoing. Among those arrested and subsequently detained was Obiora Ci-K 'Charles' Ofoedu, a Nigerian author, student and human rights activist who was one of the organizers of the antiracist demonstrations and a leading figure in several human rights organizations. The government accused Ofoedu of money-laundering, for which he spent three months in remand. During this time, *Die Neue Kronen Zeitung*, continuing to play upon the stereotype of the African drug dealer, prominently cast him as the 'boss' of the Nigerian drug mafia in Austria.

Although 'Operation Spring' had been in the planning stages for months prior to the antiracism protests in May, many have read its implementation at this moment as having been politically motivated. In particular, Angelika Schuster and Tristan Sindelgruber's 2005 documentary, *Operation Spring*, demonstrates the degree to which the legal proceedings against those arrested were less than transparent.[49] A second wave of arrests followed in late September 1999 – coincidentally just days before the parliamentary elections. For his part, the FPÖ's Jörg Haider had spent the campaign fanning the flames of xenophobia and racism with his references

---

48   *Die Neue Kronen Zeitung* is the most popular daily in Austria and regularly commands the largest market share and number of readers per issue. Rudi Renger, and Franz Rest, 'Die Neue Kronen Zeitung: Massenmediales Flaggschiff aller österreichischen Populismen', in Richard Faber, and Frank Unger, eds, *Populismus in Geschichte und Gegenwart* (Würzburg: Königshausen & Neumann, 2008), 175–209.

49   *Operation Spring*, Angelika Schuster, and Tristan Sindelgruber, dirs (Schnittpunkt, 2005).

to Omofuma as a 'Drogendealer und Mörder unserer Kinder' [drug-dealer and murderer of our children].[50]

That members of the Black community dared to challenge both the police and the government was perceived in some quarters as both transgressive and threatening. In conversation with *Der Falter*, one of Vienna's alternative papers, the spokesperson for the human rights pressure group SOS-Mitmensch [SOS-Fellow Human Being], Philipp Sonderegger, suggested that: '[t]he more people from the African Community engaged in protest against the murder of Marcus Omofuma and racist police violence, the higher investigators assumed they ranked in the alleged Nigerian drug network'.[51] Over time, this strategy took its toll, according to Ofoedu, as the Black community became paralyzed for fear of falling victim to the same fate as his own. He wrote:

> Keiner von ihnen wagte es mehr, öffentlich aufzutreten. Keine einzige Seele unter ihnen würde sich freiwillig an irgendeine Aktivität machen, mit der auch nur die geringste Gefahr verbunden war, sich einem Risiko welcher Art auch immer auszusetzen. ... Sogar unter denen, die ihre Hoffnung noch nicht ganz verloren hatten, fand sich keiner, der aufstand und für sich oder gar für die anderen sprach. Und ihre Furcht wuchs und sie wurden immer vorsichtiger. Sie waren ständig auf der Hut und verhielten sich so unauffällig wie möglich. Sie wurden zu 'guten Niggern'. Meine Ankläger hatten gewonnen.

> [None of them dared to appear publicly anymore. Not a single soul among them would voluntarily participate in any activity associated with even the slightest danger, would expose themselves to any kind of risk. ... Even among those who had not yet lost their hope, there was no one who stood up and spoke on behalf of himself, let alone the others. And their fear grew and they became ever more careful. They were constantly on guard and acted as unobtrusively as possible. They became 'good niggers'. My accusers had won].[52]

---

50 Tommy Angerer, 'Den Staat zu beobachten ist Staatsbürgerpflicht', *Augustin* (6 February 2001) <http://www.augustin.or.at/zeitung/tun-und-lassen/den-staat-zu-beobachten-ist-staatbuergerpflicht.html> accessed 6 May 2018.

51 Nina Horaczek, 'Alle waren schwarz', *Der Falter* 38 (2005) <https://www.falter.at/archiv/FALTER_20050921183313005/alle-waren-schwarz> accessed 26 June 2018.

52 Ofoedu, *Morgengrauen*, 257.

As a self-styled 'Bericht' [report], Ofoedu's book diverges from traditional narratives of incarceration by directing the reader's focus less toward himself and more at the institutional structures and cultural currents of Austrian society at the turn of the twenty-first century. Ofoedu takes great pains to appear as objective and rational as possible against what he characterizes as the raging, chaotic forces of the Austrian police – a trope that echoes the 'storm' in Onyeji's poems. The emotional volatility of the police and the servants of the justice system become a common theme throughout the book, reversing the stereotypical roles usually assigned to Africans and Europeans. Moreover, much of the behavior of the Austrian officials – from the racial epithets police officers carelessly tossed at him to the stubborn refusal of prison authorities to retrieve his glasses from his apartment – is imbued with a pettiness that encourages the reader to question the authority and credibility of the authorities.

Morgengrauen confronts not only the author's physical imprisonment, but also his sense of being held captive in a narrative web. This becomes evident in the book's preface, which was written by Marco Smoliner, a major in the Vienna police, who concludes:

> Die Erinnerungen von Charles Ofoedu an seine Festnahme und Untersuchungshaft, an glatte Polizeiwillkür und menschenverachtende Medienjustiz beschreiben den Leidensweg eines mittellosen Schriftstellers, der von Polizei und Boulevard zum bekanntesten 'Drogenboss' des Jahres gemacht wurde, weil er es gewagt hatte, sich als Afrikaner in Österreich für Menschenrechte einzusetzen.

> [The memories of Charles Ofoedu, of his arrest and pre-trial detention, of outright police arbitrariness and inhuman persecution by the media depict the path of suffering of an impoverished writer who was turned into the most famous 'drug boss' of the year by the police and tabloids because he had dared, as an African, to champion human rights in Austria].[53]

---

53   Marco Smoliner, 'Vorwort', in Obiora Ci-K Ofoedu, *Morgengrauen: Ein literarischer Bericht*, tr. Ric Maréchal (Vienna: Mandelbaum, 2000), 5.

Much like Onyeji, who laments the posthumous stigmatization of Marcus Omofuma, Ofoedu is particularly disturbed by the role of 'drug boss' in which he had been cast.

Although one might expect Ofoedu's book to seek to concentrate on his own suffering at the hands of an unjust and prejudiced system, a victim rather than a subject, the text itself bears out a rather different sensibility. He refuses to be the 'stone in the rushing river' that is eventually worn down by the constant flow of water over it. As he writes early in the book, 'Und niemals vergesse ich, daß [*sic*] von allen Dingen, die einem Menschen zustoßen können, dies das Schlimmste ist: daß [*sic*] andere Menschen über sein Schicksal entscheiden' ['And I never forget that, of all the things that can befall a person, this is the worst: that other people decide his fate'].[54] Following his release after a ten-month sentence on the charge of laundering drug money, human rights activists and liberals celebrated Charles Ofoedu as a writer-hero. Noted Austrian playwright Peter Turrini declared Ofoedu's book to be of both political and literary importance, adding: '[e]inen solchen Kollegen möchte ich einfach nicht verlieren, so viele davon haben wir in Österreich nicht' ['I just don't want to lose such a colleague – we don't have very many of his kind in Austria'].[55] Since then, Ofoedu has been awarded Austrian citizenship and inducted into the Austrian branch of the prestigious international PEN-Club.

The responses to the events of 1999 by Chibo Onyeji and Charles Ofoedu share a number of themes, perhaps the most important of which is the foregrounding of a Black community that refuses to remain silent or in the shadows. As Ofoedu notes: 'Omofumas Tod hatte die Emotionen geweckt, und viele Afrikaner hatten den Drang, auf die Straße zu stürzen und wenigstens etwas Respekt einzufordern, darauf hinzuweisen, daß [*sic*] sie Menschen wären und keine Tiere' ['Omofuma's death had awoken emotions and many Africans felt the need to take to the streets and demand at least a little respect, to point out that they were human beings, not

---

54   Ofoedu, *Morgengrauen*, 6.
55   'Turrini würdigt Ofoedu: "Verdienstvoller Österreicher"', *News* (1 November 2001) <http://www.news.at/a/turrini-ofoedu-verdienstvoller-oesterreicher-24422> accessed 6 May 2018.

animals'].[56] This determination to refuse the role of victim and to assume
the position of agent is a theme that continues to inform much of Black
Austrians' work in both the political and the aesthetic arenas.

Redressing the Past

2006 was a banner year for the Second Republic: not only did the nation
serve its six-month stint as head of the Council of the European Union, but
it also celebrated the 250th anniversary of the birth of its most famous son
– and most popular brand – Wolfgang Amadeus Mozart. Orchestrated by
creative director Peter Marboe, the WIENER MOZARTJAHR [Vienna
Mozart Year] 2006TM provided thousands of events for citizens and tour-
ists alike. The diverse programming sought to be 'not just an examination
of Mozart the genius, not simply a heroization of the "Wunderkind", but
simultaneously a self-conscious confrontation with the life and work of
the famous musician'.[57] Ethnomusicologist Eric Martin Usner characterizes this most recent iteration of the Mozart jubilee (the history of which
stretches back into the mid-nineteenth century) as 'manifesting elements
of a New Vienna, albeit one still attentive to, but no longer disciplined by,
a static sense of its past'.[58] It is in this sense that Usner describes the 2006
Mozart Year as being 'popular': 'where "popular" is that mode of cultural
activity that makes possible forms of resistance or subaltern politics, creating spaces for the contestation of dominant ideas and practices by those
excluded from or disempowered by the same'.[59]

56   Ofoedu, *Morgengrauen*, 162.
57   'Das Wiener Mozartjahr 2006', *Mozart2006* (n.d.) <http://www.mozart2006.
     at/2012/das-wiener-mozartjahr-2006/> accessed 6 May 2018.
58   Eric Martin Usner, '"The Condition of MOZART": Mozart Year 2006 and the New
     Vienna', *Ethnomusicology Forum* 20/3 (2011), 414.
59   Usner, '"The Condition of MOZART"', 420–21.

One of the approximately 180 special projects associated with the Wiener Mozartjahr 2006 was the activist-historical project 'Verborgene Geschichte/n – Remapping Mozart' [Hidden History/ies – Remapping Mozart]. This series of alternative historical narratives sought to uncover, present, enact and confront the public with aspects of the aura surrounding the cultural object of 'Mozart' that had been repressed or erased. The driving force behind 'Verborgene Geschichte/n', Araba Evelyn Johnston-Arthur,[60] described the project's aim: '[d]as Ziel von "Verborgene Geschichte/n – Remapping Mozart" ist es, im pompösen nationalen Jubel-Mozartjahr Gegengeschichten zu schreiben und sichtbar zu machen und strukturelle Rahmenbedingungen zu schaffen, die das möglich machen'] [It is the goal of 'Hidden History/ies – Remapping Mozart' to write and to make visible counter-histories and to create structural frameworks that make this possible during the ostentatious national Jubilee-Mozart Year].[61] The scope of these repressed histories ranged from the eighteenth through the twentieth centuries and into the twenty-first, as group members addressed diverse points of intersection of Black Austrian and minority histories with Vienna's codified historical narrative.[62] All told, the project

60 In 1996, Johnston-Arthur co-founded Pamoja – The Movement of the Young African Diaspora in Austria. 'Pamoja – The Movement of the Young African Diaspora in Austria' [Facebook Group] (2018) <http://www.pamoja.at/> accessed 18 June 2018. Pamoja ('together' in Swahili) is an advocacy group with the explicit aim of supporting the organization and self-definition of People of Color in Austria. Araba Evelyn Johnston-Arthur, '"*Es ist Zeit, der Geschichte selbst eine Gestalt zu geben …*" Strategien der Entkolonisierung und Ermächtigung im Kontext der modernen afrikanischen Diaspora in Österreich', in Kien Nghi Ha, Nicola Lauré al-Samarai and Sheila Mysorekar, eds, *re/visionen. Postkoloniale Perspektiven von People of Color auf Rassismus, Kulturpolitik und Widerstand in Deutschland* (Münster: Unrast, 2007), 431.

61 Sylvia Köchl, and Vina Yun, '"Let It Be Known": Die eigene Geschichte selbst schreiben. Gespräch zwischen Araba Evelyn Johnston-Arthur, Ljubomir Bratic and Stephanie Njideka Iroh', *Kulturrisse* 3 (2006) <https://igkultur.at/artikel/let-it-be-known-die-eigene-geschichte-selbst-schreiben> accessed 6 May 2018.

62 Araba Evelyn Johnston-Arthur, 'Selbst erzählen statt erzählt zu werden: Die Bedeutung von Schwarzer österreichischer Geschichtsschreibung' <https://m1.antville.org/files/writing+black+austrian+history/> accessed 6 May 2018.

produced four public installations that were mounted sequentially in various parts of the Austrian capital between March and October 2006, each with its own thematic focus.[63] Enacting the Benjaminian concept of the momentary constellation of the past and present, and employing post-structuralist and postcolonial theory, each installation – *Konfiguration* [composition] – consciously drew parallels with, and made distinctions between, contemporary cultural, economic and political practices and those during Mozart's time in order to create a space of critique and reflection.

The group curating 'Konfiguration III: What All the World Thinks Impossible' set out to uncover the extensive, but generally unknown, history of the African diaspora in Austria.[64] The researchers, most of whom were members of the *Recherchegruppe zu Schwarzer österreichischer Geschichte und Gegenwart*, sought to promote positive role models for the Black Austrian Community. Indeed, as one group member noted, the goal of the group was as much self-affirmation as it was the production of a counter-history that would illuminate the history of *Schwarze Menschen* [Black people] in Austria across the centuries.

63   Konfiguration I (9 March to 18 April 2006 in Bösendorfer Klavierfabrik, first District, Inner City): Wer alles zu verlieren hat, muss alles wagen; Konfiguration II (3 May to 11 June in the Stuwerviertel, Leopoldstadt): Frisch zum Kampfe! Frisch zum Streite; Konfiguration III (21 June to 30 July 2006 at the Kuffner Sternwarte, Ottakring): Was aller Welt unmöglich scheint; Konfiguration IV (6 September to 15 October 2006 in Das Haus Brick-5, Rudolfsheim-Fünfhaus): Es ist kein Traum!, *Verborgene Geschichte/n: remapping Mozart* (n.d.) <remappingmozart.mur.at> accessed 6 May 2018.

64   Projects such as this are by nature ephemeral. I have been unable to locate a copy of the multi-lingual DVD that documented the four installations and which was produced and distributed during the Wiener Mozartjahr 2006, and the materials that had been available, as well as the links, on the project's website have been removed. As a result, many of the details about the creation of 'Verboregene Geschichte/n – Remapping Mozart' are drawn from Claudia Unterweger's Master's thesis, as well as articles written and interviews given by various members of the group. The author apologizes in advance for any mistakes and would welcome corrections and further information about the project. Claudia Unterweger, '*Talking Back*.'

Durch das Forschen zur historischen und gegenwärtigen Situation Schwarzer Menschen als gesellschaftlich unterrepräsentierte Gruppe wollten die Aktivist/innen ein eigenes Gedächtnis erzeugen und sich in ein größeres Kollektivgedächtnis oder mehrere davon einschreiben. Dahinter stand das Anliegen der Aktivist/innen, Schwarzen Menschen unterschiedlichster Herkunft die Identifikation als spezifische soziale Gruppe zu ermöglichen und sich so gemeinsam für ihre Bürger- und Menschenrechte im heutigen Österreich stark zu machen.

[By researching the historical and current situation of Black people as a socially underrepresented group, the activists sought to create a distinct memory and thus enter themselves into a larger collective memory, or multiple collective memories. Behind it all lay the desire of the activists to facilitate the identification of Black people of different backgrounds as a specific social group and thus empower them collectively for their rights as citizens and human beings in today's Austria].[65]

As this statement suggests, the group pointedly addressed the persistent 'white-washing' of Austrian history by seeking to uncover the rich and diverse history of the African diaspora in Austria. This entailed examining everything from documents in the city morgue to paintings in Vienna's numerous art museums. As artist and group member Belinda Kazeem shared in an interview:

Auf der einen Seite ist es schmerzhaft zu wissen was alles passiert ist, was bis heute nicht wirklich dokumentiert ist. Auf der anderen Seite hat uns diese Recherche stark gemacht. Weil wir bemerkt haben, dass es schon eine lange Geschichte auch zur Darstellung Menschen afrikanischer Herkunft in Österreich gibt und wie sich das alles entwickelt hat.

[On the one hand, it is painful to know all that has happened that has still not been documented today. On the other, this research made us strong. Because we noticed that there is already a long history in Austria of the representation of people of African descent and how this all developed].[66]

---

65 Unterweger, '*Talking back*', 1.
66 Köchl, and Yun, '"Let It Be Known"'.

Coincidentally, 2006 also marked the 210th anniversary of the death of
Austria's most famous citizen of African descent, Angelo Soliman, whose
biography explicitly contradicts the perception that the Habsburg Empire
had not been involved in the slave trade. Enslaved as a child and brought
to Europe, Soliman was eventually 'gifted' to the governor of Sicily, Prince
Johann Georg Christian Lobkowitz, whom he served as a valet. 'Freed'
for having saved his 'master's' life on the battlefield, Soliman eventually
became the house tutor to the heir of the House of von Liechtenstein, as
well as a Freemason and a close associate of Emperor Joseph II. According
to Austrian historian Wolfgang Kos, it was not, however, Soliman's life
that was responsible for his 'induction into the *hall of fame* of Viennese
city mythology'. Rather, it was those 'atrocious, macabre events that overshadowed his fascinating life posthumously – the desecration of his corpse,
which was subsequently exhibited in the royal Natural History Cabinet as
a stuffed specimen in the manner of an animal'.[67]

Precisely because the research group deliberately set out to map not
only the history of Blacks in Austria as victims but also as agents, Angelo
Soliman's history represented a conflict-ridden axis of memory.[68] While
Soliman undoubtedly remains the most famous Afro-Austrian, for the
members of the group his story represented both the appropriation of
a Black life as a 'Toleranzpokal der Gesellschaft des 18. Jahrhunderts'
[trophy to validate the tolerance of eighteenth-century society], and also
the 'kümmerlicher Rest an exotisierenden Fremddarstellungen Schwarzer
Menschen, reduziert zu kuriosen (Forschungs-)Objekten' [pathetic remains

---

67   'Denn Angelo Soliman verdankt seine Aufnahme in die *hall of fame* der Wiener
     Stadtmythologie ... vor allem jenen grässlichen, makabren Geschehnissen, die sein
     faszinierendes Leben posthum überschattet haben–der Schändung seines Leichnams,
     der dann als Stopfpräparat nach Art eines Tieres im keiserlichen Naturalienkabinett
     zur Schau gestellt wurde'. Wolfgang Kos, 'Zur Ausstellung', *Angelo Soliman–Ein
     Afrikaner in Wien*, in Philipp Bloma, and Wolfgang Kos, eds, exhibition catalogue
     (Vienna: Christian Brandstätter, 2011), 7.
68   Heather Morrison has argued for viewing Soliman's multiple sartorial styles as a
     measure of his agency. Heather Morrison, 'Dressing Angelo Soliman', *Eighteenth-
     Century Studies* 44/3 (2011), 361–82.

of exoticizing representations of Black people, reduced to quaint (research) objects].[69] By choosing instead to focus on the daughter of Angelo Soliman, Josephine (sometimes spelled 'Josefine') Soliman, the group was able to emphasize the 'Eigen-Sinn' [self-will] and thus the powerful agency of this Black Austrian woman.[70]

Born in 1772 in Vienna, Josephine Soliman was the only child of Angelo and Magdalena Soliman. Josephine repeatedly protested the display of her father's body in the Museum of Natural History, demanding that his remains be returned to her for proper burial.[71] Although her aristocratic marriage to Ernst Freiherr von Feuchtersleben afforded her access to the upper echelons of Viennese bureaucracy, her pleas and demands remained un-met. It was not until 1806 that Angelo Soliman's body was moved to the attics of the Hofburg where it was destroyed in a fire during the October uprising of 1848. As Johnston-Arthur notes, 'Josephine Solimans Kampf gegen Verdinglichung ihres Vaters und ihre Forderung seiner Leichnamsbruchstücke für dessen Bestattung ist gleichzeitig auch Teil einer über den österreichischen Kontext weit hinausgehenden Widerstands- und Oppositionsgeschichte' [Josephine Soliman's battle against the objectification of her father and her demand for his remains in order to bury them is also part of a history of resistance and opposition that extends beyond the Austrian context].[72] As such, Josephine Soliman

---

69   Johnston-Arthur, 'Selbst erzählen statt erzählt werden'.

70   Literally 'self-will', the term 'Eigen-Sinn' derives from an essay by Nicola Lauré al-Samarai in which she uses it 'to underscore the subject status of Black individuals and their scope for decision-making'. Unterweger, '*Talking Back*', 56.

71   In his 1922 biography, 'Angelo Soliman. Der hochfürstliche Mohr', Wilhelm A. Bauer describes how Josephine first demanded 'Skelet und die Haut ihres Vaters zur Beerdigung' [her father's skeleton and skin for burial] in December of 1796. After several failed attempts, she enlisted the aid of Archbishop Migazzi, to no avail. Ivana Rivic, 'Die (Selbst)Inszenierung des Wiener Urbanmythos Angelo Soliman (1721–1796)', MA thesis, University of Vienna, 2015, 44–46.

72   Araba Evelyn Johnston-Arthur, '"... um die Leiche des verstorbenen M[...]en Soliman"', in Belinda Kazeem, Charlotte Martinez-Turek and Nora Sternfeld, eds, *Das Unbehagen im Museum: Postkoloniale Museologien* (Vienna: Turia + Kant, 2009), 29.

serves as both a reminder of the long history of people of African descent in Austria and a representative of the position of resistant, active Black women in the diaspora and thus a figure of positive identification.

For the group of researchers (re)contructing this neglected history of Vienna, 'as a black woman' Josephine Soliman 'demonstrated her will and resisted',[73] even as her story reveals the powerful machineries at work that sought to quell any sign of opposition to authorities.[74] As a gesture towards the significance of Josephine Soliman in the imagination of Black Austrian women, the group symbolically renamed Vienna's Löwengasse to Josefine-Soliman-Straße.[75]

Unlike some of the children born in the wake of the Allied occupation who were adopted 'out' to the United States, Black Austrians intend to remain where they are. Despite centuries of oppression – as well as the repression of any memory of their presence in, and contribution to, Austrian history and culture – they are speaking out and making themselves known. While it may be true that the generation of Black Austrians born after World War II were atomized and isolated, thanks to the internet and social media, members of the new generation need no longer be alone as websites such as afrikanet.info and publications such as *Fresh! Black Austrian Lifestyle* demonstrate.

The importance of transnational, cross-generational connection has also clearly contributed to the (re-)creation of Black Austrian identity. In her essay, "*Es ist Zeit, der Geschichte selbst eine Gestalt zu geben*" ["*It is time to instantiate history ourselves*"], Araba Evelyn Johnston-Arthur describes the continuing impact of African-American-Caribbean Audre Lorde on her own work as an activist and an academic. Referencing Lorde's call to speak in her foreword to *Farbe bekennen: Afrodeutsche Frauen auf den Spuren ihrer Geschichte* [translated as *Showing Our Colors: Afro-German*

---

73   In the German, it reads: 'als schwarze Frau Eigensinn bewiesen und Widerstand geleistet'. Roman David-Freihsl, 'Die verborgene Geschichte unserer Stadt', *Der Standard* (20 December 2006), rpt. *Der Standard* (7 January 2006) <http://derstandard. at/2702256/Die-verborgene-Geschichte-unserer-Stadt> accessed 6 May 2018.

74   Unterweger, '*Talking back*', 62.

75   David-Freihsl, 'Die verborgene Geschichte unserer Stadt'.

Women Speak Out] – the cornerstone of the Black German movement, Johnston-Arthur writes:

> Es ist die Praxis des Benennens, die das mächtige Schweigen durchbricht und den Boden für Ermächtigungs- und Dekolonisierungsprozesse bereitet und nährt. Vor diesem Hintergrund möchte ich mir mit diesem Text eine Skizze jener Unterdrückungsrealitäten von der Seele zeichnen, die bekämpft und transformiert werden müssen. Es geht auch darum, die weitgehend unsichtbar gemachte Schwarze österreichische Erfahrung als einen einzelnen, doch zugleich eigenständig-verbundenen Puzzlestein in das größe Bild der afrikanischen Diaspora einzuschreiben'...

> [It is the practice of naming that breaks through the heavy silence and prepares and nourishes the ground for the processes of empowerment and decolonization. Against this backdrop, in this text I would like to lay bare those realities of repression that must be fought and transformed. Also at stake is the inscription of the Black Austrian experience – which by and large has been rendered invisible – into the larger picture of the African Diaspora, as an individual, independent-yet-still-connected puzzle piece ...].[76]

This image of the 'independent-yet-still-connected' puzzle piece that links not only contiguous parts of the image but also contributes on a larger scale to the overall picture, powerfully underscores the importance of local or 'national' interventions within the larger project of mapping the African diaspora in Austria.

Bibliography

Akinyosoye, Clara, 'Menschen afrikanischer Herkunft in Österreich', in Simon Inou, and Beatrice Achaleke, eds, *Schwarze Menschen in Österreich 2010: Lagebericht* (Vienna: Black Publishers, 2010), 6–7 <http://www.m-media.or.at/gesellschaft/ schwarze-menschen-in-osterreich-jahresbericht-2010-die-zusammenfassung/ 2011/06/16/index.html> accessed 6 May 2018.

76 Johnston-Arthur, '"*Es ist Zeit*"', 424.

Angerer, Tommy, 'Den Staat zu beobachten ist Staatbürgerpflicht', *Augustin* (6 February 2001) <http://www.augustin.or.at/zeitung/tun-und-lassen/den-staat-zu-beobachten-ist-staatbuergerpflicht.html> accessed 6 May 2018.

APA, 'TV-Quoten 2016: ORF verliert leicht, Servus TV legt zu', *Salzburger Nachtrichten* (2 January 2017) <https://www.sn.at/panorama/medien/tv-quoten-2016-orf-verliert-leicht-servus-tv-legt-zu-564109> accessed 18 April 2017.

Bauer, Ingrid, '"Leiblicher Vater: Amerikaner (Neger)": Besatzungskinder afroamerikanischer Herkunft', in Helmuth Niederle, ed., *Früchte der Zeit: Afrika, Diaspora, Literatur und Migration* (Vienna: Vienna University Press, 2001), 49–51.

——, '*Schwarzer Peter*: A Historical Perspective. Henisch and the Postwar Austrian Occupation', paper presented at the 24th Annual Meeting of the German Studies Association, Houston, Texas, 5–8 October 2000.

Beitl, Matthias, 'Vorwort', in Niko Wahl, Phillipp Rohrbach and Tal Adler, eds, *Schwarz-Österreich. Die Kinder afroamerikanischer Besatzungssoldaten*, exhibition catalogue (Vienna: Löcker, 2016).

'BlackAustria Projektbeschreibung', *SozialMarie Prize for Social Innovation* 2007 (n.d.) <https://www.sozialmarie.org/de-AT/projects/696> accessed 6 May 2018.

Chahrour, Marcel, '"Vom Morgenhauch aufstrebender Cultur durchweht", Ägyptische Studenten in Österreich 1830–1945', in Walter Sauer ed., *Von Soliman zu Omofuma: afrikanische Diaspora in Österreich 17. bis 20 Jahrhundert* (Innsbruck: StudienVerlag, 2007), 131–49.

Chin, Rita, Heide Fehrenbach and Geoff Eley, eds, *After the Nazi Racial State: Difference and Democracy in Germany and Europe* (Ann Arbor: University of Michigan Press, 2009).

'Colonial Austria: Austria and the Overseas', special issue of *Austrian Studies* 20 (2012).

Czech, Herwig, '"Vorwiegend negerische Rassenmerkmale", AfrikanerInnen und farbige "Mischlinge" im Nationalsozialismus', in Walter Sauer, ed., *Von Soliman zu Omofuma: afrikanische Diaspora in Österreich 17. bis 20 Jahrhundert* (Innsbruck: Studien Verlag, 2007), 155–74.

'Das Wiener Mozartjahr 2006', *Mozart2006* (n.d.) <http://www.mozart2006.at/2012/das-wiener-mozartjahr-2006/> accessed 6 May 2018.

David-Freihsl, Roman, 'Die verborgene Geschichte unserer Stadt', *Der Standard* (20 December 2006), rpt. *Der Standard* (7 January 2006) <http://derstandard.at/2702256/Die-verborgene-Geschichte-unserer-Stadt> accessed 6 May 2018.

'Drei Staatspreise für die schönsten Bücher verliehen', *Hauptverband des Österreichischen Buchhandels* (2016) <http://www.buecher.at/drei-staatspreise-fuer-die-schoensten-buecher-verliehen/> accessed 6 May 2018.

Drössler, Alice, et al., 'Die Kampagne BLACKAUSTRIA in den Augen der BLACK COMMUNITY in Wien', Seminar Project (University of Vienna, 2007)

<http://www.blackaustria.at/downloads/studien/studie_black_community.pdf> accessed 20 April 2017.

Fehrenbach, Heide, 'Black Occupation Children and the Devolution of the Nazi Racial State', in Rita Chin, Heide Fehrenbach and Geoff Eley, eds, *After the Nazi Racial State: Difference and Democracy in Germany and Europe* (Ann Arbor: University of Michigan Press, 2009), 31–54.

Fuchlehner, Barbara, and Karin Röhling, 'Afrikanerinnen und Afrikaner im KZ Mauthausen: Teilauswertung der Datenblätter im Archiv der KZ-Gedenkstätte Mauthausen (Wien, Innenministerium)', Project Report (University of Vienna, 2016) <http://www.m-media.or.at/politik/neue-studie-afrikanerinnen-im-kz-mauthausen/2017/03/06/> accessed 6 May 2018.

Genner, Michael, 'ÖsterREICH – für alle GLEICH!', *asyl-in-not.org* (2001) <http://www.asyl-in-not.org/php/oesterreich_fuer_alle_gleich_,12311,4874.html> accessed 6 May 2018.

Gilroy, Paul, *The Black Atlantic: Modernity and Double Consciousness* (Cambridge, MA: Harvard University Press, 1993).

Grabovsky, Ernst, 'Österreich als literarischer Erfahrungsraum zugewanderter Autorinnen und Autoren', in Helmut Schmitz, ed., *Von der nationalen zur internationalen Literatur. Transkulturelle deutschsprachige Literatur und Kultur im Zeitalter globaler Migration* (Amsterdam: Rodopi, 2009), 275–92.

Gröpel, Irene, 'Eigen- und Fremdwahrnehemung: Afro-EuropäerInnen und Afro-ÖsterreicherInnen – Grenzen der Schwarz-Weiß-Konstruktion', MA thesis, University of Vienna, 2010.

Gürses, Hakan, 'Schwarz ist eine politische Identität: Interview mit Araba Evelyn Johnston-Arthur', in *Stimmen von und für Minderheiten* 39 (2001) <http://minderheiten.at/stat/stimme/stimme39c.htm> accessed 6 May 2018.

Heilbrunn, Jacob, 'A Disdain for the Past: Jörg Haider's Austria', *World Policy Journal* 17/1 (2000), 71–78.

'Here to Stay. Rassismus in Wien' *Filmfonds Wien* (2018) <http://www.filmfonds-wien.at/filme/here-to-stay-rassismus-in-wien> accessed 6 May 2018.

Horaczek, Nina, 'Alle waren schwarz', *Der Falter* 38 (2005) <https://www.falter.at/archiv/FALTER_2005092118331300053/alle-waren-schwarz> accessed 26 June 2018.

Inou, Simon, 'Liebe Mama Felicia Omofuma', *Der Standard* (29 April 2009) <http://derstandard.at/1240550183494/Liebe-Mama-Felicia-Omofuma-> accessed 6 May 2018.

Inou, Simon, and Béatrice Achaleke, eds, *Schwarze Menschen in Österreich 2010. Lagebericht* (Vienna: Black European Publishers, 2010) <http://www.m-media.or.at/wp-content/uploads/2015/09/Lagebericht-Schwarze-Menschen-%C3%96sterreich2010.pdf> accessed 6 May 2018.

Johnston-Arthur, Araba Evelyn, '"*Es ist Zeit, der Geschichte selbst eine Gestalt zu geben
...*" Strategien der Entkolonisierung und Ermächtigung im Kontext der modernen
afrikanischen Diaspora in Österreich', in Kien Nghi Ha, Nicola Lauré al-Samarai
and Sheila Mysorekar, eds, *re/visionen. Postkoloniale Perspektiven von People of
Color auf Rassismus, Kulturpolitik und Widerstand in Deutschland* (Münster:
Unrast, 2007), 423–44.

——, 'Selbst erzählen statt erzählt zu werden: Die Bedeutung von Schwarzer österreichischer Geschichtsschreibung' (n.d.) <https://m1.antville.org/files/writing
+black+austrian+history/> accessed 6 May 2018.

——, '"... um die Leiche des verstorbenen M[...]en Soliman"', in Belinda Kazeem,
Charlotte Martinez-Turek, and Nora Sternfeld, eds, *Das Unbehagen im Museum.
Postkoloniale Museologien* (Vienna: Turia + Kant, 2009), 11–43.

Kazeem, Belinda, Charlotte Martinz-Turek and Nora Sternfeld, eds, *Das Unbehagen
im Museum. Postkoloniale Museologien* (Vienna: Turia + Kant, 2009).

Kleine, grosse Stimme, Wolfgang Murnberger, dir. (ORF, BR and ARD Degeto, 2015).

Köchl, Sylvia, and Vina Yun, '"Let It Be Known". Die eigene Geschichte selbst schreiben. Gespräch zwischen Araba Evelyn Johnston-Aethur, Ljubomir Bratic, and
Stephanie Njideka Iroh', *Kulturrisse.at* 3 (2006) <https://igkultur.at/artikel/
let-it-be-known-die-eigene-geschichte-selbst-schreiben> accessed 6 May 2018.

Kos, Wolfgang, 'Zur Ausstellung', *Angelo Soliman–Ein Afrikaner in Wien*, in Philipp
Bloma, and Wolfgang Kos, eds, exhibition catalogue (Vienna: Christian Brand-
stätter, 2011), 7–11.

Kotrba, Franz, *k. u. k. in Ostafrika: Die Habsburgermonarchie im 'Scramble for East
Africa'* (Vienna: SADOCC, 2015).

Kravagna, Simon, 'Schwarze Stereotype und weiße Behörden: Afrikaner, Drogen-
kriminalität und Strafverfolgung durch Polizei und Justiz', *SWS-Rundschau*
45/2 (2005) <http://www.ssoar.info/ssoar/handle/document/16490> accessed
6 May 2018.

'Kreative Gegenvorurteile', *Südwind Magazin* 2 (2007) <http://www.suedwind-
magazin.at/kreativ-gegen-vorurteile> accessed 6 May 2018.

Lechhab, Hamid, 'Marokkanische Besatzungskinder in Vorarlberg nach 1945', in Walter
Sauer, ed., *Von Soliman zu Omofuma: afrikanische Diaspora in Österreich 17. bis
20 Jahrhundert* (Innsbruck: Studien Verlag, 2007), 177–86.

Lichtblau, Albert, 'Lost in Administration: Afro-Austrian GI Children – A Research
Project', University of Salzburg (n.d.) <http://www.lostinadministration.at/>
accessed 6 May 2018.

'Marcus Omofuma: "Klassischer Erstickungstod"' (6 February 2001) <http://no-
racism.net/article/485/> accessed 6 May 2018.

Morrison, Heather, 'Dressing Angelo Soliman', *Eighteenth-Century Studies* 44/3
(2011), 361–82.

Müller, Stefan, '"Das ist schrecklich"', *Zeit Online* (9 November 2015) <http://www.zeit.de/2015/45/interview-bernd-brinkmann-graz-fehlgutachten-forensikgerichtsmedizin> accessed 6 May 2018.

Ofoedu, Obiora Ci-K, *Morgengrauen. Ein literarischer Bericht*, tr. Ric Maréchal (Vienna: Mandelbaum, 2000).

Onyeji, Chibo, *Flowers, Bread, and Gold* (Ranshofen/Osternberg: edition innsalz, 2006).

Operation Spring, Angelika Schuster, and Tristan Sindelgruber, dirs (Schnittpunkt, 2005).

Özkan, Duygu, 'Österreichs vergessene Kinder', *Die Presse* (27 April 2016) <http://diepresse.com/home/leben/4974018/Oesterreichs-vergessene-Kinder> accessed 6 May 2018.

'Pamoja – The Movement of the Young African Diaspora in Austria' [Facebook Group] (2018) <http://www.pamoja.at/> accessed 18 June 2018.

Renger, Rudi, and Franz Rest, 'Die Neue Kronen Zeitung. Massenmediales Flaggschiff aller österreichischen Populismen', in Richard Faber and Frank Unger, eds, *Populismus in Geschichte und Gegenwart* (Würzburg: Königshausen & Neumann, 2008), 175–209.

Rivic, Ivana, 'Die (Selbst)Inszenierung des Wiener Urbanmythos Angelo Soliman (1721–1796)', MA thesis, University of Vienna, 2015.

Sauer, Walter, 'Afro-österreichische Diaspora heute. Migration und Integration in der 2. Republik', in Walter Sauer ed., *Von Soliman zu Omofuma: afrikanische Diaspora in Österreich 17. bis 20 Jahrhundert* (Innsbruck: Studien Verlag, 2007), 189–232.

——, *Expeditionen ins afrikanische Österreich. Ein Reisekaleidoskop* (Vienna: Mandelbaum, 2014).

——, 'Habsburg Colonial: Austria-Hungary's Role in European Overseas Expansion Reconsidered', *Austrian Studies* 20 (2012), 5–23.

——, ed., *k. u. k. Kolonial: Habsburgermonarchie und europäische Herrschaft in Afrika* (Vienna: Böhlau, 2002).

——, 'Reflexion zur afrikanischen Diaspora in Österreich', *Österreichische Zeitschrift zur Geisteswissenschaften* 17/4 (2006), 149–54.

Schad, Martha, and Horst Schad, eds, *Marie Valérie: Das Tagebuch der Lieblingstochter von Kaiserin Elisabeth 1878–1899* (Munich: Langen Müller, 1998).

Schmitz, Helmut, ed., *Von der nationalen zur internationalen Literatur: Transkulturelle deutschsprachige Literatur und Kultur im Zeitalter globaler Migration* (Amsterdam: Rodopi, 2009).

'SchwarzÖsterreich. Die Kinder afroamerikanischer Besatzungssoldaten' *Volkskundemuseum Wien* (n.d.) <http://www.volkskundemuseum.at/schwarzoesterreich_die_kinder_afroamerikanischer_besatzungssoldaten> accessed 6 May 2018.

Smoliner, Marco, 'Vorwort', in Obiora Ci-K Ofoedu, *Morgengrauen: Ein literarischer Bericht*, tr. Ric Maréchal (Vienna: Mandelbaum, 2000).

Stelzl-Marx, Barbara, 'Tagungsbericht: "Besatzungskinder in Österreich und Deutsch-land"', *H-Soz-u-Kult* (9 April 2013) <http://www.hsozkult.de/conferencereport/ id/tagungsberichte-4749> accessed 6 May 2018.

Thurman, Kira, '"Africa in European Evening Attire": Defining African American Spirituals and Western Art Music in Central Europe, 1870s–1930s', in Tiffany Florvil and Vanessa Plumly, eds, *Rethinking Black German Studies: Approaches, Interventions and Histories* (Oxford: Peter Lang, 2018) [this volume, Chapter 6].

——, 'Museum Exhibit Review: "Black Austria: The Children of African American Occupation Soldiers"', *H-Black-Europe* (20 July 2016) <https://networks.h-net. org/node/19384/discussions/135747/cross-post-exhibit-review-thurman-black-austria-children-african> accessed 6 May 2018.

Toxi, Robert A. Stemmle, dir. (Fono Film, 1952).

'Turrini würdigt Ofoedu: "Verdienstvoller Österreicher"', *News* (1 November 2001), <http://www.news.at/a/turrini-ofoedu-verdienstvoller-oesterreicher-24422> accessed 6 May 2018.

Unterweger, Claudia, '*Talking Back*. Strategien der Vergangenheitserzählung am Beispiel der *Recherchegruppe zu Schwarzer österreichischer Geschichte*', MA thesis, University of Vienna, 2013.

Usner, Eric Martin, '"The Condition of MOZART": Mozart Year 2006 and the New Vienna', *Ethnomusicology Forum* 20/3 (2011), 413–42.

Verborgene Geschichte/n – remapping Mozart (n.d.) <remappingmozart.mur.at> accessed 6 May 2018.

Wahl, Niko, 'Heim ins Land der Väter', *Die Zeit* 52 (23 December 2010) <http:// www.zeit.de/2010/52/A-Mischlingskinder> accessed 6 May 2018.

Wahl, Niko, Philipp Rohrbach and Tal Adler, eds, *SchwarzÖsterreich. Die Kinder afroamerikanischer Besatzungssoldaten*, exhibition catalogue (Vienna: Löcker, 2016).

MEGHAN O'DEA

3   Lucia Engombe's and Stefanie-Lahya Aukongo's Autobiographical Accounts of *Solidaritätspolitik* and Life in the GDR as Namibian Children

ABSTRACT

This chapter examines solidarity as expressed within the autobiographical texts *Kind Nr. 95* by Lucia Engombe and *Kalungas Kind* by Stefanie-Lahya Aukongo, who grew up in East Germany during the SWAPO liberation movement in Southwest Africa (today's Namibia). Engombe's and Aukongo's narratives share a similar criticism of East German politics of solidarity demonstrated through their contrast of official, political rhetoric on racism and equality with the social realities of everyday life. They paint a complex picture of solidarity in the GDR by, on the one hand, showing its limitations – it neither led to the eradication of 'everyday racism' nor to outright social inclusion and feelings of belonging. However, on the other hand, it inspired a culture of support and acceptance among individuals who took on advocating roles. Although critical of their political treatment, Engombe and Aukongo provide a hopeful picture of the solidarity enacted through individuals on a personal level.

The history of Namibia and Germany has a long and continuous trajectory, which Lucia Engombe and Stefanie-Lahya Aukongo – both women of Namibian decent raised in the German Democratic Republic (GDR) – recall in their respective autobiographical accounts, *Kind Nr. 95. Meine deutsch-afrikanische Odyssee* [2004, *Kid Number 95: My German-African Odyssey*] and *Kalungas Kind: Wie die DDR mein Leben rettete* [2009, *Kalungas Child: How the GDR Saved My Life*]. In their memoirs, they narrate their experiences of growing up in East Germany as Namibian children during the South West Africa People's Organization's (SWAPO) armed liberation struggle against South Africa and its imposed apartheid system. The SWAPO uprising, rooted in Namibia's expansive and fluctuating colonial history, began in 1966 and aimed to establish a free and independent Namibian state.[1] During this time, a number of Namibian civilians traveled to East Germany for refuge, medical treatment, an education and job training. East Germany supported this aid through *Solidaritätspolitik* [politics of solidarity], a key component of their foreign policy that distinguished the GDR from West German forms of international involvement. While West German SWAPO support primarily consisted of financial assistance and press coverage, East Germany declared a Treaty of Friendship and Co-operation with SWAPO.[2] Their agreement included the housing and schooling of over 400 Namibian children, among them Engombe, but with the intention of eventually returning them to an independent,

---

1   All translations are my own. Namibia's colonial history began in 1884 with Otto von Bismarck's Berlin Conference. Occurring during a period of nineteenth-century European imperialism known as the 'Scramble for Africa', Bismarck sought to expand Germany's power and claimed along with what would become German South-West Africa, the territories of Togoland and Cameroon in West Africa and German East Africa (today's Tanzania). After World War I, Germany lost all its colonies, and South-West Africa came under the Union of South Africa's control, which later in 1961 the apartheid enforcing Afrikaner National Party ruled. This officially lasted until 1990 when the Republic of Namibia declared its independence following the SWAPO's liberation struggle. See Tanja Bührer, 'Berlin Conference' in Prem Poddar, Rajeev S. Patke and Lars Jensen, eds, *A Historical Companion to Postcolonial Literatures: Continental Europe and Its Empires* (Edinburgh: Edinburgh University Press, 2008), 210; Robert Ross, *A Concise History of South Africa* (1997; Cambridge: Cambridge University Press, 2008), 91–92; Daniel Gorman, 'Berlin Conference (1884–1885)', in Carl Cavanagh Hodge, ed., *Encyclopedia of the Age of Imperialism 1800–1914*, 1 (Westport, CT: Greenwood Press, 2008), 83; and Henning Melber, 'Limits to Liberation: An Introduction to Namibia's Postcolonial Political Culture', in H. Melber, ed., *Re-examining Liberation in Namibia: Political Culture since Independence* (Uppsala: Nordic Africa Institute, 2003), 14–15.

2   Britta Schilling, *Postcolonial Germany: Memories of Empire in a Decolonized Nation* (Oxford: Oxford University Press, 2014), 148.

post-liberation Namibia.[3] The same is true for Aukongo, who was born in the GDR, where her mother had received medical treatment. In many ways, Engombe's and Aukongo's narratives reflect the development of transcultural identities common to numerous contemporary narratives of migration and return. They negotiate, for example, their identity as built upon two cultural legacies, Namibian and East German.[4] Yet, their narratives also move beyond ethnocentric notions of community and belonging by depicting the development of diverse kinship links based upon a feeling of solidarity.

While East German solidarity instilled a sense of activism in some to pursue advocacy and support roles, Engombe and Aukongo also complicate this celebratory notion by shedding critical light on problematic manifestations of *Alltagsrassismus* [everyday racism] that appear under the guise of solidarity. In their narratives, they lay the complexity of solidarity bare by not merely applauding the positive intensions of *Solidaritätspolitik*, but by furthermore portraying the exclusionary and prejudicial institutional practices and attitudes that they experienced in the GDR. In the following chapter, I briefly introduce East German *Solidaritatspolitik* and examine Engombe's and Aukongo's autobiographical texts with a focus on their narrated experiences of solidarity in East German society. Indeed, they each portray the personal effects of global politics on individuals, but they do so from different viewpoints. Engombe, for instance, narrates from the perspective of the so-called *DDR-Kinder* [GDR-Kids], a group of 428 Namibian children who were educated and raised in GDR boarding schools

3   Constance Kenna, *Die 'DDR-Kinder' von Namibia. Heimkehrer in Ein Fremdes Land* (Göttingen: Klaus Hess Verlag, 2004), 26 and 53–55. As it turned out, this group was not positioned in leadership roles in Namibia, but instead had to establish themselves within society independently and often with difficulty, especially since many of the children had been orphaned during the uprising.

4   Katrin Brandt, 'Shared Paradoxes in Namibian and German History: Lucia Engombe's *Kind Nr. 95*', in Elisabeth Bekers, Sissy Helff and Daniela Merolla, eds, *Transcultural Modernities: Narrating Africa in Europe* (Amsterdam: Editions Rodopi, 2009), 347–48, 360.

by German and Namibian teachers and caretakers.[5] Conversely, Aukongo grew up in an East German household with little contact to other Namibian children. Despite their unique situations, both narratives share a similar criticism of East German solidarity politics by contrasting the official, political rhetoric on racism and equality with the social realities of everyday life, which includes experiences of racism and exclusion. In both accounts, they frame their stories with Germany's extensive involvement abroad – initially as a colonial ruler in South-West Africa under Otto von Bismarck and later as a divided nation partnered in solidarity during the SWAPO uprising. This framing provokes questions related to Germany's colonial past and its possible paternal linkages to twentieth-century international policies. In what ways did Germany's colonial legacy affect the GDR's engagement with Namibia? How did East Germany perceive its postcolonial status? What effect did this have on East German official rhetoric on racism and international involvement? What do Engombe's and Aukongo's accounts reveal about international solidarity and *Alltagsrassismus* as well as the forging of transnational forms of identification and belonging? Within recent German scholarship, the issue of race in East Germany has received different treatment, ranging from studies that highlight the positive aspects of solidarity as a part of anti-racist and anti-colonial stances, to those that expose the everyday racism present in East German society.[6] This chapter

5   The term 'DDR-Kinder' or 'GDR-Kids' has been used in studies about this group, including early examples by Jason Owens and Constance Kenna in *Die 'DDR-Kinder' von Namibia*. The term is also used in Engombe's as well as Aukongo's texts, even though other members of this group express annoyance with the term. The 2006 documentary film *Omulaule heißt Schwarz*, Beatrice Möller, Nicola Hens and Susanne Radelhof, dirs (Omufilm, 2003) depicts a former 'GDR-Kid,' who, rolling her eyes, says: 'Nein, ich bin kein Kind mehr' ['No, I'm not a child anymore']. Many of these now adult Namibians that grew up in the GDR are identified as belonging to this former group via their German language abilities. See also Jason Owens, and Monica Nembelela, 'Can't Namibia's Ex-GDR (Ex-) Kids be Called Adults in this, the Year Namibia Itself Turned 18 Years Old?', in Cornelia Limpricht and Megan Biesele, eds, *Heritage and Cultures in Modern Namibia: A TUCSIN Festschrift* (Windhoek: Klaus Hess, 2008), 132–40.

6   See also, Chapter 7 in Höhn, Maria, and Martin Klimke, *A Breath of Freedom: The Civil Rights Struggle, African American GIs, and Germany* (New York: Palgrave Macmillan, 2010), as an example of solidarity and anti-racist, anti-colonial stances. For discussions of everyday racism in the GDR see Peggy Piesche, 'Black and German?

seeks to give voice to Engombe's and Aukongo's subjective insights by exploring how their comparative experiences as children in the GDR present new directions in approaching both solidarity and discourses of race in the former socialist state.

Engombe's and Aukongo's use of autobiographical writing is an excellent vehicle to provide individual nuance to the national, collective narrative of East German solidarity. Through their narration of personal occurrences, they detail the ways in which their lives were shaped by global events and bring lesser-known aspects of a shared East German-Namibian history to the fore. According to historian Britta Schilling, research on German colonialism and African-German transnational history has increased in the past ten years, but 'most historians still see 1945 as a stopping point, claiming that afterwards there existed only a period of colonial "amnesia".'[7] Recent publications, however, indicate that this is changing in both scholarship and cultural productions. In her chapter on Afro-German autobiographies, for instance, German film studies scholar Reinhild Steingröver draws attention to the increase in and diversity amongst Black German writers publishing in autobiographical form. Often motivated to share unique life experiences, these authors portray the lives of multiple generations of Black Germans from diverse locations and within different contexts.[8] Additionally, historian Quinn Slobodian's 2015 collection *Comrades of Color: East Germany in the Cold War World* focuses on race from a socialist perspective, where class was primarily seen as the principal vehicle of difference.[9] Historian Jason Verber's chapter in *Comrades of Color* discusses different forms of cultural diplomacy and educational assistance offered by the GDR with particular emphasis on

---

East German Adolescents Before 1989: A Retrospective View of a "Non-Existent" Issue in the GDR', in Leslie Adelson, ed., *The Cultural After-Life of East Germany: New Transnational Perspectives* (Washington DC: AICGS, 2002); and Rita Chin, and others, eds, *After the Nazi Racial State: Difference and Democracy in Germany and Europe* (Ann Arbor: University of Michigan Press, 2009).

7   Schilling, *Postcolonial Germany*, 9.
8   Reinhild Steingröver, 'From *Farbe bekennen* to *Schokoladenkind*: Generational Change in Afro-German Autobiographies', in Laurel Cohen-Pfister and Susanne Vees-Gulani, eds, *Generational Shifts in Contemporary German Culture* (Rochester, NY: Camden House, 2010), 287, 305.
9   Quinn Slobodian, 'Introduction', in Quinn Slobodian, ed., *Comrades of Color: East Germany in the Cold War World* (New York: Berghahn, 2015), 1.

the history of Mozambican children at the so-called School of Friendship (where Engombe grew up). Though unable to inculcate a uniform type of socialism according to the SED's (*Sozialistische Einheitspartei Deutschlands* [Socialist Unity Party of Germany]) ideals, the school nonetheless served as an important, tangible sign of East German support of Mozambique, in particular, and Africa as a whole, as Verber argues.[10] However, aside from the work of German Studies scholars Constance Kenna and Jason Owens, little research is devoted to the experience of the Namibian children and youth who spent their childhoods in East Germany. Engombe and Aukongo, members of this smaller group, fill the lacuna by shedding light upon the lived realities of solidarity endeavors in the GDR. Not only do they prompt critical inquiry into issues related to solidarity in its political and personal forms, but they also encourage readers to consider colonial legacies beyond 1945 as well as (East) German-Namibian historical linkages. Their personal experiences illustrate the presence of *Alltagsrassismus* and complicate understandings of *Solidaritätspolitik* while simultaneously underscoring the ways in which they developed a sense of belonging through the formation of transnational communities.

Solidarity Politics and the GDR

In order to establish diplomatic ties and partnerships, SWAPO's president Sam Nujoma initially visited the GDR's *Solidaritätskomitee* [committee for solidarity] in 1962 and eventually received aid and support to continue the SWAPO's struggle for an independent Namibia.[11] The

10   Jason Verber, 'True to the Politics of Frelimo? Teaching Socialism at the *Schule der Freundschaft*, 1981–90', in Quinn Slobodian, ed., *Comrades of Color: East Germany in the Cold War World* (New York: Berghahn, 2015), 188–89.

11   Ute Rüchel, '*Wir hatten noch nie einen Schwarzen gesehen'. Das Zusammenleben von Deutschen und Namibiern rund um das SWAPO-Kinderheim Bellin, 1979–1990* (Schwerin: Landesbeauftragten für Mecklenburg-Vorpommern für die Unterlagen des Staatssicherheitsdienstes der ehemaligen DDR, 2001), 23.

committee for solidarity functioned as a type of coordination bureau to provide international aid in cases of natural catastrophe and freedom movements. As East Germany's central actor involved in their *Afrikapolitik* [politics with Africa], the committee supported – alongside SWAPO – the liberation movements of the ANC (African National Congress) in South Africa, the ZAPU (Zimbabwe African People's Union) in Zimbabwe, and the PLO (Palestine Liberation Organization) in Palestine.[12] The GDR expanded its national commitment to solidarity in its 1974 constitution, which explicitly claimed to support the states and nations fighting for independence against imperial and colonial regimes.[13] This decision built upon previous solidarity efforts in the 1960s extended to the African American Civil Rights Movement, during which time the political activist Angela Davis famously signified the friendship between the GDR and African American community.[14] Such transnational linkages are important for understanding East Germany's international relations as well as its own self-perception, since solidarity became a defining feature of its political identity and culture. As Slobodian explains, the East German government saw and presented itself 'as an active member of the international community of world socialism'.[15] Indeed, it assisted numerous international causes and liberation struggles all within solidarity politics.

12   Ingrid Muth, *Die DDR-Außenpolitik 1949–1972. Inhalte, Strukturen, Mechanismen* (Berlin: Christoph Links Verlag, 2001), 92.

13   John J., Metzler, *Divided Dynamism: The Diplomacy of Separated Nations* (Lanham, MD: University Press of America, 2014), 29. Article 6.3 of the constitution of the GDR states: 'Die Deutsche Demokratische Republik unterstützt die Staaten und Völker, die gegen den Imperialismus und sein Kolonialregime, für nationale Freiheit und Unabhängigkeit kämpfen, in ihrem Ringen um gesellschaftlichen Fortschritt. Die Deutsche Demokratische Republik tritt für die Verwirklichung der Prinzipien der friedlichen Koexistenz von Staaten unterschiedlicher Gesellschaftsordnungen ein und pflegt auf der Grundlage der Gleichberechtigung und gegenseitigen Achtung die Zusammenarbeit mit allen Staaten'. See 'Verfassung der Deutschen Demokratischen Republik', *Dokument Archiv* (3 March 2004) <http://www.documentarchiv.de/ddr/verfddr.html> accessed 15 June 2015. See also, Rüchel, '*Wir hatten noch nie*', 12.

14   Höhn, and Klimke, *A Breath of Freedom*, 124–25, 136.

15   Slobodian, 'Introduction', 2.

Rhetorically, solidarity policies enabled the GDR to separate itself from Western forms of involvement, such as the perceived 'neocolonialist' contributions of development aid. East Germany selected different terminology to more appropriately characterize what it saw as its contribution and to linguistically distinguish itself from the West. In contrast to 'development,' the use of the term 'solidarity' sought 'to describe a relationship among equals' that was centered around 'the idea of reciprocity and the membership in a shared moral community'.[16] Alternatively, the word 'aid' became associated with a type of neocolonialism and neoimperialism located in Western countries, with which the East sought to break. Instead, East Germany preferred terms such as 'economic social assistance'.[17] All in all, East Germany's public attitude toward African countries was one that expressed a collaborative spirit and constructed a postwar East German identity based on notions of solidarity and shared responsibility to work toward an improved and positive socialist future.

West Germany, on the other hand, also contributed to SWAPO's efforts, but struggled to maintain a balance between its associations with Namibia and South Africa. While it tried to settle its difficult relationship with the apartheid state by separating economic relations in Africa from its politics, the Federal Republic of Germany still came under harsh criticisms for its ambiguity and continued economic ties to South Africa.[18] Through its *Solidaritätspolitik*, East Germany took an ideological stance to support other, socialist-leaning liberation struggles and to project an image of itself as decisively 'anti-colonial' (as opposed to postcolonial). Here, the anti-colonial stance distinguished the GDR from the 'neo-colonial' Federal Republic, which it saw in economic exploitative and militaristic terms.

16   Toni Weis, 'The Politics Machine: On the Concept of "Solidarity" in East German Support for SWAPO', *Journal of Southern African Studies* 37/2 (2011): 352 and 357.

17   Tanja R. Müller, *Legacies of Socialist Solidarity: East Germany in Mozambique* (London: Lexington Books, 2014).

18   Schilling, *Postcolonial Germany*, 151 and Rolf Hofmeier, 'Five Decades of German-African Relations: Limited Interests, Low Political Profile and Substantial Aid Donor', in Ulf Engel and Robert Kappel, eds, *Germany's Africa Policy Revisited: Interests, Images and Incrementalism* (Münster: Lit Verlag, 2002), 49.

The term 'anti-colonial' furthermore signified the GDR as actively fighting against colonial oppression. In sum, solidarity served as a key feature of the GDR's anti-colonial position and served 'to present it as the better German state, both to its African partners and to its own population'.[19] Africa in this regard thus became an ideological battleground where East and West promoted and projected their respective development, political models and national identities. This was especially important for the GDR, which was still in the process of constructing its identity, gaining international political legitimacy and trying to strengthen a new socialist world order in the then ideologically divided, bipolar world.[20] East Germany substantially supported SWAPO during its liberation struggle by providing finances, medical attention, diplomatic advocacy in the international political arena, as well as places of refuge for certain groups, including injured civilians, those seeking training or education and Namibian children.[21]

Distancing itself from German colonial memory, the GDR saw its relationships with African countries first and foremost as developing fraternal partnerships with other socialist nations. It associated colonialism with capitalist societies and, as such, perceived its endeavors as creating new relationships exemplary of international solidarity.[22] In their life narratives, Engombe and Aukongo present the complexities of *Solidaritätspolitik* that, on the one hand, appears as mere political rhetoric to project a positive public image. On the other hand, it emerges as an important part of GDR

19 Weis, 'The Politics Machine', 352 and 363.
20 Müller, *Legacies*, 20–22.
21 Interestingly, Lucia Engombe's mother was among those receiving additional training in the Soviet Union while Engombe was in school in the GDR. Members of other freedom struggles, such as the African National Congress (ANC) also sought refuge and training in the GDR. See, for instance, Sithebe Nombuso, 'Ost- oder Westdeutschland, für mich ist das kein großer Unterschied', in Ika Hügel, and others, eds, *Entfernte Verbindungen. Rassismus, Antisemitismus, Klassenunterdrückung* (Berlin: Orlanda Frauenverlag, 1993), 224–32.
22 Schilling, *Postcolonial Germany*, 149–50 and Rüchel, '*Wir hatten noch nie*', 13. See also, Gründer, Horst, 'Kolonialismus und Marxismus. Der deutsche Kolonialismus in der Geschichtsschreibung der DDR', in Alexander Fischer and Günther Heydemann, eds, *Geschichtswissenschaft in der DDR*, 2 (Berlin: Duncker & Humblot, 1990), 671–710.

identity and as something that individual citizens took seriously and acted upon. As their autobiographical accounts demonstrate, however, solidarity neither eradicated all forms of racism, particularly *Alltagsrassismus*, nor did it automatically lead to outright social inclusion and belonging.

Experiences of *Solidaritätspolitik* and *Alltagsrassismus* in *Kind Nr. 95. Meine deutsch-afrikanische Odyssee* and *Kalungas Kind: Wie die DDR mein Leben rettete*

Engombe and Aukongo traveled to the GDR during the SWAPO uprising following the then widely publicized 1978 South African attack on the Cassinga refugee camp in Angola, in which over 600 Namibians lost their lives.[23] While their personal histories cross paths at moments in their narratives, they do not come into direct contact with one another since they were part of different groups transplanted to the GDR under *Solidaritätspolitik*. Engombe, as a member of the *DDR-Kinder* group, initially resided at the *Schloss Bellin* [Bellin castle] in Mecklenburg-Vorpommern and later at the newly founded *Schule der Freundschaft* [School of Friendship] in the city of Staßfurt in Sachsen-Anhalt. Namibian and German caretakers and teachers provided education and training (including military training) to this group of children with the goal of raising them to become the future elite in Namibia.[24] After the Cassinga attack, the first group of

23   Kenna, *Die 'DDR Kinder'*, 18 and Lucia Engombe, *Kind Nr. 95. Meine deutsch-afrikanische Odyssee* (Berlin: Ullstein, 2004), 29. For more on this see also Christian A. Williams, '"Remember Cassinga?" An Exhibition of Photographs and Histories', *Kronos (Bellville)* 36/1 (2010): 213–51.

24   Kenna, *Die 'DDR Kinder'*, 26 and Engombe, *Kind Nr. 95*, 101 and 298. Upon returning to Namibia, many of the 'GDR-Kids' remark on feeling forgotten and deceived. Nothing ever became of their 'elite' training, and they were largely expected to independently reintegrate and find their way in the new Namibian state. See also, Lucia Engombe, 'Die vergessene Elite', in *Kind Nr. 95* 276–86 and the documentary film

eighty Namibian children between the ages of three and seven, including seven-year-old Lucia Engombe, were flown to East Germany to participate in this SWAPO-GDR sponsored program. Many of the children sent to the GDR were either orphaned during the Cassinga attack or were related to the high-ranking SWAPO officials living in Angola and Zambia. While Lucia Engombe was neither orphaned nor a child of such an official, she was able to go to the GDR on account of her mother's personal and later romantic relationship with the then SWAPO leader and future Namibian President Sam Nujoma.[25] Her narrative indicates that the move to the GDR was only afforded to a privileged few and that class difference indeed played a role. After German reunification, this group of children returned to Namibia, but not as the 'new elite'. Instead, many struggled to find their way into Namibian society.[26]

In contrast, a white East German family raised Aukongo before and after German reunification, following her birth in the *Solidaritätsstation* [solidarity ward] of an East German hospital. During the SWAPO uprising, a number of Namibians were flown to East German hospitals to receive treatment. Among this group was Aukongo's mother, who while pregnant with her, was badly injured during the Cassinga attack.[27] This event left Aukongo with physical disabilities that threatened her life and with which she continues to live. Her East German foster family struggled to keep Aukongo in their care and worked diligently to prevent her return to the then war-torn South-West Africa. After directly contacting Margot Honecker, Erich Honecker's wife and the Minister of Education, the family's wish to raise her was ultimately granted, albeit with the instruction that she should later grow up amongst 'afrikanische Menschen' ['African

---

Die Ossis von Namibia, Klaus-Dieter Gralow, Roger Pitann and Hans Thull, dirs (Pitann Film+Grafik, 2010).

25   Jason Owens, 'Changing Constructions of Germanness in Namibia: The "GDR Kids"', PhD dissertation, Georgetown University, 2001, 33. Engombe, *Kind Nr. 95*, 313–14.

26   See also, Engombe, 'Die vergessene Elite', 276–86.

27   Stefanie-Lahya Aukongo, *Kalungas Kind. Wie die DDR mein Leben rettete* (Hamburg: Rowohlt, 2009), 19–20.

people'], specifically with the Namibian children in Bellin and later in her native country.[28] This response illustrates the presence of *Alltagsrassismus* as well as the problematic notions of segregated communities early on in Aukongo's narrative. Nonetheless, when she was seven years old, she briefly visited the school in Bellin. However, as the only child there with disabilities, she was returned to her East German family.[29] To Aukongo the message was clear: 'Ein verschüchtertes, gehbehindertes Mädchen mit einer leicht gelähmten Hand und allen möglichen anderen Problemen erschien der Befreiungsbewegung dazu wenig geeignet' ['a shy, mobility-impaired girl with a slightly paralyzed hand and possible other issues appeared unfit for the liberation struggle'].[30] Even though existing social programs in the GDR provided some assistance to citizens with disabilities, many still experienced marginalization.[31] Yet through the solidarity efforts of her adopted family, Aukongo showed her ability to overcome adversity and obstacles, leading to both a deepening of familial ties and her personal success in life.

The two autobiographical texts articulate different stories of life in East Germany based on their distinct situations – Engombe being raised in an institutional and state-sponsored setting with a group of Namibian children, and Aukongo in a private, adopted, white German family. The different spaces they inhabited as well as their particular backgrounds led to diverse understandings and articulations of belonging, solidarity and identity. Engombe, who grew up in a boarding school that educated the students to become Namibia's new elite, developed close attachments to the other Namibian children and to some of the East German and Namibian *Erzieherinnen* [child care workers]. In her account, Engombe describes how many of the *Erzieherinnen* treated them like their own children, with several East German caretakers inviting some of the children, including Engombe on multiple occasions, to stay with them in their private homes.[32]

28   Aukongo, *Kalungas Kind*, 61–63, 80.
29   Aukongo, *Kalungas Kind*, 81.
30   Aukongo, *Kalungas Kind*, 81.
31   Carol Poore, *Disability in Twentieth-Century German Culture* (Ann Arbor: University of Michigan Press, 2007), xx.
32   Engombe, *Kind Nr. 95*, 113.

This gave the *DDR-Kinder* the opportunity to leave the school's grounds (which rarely happened) and to experience East German life in a domestic setting. This form of acceptance left Engombe with a feeling of solidarity. Over time, she depicts this feeling as more distinctly developed vis-à-vis her Namibian student community at the boarding school. Their shared experiences and consistent connection to each other at the school led to the formation of a very tight kinship bond that continued even after their return to Namibia in 1989.[33] Her close, personal linkages served as sources of strength and belonging to her.

Aukongo developed a kinship community similar to Engombe (i.e. through non-genealogical bonds), which, however, was white rather than Black and East German or Namibian, especially since she grew up in a white East German foster family. Although she was encouraged to spend time with the *DDR-Kinder* group at the boarding school and at summer camps to maintain links to her 'Namibian roots', she often felt like an outcast outside of their tight-knit community. Alternatively, the sense of belonging and familial ties to her foster family remains an important part of her life as a German citizen today.[34] Highlighting her diverse familial connections, Aukongo explains that she has multiple mothers: her Namibian biological mother Clementine, the East German sisters Petra and Ines and their parents Waltraud and Rudi Schmieder. In her account, she states that she referred to the Schmieder couple as *Oma* and *Opa* [grandma and grandpa], even though they were her actual legal foster parents, which exemplifies the development of her kinship ties.[35]

Aside from their differing circumstances, both Engombe and Aukongo portray the experience of solidarity and kinship within diverse communities that extend beyond biology and genealogy. Their narratives personify a form of solidarity that inspired individuals to act as advocates and form supportive communities. Among these individuals emerged a sense of

33 Jason Owens, 'Blood Ties and Tongue Ties: The Role of Children in Shifting the Boundaries of Namibia's German-Speaking Community', *Journal of the History of Childhood and Youth* 1/2 (2008): 232–49.
34 Engombe, *Kind Nr. 95*, 183.
35 Engombe, *Kind Nr. 95*, 18, 25.

collaboratively achieving a shared cause and an improved socialist future – a key aspect of East German identity construction. While their personal accounts demonstrate the ways in which individuals went beyond superficial practices by becoming personally involved, *Solidaritätspolitik* appears to also have another potential in their narratives. In particular, they criticize the political approach and execution of solidarity policies for having adversely affected their families and for instrumentalizing their refugee status and experiences. They were used as symbolic representations of positive political relations between the GDR and SWAPO, and they condemn the ways in which solidarity at times overshadowed existing issues related to *Alltagsrassismus*.

Beginning their narratives with a positive sense of solidarity politics, both Engombe and Aukongo describe their transfer to East Germany as having been vital to their survival. Engombe writes, 'Der Bus, der mich fortbrachte [aus Namibia], war wie ein Ticket ins Leben. Ins Überleben' [The bus that took me out [of Namibia] felt like a ticket to life. To survival].[36] Aukongo expresses a similar sentiment from the outset, in her memoir's subtitle, *Wie die DDR mein Leben rettete* [*How the GDR Saved My Life*]. Later in their narratives, Engombe and Aukongo illustrate how *Solidaritätspolitik* became a complex and conflicted affair for them. On the one hand, they applaud solidarity politics as having saved their lives, while, on the other hand, they criticize its superficiality. This is especially the case in moments in which they were objectified to project a positive self-image and serve as symbols for the cause of *Solidaritätspolitik*. Solidarity politics, as they demonstrate, also disrupted their lives by creating the conditions for their separations from family and complex self-identification. Over time, they learn to negotiate their multiple points of belonging to constitute a sense of self, especially during their return trips to Namibia. There, they eventually connect with their Namibian cultural roots and biological families, learning that they can have both Namibian and (East) German linkages.[37]

---

36 Engombe, *Kind Nr. 95*, 36.
37 In both texts, the most prominent example of this conciliation is their reconnection with their mothers and other relatives. This symbolizes the recognition and acceptance of their Namibian heritage. See also, Engombe, *Kind Nr. 95*, 369–72 and Aukongo, *Kalungas Kind*, 238–40.

This involved process empowered both women to value their difference and multifaceted feelings of belonging and to view their experiences as an opportunity to creatively construct their own unique identities across supposedly incompatible cultures. In a symbolic and telling move, Aukongo takes on her aunt's name 'Lahya', which her father wanted to name her, and explains that she found it fitting, as if it had been missing.[38] Engombe navigates her diverse ideas of belonging and identity by learning to love and understand her biological mother. She begins and ends her story with thoughts of her mother, initially expressing her desire to love and be loved by her, and in the end finding understanding and an affective link: I learned to love her 'für die Stärke mit der sie ihre Liebe geopfert hatte, um mich zu beschützen' [for the strength and love that she sacrificed to protect me], she writes.[39] Both Aukongo's and Engombe's narratives depict a particularly stressed relationship with their biological mothers – a relationship that also serves as the key for them to gain access to their alternate or second histories and cultural location. In the autobiographies, the amelioration of stressed mother-daughter relationships represents their coming to terms with and negotiation of their diverse identities. Through their biological mothers, they seek a means through which to discover their Namibian heritage as a part of themselves. In discussing and exploring their autobiographical pasts, both women are able to amend their maternal relationships and incorporate their Namibian roots as a part of their self-understanding. This is confirmed toward the end of each text with both referring to Namibia as their '*Heimat*' [homeland], while simultaneously upholding their German identity as well. Aukongo, for instance, accepts the label 'DDR-Kind' as a part of her identity and Engombe refers to both Namibia and Berlin as her '*Heimat*'.[40]

In these ways, their narratives disrupt limited perceptions of home and self by demonstrating transnational and transcultural possibilities.[41]

38   Aukongo, *Kalungas Kind*, 145.
39   Engombe, *Kind Nr. 95*, 372.
40   Aukongo, *Kalungas Kind*, 305, 319 and Engombe, *Kind Nr. 95*, 203.
41   This limited view is largely indicated by the derogatory treatment of and attitude toward white, German women who gave birth to children from African American fathers. Aukongo mentions this hostile attitude in a memory about her foster mother, Ines, who was called a 'whore' while on a walk with her. See Aukongo, *Kalungas*

The internal conflicts that they address in their narratives, including complex feelings of belonging, an initial lack of connection to their biological families and Namibian heritage and kinship within diverse communities of solidarity, reflect a resistance to the societal rejection of hybridity. For these women, their narratives of struggle, overcoming and the negotiation of difference serve as a critique of East German solidarity politics through a demonstration of its limits – it was unable to establish inclusive forms of cultural and hybrid belonging. On a personal level, they portray new possibilities for kinship inspired by a sense of solidarity that individuals took seriously as a part of a shared, socialist humanity. Yet it becomes complicated on a social level via the fact that forms of *Alltagsrassismus* persisted despite East Germany's construction of itself as anti-colonial and anti-racist.

In their narratives, the women describe forms of *Alltagsrassismus* that they experienced while growing up in the GDR.[42] Unlike articulations of racism based on instances of physical violence, *Alltagsrassismus* takes notice

---

Kind, 118. This attitude is largely reflected in the post-World War I and World War II periods with regard to white, German women, who bore children from African and African American soldiers stationed throughout Germany. It is also prominently depicted in the feature film *Toxi*, Robert A. Stemmle, dir. (Fono Film, 1952). See Patricia Mazón and Reinhild Steingröver, eds, *Not so Plain as Black and White: Afro-German Culture and History, 1890–2000* (Rochester, NY: University of Rochester Press, 2005) and Angelica Fenner, *Race Under Reconstruction in German Cinema: Robert Stemmle's Toxi* (Toronto: University of Toronto Press, 2011). Though these works focus on the West German context, Aukongo's narrative demonstrates the attitude's pervasiveness in East Germany as well.

42 Heinz Ulrich Brinkmann argues that in a German context *Alltagsrassismus* is seldom the focus of scholarly investigations but has indeed been a part of cultural constructions of society that lead to discriminatory practices and attitudes in everyday life. See Heinz Ulrich Brinkmann, 'Einführung: Diskriminierung, Fremdenfeindlichkeit und Rassismus', in Britta Marschke and H. U. Brinkmann, eds, *"Ich habe nichts gegen Ausländer, aber ...": Alltagsrassismus in Deutschland* (Berlin: Lit Verlag, 2015), 12–13, 30. But there are exceptions to this in the cultural realm, especially by People of Color in Germany. See Lara-Sophie Milagro's play performed by Label Noir *Heimat, bittersüße Heimat* [2011, *Home, Bittersweet Home*]; Grada Kilomba, *Plantation Memories: Episodes of Everyday Racism* (Münster: Unrast, 2008); and Noah Sow, *Deutschland Schwarz Weiss: Der alltägliche Rassismus* (Munich: Bertelsmann, 2008).

of the everyday, covert expressions that point to racially constructed understandings of society. The danger of *Alltagsrassismus* lies in its perpetuation of racialized stereotypes and prejudice socialized via media, politics and practices.[43] With regard to the GDR, there was a common rhetoric that racism was absent in East German society, particularly since it saw itself as anti-colonial and anti-imperialist. As historians Rita Chin and Heide Fehrenbach state, the SED in East Germany 'refused to speak the language of "race" in public in relation to its own society'. Instead, they projected '"race" and its social ills onto the contemporary capitalist West and its contemptible Nazi predecessor'.[44] Furthermore, as historians Maria Höhn and Martin Klimke claim, '[i]n the government's ideology, racism, imperialism, and anticommunism were thus intertwined and regarded as enemies of peace and progress'.[45] They argue that racism was seen as directly opposed to communism. However, the suppression of a racial discourse, as was often the case in the GDR, did not lead to the eradication of racism, especially in 'unspectacular everyday interactions' that became forms of 'identity policing', the normal use of 'evocative terms', as well as the associative color-coding

43   For more, see Toan Quoc Nguyen, '"Offensichtlich und zugedeckt" – Alltagsrassismus in Deutschland', *Bundeszentrale für politische Bildung* (6 November 2014), <https://www.bpb.de/dialog/194569/offensichtlich-und-zugedeckt-alltagsrassismus-in-deutschland> accessed 15 June 2015.

44   Rita Chin, and Heide Fehrenbach, 'Introduction: What's Race Got to Do with It? Postwar German History in Context', in Rita Chin, and others, eds, *After the Nazi Racial State: Difference and Democracy in Germany and Europe* (Ann Arbor: University of Michigan Press, 2009), 124. See also Piesche, 'Black and German?', 39 and Rüchel, 'Wir hatten noch nie', 13.

45   Höhn, and Klimke, *A Breath of Freedom*, 124. In recent oral histories and studies, there has been a focus on African contract workers and their experiences in the GDR with regard to racism and social exclusion. Peggy Piesche, for example, explains how the lack of integration programs led to social isolation and the development of ethnic rivalries that produced feelings of homelessness, a loss of inner stability, a falling away from security, uncertainty and fear of contact; 42–43. See also, Ulrich Van der Heyden, Wolfgang Semmler and Ralf Straßburg eds, *Mosambikanische Vertragearbeiter in der DDR-Wirtschaft. Hintergründe-Verlauf-Folgen* (Berlin: Lit Verlag, 2014).

of symbols in the public sphere.[46] In such cases of *Alltagsrassismus*, as cultural theorist and historian Fatima El-Tayeb explains, 'race is not mentioned yet referenced implicitly as a marker of not belonging, a strategy that relies on a shared iconography that remains unspoken.'[47] Although the GDR's self-positioning through solidarity politics aimed for positive relationships, Engombe and Aukongo recall instances of *Alltagsrassismus* in East German society that complicate the picture.

The most pervasive examples in both narratives are forms of *Alltagsrassismus* that emerged in reference to Engombe and Aukongo's integration into mainstream East German society, revealing institutional biases. As it becomes clear to both women, the East German government and SWAPO always expected that the Namibian children would return to Namibia, their supposed '*Heimat*', without regard to the limited connection to Africa that they initially felt. Historically, *Gastarbeiter* [guest workers] in East and West Germany also faced a similar response. Rita Chin explains that, in the case of West Germany, these workers were reduced to their economic function and were seen as short-term visitors who would return to their home countries.[48] A similar situation presented itself in East Germany with contract workers through the segregation of housing and employment with limited contact to 'East German natives'. Contract workers, moreover, in East Germany were either sent back at the end of their labor contracts or when they were no longer needed.[49] In both East and West Germany, these communities were not seen as members of mainstream society and were denied the possibility of integration. Engombe and Aukongo criticize the issues associated with this perspective, which, however, allowed for their appropriation as symbols representing East

46   Fatima El-Tayeb, *European Others: Queering Ethnicity in Postnational Europe* (Minneapolis: University of Minnesota Press, 2011), xxv–vi.

47   El-Tayeb, *European Others*, xxvi.

48   Rita Chin, *The Guest Worker Question in Postwar Germany* (Cambridge: Cambridge University Press, 2007), 47–48.

49   Douglas B. Klusmeyer and Demetrios G. Papademetriou, *Immigration Policy in the Federal Republic of Germany: Negotiating Membership and Remaking the Nation* (New York: Berghahn, 2009), 149–50 and Ray Taras, *Xenophobia and Islamophobia in Europe* (Edinburgh: Edinburgh University Press, 2012), 169–70.

German solidarity, the connections to SWAPO and liberation movements and East German anti-colonial and anti-racist stances. Here, the limits and contradictions of solidarity become visible. They indicate that these politicized communities were both unaccepted members of East German society and that integration into society was not the desired outcome for either the GDR or SWAPO.[50] Instead, they were used as a 'Symbol der Verbindung der beiden Völker' [symbol of the connection between both societies/peoples'].[51] This quote reinforces their linkage, but also distinguishes East Germans and the Namibian people through the use of the plural designation of *Völker* to mark distinct nationalities and, implicitly, reinforce constructed racial difference.

In a telling example, Aukongo sheds critical light on *Alltagsrassismus* through her and her mother's objectification as symbols and 'embodiments' of East German *Solidaritätspolitik*. A 1979 issue of the East German magazine *Für Dich* [*For You*], a weekly publication that catered to women, featured a personal photo of the two on the cover and included an article detailing their story. With the display of their image on the cover, the magazine draws solidarity into a personal space, giving a face to the state-sponsored program. The article itself highlights the hardship and injuries that Aukongo and her mother suffered during the Cassinga attack and how their lives were saved via transport to the GDR – all in an effort to garner sympathy from their readers. The GDR and its solidarity program are clearly championed as providing refuge and safety. According to historian Gregory Witkowski, such images 'played on recent German experiences of war and destruction', but they also 'provided an opportunity for East Germans to show that they were now a rebuilt country that could aid other lands'.[52] Images of women and children provoking sympathy as well as the evocation of German experiences served to attract support and enhance the monetary collection of charity funds from private citizens. The *Für*

---

50   Aukongo, *Kalungas Kind*, 61, 74.
51   Engombe, *Kind Nr. 95*, 61.
52   Gregory Witkowski, 'Between Fighters and Beggars: Socialist Philanthropy and the Imagery of Solidarity in East Germany', in Quinn Slobodian, ed., *Comrades of Color: East Germany in the Cold War World* (New York: Berghahn, 2015), 73, 79–80.

Dich article concludes by stressing the exemplary solidarity efforts of the Schmieder family who took Aukongo into their home. Through their hard work and the funds of the solidarity committee, they provided a positive environment for Aukongo and frequent visits between mother and daughter (her mother was still in the hospital at this time). Conveying its political message that the collective fight against apartheid and colonialism affects everyone individually, the article ends with an appeal to one's individual conscience.[53] Namibian officials also employed instrumentalized images, such as those of Aukongo, to achieve their own political goals.

The returning *DDR-Kinder* in particular, as expressed in Engombe's text, served as symbols to build positive ties and solidarity between the white and Black communities in post-apartheid Namibia.[54] The *Für Dich* article celebrates the GDR's efforts as widely successful; it also projects an East German national identity constructed upon fundamental humanitarian principals and actively engaged in a global struggle against apartheid and colonial forms of oppression. The Schmieder family is exemplary in its efforts to realize this important East German endeavor. Although the family took solidarity seriously as a part of their own personal ambitions with positive intensions, Aukongo is critical of her and her mother's exploitation in the magazine to propagate citizen support and funding and to present Namibia as her *Heimat*. 'Wie konnte ein mir unbekanntes Land meine Heimat sein?' ['How could a foreign country like Namibia be my home?'], she questions.[55] Implicated in this statement is again the denial

---

53   Hildegund Ruge, *Für Dich* 15 (1979): 7–9. The article was generously provided by the cultural organization *EWA Frauenzentrum* located in Berlin. Their library houses numerous works, including magazines (e.g. *Für Dich, Emma, Wir Frauen, Courage* and *The Advocate*) and so-called grey literature from the former GDR with a particular interest in East German feminism. *EWA e. V. Frauenzentrum* (2013) <http:// www.ewa-frauenzentrum.de/bibliothek.html> accessed 20 June 2015.

54   Jason Owens is quite critical of this and explains how there were numerous attempts to use the image of the 'GDR-Kids' and support them for personal gain: some to ward off negative accusations (often of being racist) and others to promote a rhetoric of bridge-building between white and Black communities. Owens, 'Blood Ties and Tongue Ties', 243.

55   Aukongo, *Kalungas Kind*, 18.

of her integration into East German society as an accepted permanent member, and it reasserts the manifestation of *Alltagsrassismus* experienced as an individual linked to her exclusion on a national level.

In contrast to the positive representation in the article, Aukongo draws attention to the numerous bureaucratic conflicts that attempted to block her extended stay in the GDR, revealing the limits of solidarity. Her East German foster family had to work diligently to gain permission for her to stay with them and to ensure that she received proper medical care. Particularly telling is an instance that she recalls of the *Volksbildungsministerium* [the people's ministry for education] and its decision to have her grow up with other 'afrikanische Menschen' ['African people'] instead of her adopted white, East German family.[56] Here, she uncovers the racialized construction of a white East German society that was not ready to accept her as an outright member of the GDR. Similarly revealing are the responses that the East German family faced from some hospital coworkers. One coworker, for example, advised against taking in an African child due to her 'afrikanische Mentalität' ['African mentality'], and another wondered why the family would want to take in a child with disabilities.[57] By portraying lived experiences of multiple exclusions in the GDR, these instances reflect *Alltagsrassismus* and prejudice in East German life that complicate the picture of solidarity and expose the barring of others from fully belonging. In Aukongo's case, this occurred at the intersections of her racialized and disabled body. It reveals that *Alltagsrassismus* can emerge and perpetuate prejudice and exclusion even with efforts conveying positive intentions, such as those under *Solidaritätspolitik*.

In *Kind Nr. 95*, Engombe similarly recounts early childhood memories that exemplify *Alltagsrassismus* in the GDR public sphere. On one occasion, the group of *DDR-Kinder* encountered a white East German child with his mother. The boy remarked: 'Oh, so viele Schokoladenkinder' ['Oh, so many chocolate-children'] and proceeded to touch them.[58] To

---

56   Aukongo, *Kalungas Kind*, 80.
57   Aukongo, *Kalungas Kind*, 24, 63.
58   Engombe, *Kind Nr. 95*, 66.

the boy the group seemed foreign and exotic. Another memory recalls the *DDR-Kinder*'s treatment in school, in which the group was educated and housed separately from other East German children. On hot summer days when the white GDR children in a separate class got *Hitzefrei* [time off due to hot weather], they did not. The principal of the school rationalized this by saying: 'Ihr seid doch die Hitze aus Afrika gewohnt ... Die vier namibische Klassen brauchen kaum Hitzefrei. Die halten mehr aus als die DDR-Schüler. Ihre Haut passt sich der Hitze besser an' [you are used to the African heat [...] The four Namibian classes don't need time off on account of the hot weather. They can handle more than the GDR students. Their skin is more suitable for the heat].[59] These examples are indicative of the everyday presence of racist mentalities in GDR mainstream society, and how they constructed and enacted practices of cultural and racial difference tied to the colonial imaginary, despite the socialist rhetoric of equality through solidarity partnerships.

The spatial separation of the *DDR-Kinder* provides further evidence of institutional constructions of difference and exclusion in the GDR. They were educated in separate classes and buildings and had little to no contact with white *DDRler* [East Germans from Zehna and later at the *Schule der Freundschaft*]. Initially, the newly arriving children from Namibia perceived their spatial separation from mainstream East German society as normal.[60] By the mid-1980s, however, the *Ministerium für Volksbildung* [East German ministry for national education] loosened the isolation of the Namibian children, and this enabled them to take part in sporting events and engage in extracurricular activities, such as learning to play an instrument or going on trips to local attractions.[61] Yet this interaction was still limited and not always freely permitted as Engombe recalls in her descriptions of the spatial segregation and experienced isolation. Since they were to become Namibia's new elite, the *DDR-Kinder* were placed in an education program primarily based on Namibian national principles and values. Thus, the GDR and SWAPO planned to keep these children

---

59   Engombe, *Kind Nr. 95*, 170.
60   Engombe, *Kind Nr. 95*, 90–91 and 157.
61   Rüchel, *'Wir hatten noch nie'*, 53.

segregated from the rest of East German society as a means of intentionally directing their development of cultural and national ties to the future
Namibian state.[62] To this end, they were also discouraged from interacting
with the other teenagers from Mozambique and Cuba that lived nearby and
were prompted to form relationships – even romantic ones – with other
Namibians. Specifically, the women of the group were encouraged to date
the so-called *Schönebecker Jungs* [the *Schönebecker* boys], German-speaking
Namibian men who were training in the GDR to become PLAN (People's
Liberation Army of Namibia) soldiers to fight for Namibian independence.
Engombe recalls how she and the majority of other teenage Namibian
women rejected this SWAPO-encouraged coupling, and how they instead
sought out their own connections.[63] The school's administrator shamed
some of the women, who did form relationships with non-Namibians:
'Aber ihr seid Namibierinnen, die in ihre Heimat zurückkehren werden.
Manche von euch haben ihrem Land Schande bereitet und sich mit anderen
Männern eingelassen. Damit muss Schluss sein' [You are Namibians and
will return to your homeland. Many of you have disgraced your country by
letting other [non-Namibian] men into your life. There must be an end to
this].[64] As Engombe demonstrates, this spatial separation combined with
traditional understandings of gender and national identity were both consistent with and reinforced racialized and national constructions of society
despite notions of solidarity.[65] This emerged as much from SWAPO as it
did from GDR leadership.

As the *DDR-Kinder* aged, however, they developed an acute awareness of their ethnic and racial separation, and Engombe explains how they
increasingly perceived their spatial environment as living 'hinter Zäunen'
[behind fences] and 'wie im Gefängnis' [as if in a prison].[66] Her narrative
exposes that this type of divide led to the children's exoticization and

---

62   Rüchel, *'Wir hatten noch nie'*, 50–51.
63   Engombe, *Kind Nr. 95*, 243–44 and 246–51.
64   Engombe, *Kind Nr. 95*, 246–47.
65   For this reason, Aukongo was also encouraged to join their group as a child.
66   Engombe, *Kind Nr. 95*, 172 and 230.

ensuing tensions between the *DDR-Kinder* and other *DDRler*.[67] Their institutionalized isolation allowed for the formation of rivalries, the construal of misinformation of the unknown and a sense of physical segregation. Close to their return to Namibia, Engombe details how she and the other now teenagers from Namibia did not feel safe or 'free' when leaving their school and dormitory campus.[68] The increase in xenophobic violence and racial tensions during the 1990s historically culminated in a number of horrific attacks that extremist groups committed on migrants and their families in Germany.[69] Engombe reveals how she and her fellow students looked to each other for strength and support. The group did in fact develop a very close bond and feeling of solidarity toward each other, if not always with other GDR citizens. Within their own community, they established their unique hybrid language, *Oshideutsch* [a combination of Oshiwambo, a language spoken in northern Namibia, and German], and their position as *SWAPO-Kinder* gave them a sense of identity, belonging and strength. This is particularly exemplified after their return to Namibia where they formed a community called the *Ossi-Klub* [Easterner-club] in Windhoek in order to combat their initial feelings of isolation. The club served as a

67   Engombe writes: 'So sorgte die Barriere weiterhin dafür, dass wir wie Exoten leben mussten. ... Deshalb war die DDR-Disko auch so wichtig; dort hofften wir sein zu dürfen, was wir nie waren – ganz normale Jugendliche' [Thus the barrier made certain that we had to live like exotic people. ... This is why the GDR-disco was also so important; we hoped to be allowed to be there, what we never were – totally normal youth']. Engombe, *Kind Nr. 95*, 234.

68   Engombe, *Kind Nr. 95*, 254.

69   Historically, a major event affecting groups participating in GDR solidarity sponsored programs took place in Hoyerswerda in 1991. For almost a week, a group of armed young men occupied two apartment complexes that housed former GDR contract workers from Mozambique and Vietnam. Police had difficulty containing the violence, but eventually were able to evacuate the former contract workers to safety. Xenophobic attacks also occurred in Solingen and Mölln with the murder of Turkish women and girls. Hostility and attacks took place in former West Germany as well. See Chin and Fehrenbach, 'Introduction. What's Race Got to Do With It?', 117. See also, 'Is the Boat Full? Xenophobia, Racism, and Violence', in Deniz Göktürk, David Gramling and Anton Kaes, eds, *Germany in Transit: Nation and Migration 1955–2005* (Berkley: University of California Press, 2007), 107–9.

space where they could reconnect and maintain their relationships with each other, continue to speak *Oshideutsch* and maintain a sense of their East German identity within their Namibian present.[70] In her narrative of the post-reunification period, Aukongo briefly recounts her experience of being harassed on a bus in Berlin on her way to her college by a group of five men. This exemplifies the pervasiveness of xenophobic animosity in Germany in the post-*Wende* 1990s and criticizes superficial notions of solidarity and the reality of *Alltagsrassismus*. She describes how one of the men tossed her belongings around the bus and not a single passenger came to her aid. Instead, some began to question: 'Was fährt sie denn auch hier rum! Was machen die auch alle hier?' [What is she even doing riding around! What are they all doing here?][71] This response again illustrates *Alltagsrassismus* and underlying notions of exclusion and emphasizes the distinctive political contexts for (not) coming to one's aid. Even though in this situation Aukongo believes solidarity to be forgotten in mainstream society, she is nonetheless able to find support and solidarity from her East German family, who had advocated for her from the start.[72]

Conclusion

In addition to their negotiation of diverse identities, Engombe's and Aukongo's autobiographies include a thank you section, showing appreciation and gratitude to all of the individuals who helped and supported

---

70   Engombe, *Kind Nr. 95*, 147. Owens, 'Changing Constructions', 223. For more about the 'DDR-Kinder' in Namibia today see the documentary film *Die Ossis von Namibia*; Jason Owens, 'Blood Ties and Tongue Ties', 237; Jason Owens, 'Changing Constructions'; and Jason Owens, '"Von hier, aber Deutsche?" Die DDR-Kinder und die deutschsprachige Bevölkerung Namibias', in Constance Kenna, ed., *Die 'DDR-Kinder' von Namibia. Heimkehrer in ein fremdes Land* (Göttingen: Klaus Hess Verlag, 1999).

71   Aukongo, *Kalunga's Kind*, 190.

72   Aukongo, *Kalunga's Kind*, 190.

them throughout their journeys.[73] Their narratives of overcoming adversity and self-assertion depict the important role that their support community – Engombe's group of *DDR-Kinder* and Aukongo's foster family – played on a much smaller level than that of the officially state-sponsored *Solidaritätspolitik*. While the GDR's practice of *Solidaritätspolitik* complicates the country's postwar historical narrative, making it difficult to celebrate it as a space of inclusion and acceptance, both autobiographies do present the strength and real sense of solidarity that formed between individuals who chose to take solidarity seriously and enact positive change in their day-to-day lives. Solidarity became an internalized part of the GDR's self-understanding that East Germans like the Schmieders and some caretakers at the boarding schools took to heart. Still, the political instrumentalization of solidarity, as well as the GDR's anti-colonial and anti-racist stances, did not lead to the eradication of *Alltagsrassismus* nor to outright social inclusion, acceptance and belonging. In this way, Engombe and Aukongo paint a complex picture of East German solidarity and its limitations. Their examples reveal the ways in which the GDR was indeed culturally and racially constructed, especially through practices of segregation, prejudicial attitudes and the perception of Namibia as their actual *Heimat*, even though they had largely grown up in the GDR. However, they also portray the productive potential that lies in their unique experiences – namely, their ability to negotiate their own sense of belonging within German and Namibian societies, and to construct their own diverse identities and kinship communities. Solidarity it seems is a complex endeavor. Engombe's and Aukongo's narratives encourage the consideration of underlying biases, racisms and prejudicial attitudes that existed within the context of East German solidarity. They criticize the ways in which *Alltagsrassismus* manifests in very real, and perhaps at first glance, unexpected ways.

---

73   Aukongo explains that her key motivations for telling her story was to give thanks to all the people who helped her in her life. Stefanie-Lahya Aukongo, personal correspondence with Meghan O'Dea, Skype, 27 April 2015.

Bibliography

Aukongo, Stefanie-Lahya, *Kalungas Kind. Wie die DDR mein Leben rettete* (Hamburg: Rowohlt, 2009).

Brandt, Katrin, 'Shared Paradoxes in Namibian and German History: Lucia Engombe's Kind Nr. 95', in Elisabeth Bekers, Sissy Helff and Daniela Merolla, eds, *Transcultural Modernities: Narrating Africa in Europe* (Amsterdam: Editions Rodopi, 2009), 347–62.

Brinkmann, Heinz Ulrich, 'Einführung: Diskriminierung, Fremdenfeindlichkeit und Rassismus', in Britta Marschke, and H. U. Brinkmann, eds, *"Ich habe nichts gegen Ausländer, aber ..." Alltagsrassismus in Deutschland* (Berlin: Lit Verlag, 2015), 9–44.

Bührer, Tanja, 'Berlin Conference', in Prem Poddar, Rajeev S. Patke and Lars Jensen, eds, *A Historical Companion to Postcolonial Literatures: Continental Europe and Its Empires* (Edinburgh: Edinburgh University Press, 2008), 210–11.

Chin, Rita, and others, eds, *After the Nazi Racial State: Difference and Democracy in Germany and Europe* (Ann Arbor: University of Michigan Press, 2009).

——, *The Guest Worker Question in Postwar Germany* (Cambridge: Cambridge University Press, 2007).

——, and Heide Fehrenbach, 'Introduction: What's Race Got to Do with It? Postwar German History in Context', in Rita Chin, and others, eds, *After the Nazi Racial State: Difference and Democracy in Germany and Europe* (Ann Arbor: University of Michigan Press, 2009), 1–29.

Die Ossis von Namibia, Klaus-Dieter Gralow, Roger Pitann and Hans Thull, dirs (Pitann Film+Grafik, 2010).

El-Tayeb, Fatima, *European Others: Queering Ethnicity in Postnational Europe* (Minneapolis: University of Minnesota Press, 2011).

Engombe, Lucia, *Kind Nr. 95. Meine deutsch-afrikanische Odyssee* (Berlin: Ullstein, 2004).

EWA e. V. Frauenzentrum (2013) <http://www.ewa-frauenzentrum.de/bibliothek.html> accessed 20 June 2015.

Fenner, Angelica, *Race Under Reconstruction in German Cinema: Robert Stemmle's Toxi* (Toronto: University of Toronto Press, 2011).

Göktürk, Deniz, David Gramling and Anton Kaes, eds, *Germany in Transit: Nation and Migration 1955–2005* (Berkley: University of California Press, 2007).

Gorman, Daniel, 'Berlin Conference (1884–1885)', in Carl Cavanagh Hodge, ed., *Encyclopedia of the Age of Imperialism 1800–1914*, 1 (Westport, CT: Greenwood Press, 2008).

Gründer, Horst, 'Kolonialismus und Marxismus. Der deutsche Kolonialismus in der Geschichtsschreibung der DDR', in Alexander Fischer and Günther Heydemann, eds, *Geschichtswissenschaft in der DDR*, 2 (Berlin: Duncker & Humblot, 1990), 671–710.

Heyden, Ulrich van der, Wolfgang Semmler and Ralf Straßburg, eds, *Mosambikanische Vertragsarbeiter in der DDR-Wirtschaft. Hintergründe-Verlauf-Folgen* (Berlin: Lit Verlag, 2014).

Hofmeier, Rolf, 'Five Decades of German-African Relations: Limited Interests, Low Political Profile and Substantial Aid Donor', in Ulf Engel and Robert Kappel, eds, *Germany's Africa Policy Revisited: Interests, Images and Incrementalism* (Münster: Lit Verlag, 2002), 39–62.

Höhn, Maria, and Martin Klimke, *A Breath of Freedom: The Civil Rights Struggle, African American GIs, and Germany* (New York: Palgrave Macmillan, 2010).

Kenna, Constance, *Die 'DDR-Kinder' von Namibia. Heimkehrer in Ein Fremdes Land* (Göttingen: Klaus Hess Verlag, 2004).

Klusmeyer, Douglas B., and Demetrios G. Papademetriou, *Immigration Policy in the Federal Republic of Germany: Negotiating Membership and Remaking the Nation* (New York: Berghahn, 2009).

Mazón, Patricia, and Reinhild Steingröver, eds, *Not so Plain as Black and White: Afro-German Culture and History, 1890–2000* (Rochester, NY: University of Rochester Press, 2005).

Melber, Henning, 'Limits to Liberation: An Introduction to Namibia's Postcolonial Political Culture', in H. Melber, ed., *Re-examining Liberation in Namibia: Political Culture since Independence* (Uppsala: Nordic Africa Institute, 2003), 9–24.

Metzler, John J., *Divided Dynamism: The Diplomacy of Separated Nations* (Lanham, MD: University Press of America, 2014).

Milagro, Lara-Sophie, play performed by Label Noir, *Heimat, bittersüße Heimat* [*Home, Bittersweet Home*] (2011).

Müller, Tanja R., *Legacies of Socialist Solidarity: East Germany in Mozambique* (London: Lexington Books, 2014).

Muth, Ingrid, *Die DDR-Außenpolitik 1949–1972. Inhalte, Strukturen, Mechanismen* (Berlin: Christoph Links Verlag, 2001).

Nguyen, Toan Quoc, '"Offensichtlich und zugedeckt" – Alltagsrassismus in Deutschland', *Bundeszentrale für politische Bildung* (6 November 2014) <https://www. bpb.de/dialog/194569/offensichtlich-und-zugedeckt-alltagsrassismus-in-deutschland> accessed 15 June 2015.

Nombuso, Sithebe, 'Ost- oder Westdeutschland, für mich ist das kein großer Unterschied', in Ika Hügel, and others, eds, *Entfernte Verbindungen. Rassismus, Antisemitismus, Klassenunterdrückung* (Berlin: Orlanda Frauenverlag, 1993), 224–32.

Omulaule heißt Schwarz, Beatrice Möller, Nicola Hens and Susanne Radelhof, dirs (Omufilm, 2003).

Owens, Jason, 'Blood Ties and Tongue Ties: The Role of Children in Shifting the Boundaries of Namibia's German-Speaking Community', *Journal of the History of Childhood and Youth* 1/2 (2008): 232–49.

——, 'Changing Constructions of Germanness in Namibia: The "GDR Kids"', PhD dissertation, Georgetown University, 2001.

——, '"Von hier, aber Deutsche?" Die DDR-Kinder und die deutschsprachige Bevölkerung Namibias', in Constance Kenna, ed., *Die 'DDR-Kinder' von Namibia. Heimkehrer in ein fremdes Land* (Göttingen: Klaus Hess Verlag, 1999), 192–200.

——, and Monica Nembelela, 'Can't Namibia's Ex-GDR (Ex-) Kids be Called Adults in this, the Year Namibia Itself Turned 18 Years Old?', in Cornelia Limpricht, and Megan Biesele, eds, *Heritage and Cultures in Modern Namibia: A TUCSIN Festschrift* (Windhoek: Klaus Hess, 2008), 132–40.

Piesche, Peggy, 'Black and German? East German Adolescents Before 1989: A Retrospective View of a "Non-Existent" Issue in the GDR', in Leslie Adelson, ed., *The Cultural After-Life of East Germany: New Transnational Perspectives* (Washington, DC: AICGS, 2002), 37–59.

Poore, Carol, *Disability in Twentieth-Century German Culture* (Ann Arbor: University of Michigan Press, 2007).

Ross, Robert, *A Concise History of South Africa* (Cambridge: Cambridge University Press, 2008).

Rüchel, Ute, *'Wir hatten noch nie einen Schwarzen gesehen'. Das Zusammenleben von Deutschen und Namibiern rund um das SWAPO-Kinderheim Bellin, 1979–1990* (Schwerin: Landesbeauftragten für Mecklenburg-Vorpommern für die Unterlagen des Staatssicherheitsdienstes der ehemaligen DDR, 2001).

Ruge, Hildegund, 'Stefanie und ihre Mütter', *Für Dich*, 15 (1979): 7–9.

Schilling, Britta, *Postcolonial Germany: Memories of Empire in a Decolonized Nation* (Oxford: Oxford University Press, 2014).

Slobodian, Quinn, 'Introduction', in Quinn Slobodian, ed., *Comrades of Color: East Germany in the Cold War World* (New York: Berghahn, 2015), 1–22.

Sow, Noah, *Deutschland Schwarz Weiß: Der alltägliche Rassismus* (Munich: Bertelsmann, 2008).

Steingröver, Reinhild, 'From *Farbe bekennen* to *Schokoladenkind*: Generational Change in Afro-German Autobiographies', in Laurel Cohen-Pfister, and Susanne Vees-Gulani, eds, *Generational Shifts in Contemporary German Culture* (Rochester, NY: Camden House, 2010), 287–309.

Taras, Ray, *Xenophobia and Islamophobia in Europe* (Edinburgh: Edinburgh University Press, 2012).

Toxi, Robert A. Stemmle, dir. (Fono Film, 1952).

Verber, Jason, 'True to the Politics of Frelimo? Teaching Socialism at the *Schule der Freundschaft*, 1981–90', in Quinn Slobodian, ed., *Comrades of Color: East Germany in the Cold War World* (New York: Berghahn, 2015), 188–212.

'Verfassung der Deutschen Demokratischen Republik', *Dokument Archiv* (3 March 2004) <http://www.documentarchiv.de/ddr/verfddr.html> accessed 15 June 2015.

Weis, Toni, 'The Politics Machine: On the Concept of "Solidarity" in East German Support for SWAPO', *Journal of Southern African Studies* 37/2 (2011): 351–67.

Williams, Christian A., '"Remember Cassinga?" An Exhibition of Photographs and Histories', *Kronos* (*Bellville*) 36/1 (2010): 213–51.

Witkowski, Gregory, 'Between Flighters and Beggars: Socialist Philanthropy and the Imagery of Solidarity in East Germany', in Quinn Slobodian, ed., *Comrades of Color: East Germany in the Cold War World* (New York: Berghahn, 2015), 73–94.

PART II

Theory and Praxis

KIMBERLY ALECIA SINGLETARY

4 Everyday Matters: Haunting and the Black Diasporic Experience[1]

ABSTRACT

This chapter uses the Black American and Afro-German populations as two instances of haunting in relation to the material presence of the Black diasporic experience in Germany. In addition to German Blackness haunting the German nation, another layer of haunting – that of American Blackness toward Afro-Germanness – impacts Germany, creating a *stratified haunting*. U.S. Blackness is represented in nearly every facet of German public and popular culture from politics to street culture while Afro-Germans still fight to be recognized as both German and Black; that overrepresentation edges out Afro-German visibility by a public too willing to privilege the whiteness of German identity. This chapter asks: what is the political, social and racial environment that make racial hauntings possible? How have they been represented in visual and written texts? How can we effectively use the concept of haunting to productively discuss Black diasporic populations in Germany?

We stood, contemplating the satisfying flavor, but uncomfortable psychic experience of our 'Lumumbas' – rum-flavored hot cocoa named after the Congolese independence leader – at the Berlin Christmas market in the Alt Tegel neighborhood in December 2013. Two Black girls, both American

---

1   In this text, all translations of German are my own. I use 'Afro-German' and 'Black German' somewhat interchangeably, recognizing of course that this may not be everyone's preferred usage; rather, it reflects my interactions with Black German friends who use both reciprocally.

but one also German, wondering if we were committing some sort of Black diasporic sin by enjoying such a drink. Would we have enjoyed it as much – or even more – if it were a white chocolate drink served in an iron cup called the Thatcher? Or vodka-laced hot lemon water named the Lech Wałęsa? Leave it to graduate students to overthink a beverage. We had had the kind of experience at the market that is par for the course for Brown bodies in white spaces. Men enamored by our 'exotic' look flirted with us. Those surprised by our exoticness stared in amazement. Those who could not fathom our exotic existence in their decidedly 'normal' space pointed at us. When we stopped to drink our freedom-flavored cocoa, two older, but not elderly, white Germans, a man and woman, approached us and politely inquired if they could share our table. 'Other people wouldn't want to stand next to you', the woman said in English. 'But we will'. Amused more than offended, we smiled as the pair settled near us. My friend spoke with the man, and I, the woman. Toward the end of our conversation, when I disclosed my American nationality, I began to understand why my drink was named after Lumumba: drinking just a few could free your mind from having to remember where you were. 'Oh', she said, lowering her voice and leaning just a little bit closer. 'It must be so hard for you there'.

Our encounter with the white German couple was indicative of how the borders of national identity are porous for some and impenetrable for others. The misperception that Germans are white led to the assumption that our visible Blackness barred us from claiming an authentic German identity. Our visible incompatibility with the mythos of white *Volkishness* wrote the script that directed our interaction.[2] The couple's initial salvo was an unspoken but spoken, implicit but explicit, reaffirmation of the barriers that are fortified against People of Color in countries where a white majority must come to grips with a Brown minority wishing to claim more

---

2   See Alexander G. Weheliye, 'My Volk to Come: Peoplehood in Recent Diaspora Discourse and Afro-German Popular Music', in Darlene Clark Hine, Trica Danielle Keaton and Stephen Small, eds, *Black Europe and the African Diaspora* (Urbana: University of Illinois Press, 2009), 161–79.

than liminal citizenship.[3] What happened at the market, while I drank my colonial hot cocoa and was probed for affirmation that Germany really was the most racially tolerant country in the Western Hemisphere, was a complicated dance of the acknowledgment of race coupled with its denial.

My racial and national identity produced a situation in which a larger discussion on why (white) Germans would not have wanted to stand next to us was rendered impossible because my American Blackness overrode and elided a discussion of race and Germanness. It provided a perfect foil by which an individual could claim righteous superiority for him or herself and on behalf of the nation. The encounter at the Christmas market illustrates my concept of racial haunting: how Blackness haunts the German national imaginary in ways that undermine the use of whiteness to organize conceptions of German national belonging. I also tease out how Black Germanness becomes erased from the national imaginary and Black Americanness added. Racial haunting encourages us to contemplate how race is a socially constructed designation with a deep and lasting impact on Communities of Color worldwide and to think more deeply about the limitations of using a broad brush to paint the outlines of the African diaspora.

Racial haunting uses principles of rhetoric and critical race theory, escaping the intellectually impoverished notion of colorblindness, to examine how race becomes inextricably intertwined with societal inclusion or exclusion. A rhetorical study examines, in part, how people are influenced to think, act or respond. Relatedly, critical race theory examines, in part, how race inflects our everyday encounters which, in turn, impacts our thoughts, actions and responses. Racial haunting provides a window into analyzing how the ideologies and actions of those who came before us shaped and influenced discourses and cultures. In this chapter I ask: What are the environments that make racial hauntings possible? How can we effectively use the concept of racial haunting to productively discuss African diasporic populations in Germany? This essay outlines the theoretical side of the concept of racial haunting and the role of race in German nationality using popular media to elucidate the ways race is included in – or exacted

---

3   I use the word 'salvo' in relation to its definition as a spirited attack or a series of shots from artillery.

from – German popular culture. In particular, I will concentrate on the German film *Leroy* (2007), and to a certain extent its precursor, the short film *Leroy Räumt Auf* [*Leroy Cleans Up*] (2006). Both films are about an Afro-German teen finding his Black identity and are illustrative of a mode of erasure relating to Black German subjectivity in the German nation-state.

Colorblind Binds

There has been a longstanding project of amnesia in relation to the treatment of racialized minority populations in larger continental Europe. We may celebrate the cosmopolitanism of the Dutch without registering claims from Afro-Dutch, Afro-Europeans and others, that the Dutch 'Zwarte Piet', Saint Nicholas' helper with big red lips, round white eyes, and soot Black skin, is racist.[4] We may marvel at the variety of people and ethnicities represented in France without reflecting on France's role as a colonial power throughout Africa, Asia and Oceania and the role racism plays in their lives in the most quotidian of encounters. We may applaud Germany's desire to atone for atrocities committed decades ago while ignoring the pleas of current refugees who live in constant fear of racist attacks and deportation.[5] Uplifting stories about racial conciliation and

---

4   See Mitchell Esajas, 'Beyond Blackface: Emancipation Through the Struggle Against
     Black Pete and Dutch Racism', *Stop Blackface* (12 December 2014) <http://stop-
     Blackface.com/beyond-Blackface-emancipation-through-the-struggle-against-Black-
     pete-and-dutch-racism/> accessed 15 December 2014; Philomena Essed, and Isabel
     Hoving, eds, *Dutch Racism* (New York and Amsterdam: Rodopi B. V., 2014); and
     Philomena Essed, *Understanding Everyday Racism: An Interdisciplinary Theory*
     (Thousand Oaks, CA: Sage Publications, 1991).
5   Jack Ewing, 'German Town to Add Security After Anti-Refugee Protests', *New York
     Times* (23 August 2015) <http://www.nytimes.com/2015/08/24/world/europe/
     germany-heidenau-anti-immigration-protest-police. html?&moduleDetail=section-
     news-2&action=click&contentCollection=Europe&region=Footer&module=
     MoreInSection&version=WhatsNext&contentID=WhatsNext&pgtype=article>

collaboration undergird arguments about the minimalist role race plays in contemporary society, drowning out those who might argue otherwise. Afro-German theorist Fatima El-Tayeb believes that there is an 'invisible' racialization that takes place in Europe leading to 'the peculiar co-existence of, on the one hand, a regime of continent-wide recognized visual markers that construct non-whiteness as non-Europeanness with on the other, a discourse of colorblindness that claims to "see" radicalized difference'.[6] The language of colorblindness has infiltrated our political and social realms to the extent that it has done serious harm to Populations of Color because it eliminates their ability to argue the presence of racial bias, thus allowing racial injustice to persist. As Ian F. Haney Lopez argues, '[c]olorblindness is a form of racial jujitsu. It co-opts the moral force of the civil rights movement, deploying that power to attack racial remediation and simultaneously defend embedded racism. It defends racial injustice directly, for instance, by insisting that massive racial disparities are "not racism"'.[7] Haney Lopez' argument is in relation to the U.S. context, but the thrust of his argument also may be applied to Germany in that Afro-Germans expose the flaw in European discourses of colorblindness. El-Tayeb writes that despite the majority of Afro-Germans growing up in predominantly white neighborhoods, matriculating in the German school system, and holding German citizenship: 'they are the minority generally perceived as being most "un-German" ... the stubborn conviction persists that Black Germans must "really" come from either Africa or the Americas'.[8] Scholars

---

accessed 23 August 2015 and Daniel Trilling, 'Germany Refugees Seek Fair Treatment', *Al Jazeera* (3 April 2014) <http://www.aljazeera.com/indepth/features/2014/04/germany-refugees-seek-fair-treatment-berlin-oranienplatz-20144211253138114.html> accessed 1 May 2014.

6   Fatima El-Tayeb, *European Others: Queering Ethnicity in Postnational Europe* (Minneapolis: University of Minnesota Press, 2011), xxiv.

7   Ian F. Haney Lopez, 'Is the "Post" in Post-Racial the "Blind" in Colorblind?', *Cardozo Law Review* 32/3 (2011): 817.

8   El-Tayeb, *European Others*, 61. See also Charles Mills, *The Racial Contract* (Ithaca, NY: Cornell University Press, 1999); Lisa Lowe, *Immigrant Acts: On Asian-American Cultural Politics* (Durham, NC: Duke University Press, 1996), ix.; Paul C. Taylor, *Race: A Philosophical Introduction* (Cambridge: Polity Press,

have long debated the moral issues involved in using a socially constructed term as a means by which to empirically categorize people.

The realities of racial subjugation are far-reaching.[9] U.S. philosopher Lucius T. Outlaw argues that race is 'socially and historically constructed and changes as a consequence of social struggle', making it 'irreducibly political'.[10] Race is a value-laden concept that organizes our treatment of [O]thers. We naturally group people, places and things according to a culturally influenced rubric. House pet or wild animal, man or child, holy or blasphemous, these are designations that are greatly influenced by the people and traditions around us. Race, however, is an unnatural designation related to an inborn characteristic. As Outlaw notes, '"Race" continues to function as a critical yardstick for the rank-ordering of racial groups ... "race" – sometimes explicitly, quite often implicitly – continues to be a major fulcrum of struggles over the distribution and exercise of power'.[11] Yet a move to extract race from the national conversation allows for the maintenance of white privilege and engenders public ignorance of how race has created an imbalance of economic and social privileges.[12]

2004), esp. Chapter 2; and George Yancy, ed., *What White Looks Like: African-American Philosophers on the Whiteness Question* (New York: Routledge, 2004), esp. Chapter 1.

9   Racing a body is as important as its policing. Images, which put a face with the name, play a part in both naming and policing. Naomi Zack writes that word usage within a community leads to the widespread application and solidification of terms like 'Black', which, even if 'not in accord with scientific study are nonetheless meaningful, due to folk experience'. Naomi Zack, 'Race and Philosophic Meaning', in Bernard Boxill ed., *Race and Racism* (Oxford: Oxford University Press, 2001), 52.

10   Lucius T. Outlaw, 'Toward a Critical Theory of Race', in Bernard Boxill, ed., *Race and Racism* (Oxford: Oxford University Press, 2001), 81.

11   Outlaw, 'Toward a Critical Theory of Race', 69.

12   See Arnold Farr, 'Whiteness Visible: Enlightenment Racism and the Structure of Racialized Consciousness', in George Yancy, ed., *What White Looks Like: African-American Philosophers on the Whiteness Question* (New York: Routledge, 2004), 143–58; and Clevis Headley, 'Delegitimizing the Normativity of "Whiteness": A Critical Africana Philosophical Study of the Metaphoricity of "Whiteness"', in George Yancy, ed., *What White Looks Like: African-American Philosophers on the Whiteness Question* (New York: Routledge, 2004), 87–106, esp. 94–96.

Although this chapter is focused on how racial Others enact racial haunting, it is also the case that those in the racial majority can haunt racial Others. The racial terror enacted against Brown bodies by white people has produced generations of people afraid to live and speak fearlessly.[13] That, however, is a haunting powered by outsized advantages borne of uneven racial, economic and social hierarchies. Racial haunting is a reminder of lingering racial imbalances.

Imagining Racial Haunting

Haunting as a concept has been taken up earnestly within diverse academic fields. In *Ghostly Matters*, sociologist Avery Gordon attends to the psychic experience of haunting within popular culture and literature. Literary and cultural studies scholar Janice Radway argues that Gordon's work on haunting is a meditation on 'the historically constituted divide between the social and the individual, the abstract and the concrete, the analytical and the imaginary'.[14] Remembrance as a conscious act is central to the idea of a ghostly haunting. As Gordon details it, 'If haunting describes how that which appears to be not there is often a seething presence, acting on and meddling with taken-for-granted realities, the ghost is just the sign or the empirical evidence [...] that tells you a haunting is taking place'.[15] It is the ghost, she details, that makes that which has been 'lost' or barely visible known to us. Ghosts are a common trope in literature and popular

---

13   See Dana Cloud, 'The Null Persona: Race and the Rhetoric of Silence in the Uprising of '34', *Rhetoric and Public Affairs* 2/2 (1999), 177–209 and Frederick Harris, 'The Rise of Respectability Politics', *Dissent* 2014, <https://www.dissentmagazine.org/article/the-rise-of-respectability-politics> accessed 26 August 2015.

14   Janice Radway, 'Foreward', in Avery F. Gordon, *Ghostly Matters: Haunting and the Sociological Imagination* (Minneapolis: University of Minnesota Press, 2008), ix.

15   Avery F. Gordon, *Ghostly Matters: Haunting and the Sociological Imagination* (Minneapolis: University of Minnesota Press, 2008), 8.

culture to signify loss or regret. Ghosting indicates that a task has yet
to be completed, or a soul mollified. Locating ghosts as the entities that
haunt narrows our ability to use haunting to discuss contemporary issues
of race and racial belonging. It is important to regard racial haunting as
an embodied practice enacted by the living, not an act belonging to the
province of the dead.

Our first inclination is to treat a haunting as happening only after a
division from the family, the people and the nation; in order to come back
as a spirit, the ties that bind one to the earthly realm must be severed. The
entities that haunt become the nearly forgotten or the never shall be and
are thought of as trying to take something from the living: livelihood, peace
of mind, sanity. Ghosts are often represented as threatening presences. In
Germany, the Boogeyman children's game, 'Wer hat Angst vorm schwarzen
Mann' [Who is afraid of the Black man] specifically references Blackness
as the frightening element. Haunting often refers to the physical absence
of matter that is psychically felt. It is the impact on our mental state that
makes haunting such a powerful act.

Haunting, as a means to discuss Jewish histories in Central Europe,
has also been instructive in thinking about the connection between racialized bodies and their presence in spaces erroneously understood as white
and Christian.[16] That conflation indicates an erasure of difference that was
needed for survival but also promulgated an uneven privilege in favor of a
specific type of whiteness that Othered those who shared a skin color but
not a religious history. Jonathan Schorsch examines how Jews and Germans
reflected on their shared histories, particularly in Jewish literature. Schorsch
likens the eradication of Jews from Germany and Poland to an amputated
limb that haunts the nation with its resurgence. 'When the ghostly limb

16   See Josef Nassy's paintings from his incarceration in Germany during World War II.
     As a Black naturalized American of Jewish descent born in Paramaribo, Suriname
     (Dutch Guiana), Nassy was afforded some privileges as a prisoner in internment
     camps in Upper Bavaria, among them, materials for his artwork. His work illustrates
     the variety of races and ethnicities of the people that German forces imprisoned.
     Monica C. Rothschild-Boros, *In the Shadow of the Tower: The Works of Josef Nassy
     1942–1945* (Irvine, CA: Severin Wunderman Museum, 1989).

voices its own needs [...] as ghosts so often do, the conflict of memory and desires can only result in complications that far transcend the sphere of political medicine', he writes.[17] Schorsch argues that an 'irritation' in the form of guilt, lamentation and even romanticization, 'marks one of the many ways in which the collective consciousness and conscience relates to the former limb amputated from the national body'. I see this 'irritation', however, as an acknowledgment that Jewish people were just as important to the functioning body (politic) as those who sought to terrorize them. Although a critical discussion of the Holocaust is beyond the scope of this chapter, it does engage important questions in relation to my idea of racial haunting. How might we understand attempts to acknowledge a racialized national minority as both embracing and keeping at arm's length that very same population? How does Blackness, in particular, provide an avenue for understanding the hypervisibility of certain *kinds* of Blackness in Germany at the expense of an authentic Black German experience?

Although this chapter uses racial haunting to discuss the Black German experience, its application is not strictly limited to Black populations. One might just as easily use it in relation to the Turkish population in Germany, who arrived in large numbers in the 1960s and 1970s in West Germany as guest workers and stayed in the country, creating enclaves and raising families. Germans who see them as interlopers still discriminate against and treat poorly those of Turkish descent. Racial haunting might also be applied to the Roma and Sinti, who have been persecuted across Europe over centuries and remain subject to vicious attacks; they are commonly derided as thieves and beggars and often forced to live on the outskirts of towns and cities in substandard living conditions.[18] Their presence in

---

17 Jonathan Schorsch, 'Jewish Ghosts in Germany', *Jewish Social Studies* 9/3 (2003), 140.

18 Citing the European Union Agency for Fundamental Human Rights, CNN reports that, 'One in three Roma in Europe are unemployed and 90% live below the poverty line'. See also Emily Dugan, 'Nine Out of 10 Gypsy and Traveller Children Have Suffered Racial Abuse', *The Independent* (22 October 2014) <http://www.independent.co.uk/news/uk/home-news/nine-out-

and around Europe is a daily reminder of the irrational prejudice directed at them. While racial haunting can be used to consider Othered populations, there should be some hesitation before applying it outright to the Holocaust. Largely, racial haunting centers on that which remains to be addressed. The German government has officially addressed the issues related to the Holocaust, although those issues are not solved by any measure. The plethora of memorials and museums, and public art and remembrance installations, such as the *Stolpersteine*, serve as constant reminders of the Third Reich's attempt at racial control and engineering.[19] Yet public conversations on Germany's colonial past have, until late, been relatively quiet or ignored.[20] Referring to Hitler and the Holocaust has become cultural shorthand for racism; keeping racial haunting distinct from the Holocaust is an attempt to parse out the nuances of how racial bias continues unabated, under what circumstances and with which populations.[21] The danger in applying shortcut phrasings is that it gives the impression that an issue is an open and shut case. Separating racial haunting from the Holocaust hopefully will encourage understanding of the concept without lumping it under a larger umbrella term that already is freighted with enormous cultural meaning. Racial haunting is a concept that might be applied broadly across fields and groups. I now turn to film as an entry point to examine how Blackness haunts the German nation.

---

of-10-gypsy-and-traveller-children-have-suffered-racial-abuse-9811861.html> accessed 15 June 2015.

19   For instance, German artist Gunter Demnig began the Stolpersteine Project, installing more than 48,000 stones in 610 places in Austria, Belgium, the Czech Republic, Germany, Hungary, Norway and the Ukraine; the 'stumble stones' seek to draw attention to victims of National Socialism. Gunter Demnig, 'Stolpersteine', <http://www.stolpersteine.eu/en/> accessed 2 June 2018.

20   See Eric Ames, Marcia Klotz and Lora Wildenthal, eds, *Germany's Colonial Pasts* (Lincoln: University of Nebraska Press, 2005) and *White Charity: Schwarzsein und Weißsein auf Spendenplakaten*, Carolin Philipp, and Timo Kiesel, dirs (Berlin, 2011).

21   I do not suggest, however, that anti-Semitism has abated with official redress by the German government, but rather, that there is room for extended conversations in relation to other marginalized groups in Germany.

Soul *Bruder* [Brother] Number 1

In *Leroy* (2007) and the short film *Leroy Räumt Auf* [*Leroy Cleans Up*] (2006), both directed by white German Armin Völcker, German audiences encounter a teenager who represents a 'new' Germany. Young, smart, handsome and funny, Leroy, played by Alain Morel, is half African and half white German. He learns about love from his first girlfriend Eva, and the politics of racialized national belonging from Eva's five skinhead brothers, her hyper-nationalist, pro-Nazi parents and a host of characters that help Leroy make sense of his racial hybridity. Although Leroy knows he is Black, he does not seem to know how to reconcile his Blackness with his Germanness. In the opening scene in *Leroy Räumt Auf*, Eva and her brothers sit patiently while Leroy cleans his room and discusses activist politics. Eva's brothers continue their campaign to recruit him as a Neo-Nazi because they have decided to focus on attacking Russians and Albanians rather than Black people. Leroy's concern, however, is what would happen to his hair should he join them. 'Hanno, Ich kann kein Skinhead werden. Da müsste ich mir alle Haare abrasieren' [I can't become a skinhead because I'd have to shave off all of my hair]. They counter with the argument that Leroy is as German as any one of them, and they would even allow him to keep his afro. 'Niggers are cool', says one. The scene ends with the eldest brother Hanno calling Leroy a *Geile Negersau* [horny nigger] threatening to kill him if he breaks up with Eva and declaring it all a joke to an alarmed Leroy.[22] Leroy is set up as both a welcomed insider and an unwelcomed interloper. Nowhere are the tensions of Leroy's identity more evident than in his bedroom. The walls are decorated in ephemera from the 1960s U.S. Civil Rights Movement; on the shelves are knickknacks that link him to a German and a general Black heritage. In the opening scenes of *Leroy Räumt Auf*, both Germanness and Blackness are represented using well-worn tropes: a bust of Goethe representing Germany's wealth of pre-eminent philosophers; a

---

22   *Leroy Räumt Auf*, Armin Völckers, dir. (Berlin: Stormfilm Berlin & Dreamer Joint
Venture Filmproduktion 2006), <https://www.youtube.com/watch?v=ymxB7rcPATc>,
2:00–3:45 minutes.

model Volkswagen car representing Germany's stellar engineering history and posters of Black American activists. The objects act as cultural touchstones directing the audience to recognize the space as distinctly German with a worldly outlook. It is not until the camera rests on Leroy's outsized afro labeled with his name that audiences are presented (surprised) with his Blackness. The only nod to his African roots is a book titled *Africa*. In Leroy's room, it is apparent that essentialized notions about high culture constitute Germanness while Blackness is encapsulated in historical appeals for equality and civil rights in an explicit *U.S.* context. In the opening sequence of *Leroy*, Black Germanness is erased from both of these racialized, nationalized conceptions of identity which ultimately instructs audiences to regard Leroy as a liminal subject, who is neither here nor there. With the concept of racial haunting, the move toward division becomes the point at which Brown bodies can be distanced from the nation.

In nations that are organized and defined by the possession of whiteness, division preserves the assumption of a national racial identity that rests on maintaining its historical and racial configurations. In this way, racial haunting first marks the importance of race in regard to the relationship between citizens in a state, and second, it allows the presence of 'contact', or more precisely, 'making a contact that changes you and refashions the social relations in which you are located'.[23] The moment of seeing difference and attempting to remove it enacts racial haunting. Part of that removal rests on a shared cultural conception and memory of what a people are *supposed* to be, which may or may not reflect reality.

Leroy's language, heritage and omnipresent white German mother anchor him to a German identity, even though his African father lives with him. Viewers are to understand Leroy as not specifically African. The narrowness in how Germanness is delineated – through classical music, philosophy or neo-Nazism – and the positioning of authentic Blackness as American preclude an honest rendering of Germanness as multicultural and racially diverse. In refusing to give Leroy an American or specifically African genealogy, Völcker denies Leroy an important part of his history.

---

23   Gordon, *Ghostly Matters*, 22.

Leroy's inability to fit well into any space he occupies signifies his 'amputation' from his communities and the larger German populace.

Blackening Europe

The history of Blackness in Europe is one defined by misconception and bigotry. Denigrating the racialized Other became the means by which white Europeans, Germans included, created a positive sense of self as well as the boundaries of citizenship. Blackness, then, began not with a physical encounter, but an imagined understanding of difference and inferiority that shaped white German understandings of race.[24] As philosopher George Yancy asserts, 'the Black body's subjectivity, its lived reality, is reduced to instantiations of the white imaginary [...] These instantiations are embedded within and evolve out of the complex social and historical interstices of whites' efforts at self-construction through complex acts of erasure vis-à-vis Black people'.[25] German Studies scholar Beverly Harris-Schenz argues that before Germans sent their first colonizing forces to Africa, white Germans learned about the continent through the books and missives from other European world powers; that written material had a formative effect on the German popular imagination in regard to

---

24   For example, Jan Pieterse writes, '[t]he explorers created the image of the Dark Continent, the churches created the images of the fallen heathen and the ignoble savage, stereotypes which colonialism would build on and elaborate'. See Jan Nederveen Pieterse, *White on Black: Images of Africa and Blacks in Western Popular Culture* (New Haven, CT: Yale University Press, 1992), 75. See also Michelle M. Wright's assertion that '[t]his is the fundamental contradiction in Hegel's *Philosophie der Geschichte:* determining the Negro to be outside the dialectic, outside history itself, and simultaneously within that dialectic as the antithesis of the European subject'. Michelle M. Wright, *Becoming Black: Creating Identity in The African Diaspora* (Durham, NC: Duke University Press, 2004), 39.

25   George Yancy, 'Whiteness and the Return of the Black Body', *Journal of Speculative Philosophy* 19/4 (2005), 216.

the perception of African people.[26] Depictions presenting the colonized as 'natural' laborers and the colonizers as 'natural' leaders created a visual environment that made Africans appear fit to be ruled over and subjugated. Historian Joachim Zeller notes that dehumanizing the African Other 'formed the necessary precondition for consolidating and safeguarding the superior European identity'.[27] The perception of the African as from outside of Western civilization and culture provided the opportunity to compare oneself favorably against a decidedly inferior subject. Prejudiced public opinion laid the foundation for racial haunting beginning with the generation of Afro-Germans who were conceived during and after World War I.[28] The increase in their visibility contributed to the hysteria about the impact they had on white German identity. Black Germans 'had been defined through a racialized difference that was conceived of in exclusively negative terms, in itself enough to justify their exclusion from the collective of Germans ...', contends El-Tayeb.[29] During World War II, when Black American forces began to experience greater mobility and freedom, traveling overseas as part of the war effort, many Germans found that the image of Blackness as savage did not match the presence of Black American soldiers in front of them.

26   Beverly Harris-Schenz, *Black Images in Eighteenth-Century Literature* (Stuttgart: Heinz, 1981), 13.

27   Joachim Zeller, 'Harmless "*Kolonialbiedermeier*"?: Colonial and Exotic Trading Cards', in Volker Langbehn ed., *German Colonialism, Visual Culture, and Modern Memory* (New York: Routledge, 2010), 71–86.

28   This is not to say that Black mobility before the war was non-existent or confined strictly to Germany. Several scholars have discussed how Black people migrated to and moved around Europe prior to World War I. See Robbie Atiken and Eve Rosenhaft, *Black Germany: The Making and Unmaking of a Diaspora Community* (Cambridge: Cambridge University Press, 2013). David Ciarlo, *Advertising Empire: Race and Visual Culture in Imperial Germany* (Cambridge, MA: Harvard University Press, 2011); Darryl Glenn Nettles, *African American Concert Singers Before 1950* (Jefferson, NC: McFarland & Co, 2003) and Kira Thurman, 'Singing the Civilizing Mission in the Land of Bach, Beethoven, and Brahms: The Fisk Jubilee Singers in Nineteenth-Century Germany', *Journal of World History* 27/3 (2016), 443–71.

29   El-Tayeb, *European Others*, 68.

Romantic relationships between white German women and Black American GIs stationed in Germany during and after World War II forced white Germans to come to terms with their wartime loss, the German women who loved Black men and the mixed-raced children born of those relationships. As historian Heide Fehrenbach writes, '[r]elations between Black G.I.s and white German women were condemned not because they were perceived as coercive – as in the case of 'Moroccan' or Soviet troops [who occupied Germany during World War I] – but because women willfully embraced them for material advantage, sexual pleasure, and romance' … Black G.I.s posed an imminent threat to the national order that 'linked racialized American masculinity with unrestrained native female sexuality, criminality, and materialism'.[30] The children of those relationships, unflatteringly called *Besatzungskinder* [Occupation Babies/Children] or *Mischlingskinder* [Mixed-Breed Children], were unable to escape what Fehrenbach has deemed 'a socially ascribed identity of immutable difference'.[31] Those Afro-German children symbolically represented the purported violation of white German women as well as the German nation by foreign enemies. 'While the actual demographic presence of Black occupation children in West Germany was miniscule, the hyperbolic response to the children indicates the disproportionate symbolic significance accorded them', writes Fehrenbach.[32] Afro-German children were a living reminder of the porousness of German borders, real and imagined, and the fragility of Germans' self-conception as ethnically and homogenously white.

Those children, like the generation of Afro-German children conceived during World War I, enacted racial haunting as they represented the desecration of the German race and, by extension, the nation. Labeling Afro-Germans differently brings even more attention to how racial haunting can undermine a national identity reliant upon racial exclusion. Haunting is an indication of the tension that exists between groups. It is a reminder that something remains unresolved or unaddressed. Rather than create avenues to enfold Black Germans in the larger German community, white

30   Heide Fehrenbach, *Race after Hitler: Black Occupation Children in Postwar Germany and America* (Princeton, NJ: Princeton University Press, 2005), 65.
31   Fehrenbach, *Race after Hitler*, 74.

Germans attempted to exacerbate the terms of their difference. Labeling Afro-German children as 'Mixed-Breeds' or 'Occupation Babies' disenfranchised them from the nation, denying their claims to Germanness and national belonging. Much like the efforts encouraging Black Americans to adopt Afro-German children, the official response toward German Blackness was to erase the possibility of its normalization in German society.

Naming Rights

One cannot discount the power language plays in categorizing racial difference.[32] The German concept of *Volk*, for instance, remains an explicit organizing principle that implicitly excludes non-white Germans. *Volk* is exemplary as a colorblind term; it does not on the surface refer specifically to racial exclusion. As Alexander Weheliye argues, 'a distinction should be made between *das* Volk, which signifies the people as an undifferentiated mass of humans, including the oppressed, and *ein* Volk as a specific and supposedly homogeneous ethnic, cultural and/or linguistic group'.[33] A change in article from *das* (the) to *ein* (one) upends the entire understanding of who belongs to the nation. It is an important slippage to note, for as white Germans claim unity, there is a visual interpretation of Blackness that indicates fundamental difference. White Germans' constant questioning of Afro-Germans' origin and the consistent conflation of Afro-German identity with foreignness demonstrates a conscious attempt to render Afro-Germans invisible. As philosopher Charles Mills writes, '[f]or Blacks, the body thus necessarily becomes central in a way it does not for whites, since this is the visible marker of Black invisibility'.[34] There is both a case of

32   See Frantz Fanon, *Black Skin, White Masks* (New York: Grove Press, 1967), esp. Chapter 1.

33   Weheliye, 'My Volk to Come', 165.

34   Charles Mills, *Blackness Visible: Essays on Philosophy and Race* (Ithaca, NY: Cornell University Press, 1998), 16.

displacement and replacement of the Afro-German body, owing, in part, to the overrepresentation of U.S. Blackness in German public culture. That overrepresentation, however, often relies on preconceived or well-worn notions about what 'authenticity' looks like or how it acts.

In both *Leroy* films, Black identity comes not from the source of Blackness but the assumed source of 'Black cool.'[35] American Blackness becomes that which displaces and haunts Leroy's Black Germanness. The unresolved issues of Afro-Germans being understood as 'imitative' of the Black American experience, and 'com[ing] into existence only when it is recognized and created by a diaspora whose consciousness is firmly situated in African-American experiences', engenders the space for U.S. Blackness to haunt Afro-Germanness.[36] When Leroy stumbles into Scratch Records, with its poster of Malcolm X next to the text, 'Black Power'! in the window, he asks Rudy the Black shopkeeper, 'Ist Black Power ein Plattentitel'? [Is Black Power a record title]. Rudy, taking pity on the boy, explains the concept of Black Power and lists the names of famous funk and soul musical titles. Leroy, 'Das ist Soul' [That is Soul], he stresses, bringing from behind the counter his own copy of the film *Shaft* starring Richard Roundtree, which he lends to Leroy. A regular customer joins the conversation, telling Leroy, '[d]u siehst intelligent aus. Aber dir fehlt Bewusstsein. Schwarzes Bewusstsein' [You look intelligent. But you lack consciousness. Black consciousness]. The customer, who also is Black, implores Leroy to watch *Blacula* (1972) for a lesson in Black/white relations.[37] That Leroy's mentors implore him to find Black consciousness through an exported cultural artifact from the United States instead of through a specifically Black German context is another way that Völckers erases Afro-German subjectivity. *Shaft* (1971), like *Blacula*, also was part of the Blaxploitation film movement in U.S. history, and many regarded it as empowering for Black movie-going audiences accustomed to seeing Black characters in subservient or menial

35   See Rebecca Walker, *Black Cool: One Thousand Streams of Blackness* (Berkeley, CA: Softskull Press, 2012).

36   El-Tayeb, *European Others*, 64.

37   *Leroy*, Armin Völckers, dir. (Berlin: Stormfilm Berlin & Dreamer Joint Venture Filmproduktion 2007), 25:40–26:41 minutes.

roles in films. That both Afro-German men in the record shop have their individual racial awakenings underneath the umbrella of American race relations signifies their weak grasp of their own racial consciousness; it creates a moment for audience members to laugh at – not with – Rudy and his customer as they push Leroy toward a Black political consciousness that has nothing to do with their shared German nationality. The placement of U.S. Blackness at the top of a hierarchy of authentic soul opens up a space by which other representations of Blackness become lesser than and not equal to. It reflects Michelle M. Wright's assertion of the existence of, 'an unspoken level of discourse that structures black Diasporic identities into a hierarchy from most authentic to least authentic'.[38] Unlike Afro-German scholar/activists who have been inspired by U.S. scholar/activists, Leroy's mentors do not explain how his Black consciousness should be translated into German(y) and never challenge the hierarchy, ultimately positioning Afro-German subjectivity as an afterthought. Yet when the men take Leroy under their wings, calling him 'brother', and offering him advice, that moment of recognition proves to be a pivotal moment for Leroy. He suddenly begins to notice all the Black people – and the Black couples – in Berlin. He sees an ad featuring Martin Luther King Jr. and another for 'Black arts'. He notices all the places where Black people, and, by extension he, fit in – but only within a U.S.-centric milieu.[39] Now that Leroy registers the everyday presence of Blackness across Berlin, he begins to treat Blackness as a commodity that can be bought. He illustrates mixed race studies scholar Michelle Elam's discussion on Black performative modes that 'recognize preexisting racial codes and expectations for behavior but do not necessarily require their re-inscription'.[40] As a German teenager new to engaging his racial, political and sexual identity, the soulful, cool Blackness that Leroy

---

38   Michelle M. Wright, 'Can I Call You Black? The Limits of Authentic Heteronormativity in African Diasporic Discourse', *African and Black Diaspora: An International Journal* 6/1 (2013), 5.

39   *Leroy*, Armin Völckers, dir. (Berlin: Stormfilm Berlin & Dreamer Joint Venture Filmproduktion 2007), 25:30–28:30 minutes.

40   Michelle Elam, *The Souls of Mixed Folk: Race, Politics, and Aesthetics in the New Millennium* (Stanford, CA: Stanford University Press, 2011), 160.

covets is out of his reach. But he performs a Blackness-within-reach in his clothing, speech and even his hair that allow him to fake it until he makes it. Leroy begins wearing t-shirts advertising long-past Black American community events and refers more often to Black Power. Leroy, in short, observes within Black *America*, a means for him to merge his dual African and German identities.

In both *Leroy* films, American Blackness becomes the 'insistent, underlying subtext, a nagging assumption or question that cannot be ignored'.[41] In other words, U.S. Blackness is presented as the gold standard of Blackness, of living, of *soul*. That supposition, however, produces what Tina Campt defines as diasporic asymmetries:

> The frequent citation of Black America within scholarly discourse on the African Diaspora as an almost privileged site or referent in the trajectory of diasporic cultural, community, and identity formation, and the increasing use of the African-American context in articulating a politics of diasporic relation, may be read as a discourse that refers not so much to a relation of equity than of hegemony.[42]

The diasporic asymmetry in *Leroy* is created, in part, by erasing the emotional value that Africa would have for Leroy despite his easy access to a source of cultural and historical knowledge: his father. By erasing Leroy's last name, Völckers makes it easier for Leroy to adopt U.S. Blackness as part of his political identity and for Germans to extract – to cut – him from the conception of a 'real' German. His first name, which is commonly associated with Black Americans, also distances Leroy from his Germanness. Therefore, Leroy becomes a 'green screen' onto which audiences can project their fantasies and a space for a racialized imagination.[43] Leroy is consistently presented as more deeply connected to his German rather than his

41 Tina Campt, *Other Germans: Black Germans and the Politics of Race, Gender, and Memory in the Third Reich* (Ann Arbor: University of Michigan Press, 2004), 178.
42 Campt, *Other Germans*, 178.
43 Melissa Harris-Perry discusses a 'green screen identity' in relation to U.S. President Barack Obama and his ability to appeal to voters of various races and ethnicities. Melissa Harris-Perry, *Sister Citizen: Shame, Stereotypes, and Black Women in America* (New Haven, CT: Yale University Press, 2011), 272.

Black roots. Giving him an African last name – or a hyphenated German and African name – would then open the door for that African name to be included in the lexicon of 'German' names.

Without a last name, audiences are free to write an alternate history, to avoid the cognitive reality of Leroy's authentic Germanness. What is more, Leroy's father, who is a college-educated inventor and fluent in German, is positioned as a-historical, without family or life before his emigration and marriage, widening the distance between Leroy and Africa. Leroy's mother's background also is erased but her representation as a government worker distances her from the migrant background Leroy's father so clearly occupies. Leroy's parentage further enacts racial haunting as both of his parents represent problematic entities in German national history: the white German woman without 'racial pride' because of her marriage to a foreigner and the African immigrant interloper. Leroy's family stands in contrast to Eva's family, whose naming, if not coded as specifically representing Nazism such as in their surname 'Braun', nod to a stereotypical understanding of white Germanness.[44] For example, their dog's name is Goebbels, and the brothers are called Hanno, Horst and Siegfried. If Leroy were half American, then his discovering of U.S. political actors would be less revelatory because an American background would give him a pre-existing historical narrative that assumed that Leroy knew that Black Power was a political movement, not a record.

In one telling scene in *Leroy*, Leroy's identity is presented as a zero-sum game in which he is either African or German but not both. Leroy's mother pressures him to break up with Eva because of her family's politics. Leroy refuses to speak further with her about his problems because she is white. 'Ich bin deine Mutter, Freundchen' [I am your mother, my little friend!], she implores. 'Ich bin Afrikaner' [I am an African!], Leroy exclaims. His father steps in, demanding Leroy apologize to her. Leroy is sent to his room where he destroys everything in it, including throwing his prized bust of Goethe out of the window. Just before he throws his cello out of the window, his father stops him, asking 'Glaubst du, in Afrika, schmeißen sie

---

44   Eva Braun was also the name of Adolf Hitler's longtime partner.

den ganzen Tag Goethe-Köpfe und Cellos auf die Strasse' [Do you believe that in Africa they throw busts of Goethe and cellos on the streets all day]? His words are an explicit challenge to Leroy's knowledge of African culture and people and force Leroy to examine his actions. Throughout this scene, Leroy, the African, who has spent the better part of the movie asserting his Germanness and identifying with a Black American political movement, is wearing a shirt that advertises a Harlem, New York, community event. Yet again, Black Americanness haunts Black Germanness as Black Germanness haunts white Germanness.

Leroy presents the problems and possibilities in adopting an identity based on clichés and narratives of racial struggle made rosy with the passage of time. On the one hand, Leroy is free to identify with the positive aspects of Black America without having had to endure systematic terror and oppression at the hands of white Americans. His identity is based on an idea about solidarity without any of the hard work done to attain it. Leroy's inability to organically draw on an *Ami* (American) coolness as part of his identity is what makes his adoption of U.S. Blackness that much more poignant and illustrates the concept of a stratified racial haunting. Despite Leroy's assertion that he is an African, he never claims the country of his father, thus permitting him to take ownership of a Black diasporic identity that encompasses Americanness. At times, U.S. Blackness can structure, if not dictate, the articulations of Blackness in intercultural interactions far from U.S. shores; some populations in the African Diaspora 'accrue', Campt opines, 'forms [of] cultural capital some Black communities, particularly the African-American community, have come to command'.[45] In *Leroy*, Leroy's presence engages a racial haunting with Afro-Germans and Germany, but the asymmetrical value given to U.S. Blackness enacts racial haunting within the diasporic community at the same time. As a half-African, Leroy lacks the rhetorical power he desires only up until he begins to voice a racial consciousness expressed first by Americans. To find his place in society, Leroy, the Black German, must first become Black American, thus creating the impossibility of his Black German identity. It also erases the

45   Campt, *Other Germans*, 178.

opportunity for him to engage with the Black German political movement. Black German political activism and cultural practices are sublimated and rendered inadequate in the shadow of American Blackness. It is also the case that Blackness, and U.S. Blackness specifically, becomes represented as something that is collected and consumed, not experienced.

Erasing Identities

The erasure of differences in *Leroy* allows for an understanding of Black political rhetoric not as culturally specific, but racially applicable. Blackness becomes something visible onto which we can map pre-existing ideas without much cognitive dissonance. As rhetorician Nicole Fleetwood remarks in her discussion of de-contextualized images, 'Black iconicity serves as a site for Black audiences and the nation to gather around the seeing of Blackness. However, in the focus on the singularity of the image, the complexity of Black lived experience and discourses of race are effaced'.[46] In *Leroy*, non-Black audiences and in this case, non-Black and/or non-U.S. audiences are encouraged to create a shared understanding of the universality of Blackness based on the same decontextualized, essentialized images. 'The icon is a fixed image so immersed in rehearsed narratives that it replaces the need for narrative unfolding', Fleetwood writes.[47] Leroy's de-regionalized use of icons of the U.S. Black political struggle – Malcolm X, Martin Luther King Jr., *Shaft* and even his own afro – mute the specificity of those icons, erasing the uniqueness of both the Afro-German and Black American experiences.

The danger is that these iconic decontextualizations can have an impact on the whole of the African Diaspora. *Leroy* maps culturally specific experiences of one racialized group onto another with a completely different racial and political history. It falsely centers the United States in a global

---

46   Nicole R. Fleetwood, *Troubling Vision: Performance, Visuality, and Blackness* (Chicago, IL: University of Chicago Press, 2011), 10.
47   Fleetwood, *Troubling Vision*, 46

discussion that threatens to overwhelm, if not render silent, injustices aimed at non-U.S. Black diasporic populations in non-U.S. contexts. Völckers' prominent placement of U.S. Blackness in front of the camera suggests that it is possible to use culturally and temporally specific rhetorical arguments and apply them wholesale to foreign populations. It leads to an assumption that the Black populations in the United States and Germany, especially, are one-dimensional communities without separate racial histories and experiences. It begs the question as to whether that asymmetrical focus on U.S. Blackness would make it more difficult for smaller, less visible, or less politically active Black communities in other countries to gain traction in their own fights for political, social and civil visibility.

The tension of being German but not 'looking' German is a constant theme in *Leroy*. Leroy's Germanness, even as it is exemplified by his deep knowledge of German history, his love of classical music and his extensive vocabulary, is rejected as being indicative of a German nationality and upbringing. Even as he has to explain key aspects of German culture to others around him, his Germanness is read as inauthentic. His later adoption of U.S. culture allows him to carve a space of belonging for himself within Germany, but only by placing himself outside of the nation, albeit on his own terms. Leroy's ambiguity is meant for viewers to simply assume that his Blackness is of the sort we have always known. Blackness is vaguely related to the United States and identified by clothing and hairstyles that are assumed to 'belong' to an authentic Black American identity. Leroy's search for belonging outside of his immediate reference groups is not novel. As El-Tayeb has discovered in her examination of diasporic and urban spaces, there is a history of

> minority youths – misfits within the strict identity ascriptions characterizing contemporary Europe, not meeting the criteria of 'authentic Europeanness' nor being authentic migrants since they never in fact migrated – circumvent the complicated question of national belonging by producing a localized, multicentered, horizontal community, in which a strong identification with cities or neighborhoods, perceived as spaces both created by and transcending national and ethnic limits, combines with a larger diasporic perspective.[48]

48 El-Tayeb, *European Others*, xxxvii.

For many people, finding one's way in the world means looking beyond the obvious to create welcoming spaces for marginalized communities. What is problematic in *Leroy*, however, is that there is an assumption that his Blackness grants him natural *carte blanche* to adopt Black Americanness. Blackness is presented as something to cloak oneself in at will, leaving it to be identified through hairstyles, clothing choices and one-dimensional catchphrases. Furthermore, in not engaging with any Black Germans his age, Afro-German identity is never explored and never represented as an equally valid identity for Leroy to adopt. Both *Leroy* films then, maintain the division between Germanness and Blackness that makes racial haunting possible because the division between races is never fully addressed or remedied.

Conclusion

Afro-Germans are living proof that Blackness and Germanness are one in the same and that Germanness does not rest solely in the province of whiteness. That is to say, the racial delineations of the German nation are no longer so clearly tied to one racial grouping and in fact never have been, despite attempts to imagine the nation as racially homogenous. Yet the desire to maintain the illusion of national German whiteness in a country with its fair share of people of African descent has engendered a situation whereby a stereotypical U.S. Blackness is used to epitomize the definition of *authentic* Blackness. That authenticity, however, is reliant upon a hyper-stylized, often *theatrical* Blackness. This easily separates Blackness from respectable and respected whiteness; representations of *theatrical* Blackness reflect existing racial stereotypes about Blackness producing a popular understanding of Blackness that is always already *un*German. Afro-German journalist and activist Noah Sow observes that in contemporary German society Blackness still is understood as a threat to the German nation. She argues:

> Rassismus ist bei uns schon so sehr Normalität, dass wir ihn in unseren alltäglichen Handlungen und Überzeugungen noch nicht einmal mehr bemerken: Wir bauen meterhohe Zäune um die Festung Europa ... Sind sie aber Schwarz oder Afrikaner, sind

Leute mit genau dem gleichen Verhalten für uns plötzlich 'Wirtschaftsflüchtlinge' und 'naiv' und werden nicht als Helden oder mutig, sondern als Bedrohung, empfunden, und dementsprechend behandelt.

[Racism is, for us, so very normal, that we in our everyday actions and beliefs don't even notice it; we build meter-high fences around the 'Fortress Europe' [...] [but] if they are Black or African, [and] act like us, they are suddenly considered economic refugees and naïve, not heroes or brave and will be treated accordingly, as a perceived threat].[49]

My larger point is not to posit that Afro-Germans are helpless to fend off misapprehensions about Black Germanness. Rather, it is to illustrate how there are varying layers of race and representation that comingle and interact simultaneously. 'Holistic representations' of Blackness, in Wright's conception, can often serve to narrow how Black people are regarded. 'As certain bodies crowd the foreground of our representations, we begin to assume and look for only similar bodies, producing an inaccurate history of which peoples, groups, movements or individuals were part of which events, much less of the (interpretive) effect of those moments in their lives', she argues.[50] The overrepresentation of Blackness from outside of Germany, coupled with the erroneous assumption about the impossibilities of Black Germanness, create a national situation in which Blacks must always fight for their right to be both German and Black. As Berlin-based, African-Portuguese scholar Grada Kilomba argues:

The constant questioning about where [one] comes from is not only an exercise of curiosity or interest, but also an exercise in confirming dominant fantasies around 'race' and territoriality [...] Within contemporary racisms there is no place for 'difference.' Those who are 'different' remain perpetually incompatible with the nation; they can never actually belong, they are irreconcilably *Ausländer* [foreigner].[51]

---

49   Noah Sow, *Deutschland Schwarz Weiss* (Munich: Goldmann, 2009), 44.
50   Michelle M. Wright, *Physics of Blackness: Beyond the Middle Passage Epistemology* (Minneapolis: University of Minnesota Press, 2015), 13.
51   Grada Kilomba, *Plantation Memories: Episodes of Everyday Racism* (Münster: Unrast, 2008), 65.

While one might argue that the opening scenes of *Leroy* and *Leroy Räumt Auf* normalize his Blackness, the entirety of the rest of the films set about making his Blackness strange, such as when he dresses as a Neo-Nazi and becomes the manager for Eva's brothers' Nazi boy band, or when his best friend makes Leroy the butt of a joke about Black slaves. What the *Leroy* films illustrate is how identity can be considered fluid and performative. At the same time, they also reify misperceptions that Blackness is generalizable and easily adopted, and that Germanness is distinct in its singularity – and whiteness. Postcolonial theorist Frantz Fanon posits, '[t]here is a quest for the Negro, the Negro is in demand, one cannot get along without him, he is needed, but only if he is made palatable in a certain way'.[52] And so it is that palatable Blackness – Blackness that can be shaped and conformed into our fantasies – is sought. Yet racial haunting is evidence that an easily digestible Blackness – one that replicates stereotypes and misconceptions – is not available. It is evidence that racial disparity and diasporic imbalances must be addressed. Black Germans have not given up their claim to the nation and, in doing, so they refuse to become palatable.

Returning to the Christmas market in Alt-Tegel, when the couple approached my friend and me, the explicit statement that our perceived foreignness would repel others was an implicit rejection of our ability to authentically partake in a distinctly (white) *German* tradition. The communal nature of the drinks table at a Christmas market is meant to encourage people to talk to their neighbors. We might have been residential neighbors, but there was an unspoken assumption that we were not connected by heritage because our heritage was irrepressibly *Black*. The concrete presence of a physical Black body overrode the abstract idea of political, social and racial equality; that is, the physical presence of our Blackness produced a moment of dissonance, a clashing of the ideal versus reality that revealed itself in the external moment of contact. The idea of a national kinship was obliterated when the fact of our Blackness came to the fore. Historian and political scientist Benedict Anderson has argued that, 'racism dreams of eternal contaminations [...] Niggers are [...] forever niggers; Jews [...] forever

52   Fanon, *Black Skin, White Masks*, 176.

Jews no matter what passports they carry or what languages they speak and read (Thus, for the Nazi, the *Jewish* German was always an imposter)'.[53] In other words, the act of racialization has been strengthened with the privileging of visual markers as proof of national belonging, but there must be an idea of what is *not* included, which ultimately solidifies categories of difference. If Blackness is from somewhere else, no one needs to make an effort to include it. The elaborate game of make believe that societies with histories of oppression and racial injustice play can be continued insofar as the game pieces always remain foreign.

To put aside the false premise that a society and a people can be 'over' racism would be a tacit acknowledgment that there are problems yet to be addressed, lessons that have yet to be learned and privileges that must be re-allocated. It would threaten the national narratives of racial inclusion that for so long have allowed those in power to avoid addressing the claims of the racially excluded. The resistance to seeing Black people as part of the body politic is a refusal to see them as equally deserving of the spoils of whiteness.[54] The tactics employed to exclude other racialized Others such as passport restrictions, limits on immigration, cripplingly slow bureaucracy, or crowds of mythic proportions at regional foreigner registration offices do not apply to Afro-Germans, whose only home might be Germany.[55] Racial haunting is not about an emphasis on the absence of something but, rather, the abundance of an element that reminds us of our own fragility

---

53 Benedict Anderson, *Imagined Communities: Reflections on the Origin and Spread of Nationalism* (London: Verso, 1983), 149.

54 For instance, in May 2015, there was intense debate after members of the Pegida anti-Islamic group criticized the Ferrero group, makers of 'Kinder Schokolade', for using the childhood photos of minority German national soccer team members on their packaging. Although white players' images were used, many of the players represented the racial and ethnic diversity of Germany, including Jerome Boateng, whose father is a Ghanaian immigrant. Michael Nienaber, 'Chocolate Bar Wrappers Ignite German Row Over Racism', *Reuters*, 25 May 2016 <http://uk.reuters.com/article/uk-soccer-euro-germany-chocolate-idUKKCN0YG25D> accessed 25 May 2016.

55 This would also apply to a larger number of Germans of Color such as Germans of Turkish and East Asian descent, among others.

and our fallibility. It is not simply Brown bodies in white spaces that prove problematic, but rather *free* Brown bodies that are free to speak, to act and to fight back, which prove so dangerous.

Bibliography

Ames, Eric, Marcia Klotz and Lora Wildenthal, eds, *Germany's Colonial Pasts* (Lincoln: University of Nebraska Press, 2005).

Anderson, Benedict, *Imagined Communities: Reflections on the Origin and Spread of Nationalism* (London: Verso, 1983).

Atiken, Robbie, and Eve Rosenhaft, *Black Germany: The Making and Unmaking of a Diaspora Community* (Cambridge: Cambridge University Press, 2013).

Campt, Tina, *Other Germans: Black Germans and the Politics of Race, Gender, and Memory in the Third Reich* (Ann Arbor: University of Michigan Press, 2004).

Ciarlo, David, *Advertising Empire: Race and Visual Culture in Imperial Germany* (Cambridge, MA: Harvard University Press, 2011).

Cloud, Dana, 'The Null Persona: Race and the Rhetoric of Silence in the Uprising of '34', *Rhetoric and Public Affairs* 2/2 (1999), 177–209.

Demnig, Gunter, 'Stolpersteine', <http://www.stolpersteine.eu/en/> accessed 2 June 2018.

Dugan, Emily, 'Nine Out of 10 Gypsy and Traveller Children Have Suffered Racial Abuse', *The Independent* (22 October 2014) <http://www.independent.co.uk/news/uk/home-news/nine-out-of-10-gypsy-and-traveller-children-have-suffered-racial-abuse-9811861.html> accessed 15 June 2015.

Elam, Michelle, *The Souls of Mixed Folk: Race, Politics, and Aesthetics in the New Millennium* (Stanford, CA: Stanford University Press, 2011).

El-Tayeb, Fatima, *European Others: Queering Ethnicity in Postnational Europe* (Minneapolis: University of Minnesota Press, 2011).

Esajas, Mitchell, 'Beyond Blackface: Emancipation Through the Struggle Against Black Pete and Dutch Racism', *Stop Blackface* (12 December 2014) <http://stop-Blackface.com/beyond-Blackface-emancipation-through-the-struggle-against-Black-pete-and-dutch-racism/> accessed 15 December 2014.

Essed, Philomena, and Isabel Hoving, eds, *Dutch Racism* (New York and Amsterdam: Rodopi B. V., 2014).

Essed, Philomena, *Understanding Everyday Racism: An Interdisciplinary Theory* (Thousand Oaks, CA: Sage Publications, 1991).

Ewing, Jack, 'German Town to Add Security After Anti-Refugee Protests', *New York Times* (23 August 2015) <http://www.nytimes.com/2015/08/24/world/europe/germany-heidenau-anti-immigration-protest-police.html?&moduleDetail=section-news-2&action=click&contentCollection=Europe&region=Footer&module=MoreInSection&version=WhatsNext&contentID=WhatsNext&pgtype=article> accessed 23 August 2015.

Fanon, Frantz, *Black Skin, White Masks* (New York: Grove Press, 1967).

Farr, Arnold, 'Whiteness Visible: Enlightenment Racism and the Structure of Racialized Consciousness', in George Yancy, ed., *What White Looks Like: African-American Philosophers on the Whiteness Question* (New York: Routledge, 2004), 143–58.

Fehrenbach, Heide, *Race after Hitler: Black Occupation Children in Postwar Germany and America* (Princeton, NJ: Princeton University Press, 2005).

Fleetwood, Nicole R., *Troubling Vision: Performance, Visuality, and Blackness* (Chicago: University of Chicago Press, 2011).

Gordon, Avery F., *Ghostly Matters: Haunting and the Sociological Imagination* (Minneapolis: University of Minnesota Press, 2008).

Haney Lopez, Ian F., 'Is the "Post" in Post-Racial the "Blind" in Colorblind?', *Cardozo Law Review* 32/3 (2011), 807–31.

Harris, Frederick, 'The Rise of Respectability Politics', *Dissent* 2014, <https://www.dissentmagazine.org/article/the-rise-of-respectability-politics> accessed 26 August, 2015.

Harris-Perry, Melissa, *Sister Citizen: Shame, Stereotypes, and Black Women in America* (New Haven, CT: Yale University Press, 2011).

Harris-Schenz, Beverly, *Black Images in Eighteenth-Century Literature* (Stuttgart: Heinz, 1981).

Headley, Clevis, 'Deligitimizing the Normativity of "Whiteness": A Critical Africana Philosophical Study of the Metaphoricity of "Whiteness"', in George Yancy, ed., *What White Looks Like: African-American Philosophers on the Whiteness Question* (New York: Routledge, 2004), 87–106.

Kilomba, Grada, *Plantation Memories: Episodes of Everyday Racism* (Münster: Unrast, 2008).

Lowe, Lisa, *Immigrant Acts: On Asian-American Cultural Politics* (Durham, NC: Duke University Press, 1996).

Mills, Charles, *Blackness Visible: Essays on Philosophy and Race* (Ithaca, NY: Cornell University Press, 1998).

——, *The Racial Contract* (Ithaca, NY: Cornell University Press, 1999).

Nettles, Darryl Glenn, *African American Concert Singers Before 1950* (Jefferson, NC: McFarland & Co, 2003).

Nienaber, Michael, 'Chocolate Bar Wrappers Ignite German Row Over Racism', *Reuters* (25 May 2016) <http://uk.reuters.com/article/uk-soccer-euro-germany-chocolate-idUKKCN0YG25D> accessed 25 May 2016.

Outlaw, Lucius T., 'Toward a Critical Theory of Race', in Bernard Boxill, ed., *Race and Racism* (Oxford: Oxford University Press, 2001), 58–82.

Pieterse, Jan Nederveen, *White on Black: Images of Africa and Blacks in Western Popular Culture* (New Haven, CT: Yale University Press, 1992).

Radway, Janice, 'Foreword', in Avery F. Gordon, *Ghostly Matters: Haunting and the Sociological Imagination* (Minneapolis: University of Minnesota Press, 2008), vii–xiv.

Rothschild-Boros, Monica C., *In the Shadow of the Tower: The Works of Josef Nassy 1942–1945* (Irvine, CA: Severin Wunderman Museum, 1989).

Schorsch, Jonathan, 'Jewish Ghosts in Germany', *Jewish Social Studies* 9/3 (2003), 139–69.

Sow, Noah, *Deutschland Schwarz Weiss* (Munich: Goldmann, 2009).

Taylor, Paul C., *Race: A Philosophical Introduction* (Cambridge: Polity Press, 2004).

Thurman, Kira, 'Singing the Civilizing Mission in the Land of Bach, Beethoven, and Brahms: The Fisk Jubilee Singers in Nineteenth-Century Germany', *Journal of World History* 27/3 (2016), 443–71.

Trilling, Daniel, 'Germany Refugees Seek Fair Treatment', *Al Jazeera* (3 April 2014) <http://www.aljazeera.com/indepth/features/2014/04/germany-refugees-seek-fair-treatment-berlin-oranienplatz-20144211253138114.html> accessed 1 May 2014.

Völckers, Armin, *Leroy Räumt Auf* (Berlin: Stormfilm Berlin & Dreamer Joint Venture Filmproduktion 2006), <https://www.youtube.com/watch?v=ymxB7rcPATc>, 2:00–3:45 minutes.

Walker, Rebecca, *Black Cool: One Thousand Streams of Blackness* (Berkeley, CA: Softskull Press).

Weheliye, Alexander G., 'My Volk to Come: Peoplehood in Recent Diaspora Discourse and Afro-German Popular Music', in Darlene Clark Hine, Tricia Danielle Keaton and Stephen Small, eds, *Black Europe and the African Diaspora* (Urbana: University of Illinois Press, 2009), 161–79.

White Charity: Schwarzsein und Weißsein auf Spendenplakaten, Carolin Philipp, and Timo Kiesel, dirs (Berlin, 2011).

Wright, Michelle M., *Becoming Black: Creating Identity in the African Diaspora* (Durham, NC: Duke University Press, 2004).

——, 'Can I Call You Black? The Limits of Authentic Heteronormativity in African Diasporic Discourse', *African and Black Diaspora: An International Journal* 6/1 (2013), 3–16.

——, *Physics of Blackness: Beyond the Middle Passage Epistemology* (Minneapolis: University of Minnesota Press, 2015).

Yancy, George, ed., *What White Looks Like: African-American Philosophers on the Whiteness Question* (New York: Routledge, 2004).

——, 'Whiteness and the Return of the Black Body', *Journal of Speculative Philosophy* 19/4 (2005): 215–41.

Zack, Naomi, 'Race and Philosophic Meaning', in Bernard Boxill, ed., *Race and Racism* (Oxford: Oxford University Press, 2001), 43–57.

Zeller, Joachim, 'Harmless "*Kolonialbiedermeier*"?: Colonial and Exotic Trading Cards', in Volker Langbehn ed., *German Colonialism, Visual Culture, and Modern Memory* (New York: Routledge, 2010), 71–86.

KEVINA KING

5 Black, People of Color and Migrant[1] Lives Should Matter: Racial Profiling, Police Brutality and Whiteness in Germany

ABSTRACT

Incidents of racial profiling and police brutality are common in Germany. They represent the daily realities and encounters with law enforcement and the judiciary that are institutional racist structures. Federal and local police measures rely on paragraph 22(1a) of the Federal Police Act, which empowers law enforcement officials to stop, search and question anyone without reasonable suspicion. Yet Black, People of Color and Migrant communities are primarily targeted. They are racially profiled in stores, parks, bars, discotheques and even their own homes. Drawing on the groundbreaking work of anti-racism initiatives, the scholarship of Fatima El-Tayeb, Yasemin Yildiz, Maisha Eggers and other critical race theorists, I highlight how this practice is fostered, reviewing current racial dynamics and recounting the most recent and widely covered incidents of racial profiling in Germany. I then illustrate how pervasive this practice is, and what it reveals about the normalization of whiteness in society.

1 Here, I refer to the Black, People of Color and Migrant communities not as one homogenous group, but as people whom law enforcement in Germany targets and against whom it discriminates. I do not aim to obscure the crucial roles colorism and white skin privilege play or to negate the specificities of anti-Black racism, Islamophobia and xenophobia, but to point to the commonalities of racial criminalization, racialized experiences and the effects of institutional racism people face daily in Germany. To denote each of these terms as political and socially constructed markers, which may intersect at times and refer more to lived experiences than essential characteristics, I capitalize them throughout.

The 4th of December 2014 was the day after a Staten Island grand jury failed to indict the white police officer David Pantaleo for choking Eric Garner to death. Although the cell phone footage of Eric Garner's murder and his last words 'I can't breathe' echoed – as if on constant replay – on nearly all media outlets for weeks, university business at the predominately white institution of the University of Massachusetts, Amherst continued as usual. As I walked across campus, it felt like the majority of white students, administrators, faculty and staff had not even heard about what had happened. Whiteness, and by extension white privilege, seemed especially palpable that day. However, the majority of Black students, administrators, faculty and staff that I came across were just as weary as I was, in mourning, anxious or experienced what psychologists call race-based trauma and stress.[2]

One of my favorite students has said that 'Whiteness is exhausting' and made a t-shirt out of it.[3] And this student is certainly right. Entering spaces in which the majority of the people do not experience this race-based trauma, but also do not *have* to concern themselves with the daily dangers of racist practices such as racial profiling, is just one way that whiteness asserts itself daily. But there are many manifestations of whiteness. Eric Garner's haunting last words before he was slammed to the ground repeating 'I can't breathe' eight times alluded to the constant racial profiling he experienced: 'Every time you see me, you want to mess with me. I'm tired of it. It stops today [...] every time you see me, you want to harass me'.[4] Whiteness can seem omnipresent and, as a socio-historical dynamic embedded in cultural practices, institutions and national narratives, it is. A society entrenched in whiteness offers individuals who appear to be white

2   Sumie Okazaki, 'Impact of Racism on Ethnic Minority Mental Health', *Perspectives on Psychological Science*, 4/1 (2009), 103–7.
3   See Josh Odam, 'Free Negro University' (2018) <https://teespring.com/stores/fnu> accessed 5 May 2018. See also Stuart Foster, 'Josh Odam Spreads Succinct Messages Through Free Negro University Clothing Line', *Massachusetts Daily Collegian* (28 March 2017) <https://dailycollegian.com/2017/03/josh-odam-spreads-succinct-messages-through-free-negro-university-clothing-line/> accessed 5 May 2018.
4   Susanna Capelouto, 'Eric Garner's Haunting Last Words', *CNN* (8 December 2014) <http://www.cnn.com/2014/12/04/us/garner-last-words/> accessed 2 May 2017.

multiple opportunities, advantages and freedoms. According to a study the *Washington Post* conducted, the police in the United States shot and killed 963 people in 2016 and 991 people in 2015.[5] Black people, compared to white people, were two and a half times more likely to be killed during an encounter with the police. It is this reality and context out of which the following chapter emerges.

As a Black German woman scholar in the United States, witnessing the police brutality and racial profiling directed at Black people has made me keenly aware of parallel instances in Germany. In the following, I argue that incidents of racial profiling and police brutality are not examples of few and far between occurrences in Germany, but they entail daily realities and encounters with law enforcement and the judiciary that structural racism enables. While the 4th Amendment of the U.S. Constitution ensures one's personal rights and stipulates that probable cause is needed for the police to arrest, search and seize, the German Federal Police is empowered to stop, search and question every person in transit zones without probable cause or suspicion and based on their location-specific knowledge [*Lageerkenntnisse*] or experience policing the border [*grenzpolizeiliche Erfahrung*]. Paragraph 22 section 1a of the Federal Police Act states:

> Zur Verhinderung oder Unterbindung unerlaubter Einreise in das Bundesgebiet kann die Bundespolizei in Zügen und auf dem Gebiet der Bahnanlagen der Eisenbahnen des Bundes (§ 3), soweit auf Grund von Lageerkenntnissen oder grenzpolizeilicher Erfahrung anzunehmen ist, daß [*sic*] diese zur unerlaubten Einreise genutzt werden, sowie in einer dem Luftverkehr dienenden Anlage oder Einrichtung eines Verkehrsflughafens (§ 4) mit grenzüberschreitendem Verkehr jede Person kurzzeitig anhalten, befragen und verlangen, daß [*sic*] mitgeführte Ausweispapiere oder Grenzübertrittspapiere zur Prüfung ausgehändigt werden, sowie mitgeführte Sachen in Augenschein nehmen.

---

5   Julie Tate, and others, 'How *The Washington Post* Is Examining Police Shootings in the United States', *Washington Post* (7 July 2016) <https://www.washingtonpost.com/national/how-the-washington-post-is-examining-police-shootings-in-the-united-states/> accessed 2 May 2017.

[To prevent unauthorized entry into Federal territory, the Federal Police can briefly stop every person, question them, and demand that carried identification papers or border-crossing documents as well as all goods and things shall be handed in for inspection. The Federal Police can do this in air traffic facilities (§ 4) or in trains, and in the area of federal railway facilities (§ 3) with cross-border traffic as long as they can assume, based on their location-specific knowledge or experience policing the border, that these transit zones are used for unauthorized entry].[6]

However, in reality, officials do not confront just *every person* in these transit areas but primarily racially profile members of Black, People of Color (PoC) and Migrant communities in Germany. While these practices are aimed at preventing illegal immigration, Germany's Black, PoC and Migrant communities have argued that their phenotypes alone raise the police's suspicion.

Incidents of racial profiling like these reflect an antiquated understanding of Germans as a white ethnic group with essentialized *völkisch* characteristics linking Germanness to blood, descendance and world views.[7]

6   For more about the law, see Hendrik Cremer, *'Racial Profiling' – Menschenrechtswidrige Personenkontrollen nach § 22 Abs. 1 a Bundespolizeigesetz: Empfehlung an den Gesetzgeber, Gerichte und Polizei* (Berlin: Deutsches Institut für Menschenrechte, 2013), 9 and footnote 4, <https://www.institut-fuer-menschenrechte.de/uploads/tx_commerce/Studie_Racial_Profiling_Menschenrechtswidrige_Personenkontrollen_nach_Bundespolizeigesetz.pdf> accessed 2 June 2018.

7   One way that German whiteness adds a complicated dimension to European notions of whiteness is that white Germans vehemently resist the term 'white', as Maureen Maisha Eggers points out in Maureen Maisha Eggers, among others, eds, *Mythen, Masken und Subjekte: Kritische Weißseinsforschung in Deutschland* (Münster: Unrast Verlag, 2009), 19–20. Paradoxically, Germany's white hegemony is based on a biological conception of whiteness linking Germanness to bloodlines, paternity and descent instead of citizenship or merely appearing white. As such, whiteness stratifies racially and functions as a tool to concentrate power, in essence contributing to its uneven distribution and power relations. Eggers termed this German whiteness a form of 'super-whiteness'. Eggers, Mythen, 20. Michelle M. Wright also recognizes this more exclusive and superlative form of German whiteness in her manuscript. In it, she asserts that German whiteness is a very specific reading of whiteness where 'white Germans do not read themselves as racially selfsame with other white Western Europeans but rather as a distinct *Volk* with a specific cultural and *racial* heritage'. Michelle M. Wright, *Becoming Black: Creating Identity in the African Diaspora*

Racial profiling and police brutality, especially when occurring in public, nurture stereotypes of the criminality of racialized people. The humiliating, violent and occasionally fatal practices of racial profiling and police brutality do not just play out on trains or in airports. While the press has covered racial profiling on trains or around train stations more and more in recent years, I illustrate how pervasive this practice is by showcasing how racial profiling is a reality of Black, PoC and Migrant communities while driving or walking. These communities are often racially profiled in stores, parks, bars, discotheques and in their own homes. I draw my sources from the groundbreaking work of anti-racism initiatives like the *Kampagne für Opfer rassistischer Polizeigewalt*, KOP [Campaign for Victims of Racist Police Violence], *Initiative Schwarze Menschen in Deutschland*, ISD [the Initiative of Black People in Germany] and the intersectional scholarship of Fatima El-Tayeb, Yasemin Yildiz, Maisha-Maureen Auma (formerly Maureen Maisha Eggers) and many more. Also included are sources from newspapers, social media platforms, press releases and statements from attorneys and human rights organizations like the Office of the United Nations High Commissioner for Human Rights (OHCHR). I offer examples of this process by briefly reviewing current racial dynamics in Germany and then recounting the most recent and widely covered incidents of racial profiling. One of these is the 2016/2017 Cologne New Year's Eve incident, in which the local police racially profiled around 650 men. Because the men were assumed to be 'seemingly of African descent',[8] they were held outside of Cologne's main train station. This controversy was preceded by the prior New Year's Eve festivities near the Cologne Central

---

(Durham, NC and London: Duke University Press, 2005), 184. In this way, the unmarked and biological notion of whiteness in Germany reaffirms a national narrative around Germany's identity that is constructed as necessarily white and racially homogeneous. This construction is pervasive and reverberates throughout social systems.

8   Polizei NRW Köln, 'Several hundreds of people, seemingly of African descent, have been tracked at Cologne main railway station ...', *Silvester 2016* [Facebook photo album, 4th image and caption] (edited 31 December 2016) <https://www.facebook. com/Polizei.NRW.K/photos/a.964212580377305.1073741845.127899314008640/9 64557803676116/?type=3&theater> accessed 3 May 2017.

Station, during which reports of sexual violence were made, accusing hundreds of men of North African and/or Arab descent. Another incident involved the case of a Black German architecture student racially profiled while commuting on a train. After covering those occasions as exemplary of racial profiling while people are in transit, the focus then turns to instances of racial profiling and police brutality that occur in other public and private realms. I conclude that these forms of structural racism shed light on the pervasiveness and complex specificity of whiteness in Germany. The incidents of racial profiling and police brutality discussed here should, more importantly, remind us that Germany has not yet become 'an anchor of hope' for all and that financial support for the organizations on the ground, who have been networking and serving these communities, is crucial.[9]

9   In his 2017 acceptance speech, President Frank-Walter Steinmeier recalled a young activist in Tunisia, two years prior, who told him that he gave her courage: '"Ihr macht mir Mut!", das heißt unser Land. Deutschland war gemeint. "Ihr Deutschen macht mir Mut!", war die Aussage dieses Satzes.' 'Ist es nicht erstaunlich, ist es nicht eigentlich wunderbar, dass dieses Deutschland, "unser schwieriges Vaterland", wie Gustav Heinemann es einmal nannte, ist es nicht wunderbar, dass dieses Land für viele in der Welt ein Anker der Hoffnung geworden ist?' [Her 'You give me courage!' referred to our country. She meant Germany. 'You Germans give me courage', was what she meant. Is it not surprising, is it not wonderful that this Germany, 'our difficult fatherland', as former President Gustav Heinemann once called it, is it not wonderful that this country has become an anchor of hope for many in the world?] Frank-Walter Steinmeier, 'Designierter Bundespräsident Frank-Walter Steinmeier nach seiner Wahl zum Bundespräsidenten durch die Bundesversammlung' [transcript of speech] (12 February 2017) <http://www.bundespraesident.de/SharedDocs/Reden/DE/Frank-Walter-Steinmeier/Reden/2017/02/170212-Bundesversammlung.html> accessed 3 May 2017. Frank-Walter Steinmeier, 'Word of Thanks to the 16th Federal Convention' [translated transcript] (12 February 2017) <http://www.bundespraesident.de/SharedDocs/Reden/EN/Frank-Walter-Steinmeier/Reden/2017/02/170212-Federal-Convention.html> accessed 3 May 2017.

Current Racial Dynamics in Germany

After their seven-day trip through Germany in February 2017, the United Nations Working Group of Experts on People of African Descent released a damning statement echoing what Black, PoC and Migrant communities in Germany have long been saying. While Article 3(3) of Germany's *Grundgesetz* (*GG*) [constitution] prohibits racial discrimination, they argue that Black, People of Color and Migrant communities who face racist police practices inevitably learn it is not enforced:

> [R]acial profiling by police officials is endemic. Stop and search and controls by police are usually targeted at minority groups including people of African descent ... The repeated denial that racial profiling does not exist in Germany by police authorities and the lack of an independent complaint mechanism at federal and state level fosters impunity.[10]

Many of us know intuitively what the UN Group's research bears out: racial profiling is a daily lived experience within all spheres of society and simply cannot be mitigated by employing the 'bad-apple' mythos that is often articulated as a counter narrative. The United Nation's Group states that Black people in Germany 'are subjected to racial discrimination by their classmates, teachers, workmates, and structural racism by the government and criminal justice system.'[11] As such, their lived experiences point to systemic and individual racism(s) existent in all levels of German society and have to be understood as reflective of the national narrative. The UN Working Group reasons that Germany's prevalent racism targeted at people of African descent is in part possible because Black people 'have not been recognized as a significant minority within the German population

10   Office of the United Nations High Commissioner for Human Rights (OHCHR), 'Statement to the Media by the United Nations' Working Group of Experts on People of African Descent, on the Conclusion of its Official Visit to Germany 20–7 February 2017' (27 February 2017) <http://www.ohchr.org/EN/NewsEvents/Pages/DisplayNews.aspx?NewsID=21233&LangID=E>, accessed 2 May 2017.

11   OHCHR, 'Statement to the Media by the United Nations' Working Group'.

deserving specific action'.[12] The events of World War II overshadowed 'Germany's crimes against Africans'. The group adds that 'Germany's colonial past, the genocide of the Ovaherero and Nama peoples and the sterilization, incarceration, and murder of Black people during Nazi Germany, is not adequately addressed in the national narrative'.[13] The absence of Black, PoC and Migrant histories in the German imagination – instead of understanding that these communities have been a part of Germany for a long time – enables a falsehood about Germany's homogenous racial makeup upon which racial discrimination (structural and individual) can rely.

Fatima El-Tayeb expounds upon this silencing that enables racial inequality and enforces whiteness within the German national narrative in her 2016 book, *Undeutsch: Die Konstruktion des Anderen in der Postmigrantischen Gesellschaft* [*UnGerman: The Construction of the Other in the Postmigrant Society*]. Germany is afflicted with what El-Tayeb termed *Rassismusamnesie* [an amnesia about racism]: a dialectical process of a racial moral panic accompanied by the repression of the historical presence of racialized citizens already in the midst of Germany.[14] One reason that accounts for this amnesia about racism, she argues, is the preferred European and specifically German narrative of characterizing both Europe and Germany as white. Europeans, El-Tayeb writes, have a very static and racialized understanding of who can be European and who cannot: '[t]hose who are not white, are also not European'.[15] She further explains that the construction of European identity as white also means white *and* Christian or white *and* socialized within Christian secularism.[16] This reveals the complex intersections that so-called Others finds themselves in when staking a claim to Europeanness or Germanness. The notion that only a specific race/ethnicity and religion can account for someone's belonging to Europe or Germany creates peculiar potential dangers for racialized people

12   OHCHR, 'Statement to the Media by the United Nations' Working Group'.
13   OHCHR, 'Statement to the Media by the United Nations' Working Group'.
14   Fatima El-Tayeb, *Undeutsch: Die Konstruktion des Anderen in der Postmigrantischen Gesellschaft* (Bielefeld: transcript, 2016), 15.
15   El-Tayeb, *Undeutsch*, 7.
16   El-Tayeb, *Undeutsch*, 8.

and their descendants, especially when interacting with law enforcement.[17] Because of this white narrative, racialized people and their descendants are not understood as European or German. Instead, El-Tayeb argues, they are positioned in the imposed category of the so-called 'immigrant' or that of a 'citizen with a migrant background' who, because of this othering, is repeatedly assumed to have come to Germany from some other place.[18] Michelle M. Wright refers to this phenomenon in regards to Black Germans as an 'Afro-German Subject Formation' positioning them as 'Others-from-Within (members of that country)' and 'Others-from-Without (misrecognized as Africans)'.[19] Other racialized people share this experience with Black Germans. Fatima El-Tayeb writes in *Undeutsch* that racialized people and their descendants are condemned to continuously relive a moment akin to just arriving.[20] This moment is often described as one where the white German recognizes the racialized Other as such and reifies this othering by asking: 'Where are you from'? 'No, I mean where are you *really* from'?

This moment of recognition and othering is accompanied by a public discourse that constructs and sensationalizes each encounter with the Other as brand new. In fact, the Other of Color or Migrant Other has been in Germany for a long time and is not new at all. Black people, for example, have been living in Germany, albeit in varying numbers, since the Middle Ages and in greater numbers later. After World War I, 'Black colonial troops' from the French colonies occupied the Rhineland. A national and international campaign followed this, entitled the *Schwarze Schmach* [Black Horror], which labeled these Black soldiers as rapists. These colonial forces were mostly made up of France's colonized subjects from northern Africa, specifically Algeria and Morocco, but also Tunisia, Madagascar

---

17   Here, I refer to religion not necessarily as religious practices, theological concepts or traditional/cultural rituals. The term, instead, functions as a category identifying the Other in an effort to essentialize the behaviors of racialized people.

18   El-Tayeb, *Undeutsch*, 8.

19   Michelle M. Wright, 'Others-from-Within from Without: Afro-German Subject Formation and the Challenge of a Counter-Discourse', *Callaloo* 26/2 (2003), 296–305.

20   El-Tayeb, *Undeutsch*, 8.

and Senegal.[21] The construction of a dangerous, sexually deviant 'North African' aggressor was especially prevalent during the *Schwarze Schmach* campaign. Today, as seen during the New Year's Eve scandals in Cologne, the construction is still in effect. The difficulties that ensued from the *Schwarze Schmach* campaign for the children of these Black soldiers and predominantly white German women reached their height under National Socialism when many of them were forced to undergo sterilization in the latter half of the 1930s.[22] After World War II, the fate of the so-called 'Brown Babies' of mostly Black American GIs and white German women was also publicly debated in the Bundestag and press during the 1950s and 1960s.[23] Black people are obviously not the only Others in Germany. In fact, they are amongst the smallest minorities. By the 1970s, the efforts to rebuild Germany's economy led to an influx of Turkish migrants, who currently constitute the largest minority in the nation. Migrant workers, students and refugees from Italy, Greece, Morocco, Tunisia, Portugal, Yugoslavia, Poland, Iran and Mozambique, to name but a few, have also made Germany their home.[24]

Thus, Migrants, Black people and Others of Color are not only nothing new to the nation, but they also have long been a part of public discourses and contribute to the social and cultural fabric of Germany. Fatima El-Tayeb posits that this repression of the historical presence of racialized people underscores Germany's identity crises.[25] However, what we learn from El-Tayeb and Yasemin Yildiz, who also speaks to this amnesia,

---

21   See Tina Campt, *Other Germans: Black Germans and the Politics of Race, Gender, and Memory in the Third Reich* (Ann Arbor: University of Michigan Press, 2005).

22   See Reiner Pommerin, *Sterilisierung der Rheinlandbastarde: Das Schicksal einer farbigen deutschen Minderheit 1918–1937* (Düsseldorf: Droste, 1979).

23   See Yara-Colette Lemke Muniz de Faria, *Zwischen Fürsorge und Ausgrenzung: Afrodeutsche "Besatzungskinder" im Nachkriegs-Deutschland* (Berlin: Metropol, 2002) and Heide Fehrenbach, *Race after Hitler: Black Occupation Children in Postwar Germany and America* (Princeton, NJ: Princeton University Press, 2007).

24   See Rita Chin, *The Guest Worker Question in Postwar Germany* (Cambridge: Cambridge University Press, 2009) and Yasemin Yildiz, *Beyond the Mother Tongue: The Postmonolingual Condition* (New York: Fordham University Press, 2011).

25   El-Tayeb, *Undeutsch*, 33.

defining it as a 'willful amnesia', is that these moments of crises are possible due to discursive shifts.[26] El-Tayeb, in *Undeutsch*, points out that while the labeling for the Other might change, the themes change very little. The contemporary asylum crisis is now constructed as a refugee crisis. The problem with 'Turks' is now labeled as a problem with 'Muslims',[27] and instead of scapegoating the alleged rapists in the French colonial forces, who occupied the Rhine area as *Die Schwarze Schmach* [The Black Shame], the alleged 'North African' criminal, just arriving as a refugee in Germany, serves as a stand in. Yildiz explains that there was a discursive shift around the year 2000 which re-labeled the 'Turk' as the 'Muslim'.[28] She argues that this shift functioned to demarcate transnational and civilizational differences. To signify the Other, who was becoming less of an Other with each generation, into the Other yet again, 'the Muslim' was constructed to 'mark large-scale, hard-to-control incidents of violence [...] indicative of the threat posed by "Muslims"'.[29] These discursive shifts reflect a constant repetition of played out racist tropes while making space for new ones and simultaneously reifying whiteness in Germany's national narrative.

Racial Profiling in Germany

When the whiteness of the national narrative permeates the German law enforcement system, officials of the state acting upon it can engage in particularly damaging actions. Since they are understood to be representative of the state, their actions reproduce and strengthen racial inequality and normalize the assumption that Germany is white. Incidents of racial profiling recently highlighted in the German and international press shed light

26 Yasemin Yildiz, 'Turkish Girls, Allah's Daughters, and the Contemporary German Subject: Itinerary of a Figure', *German Life and Letters* 62/4 (2009), 465–81.
27 El-Tayeb, *Undeutsch*, 33.
28 Yildiz, 'Turkish Girls, Allah's Daughters', 466 and 474.
29 Yildiz, 'Turkish Girls, Allah's Daughters', 475.

on the discriminatory practices that People of Color face especially on trains and in or around train stations when commuting. One particularly important case is that of a Black German architecture student, who in 2010 traveled on train between Kassel and Frankfurt. The young man, whose name has not been shared with the public, was the only person on the full train 'spot-checked' for his identification by federal police officers. When he refused to comply, he was taken off the train and into custody. There, he remarked that the methods of the police resembled those of the Nazi SS, for which he was formally charged with slander.[30] While the charges against the man were dropped, he later sued the police for discrimination. But sadly, he lost his suit in February 2012, even though the police had admitted that the young man aroused suspicion solely as a result of his skin color.[31] The *Verwaltungsgericht*, or VG [Administrative Court], in Koblenz ruled that 'skin color' is a legitimate criterion for the police to use as a point of reference when stopping and checking for illegal immigration under the German Federal Police Act from 1994, which was enacted after the Schengen Agreement abolished formal internal border controls in the European Union in 1993. According to paragraph 22 section 1a, to prevent unauthorized entry, the German Federal Police is empowered to stop, search and question every person in transit zones without probable cause or suspicion and based on their location-specific knowledge or experience policing the border. The case of the Black German architecture student was overturned by the same state's *Oberverwaltungsgericht*, or OVG [Higher Administrative Court], in Koblenz eight months later. The Higher Administrative Court decided that the ruling of the lower Administrative Court violated the discrimination ban of Germany's constitution under Article 3(3). The young man received an official apology.[32]

There are two particularly important points about this case. First, the case demonstrates that racist and discriminatory practices had been taking

30   Anwaltskanzlei Sven Adam, 'Urteil des VG Koblenz vom 28. 02. 2012' [scanned copy online], (1 September 2012) <http://www.anwaltskanzlei-adam.de/index.php?sonderseite-vg-koblenz-dokumente> accessed 2 May 2017.
31   Adam, 'Urteil des VG Koblenz vom 28. 02. 2012'.
32   Cremer, *"Racial Profiling"*, 9 and footnote 3.

place every time the Federal Police engaged a member of the Black, PoC or Migrant community based solely on phenotype and or assumed origin. Second, the case helped to establish a precedent that then paved the way for a landmark decision made by the same Higher Administrative Court for a similar case in April 2016.[33] With the 2016 case, a Black family was taking the train between Mainz and Koblenz, and three Federal Police officers entered the train and asked them alone for identification papers. After calling-in their information, the officers exited the train at the next stop, passing approximately twenty other passengers without checking their identification. According to the findings of the evidentiary hearing, the plaintiffs' skin color was at least one of the reasons for the family to be stopped and as such a violation against the discrimination ban in Germany's constitution.[34] The attorney for both cases, Sven Adam, remarked on the importance of this case:

> Das Urteil des OVG ist ein Meilenstein für den Kampf gegen die rechtswidrige Praxis des Racial Profiling ... Denn von nun an wird die Bundespolizei nachweisen müssen, gerade nicht diskriminierend kontrolliert zu haben, wenn der äußere Anschein eine Kontrolle aufgrund der Hautfarbe nahelegt.

> [The ruling of the Higher Administrative Court is a milestone in the fight against the illegal practice of racial profiling ... From now on, the Federal Police have to prove that they indeed did not act racially discriminatorily].[35]

Despite this landmark decision, however, these practices continue since the individual states in Germany and their State Police authorities have adopted versions of the Federal Police Act paragraph 22 section 1a to varying degrees.

In Berlin, for example, 'dangerous places' are defined by the police as places where infringements of provisions relating to residence permits as

---

33 Anwaltskanzlei Sven Adam, 'Grundsatzentscheidung des Oberverwaltungsgerichts Rheinland-Pfalz gegen diskriminierende Polizeikontrollen anhand der Hautfarbe' [online press release] (22 April 2016) <http://www.anwaltskanzlei-adam.de/index.php?id=36,1136,0,0,1,0> accessed 2 May 2017.

34 Adam, 'Grundsatzentscheidung des Oberverwaltungsgerichts Rheinland-Pfalz'.

35 Adam, 'Grundsatzentscheidung des Oberverwaltungsgerichts Rheinland-Pfalz'.

well as the harboring of criminals happen.[36] As such, the police in Berlin
are empowered to control, stop, question and search individuals without
probable cause or suspicion and based on their location-specific knowledge or experience policing the border, as previously noted. However, the
lack of transparency the authorities and criminal law enforcement display
is problematic. These places are defined by the police based on the same
principle employed in paragraph 22 section 1a. Thus, here too, dangerous
places are determined by the police's knowledge of the current conditions
and/or these places have warranted policing. Yet, the statistics that are
supposed to account for these experiences and data are not shared publicly.[37] This authorization is also given to the police to secure endangered
sites such as synagogues and train stations as well as control points, for
example, at soccer games and demonstrations. Anyone within these areas
can be considered a suspect. These stop, check and search practices conducted without probable cause or suspicion are implemented to varying
degrees not only by the Federal Police, but also by local and state police
authorities. According to Anke Borsdorff, an expert on the German Federal
Police and professor of Legal Studies, and her article 'Die Rechtsfigur der
Schleierfahndung' [the Legal Concept of Dragnet Controls], the term
commonly used to refer to these types of practices loosely translates and
connotes a metaphorical veil, blanket or net used to conduct a search. More
aptly the term *Schleierfahndung* describes dragnet measures to apprehend
criminals.[38] In 1995, she writes, the German state of Bavaria was the first to
sign this practice into law, mandating that their State Police officers could
stop, check and search anyone within 30 kilometers inland of the border
without probable cause or suspicion. In addition to border-crossing airports and train stations, lawmakers expanded their reach onto major roads,

36   Kampagne für Opfer rassistischer Polizeigewalt (KOP), *Alltäglicher Ausnahmezustand:*
     Institutioneller Rassismus in deutschen Strafverfolgungsbehörden (Münster: edition
     assemblage, 2016), 14.
37   Kampagne für Opfer rassistischer Polizeigewalt, *Alltäglicher Ausnahmezustand*, 14.
38   Anke Borsdorff, 'Die Rechtsfigur der Schleierfahndung', in Hartmut Brenneisen,
     and others, eds, *Polizeirechtsreform in Schleswig-Holstein: Materialien zur Auslegung*
     und Bewertung der Gesetzesnovellierung (Münster: LIT Verlag, 2008), 58.

highways and important facilities along them, such as rest stops and gas stations. Furthermore, Bavarian police officers are legally authorized to conduct searches of items and persons.[39] The state of Baden-Württemberg followed Bavaria's lead and adopted *Schleierfahndung* measures in 1996, although latter aspects of the measure, the search of items and persons, was not adopted at first.[40] Most of the other German states have adopted versions of the measure, including North-Rhine Westphalia.

The Cologne Controversies

North Rhine-Westphalia's largest city, Cologne, has made international headlines due to its controversial handling of the New Year's Eve incidents of 2015 and 2016. During the festivities near the Cologne Central Station, a slew of incidents of sexual violence were reported; hundreds of men were accused of forming crowds around women and then groping, harassing, robbing and intimidating them. According to many of the survivors, their attackers were of North African or Arab descent. In the days that followed the attacks, accounts of the assaults appeared on social media and in smaller local newspapers.[41] While it took the police, the national media and the mayor of the city days to respond, reports of similar incidents emerged across other German cities – from Hamburg to Stuttgart – triggering an outcry on social media. Although reports of the actual numbers and specific origins of each assailant are still murky, one of Germany's largest weekly news magazines *Focus* published its second edition of the year on 9 January 2016, addressing the allegations. The magazine's cover image,[42]

39   Borsdorff, 'Die Rechtsfigur der Schleierfahndung', 59.
40   Borsdorff, 'Die Rechtsfigur der Schleierfahndung', 60.
41   See Beverly Weber, '"We Must Talk about Cologne": Race, Gender, and Reconfigurations of "Europe"', *German Politics and Society* 34/4 (2016), 68–86.
42   See Weber for a detailed analysis of the *Focus* cover image, '"We Must Talk about Cologne"' and Vanessa Plumly, 'Refugee Assemblages, Cycles of Violence, and Body

printed independent of specific articles, depicts a black-and-white image of a young and slender white woman with blond hair almost reaching to her shoulders. She stands in front of a grey background, using her hands and arm to cover herself. Everything above the tip of her nose is cropped off; the magazine's title serves as a header in big block font to anonymize her. Her lips are slightly parted. She is covered in five black and muddied handprints on her stomach, shoulders, arm and hip. Additionally, there are three red bands with white lettering covering her breasts, navel and hip bones proclaiming: '*Frauen klagen an / Nach den Sex-Attacken von Migranten: / Sind wir noch tolerant oder schon blind*'? [Women accuse/ After the sex-attacks of migrants: / Are we still tolerant or already blind?] Here, the anonymous woman stands in as an embodiment of the German nation precisely illustrating a phenomenon Yildiz and Chin describe as what became a litmus test for foreigners. The oppression and mistreatment of women determines whether the racialized Other is capable of assimilating to Germany's liberal values, which are suggested to be absent of sexism.[43]

The image is striking for its blatant racism and sexism. By cropping out the anonymous woman's eyes, *Focus* magazine provides an answer to its question. We are blind. But not blind enough to notice that the woman's body, chosen for this cover, is objectified and reaffirms the quintessential standards of beauty: white, slim and blond. With her slightly parted lips, she seemingly wants to say something or, conversely, is portrayed as sexually suggestive. In the former scenario, her attempt to speak out in protest is muted. In the latter reading, her flirty demeanor would only position her for more scrutiny and victim blaming. The survivors of the sexual assaults during the New Year's Eve celebrations experienced both blaming and silencing and had to relive those moments as the *Focus* cover depicted their lose-lose situation. The five muddied handprints soiling her naked body remind us not only of the sexual violence she experienced but that her attacker or attackers' filth remains with her on her body and for the

---

Politic(s) in Times of "Celebratory Fear"', *Women in German Yearbook: Feminist Studies in German Literature & Culture* 32 (2016), 163–88.

43   Yildiz, 'Turkish Girls, Allah's Daughters', 471 and 477; also Chin, *The Guest Worker Question*, 143.

public to witness. Germanist Beverly Weber draws connections between the 'fears about dangerous Muslim masculinity [...] and a contamination of whiteness',[44] which is precisely the message of the photo. The image invokes not only sexualized stereotypes about the passivity of women and dialectically the promiscuity of young white sexually liberated women in Germany, but it also represents notions of the sexual deviancy of non-white men incapable of controlling their sexual urges around white women, inscribing the men's Otherhood or foreignness and color. Germanist Vanessa Plumly draws important connections to the historicity of these images in Germany:

> Colonizing structures of white fear have been embedded in German culture for centuries. The children's game 'Who's afraid of the boogeyman?' (literally, 'Who's afraid of the black man?') is but one example of this. Racial violence and fear – particularly of miscegenation – are sociopolitically and historically anchored in Germany in the black male body. The politicized refugee framework and the socio-historical conditions of the post-Wende era only served to add to the overlapping layers of this already existing racializing assemblage of fear.[45]

The overlap in racialized stereotypes that Plumly highlights exemplifies El-Tayeb's notion of an amnesia about racism in Germany and Yildiz' assertion that discursive shifts from 'Turk' to 'Muslim' allow for the remaking of the dangerous Other of Color. The *Focus* cover is powerfully evocative of the images used during racist campaigns against France's Black soldiers during the 1920s, reminding us of a familiar racist trope where the savage and hypermasculinity of the Other endangers white German womanhood. Then and now the 'North African' is constructed as a rapist and primitive. He is often depicted as lacking humanity, in which media outlets and white Germans represent him as an ape or ape-like, reducing him to body parts only and/or enlarging certain body parts grotesquely. *Focus* magazine replicates this imagery by representing the Other as dirtied hand prints. In opposition to what is understood to be quintessential Germanness, the racist trope of the image is accompanied by the magazine's assertion that

---

44   Weber, '"We Must Talk about Cologne"', 69.
45   Plumly, 'Refugee Assemblages', 173.

'migrants' violated the white German woman, marking the threat as necessarily coming from outside the nation.

Lacking an intersectional perspective, the image and the messaging on the magazine's cover mark the women surviving the sexual assaults as necessarily white and German, assuming Women of Color or Migrant women were not targeted and attacked during the festivities. Conversely, the racialized man, not the white German man, is positioned as the attacker, implying that white German men are not the source of danger, which is reminiscent of racist tropes positioning the white (German) man as savior. Paradoxically, this attempt to address sexual violence with the sexist image of a naked woman tells us much about racist stereotypes that Germany continues to harbor, reflecting the turning around of the litmus test Yildiz and Chin highlighted. The woman on the magazine is not only symbolic of the women surviving the attacks, but she also embodies the nation, German values and the narrative Germany envisions. With her young and fit physique standing straight and facing the camera, she might have slightly parted her lips to say: 'It's enough', but the magazine does it for her and addresses the German nation by perpetuating an 'us' versus 'them' dichotomy.

The similar racist and sexist stereotypes constructing the so-called 'Muslim,' 'Migrant,' 'North African' or 'Refugee' man as a rapist or a dangerous or sexual deviant reveal the appropriation and overlapping of racist tropes at play within Germany society. This, however, does not only affect people discursively. Indeed, these tropes have real and material consequences that have resulted in violence against and racial profiling of non-white Communities of Color in Germany. Days after the sexual assaults took place, gangs of right-wing extremists organized a manhunt through social media in Cologne, attacking 'two Pakistanis, two Syrians and a group of Africans'.[46] The criminalized depiction of the Other in the media, politics and research as well as individual racist stereotypes are promoting the racist

---

46   Josie Le Blond, 'Cologne gangs attack groups of foreigners as New Year's Eve assault complaints grow', *The Guardian* (11 January 2016) <https://www.theguardian.com/world/2016/jan/11/two-pakistanis-and-a-syrian-man-injured-in-attacks-by-gangs-in-cologne> accessed 3 May 2017.

development of suspicion within the police. There have been no-go areas for People of Color for many decades,[47] but a rise in far-right extremism over the last years with the emergence of the far-right political movement *Patriotische Europäer gegen die Islamisierung des Abendlandes*, or PEGIDA [Patriotic Europeans against the Islamization of the West], and its various offshoots in other German cities expanded them. People who normally would not have been vocal with their racist views are now more vocal and mainstream, gaining additional cultural currency.[48]

One year after the *Focus* cover and the sexual assaults in Cologne, the police, in an effort to prevent a repeat of the prior year, detained nearly 650 men at Cologne's main train station. During the 2016 New Year's Eve festivities, Cologne police's Twitter page announced that hundreds of so-called *Nafris*—a term that stands for *Nordafrikanischer Intensivtäter* [North African intensive offenders], an internal police abbreviation used primarily to describe repeat or 'intensive' offenders of North African descent, were being held and searched at Cologne's central train station.[49] The edited Facebook post from the Cologne police used different language and clarified that the hundreds of men held and checked were 'seemingly of African descent'.[50] After a public outcry on social media criticizing law enforcement officials for racial profiling, Cologne's police chief apologized for the use of the term, asserting that it was an internal term never meant to be used in public. According to him, Cologne police officers stopped nearly 650 so-called North Africans before they were able to enter the inner city

---

47   These are areas PoC, Black and Migrant communities know to avoid due to rampant neo-Nazism.

48   Weber, "'We Must Talk about Cologne'", 68–70.

49   @polizei_nrw_k, '#PolizeiNRW #Silvester2016 #SicherInKöln: Am HBF werden derzeit mehrere Hundert Nafris überprüft. Infos folgen. http://url.nrw/silvester2016' [Twitter tweet] (posted 31 December 2016) <https://twitter.com/polizei_nrw_k/status/815318640094572548> accessed 3 May 2017.

50   Polizei NRW Köln, 'Several hundreds of people, seemingly of African descent, have been tracked at Cologne main railway station ...', *Silvester 2016* [Facebook photo album, 4th image and caption] (edited 31 December 2016) <https://www.facebook.com/Polizei.NRW.K/photos/a.964212580377305.1073741845.127899314008640/964557803676116/?type=3&theater> accessed 3 May 2017.

because a certain level of aggression was detectable, leading the officers to conclude there would be criminal offenses. Later, the police released a report clarifying that out of the 674 men apprehended, the nationality of only 425 could be determined: 99 men were from Iraq, 94 from Syria, 48 from Afghanistan, 46 from Germany, 17 from Morocco and 13 from Algeria.[51] It is, nevertheless, essential to note that activist groups and initiatives have been addressing and continue to expose the racism and sexism that the Cologne incidents illuminated, as they fight against the embedded institutional structures in policing, dragnet measures and surveillance that place a target on People of Color, while eluding a critical engagement in the normalization and erasure of whiteness in the masking of sexual violence within broader societal contexts.

Resisting Racial Profiling

While the aforementioned incidents of racial profiling and their aftermath are of great importance, it would be naive to assume that the German police racially profile people only while they are in places of transit and to prevent illegal immigration. This would exclude the narratives of Black, People of Color and Migrant communities who face these practices daily in the public and private spheres. One activist group fighting against racism that stands out in particular is an initiative called the *Kampagne für Opfer rassistischer Polizeigewalt*, or KOP [Campaign for Victims of Racist Police Violence]. In 2002, KOP was founded by a number of groups, including members of ReachOut, an advice center for victims of right-wing, racist and anti-Semitic violence in Berlin; Netzwerk Selbsthilfe [Network Self-Help], a left-leaning financial support group involved in various projects

---

51   Peter Maxwill and Ansgar Siemens, 'Silvester in Köln: Polizei relativiert Angaben zu Nordafrikanern', *SPIEGEL ONLINE* (13 January 2017) <http://www.spiegel.de/panorama/justiz/silvester-in-koeln-polizei-korrigiert-eigene-angaben-ueber-kontrollierte-a-1129870.html> accessed 3 May 2017.

promoting solidarity; Antidiskriminierungsbüro Berlin, or ADB [the Bureau for Anti-Discrimination in Berlin], and a legal support group called Ermittlungsausschuss Berlin [Investigation Committee Berlin]. KOP first aimed at creating a legal assistance fund for survivors of racial profiling and police brutality.[52] After its inception, founding members and activists transformed the organization into a more extensive campaign archiving and fighting racial profiling and police brutality in Berlin. Since then, KOP has published a groundbreaking chronicle in 2014 detailing 150 cases of racist police brutality in Berlin from 2000 until 2013 *Chronik rassistischer Polizeigewalt in Berlin 2000 bis 2013* [Chronicle of Racist Police Brutality in Berlin 2000–2013], the first film documentary on racial profiling in Germany *ID WITHOUT COLORS* accompanying the *Chronik* and the 2016 edited volume *Alltäglicher Ausnahmezustand* [Daily State of Emergency].

Reviewing individual cases archived in KOP's *Chronik* shows that men and women experienced racial profiling and police brutality while driving or walking in their neighborhoods, in parks, stores, bars and discos and even in their own homes. Sources are based on the reports of survivors, witnesses and daily newspapers. Most often there are no legal complaints filed. In fact, KOP estimates that approximately 5 per cent of the complaints made against the police are brought to court.[53] Survivors are hesitant to file a suit against the police for numerous reasons. However, one particularly egregious reason, highlighting a common pattern, is that police officials often make formal complaints against the survivors to prevent the filing of a complaint against them or their colleagues.[54] Common offenses survivors are charged with by the police are *Beleidigung* [insult], *Widerstand gegen Vollstreckungsbeamte* [resisting arrest] and '*(schwere) Körperverletzung*' [(aggravated) assault].[55] These retaliation practices sustain and nurture stereotypes of racialized survivors as dangerous criminals, which

---

52 KOP, *Alltäglicher Ausnahmezustand*, 5.
53 Kampagne für Opfer rassistischer Polizeigewalt (KOP), *Chronik rassistischer Polizeigewalt in Berlin 2000 bis 2013* (Berlin: KOP, 2014), 3.
54 KOP, *Alltäglicher Ausnahmezustand*, 5.
55 KOP, *Alltäglicher Ausnahmezustand*, 17.

simultaneously discredits them. One example of this is the case of Lennis H.*.[56] On the evening of 4 January 2002, according to the KOP's *Chronik*, the man was in the backseat of his car fixing a defective seatbelt.[57] Suddenly, a police patrol car pulled up next to him, in which four officers and a German Shepherd exited. Although Lennis' car keys were stuck in the lock of his car door, he was prompted to hand over his identification papers. Since he did not have them on his person, he wanted the police to accompany him to his nearby apartment where his wife could also attest to his identity. When he exited his car, one of the police officers took her German Shepard off the leash, which attacked him immediately. A second officer pepper-sprayed him. Lennis was slammed to the ground, handcuffed and his head was pressed against the concrete. He was dragged to the other side of the street and thrown on the ground once more. On the way to the station, a third officer punched Lennis in the face. Lennis was held for five hours. According to the police, Lennis hurled insults such as 'Nazi Pigs' at them, kicked and screamed and could be detained only after the use of pepper spray. In October 2002, Lennis was sentenced to pay a fine of 1,600 Euro for the crimes of insult, resisting arrest and assault. Lennis' appeal was dismissed in March 2003.[58]

Another reason that prevents survivors from bringing their case to court are the expenses that they would accrue. Maren Burkhardt, attorney with *Justiz Watch* [Justice Watch], formerly known as *Prozessbeobachtungsgruppe Rassismus und Justiz* [Trial Observation Group Racism and Justice], 'a group that monitors racism in the judiciary in Berlin', explains that defendants in criminal proceedings do not qualify for *Prozesskostenhilfe* [legal aid].[59] Administrative proceedings, such as the case of the Black German architecture student outlined above, can be costly as well. She explains the difficulties of focusing on racial profiling in either court system. Cases between the people and the state, government agencies and regulatory practices are adjudicated in administrative proceedings. Thus, a person

---

56   KOP indicates with the asterisk symbol (*) that the name was anonymized.
57   KOP, *Chronik*, 17.
58   KOP, *Chronik*, 17.
59   *KOP, Alltäglicher Ausnahmezustand*, 27.

bringing forth a case of discriminatory identity checks, etc. would fall under this category. Burkhardt outlines that keeping the focus on racial profiling within administrative procedures is relatively straightforward.[60] However, as in the case of Lennis above, the situation is more complicated when officials allege that resistance, insults or obstruction have occurred. The problem is that the judiciary can criminalize 'jedes noch so kleine Zappeln' [every tiny bit of fidgeting].[61] Keeping the focus on racial profiling and police brutality in criminal proceedings when the survivor is charged by the police is therefore extremely difficult. Even if the officer's initial actions are ruled to be unlawful, the survivor's response to violence and racism can be criminalized.

Not all incidents of racial profiling and police brutality result in a fine for survivors or a dismissed case. Some are fatal. Such was the case with Sejad M.* whom police killed on 28 February 2010. In the early morning hours, someone called the police presumably in response to the loud music one of Sejad's neighbors was playing. Sejad was woken by the music as well and was angry. Sejad's family did not want him to start an argument with the neighbors and asked him to stay inside the apartment, but he did not. When the police arrived, they assumed he was the troublemaker and wanted to expel him from the building. Sejad wanted to go back to his parent's apartment, but then the police became violent. He was kicked, beaten and handcuffed. When three additional officers arrived on the scene for backup, they pepper sprayed Sejad and the entire corridor filled up with fumes. Sejad was held on the floor lying on his stomach handcuffed. Unconscious, he was dragged down the stairway. No one called an ambulance for Sejad; instead, the paramedics were called for some of the police officers affected by the indoor pepper spray action. When the paramedics arrived, they attempted to resuscitate him, but his injuries were fatal. Sejad M. died due to internal bleeding. He was only thirty-two.[62] Sejad is not the only fatal case of police brutality in Germany: police officers fatally shot Mareame N'Deye Sarr in July 2001; Oury Jalloh burned to death in a prison cell in

---

60   KOP, *Alltäglicher Ausnahmezustand*, 22.
61   KOP, *Alltäglicher Ausnahmezustand*, 23.
62   KOP, *Chronik*, 114.

January 2005; police officers fatally shot Dominique Koumadio in April 2006; the police fatally shot Dennis Jockel in December 2008; Slieman Hamade died of asphyxiation due to pepper spray in February 2010 and Christy Schwundeck was fatally shot by police officers in May 2011, to name but a few.[63]

Conclusion

KOP in its 2016 publication highlights how pervasive institutional racism affects Black, PoC and Migrant communities. They argue that racist law enforcement practices in Germany have always been a part of the lived experiences these communities face.[64] Yet, these realities are widely unknown to the majority of non-Black, -PoC and -Migrant communities.[65] These lived experiences, especially those of racism and its practices, are valuable sources of knowledge. In *Mythen, Masken und Subjekte*, Maisha Eggers argues for the importance of tapping into this knowledge, which she terms a 'Black Archive of Knowledge'.[66] Eggers, similarly to bell hooks,[67] argues that,

---

63   Denise Bergold-Caldwell, and others, eds, *Spiegelblicke: Perspektiven Schwarzer Bewegung in Deutschland* (Berlin: Orlanda Verlag, 2016), 256–57.

64   KOP, *Alltäglicher Ausnahmezustand*, 5.

65   KOP, *Alltäglicher Ausnahmezustand*, 5.

66   Maureen Maisha Eggers, 'Ein Schwarzes Wissensarvhiv' in Maureen Maisha Eggers, and others, eds, *Mythen, Masken und Subjekte: Kritische Weißseinsforschung in Deutschland* (Münster: Unrast Verlag, 2009), 18.

67   See bell hooks, 'Representations of Whiteness in the Black Imagination', in Paula Rothenberg, ed., *White Privilege: Essential Readings on the Other Side of Racism* (New York: Worth, 2008), 19: 'black folks have, from slavery on, shared in conversations with one another "special" knowledge of whiteness gleaned from close scrutiny of white people. Deemed special because it was not a way of knowing that has been recorded fully in written material, its purpose was to help black folks cope and survive in a white supremacist society. For years, black domestic servants, working in white homes, acting as informants, brought knowledge back to segregated communities – details, facts, observations, and psychoanalytic reading of the white Other'.

especially when examining whiteness critically, white people and scholars should rely on Black and PoC voices to stay accurate. By centering what Black, People of Color and Migrant communities write and say about their experiences with racial profiling, police brutality and whiteness (and by extension white supremacy), we attempt to progress from racial inequality. The voices and experiences of these communities disrupt hegemonic conceptions and practices of Germany's whiteness. Institutional racism defines not only where racism happens but also how. Moreover, institutional racism speaks to how racism is embedded in an institution so that it systematically organizes itself into practices and structures. It is of secondary importance whether the actors within these institutions intend to act in a racist way. To critically engage with the criminalization of racialized groups, investigating institutional racism must first include the calling-out of the problem. The accounts detailed in this chapter suggest how law enforcement officials, courts and the media stand in the way of honest and critical engagements with this topic. It is crucial to view these quotidian forms of racial discrimination within the contexts of other individualized, and more importantly, other institutionalized forms of racial discrimination, such as in the media. To show solidarity with the survivors and engage in a critique of institutional racism on a scholarly and personal level is only a small portion of our engagement with this. It is important to center the experiences of Black, PoC and Migrant communities, since their experience is underrepresented in the media, judiciary, politics, education and scientific research.

Bibliography

@polizei_nrw_k, '#PolizeiNRW #Silvester2016 #SicherInKöln: Am HBF werden derzeit mehrere Hundert Nafris überprüft. Infos folgen. http://url.nrw/sil vester2016' [Twitter tweet] (posted 31 December 2016) <https://twitter.com/polizei_nrw_k/status/815318640094572548>, accessed 3 May 2017.

Anwaltskanzlei, Sven Adam, 'Grundsatzentscheidung des Oberverwaltungsgerichts Rheinland-Pfalz gegen diskriminierende Polizeikontrollen anhand der

Hautfarbe' (22 April 2016) <http://www.anwaltskanzlei-adam.de/index. php?id=36,1136,0,0,1,0> accessed 2 May 2017.

——, 'Urteil des VG Koblenz vom 28. 02. 2012' (1 September 2012) <http://www. anwaltskanzlei-adam.de/index.php?sonderseite-vg-koblenz-dokumente> accessed 2 May 2017.

Bergold-Caldwell, Denise, and others, eds, *Spiegelblicke: Perspektiven Schwarzer Bewegung in Deutschland* (Berlin: Orlanda Verlag, 2016), 256–57.

Borsdorff, Anke, 'Die Rechtsfigur der Schleierfahndung', in Hartmut Brenneisen, among others, eds, *Polizeirechtsreform in Schleswig-Holstein: Materialien zur Auslegung und Bewertung der Gesetzesnovellierung* (Münster: LIT Verlag, 2008), 58–60.

Campt, Tina, *Other Germans: Black Germans and the Politics of Race, Gender, and Memory in the Third Reich* (Ann Arbor: The University of Michigan Press, 2004).

Capelouto, Susanna, 'Eric Garner's Haunting Last Words', *CNN* (8 December 2014) <http://www.cnn.com/2014/12/04/us/garner-last-words/> accessed 2 May 2017.

Chin, Rita, *The Guest Worker Question in Postwar Germany* (Cambridge: Cambridge University Press, 2009).

Cremer, Hendrik, *"Racial Profiling" – Menschenrechtswidrige Personenkontrollen nach § 22 Abs. 1 a Bundespolizeigesetz: Empfehlung an den Gesetzgeber, Gerichte und Polizei* (Berlin: Deutsches Institut für Menschenrechte, 2013).

Eggers, Maureen Maisha, 'Ein Schwarzes Wissensarchiv', in Maureen Maisha Eggers, and others, eds, *Mythen, Masken und Subjekte: Kritische Weißseinsforschung in Deutschland* (Münster: Unrast Verlag, 2009), 18–21.

El-Tayeb, Fatima, *Undeutsch: Die Konstruktion des Anderen in der Postmigrantischen Gesellschaft* (Bielefeld: transcript, 2016).

Fehrenbach, Heide, *Race after Hitler: Black Occupation Children in Postwar Germany and America* (Princeton, NJ: Princeton University Press, 2007).

Foster, Stuart, 'Josh Odam Spreads Succinct Messages Through Free Negro University Clothing Line', *Massachusetts Daily Collegian* (28 March 2017) <https:// dailycollegian.com/2017/03/josh-odam-spreads-succinct-messages-through-free-negro-university-clothing-line/>, accessed 5 May 2018.

hooks, bell, 'Representations of Whiteness in the Black Imagination', in Paula Rothenberg, ed., *White Privilege: Essential Readings on the Other Side of Racism* (New York: Worth, 2008).

Kampagne für Opfer rassistischer Polizeigewalt (KOP), *Alltäglicher Ausnahmezustand: Institutioneller Rassismus in deutschen Strafverfolgungsbehörden* (Münster: edition assemblage, 2016).

——, *Chronik rassistischer Polizeigewalt in Berlin 2000 bis 2013* (Berlin: KOP, 2014).

——, *ID-WITHOUTCOLORS: Der erste Dokumentarfilm über Racial Profiling in Deutschland*, dir. Riccardo Valsecchi (Migrationsrat Berlin-Brandenburg e.V., 2013).

Le Blond, Josie, 'Cologne gangs attack groups of foreigners as New Year's Eve assault complaints grow', *The Guardian* (11 January 2016) <https://www.theguardian.com/world/2016/jan/11/two-pakistanis-and-a-syrian-man-injured-in-attacks-by-gangs-in-cologne> accessed 3 May 2017.

Lemke Muniz de Faria, Yara-Colette, *Zwischen Fürsorge und Ausgrenzung: Afrodeutsche "Besatzungskinder" im Nachkriegs-Deutschland* (Berlin: Metropol, 2002).

Maxwill, Peter and Ansgar Siemens, 'Silvester in Köln: Polizei relativiert Angaben zu Nordafrikanern', *SPIEGEL ONLINE* (13 January 2017) <http://www.spiegel.de/panorama/justiz/silvester-in-koeln-polizei-korrigiert-eigene-angaben-ueber-kontrollierte-a-1129870.html> accessed 3 May 2017.

Odam, Josh, 'Free Negro University' (2018) <https://teespring.com/stores/fnu> accessed 5 May 2018.

Office of the United Nations High Commissioner for Human Rights (OHCHR), 'Statement to the Media by the United Nations', Working Group of Experts on People of African Descent, on the Conclusion of its Official Visit to Germany 20–7 February 2017', *OHCHR* (press release from 27 February 2017) <http://www.ohchr.org/EN/NewsEvents/Pages/DisplayNews.aspx?NewsID=21233&LangID=E> accessed 2 May 2017.

Okazaki, Sumie, 'Impact of Racism on Ethnic Minority Mental Health', *Perspectives on Psychological Science*, 4/1 (2009), 103–7.

Plumly, Vanessa, 'Refugee Assemblages, Cycles of Violence, and Body Politic(s) in Times of "Celebratory Fear"', *Women in German Yearbook: Feminist Studies in German Literature & Culture* 32 (2016), 163–88.

Polizei NRW Köln, 'Several hundreds of people, seemingly of African descent, have been tracked at Cologne main railway station ...', *Silvester 2016* [Facebook photo album, 4th image and caption] (edited 31 December 2016) <https://www.facebook.com/Polizei.NRW.K/photos/a.964212580377305.1073741845.127899314008640/964557803676116/?type=3&theater> accessed 3 May 2017.

Pommerin, Reiner, *Sterilisierung der Rheinlandbastarde: Das Schicksal einer farbigen deutschen Minderheit 1918–1937* (Düsseldorf: Droste, 1979).

Steinmeier, Frank-Walter, 'Designierter Bundespräsident Frank-Walter Steinmeier nach seiner Wahl zum Bundespräsidenten durch die Bundesversammlung' [transcript of speech] (12 February 2017) <http://www.bundespraesident.de/SharedDocs/Reden/DE/Frank-Walter-Steinmeier/Reden/2017/02/170212-Bundesversammlung.html> accessed 3 May 2017.

——, 'Word of Thanks to the 16th Federal Convention' [translated transcript] (12 Febuary 2017) <http://www.bundespraesident.de/SharedDocs/Reden/ EN/Frank-Walter-Steinmeier/Reden/2017/02/170212-Federal-Convention. html> accessed 3 May 2017.

Tate, Julie, and others, 'How *The Washington Post* Is Examining Police Shootings in the United States', *Washington Post* (7 July 2016) <https://www.washingtonpost. com/national/how-the-washington-post-is-examining-police-shootings-in-the-united-states/> accessed 2 May 2017.

Weber, Beverly, '"We Must Talk about Cologne": Race, Gender, and Reconfigurations of "Europe"', *German Politics and Society* 34/4 (2016), 68–86.

Wright, Michelle M., 'Others-from-Within from Without: Afro-German Subject Formation and the Challenge of a Counter-Discourse', *Callaloo* 26/2 (2003), 296–305.

——, *Becoming Black: Creating Identity in the African Diaspora* (Durham, NC and London: Duke University Press, 2005).

Yasemin Yildiz, *Beyond the Mother Tongue: The Postmonolingual Condition* (New York: Fordham University Press, 2011).

——, 'Turkish Girls, Allah's Daughters, and the Contemporary German Subject: Itinerary of a Figure', *German Life and Letters* 62/4 (2009), 465–81.

PART III

Art and Performance

KIRA THURMAN

6 'Africa in European Evening Attire': Defining African American Spirituals and Western Art Music in Central Europe, 1870s–1930s

ABSTRACT

This chapter examines how white Germans and Austrians defined the relationship between art music and Black musicianship in the nineteenth and twentieth centuries. It argues that listeners came to believe that African American spirituals – more than any other form of 'Black music' or 'Negro music' – were capable of entering the realm of high art music. Audiences worked out fluid, contradictory and fragile constructs of Blackness and culture in the nineteenth and twentieth centuries as they struggled to locate spirituals within the world of 'Black music'. What if, Germans wondered, African American spirituals were proof that Blacks were capable of civilization? What if these spirituals belonged in the opera house more than in an ethnological exhibit? Debates about African American spirituals and 'Negro music' in cities such as Berlin and Vienna illustrate how Austro-German musical culture accepted or denied Black people's ability to create high art.

What shocked famous Viennese vocal pedagogue Dr. Theodore Lierhammer was not that the African American spirituals that his pupil tenor Roland Hayes performed for him in 1923 were beautiful. It was that they sounded like Western art music. 'I vividly remember his astonishment on hearing me sing some Aframerican [*sic*] folk songs', Hayes recalled, 'an astonishment caused by the spiritual affinity of my songs with the spirit and style of the great German master [Johann Sebastian Bach]. "But you have it all there," he assured me; "it is the same language"'.[1] Like the music in Bach's *Saint Matthew Passion* or the works of composers such as Heinrich Schütz, African American spirituals, Lierhammer told Hayes, met 'on the common ground of purpose, feeling and fitting form' and shared the same musical poetic style and religious spirit.[2] What inspired Dr. Lierhammer to compare these two different musical traditions to each other?

This chapter examines how white Germans and Austrians defined the relationship between art music and Black musicianship in the nineteenth and twentieth centuries. I argue that some listeners came to believe that African American spirituals – more than any other form of 'Black music' or 'Negro music' – were capable of entering the realm of high art music.[3] The purpose of this chapter is not to demonstrate that African American spirituals ultimately gained wide acceptance as a form of art music in Central Europe. As I explain below, African American musicians often received praise for having the *potential* to become cultured in a European sense but rarely fully achieved that potential to the ears of their white German and Austrian listeners. The musical yardstick determining their eligibility into the social and cultural world of art music shifted from decade to decade. Central European debates about African American spirituals illustrate how Austro-German musical culture accepted or denied Black people's ability to create high art.

In his essay, 'Strategic Inauthenticity', ethnomusicologist Tim Taylor asks, '[s]o what has happened? Westerners – including musicians – now allow others a culture, but it is a culture in the anthropological sense. Western culture is still a culture in the opera house sense – civilization'.[4] In this chapter, I demonstrate that this racialized bifurcation of cultures – an

---

1   Roland Hayes, *My Favorite Spirituals: 30 Songs for Piano and Voice* (Mineola, NY: Dover Publications, 2001), 12.

2   Hayes, *My Favorite Spirituals*, 12. 'But the incomparable freedom of the speech of Bach in "Saint Matthew Passion", and his musical poetic style, at times find their counterpart in the religious spirit of the artless outpourings of a musical race'.

3   For this chapter, I use the phrases 'Negro music' and 'Black music' interchangeably.

4   Timothy Taylor, *Global Pop: World Music, World Markets* (New York: Routledge, 1997), 126.

anthropological primitive culture vs. Western high culture – was a historical process. High culture *became* European and Black diasporic cultures
became primitive.[5] But African American spirituals posed a challenge to
this cultural and racial segregation. Audiences worked out fluid, contradictory and fragile constructs of Blackness and culture in the nineteenth and
twentieth centuries, as they struggled to locate spirituals within the world
of 'Black music'. What if, Germans wondered, African American spirituals
were proof that Blacks were capable of civilization? What if these spirituals
belonged in the opera house more than in an ethnological exhibit?

It matters greatly what audiences in Germany and Austria thought of
African American spirituals because Central Europe was the epicenter of
Western art music. As the nation of Bach, Beethoven and Brahms, Germans
saw themselves as the purveyors of art music. They were the tastemakers,
determining what constituted beautiful art music and what had missed the
mark. Their criticisms were of global importance by the late nineteenth
century, a time when Western art music reached even more audiences
and markets around the world. African American musicians intentionally
sought out their endorsements, knowing that German praise could boost
their careers upon return to the United States. Aware of their own value,
German audiences, in turn, invested in attending Black musical concerts
and discussing their merits. Examining how audiences responded to African
American spirituals, then, grants us an opportunity to explore how Central
European listeners responded to and sought to shape transatlantic musical discourses.

German reception of African American spirituals also affords us a
new opportunity to see the constant tension humming in German musical

---

5   For more information on this theory, see Andrew Zimmerman, *Anthropology and
     Anti-Humanism in Imperial Germany* (Chicago: University of Chicago Press, 2001).
     Zimmerman argues that by the late nineteenth century, German anthropologists
     had divided people into the categories of *Kulturvölker* [civilized peoples, namely
     Europeans] and *Naturvölker* [natural or primitive peoples, namely from Africa, Asia
     and the Americas]. They assumed, in other words, that *Naturvölker* lacked the defin-
     ing characteristics of civilization such as history, a written tradition and identifiable
     cultural norms and therefore were culturally inferior to Europeans.

culture between Western art music that served the purpose of uplifting and edifying its audience and popular music that served the purpose of entertaining. The popular assumption remains that throughout the twentieth century Black music-making fell (and continues to fall) into the category of entertainment, that it provided little intellectual or spiritual fulfillment and that its value to European listeners lay precisely in its primeval difference. In the 1920s, for example, the Black popular music that had wormed its way into the ears of German and Austrian audiences appealed to listeners because they thought it was wild and liberating, not serious or cultivated. German critics such as Ivan Goll and Alice Gerstel depicted 'Black music' as the antithesis to European art music and its bourgeois values. Central European audiences therefore frequently expressed skepticism over the question of whether Blacks were capable of producing not simply Black entertainment but Black high art. Black performances of spirituals, however, encouraged listeners to consider the possibility that Black high art or Black high culture was not oxymoronic. What were they to do with a musical genre that appeared to hold spiritual, moral, cultural and aesthetic values that moved it beyond the marketplace?[6]

German debates about the meaning of Black high art reveal the ways in which Blackness and high culture could become intertwined or forcefully separated. Throughout the nineteenth and twentieth centuries, German and Austrian praise of African American spirituals was contingent upon how closely the listener perceived the performance to be in proximity to whiteness or to a perceived shared sense of European culture. The more, in other words, the nature of a Black performance sounded European, the more audiences praised its beauty. Yet a Catch-22 lurked in German criticism of African American Black art music: the more they praised Black art music for incrementally encroaching upon the realm of European art music, the more critics dismissed the music as inauthentic and complained that its creators were merely imitators. Even if the music was indeed

---

6   H. Wiley Hitchcock, *Music in the United States: A Historical Introduction*, 4th edn (Upper Saddle River, NJ: Prentice Hall, 2000), 56. See also Ralph Locke, 'On Exoticism, Western Art Music and the Words We Use', *Archiv für Musikwissenschaft* 69/4 (2012), 318–28.

thought to be an authentic expression of the Black Diaspora, it still had to be made European in order for it to be musically relatable or understood on European terms. German reception of Black high art functioned as a zero-sum game, one in which German listeners sought to make Black art European or to make it authentically Black. The assumption that undergirded debates in German musical discourse about Black music was that it was impossible for it to be authentically Black while also meeting the (European) criteria that deemed it high art.

Nowhere do we see the process of coming to terms with Black high art in German culture more powerfully than with African American spirituals and the performers who sang them. As we will see, African American musicians insisted that spirituals belonged to the world of folk songs at the very least and to the genre of art songs at their very best. By performing in custom gowns and tuxedos on some of Europe's most famous concert stages, they strove to elevate African American culture specifically and the Black Diaspora more generally in the eyes and ears of the white societies in which they participated. Their performances of respectability on and off stage resonated with their audiences, while their carefully arranged music appealed to Central European listeners' ears because it had been musically prepared to their tastes. In one sense, African American musicians had done everything right to make their music sonically and therefore culturally acceptable to German audiences and to prove they were capable of culture and civilization in the opera house sense.

But African American spirituals became caught in a double bind. The only genre that white German audiences willingly applauded for its cultivated and sophisticated nature, spirituals, also faced dismissal from audiences for the same reasons they claimed to love them: for their perceived European qualities. Their harmonic, polyphonic and melodic characteristics deemed them not authentically Black enough in an anthropological sense, since they failed to meet listeners' primitivist expectations. Their lack of rhythmic vibrancy and entertainment value in the interwar era also marked them as a (sometimes unwelcome) departure from jazz and American syncopated music as well. I argue that German conversations on how to define, locate and listen to African American spirituals throughout the nineteenth and twentieth centuries reveal the fragility of their constructed hierarchies of Black sounds, cultures and creativity.

Performing Against Primitivism: African American Musicians as Creators of High Art

Negersänger

Nachdem sie leibhaftig in einem Konzert aufgetre-
ten sind, weiß man erst, was man doch noch verliert,
wenn man glückstrahlend vor seinem Grammophon
sitzt und zusieht, wie die Nadel über die Platte
schürft, weil die Augen doch irgendwo sinngemäß
deponiert werden müssen. Sehen muß man diese Neger,
wenn sie singen. Denn während es dem europäischen
Kunstgesang entspricht, daß der Sänger — besonders
der Chorsänger — seine Eigenart möglichst unter-
drückt zugunsten dessen, was objektiv in den Noten
einmal für Alle niedergelegt ist, singt so ein Neger zu-
nächst einmal sich selbst und bedient sich dazu der

15

Figure 6.1. Rudolf Arnheim, 'Negersänger', *Stimme von der Galerie: 25 kleine Aufsätze zur Kultur der Zeit* [Voice from the Gallery: 25 Short Essays on the Culture of the Time] (Berlin: Verlag Dr. Wilhelm Bernary, 1928).

In his 1928 collection of vignettes, German writer and theorist Rudolf Arnheim describes in one of his sketches his experience hearing African American singers perform spirituals at a concert in Germany (see Figure 6.1). It is not enough, he writes, to simply hear a recording of them. 'One must see these Negroes when they perform', he urges.[7] What they offer in their renditions of 'fresh and lively folk songs' – such as 'Every Time I Feel the Spirit' and 'Hand Me Down the Silver Trumpet, Gabriel' – is a curious mixture of barbarism and *musikalische Feinfühligkeit* [musical refinement and sensitivity].[8] 'These songs are seldom true choral works', he writes. 'They have a muted if brisk march-like rhythm, and one time the beat was promptly paused as a small Negro angel sang a cadence quite high over everything, light and free, monotone, always oscillating between the same interval like an Oriental peddler'.[9] The image accompanying his sketch – drawn for the volume – visualizes Arnheim's description of African American singers as exotic primitive moderns in the minstrel tradition. Short and rotund or tall and skinny, wearing black tuxedos and white gloves, with pitch-black skin, big, white lips and wide grins revealing only a few teeth, Arnheim's black figures are well-established caricatures of Black entertainers disseminated in Central Europe since the mid-nineteenth century.[10]

The German media also depicted the now-famous Fisk Jubilee Singers in a similar manner during their landmark tour of Germany in 1877. The first large-scale musical ensemble to perform African American music in Germany, they received notable attention from the German royal family,

7   Rudolf Arnheim, *Stimme von der Galerie: 25 kleine Aufsätze zur Kultur der Zeit* (Berlin: Verlag Dr. Wilhelm Bernary, 1928), 15. All of the translations provided in this chapter are the author's own.

8   Arnheim, *Stimme von der Galerie*, 17.

9   Arnheim, *Stimme von der Galerie*, 17.

10   For more information, see David Ciarlo, *Advertising Empire: Race and Visual Culture in Imperial Germany* (Cambridge, MA: Harvard University Press, 2011); Volker Langbehn, ed., *German Colonialism, Visual Culture and Modern Memory* (New York: Routledge, 2010); Anne McClintock, *Imperial Leather: Race, Gender and Sexuality in Colonial Conquest* (New York: Routledge, 1995); and Jan Nederveen Pieterse, *White on Black: Images of Africa and Blacks in Western Popular Culture* (New Haven, CT: Yale University Press, 1992).

from audiences throughout Germany and from the German press during their ten-month tour. They deliberately performed polished renditions of African American spirituals that were accommodating to white American and European ears in order to raise funds for their newly established university (Fisk University) in Nashville, Tennessee.[11] The images that proliferated in the press of the Fisk Jubilee Singers, however, contradicted the musical, religious and cultural agenda of the Jubilee Singers. Although the ensemble was actually composed of about a dozen men and women who performed in prim and proper Victorian dress, the satirical magazine *Kladderadatsch* erased the women from their portrait of the Fisk Jubilee Singers in their depiction of them (see Figure 6.2).

By omitting women from their caricature, *Kladderadatsch* removed visual representations of modesty, respectability and moral purity that Wilhelminian values located in womanhood.[12] Instead only four men appear in the caricature, portrayed as stereotypical minstrels with big lips, unkempt hair and pitch-black skin. Their sloppy tuxedos, ape-like features and jocular posture reinforce a popular imagination of Black performers as lowbrow entertainers of low intelligence, an ensemble to be mocked rather than listened to.

Both Arnheim and *Kladderadatsch's* depictions of Black American figures belong to a greater discourse on primitivism that permeated Central European reception of Black musicians in the nineteenth and twentieth centuries. Developing in earnest in the late nineteenth century with the rise of mass culture, Central European visual, textual and musical depictions of American Blackness fixated on Black minstrelsy, jazz and other forms of Black popular entertainment they deemed primitive.[13] The notion of the

---

11   Kira Thurman, 'Singing the Civilizing Mission in the Land of Bach, Beethoven and Brahms: The Fisk Jubilee Singers in Nineteenth Century Germany', *Journal of World History* 27/3 (2016), 443–71.

12   For more information, see Karen Hagemann, and Jean Quataert, eds, *Gendering German History: Rewriting Historiography* (New York: Berghahn, 2007) and James Retallack, ed., *Imperial Germany, 1871–1918* (Oxford: Oxford University Press, 2008).

13   Sieglinde Lemke, *Primitivist Modernism: Black Culture and the Origins of Transatlantic Modernism* (Oxford: Oxford University Press, 1998); Jill Lloyd, *German Expressionism: Primitivism and Modernity* (New Haven, CT: Yale University Press,

Figure 6.2. 'A Black Attack', *Kladderadatsch* (16 December 1877), 1.

'primitive', Sieglinde Lemke writes, 'was the antonym of discipline, order, rationality – the antithesis of "civilized." The racist imagination conflated these two versions of alterity and defined people of African descent as irrational, uncivilized and not-yet-modern'.[14] What made Black people primitive was not merely their supposed lack of rational intelligence but, rather, the more serious and deeper problem of a lack of a sophisticated culture from which to draw inspiration and intellectual curiosity.

In the 1920s, the discourse of primitivist modernism focused on jazz, popular music and avant-garde aesthetics.[15] Tying Black popular performance to animalism and commercialism, to superficiality and to mimicry, primitivist modernism praised Black American entertainers for freeing Europeans from their own civilization to dance to the tune of wild self-abandonment. African American musicians such as the Chocolate Kiddies traveled across the Atlantic Ocean and enthralled their white European audiences with their exciting new instruments (the banjo, drums and

---

1991); James Deaville, 'African-American Entertainers in *Jahrhundertwende* Vienna: Austrian Identity, Viennese Modernism and Black Success', *Nineteenth-Century Music Review* 3/1 (2006), 89–112; Jonathan Wipplinger, 'The Racial Ruse: On Blackness and Blackface Comedy in "Fin-de-Siècle" Germany', *The German Quarterly* 84/4 (2011), 457–76 and Ronald Radano, *Lying Up A Nation: Race and Black Music* (Chicago: University of Chicago Press, 2003).

14   Lemke, *Primitivist Modernism*, 4. The European intellectual tradition degrading people of African descent as primitive and inferior goes back further than the twentieth century, of course. Many scholars see the origins of such thinking in the Enlightenment. See, for example, Emmanuel Chukwudi Eze, *Race and the Enlightenment: A Reader* (Hoboken: Wiley-Blackwell, 1997). Others argue that racist depictions of Black people as primitive date back to the Middle Ages. See Lynn Ramey, *Black Legacies: Race and the European Middle Ages* (Gainesville: University of Florida Press, 2014) and Geraldine Heng, 'The Invention of Race in the European Middle Ages I: Race Studies, Modernity and the Middle Ages', *Literature Compass* 8/5 (2011), 258–74.

15   See Jonathan Wipplinger, *The Jazz Republic: Music, Race and American Culture in Weimar Germany* (Ann Arbor: University of Michigan Press, 2017). For more information on primitivist modernism in Austria in the 1920s and 30s, see Ingeborg Harer, '"Dieses böse Etwas, der Jazz" Varianten der Jazz-Rezeption in Österreich von der Jahrhundertwende bis zu den 1920er Jahren', in Rudolf Flotzinger, ed., *Fremdheit in der Moderne* (Vienna: Passagen, 1999), 138–72.

saxophone, in particular) and rhythmic vibrancy. Audiences in cities such as Berlin, Frankfurt and Vienna shimmied away their post-World War I troubles and anxieties for a night, moving their bodies to the beat Black musicians pounded out. Praising jazz in racialized terms, German critic Arthur Rundt writes, '[i]t is the animal freedom, to which the Negro, having landed in the teeming jungle of the world, gives keen expression.'[16] Above all, Black performers were popular entertainers whose music was supposedly light-hearted but inconsequential in comparison to serious art music.[17]

It is precisely these primitivist discourses of the Black Diaspora – ones that depicted people of African descent as crass, highly sexualized and animalistic performers – that African American performers of spirituals were performing *against*. It was essential for performers of spirituals to present themselves as respectable, polite and mild-mannered to the European public in order to distance themselves from Black popular musicians and to position themselves as serious artists. These African American musicians practiced a politics of respectability that had been inculcated in the United States at Black institutions of higher learning and in their communities. Their efforts to create a proper appearance and to perform a moral purity, scholars such as Kevin Gaines have argued, had much to do with the politics of racial uplift in twentieth-century America.[18] 'For many black elites', Kevin Gaines writes, 'uplift came to mean an emphasis on self-help, racial solidarity, temperance, thrift, chastity, social purity, patriarchal authority

---

16 Earl R. Beck, 'German Views of Negro Life in the United States, 1919–1933', *Journal of Negro History* 48 (1963), 31, quoted in Neil McMaster, *Racism in Europe, 1870–2000* (New York: Palgrave, 2001), 136.

17 Nancy Nenno, 'Femininity, the Primitive and Modern Urban Space: Josephine Baker in Berlin', in Katharina von Ankum, ed., *Women in the Metropolis: Gender and Modernity in Weimar Culture* (Berkeley: University of California Press, 1997), 157. Figures such as Josephine Baker, Nenno writes, 'actively replicated stereotypes of the primitive'.

18 Kevin Gaines, *Uplifting the Race: Black Leadership, Politics and Culture in the Twentieth Century* (Chapel Hill: University of North Carolina Press, 1996) and Lawrence Schenbeck, *Racial Uplift and American Music, 1878–1943* (Jackson: University of Mississippi Press, 2012).

and the accumulation of wealth'.[19] Seeking social advancement and political equality in the United States, African American elites fought back against racism through their presentation of themselves as upper-class, respectable citizens.[20] The belief that they could challenge myths of Black inferiority through proper musicianship partly formed the basis of Black American cultural politics in the Jim Crow era and traveled with them across the Atlantic when they performed in Central Europe.

Their efforts to present a positive Black musical identity came at a cost. African American elites depended on patriarchal gender relations to signify their respectability and denounced performances of Blackness that did not conform to their (bourgeois) notions of culture and morality.[21] Moreover, many of these musicians participated in the devaluation of Black popular cultures globally. They saw themselves as successful models of the civilizing mission at work: they were more sophisticated and refined than their fellow African American popular entertainers and also more civilized than Africans.[22]

Who were these musicians, and why were they in Central Europe in the 1920s and 1930s? Overwhelmingly well-educated, middle- or upper-class and well-traveled, African American performers of spirituals represented an elite group of African American musicians in the United States. Some traveled to Europe as a choir from institutes of higher education such as Fisk University, the Hampton Institute or the Utica Normal and Industrial Institute, in search of sponsors and charitable donations. Led by some of the most prominent African American musicians of the day, including composer R. Nathaniel Dett, these vocal ensembles wooed audiences with their musical precision, vocal blend and classical training. The Utica Singers

---

19   Gaines, *Uplifting the Black Race*, 2.
20   Lawrence Schenbeck, 'Representing America, Instructing Europe: The Hampton Choir Tours Europe', *Black Music Research Journal* 25/1–2 (2005), 15. See also Schenbeck, *Racial Uplift and American Music*.
21   Gaines, *Uplifting the Black Race*, 5.
22   For more information, see Tunde Adeleke, *UnAfrican Americans; Nineteenth-Century Black Nationalists and the Civilizing Mission* (Lexington: University of Kentucky Press, 1998).

received ten encores after their Berlin debut in February 1930, and when the Hampton Choir performed in Dresden that same year, the *Pittsburgh Courier* reported that 'the lights of the hall had to be turned out before the enthusiastic audience would leave the building.'[23]

African American concert singers such as Marian Anderson, Abbie Mitchell, Paul Robeson, Aubrey Pankey, Lilian Evanti and Roland Hayes also flocked to Central Europe in the 1920s and 1930s. There to study classical music, they also offered song recitals to critical acclaim.[24] When Robeson decided to sing in Europe in 1929, he had just completed a successful run in London as a stage actor in the musical *Show Boat*. Building upon his newfound success, Robeson decided to embark on a tour of Central Europe – including Prague, Brno, Vienna, Berlin and Dresden – with his wife, Essie, choosing to present concert programs consisting mostly of spirituals.[25] Later in 1930, observing the large and enthusiastic crowd gathered in Vienna to hear the Hampton Choir perform, the *New York*

23   'Hampton Choir Making Triumphant Tour of England and Scotland', *The Pittsburgh Courier* (7 June 1930).

24   Abbie Mitchell, who studied in Vienna in the 1920s, became an avid supporter and performer of a new collection of art songs put together by a group of modern Viennese composers interested in the Harlem Renaissance. Called 'Afrika Singt' [Africa Sings], the musical anthology of 27 poems from Harlem Renaissance poets such as Langston Hughes and Countee Cullen featured music by Wilhelm Grosz, Fritz Kramer, Edmund Nick, Kurt Pahlen, Erich Zeisl and Alexander Zemlinsky. In a recital in the United States in 1931, Mitchell sang a collection of these songs, including 'Angst' [Fear], 'Erlebnis' [Experience], 'Erkenntnis' [Insight], 'Vor Uns Liegt Morgen' [Tomorrow Lies Before Us], 'Elend' [Suffering] and 'Ich Bin Amerika' [I Am America]. Considering that Mitchell performed these pieces in 1931 – around the time of their publication – it is possible that she acquired copies of these pieces prior to their publication during her tenure in Vienna. For more information on this musical endeavor, see Malcolm S. Cole, '"Afrika singt": Austro-German Echoes of the Harlem Renaissance', *Journal of the American Musicological Society* 30/1 (1977), 72–95.

25   Robeson's success followed him around continental Europe, and he frequently had to reschedule more appearances to his sold-out concerts throughout Central Europe. For more information on Robeson's career in Central Europe, see Martin Duberman, *Paul Robeson* (New York: Knopf, 1989).

Times explained, 'Vienna, despite a reputation for musical conservatism, had already acclaimed Negro music when it was introduced some time ago by Paul Robeson and other soloists'.[26]

German and Austrian adoration of African American spirituals had everything to do with the musicians who performed them. African American performers of spirituals sought to convince audiences of the edifying and uplifting virtues of their music in four ways: first, by giving public lectures and promotional interviews with the press to instruct their audiences on what 'Negro music' was and what it sounded like; second, by performing their music in elite social spaces associated with European high art music; third, by presenting their own bodies as respectable vessels for musical performance; and lastly, by juxtaposing African American spirituals with Western art music in their concert programs. Their performative efforts on and off stage strove to place African American spirituals at the top of a Black diasporic musical pyramid: more beautiful than 'primitive' African music and more dignified and refined than Black American popular entertainment; their music was proof, they countered, of the sophisticated and cultivated nature of African Americans in the modern era. African American spirituals were sonic evidence that all Black people had the potential to become civilized.[27]

African American musicians' desire to inform or correct European ideas about African American music and culture through their interviews with the press was evident throughout the interwar period. Dett, a conductor and composer who had studied at the Oberlin Conservatory of Music, told European newspapers in 1930, for example, that 'the Negro is more than a minstrel. We are not all Josephine Bakers'.[28] Prominent African American public intellectual William Pickens gave a lecture in Vienna, called 'Negro Spirituals and Other Music', on 18 July 1932, and in May 1931, Howard University chemistry professor Julian Percy, who had studied chemistry at the University of Vienna, delivered a lecture in German that was broadcast through Germany and Austria, called 'The Negro Which Europe Does Not

26   'Hampton Choir in Vienna', *New York Times* (24 May 1930).
27   See Thurman, 'Singing the Civilizing Mission'.
28   *New York Amsterdam News* (21 May 1930).

Know'.[29] For many African American elites, it was essential to disseminate *their* interpretation of African American music and culture to the press. Their words further cemented in listeners' minds the serious nature of African American spirituals.[30]

Anderson, for example, sought to dignify African American spirituals in her interviews with Central European presses in the interwar period: 'I prefer to sing above all whatever is good. [I sing] Handel and the great Italian masters just as fondly as spirituals, which express the soul of my people the most beautifully. Above all I love music in which lies the possibilities to portray profound emotions and produce [beautiful] tones'.[31] In the same interview, she also cited African American tenor Hayes's musicianship as another example of how African American music and musicians channeled the same spirit as European art music and musicians:

> The first significant impression that really connected with me was the singing of Roland Hayes, who everyone in Vienna already knows. As I heard him – he sang Handel – I knew for the first time what expression truly was. ... For this reason one can find it understandable that I portray Handel or Bach with the same devotion as my spirituals. Behind such music lie eternal values. And only those [values] should we as artists seek.[32]

29 'Pickens Gives Six Austrian Talks', *Atlanta Daily World* (14 August 1932), 6 and *Afro-American* (2 May 1931).

30 *Neues Wiener Journal* (8 October 1925).

31 'Die Negersängerin mit der weissen Seele', found in the Annenberg Rare Books and Manuscript Collection at the University of Pennsylvania: MS Coll 200 Box 225, 09577.

32 'Die Negersängerin mit der weissen Seele'. In a separate interview for the *Neue Freie Presse*, Anderson remarked: '[r]egardless of the many unfortunate isolated cases, racial prejudice against us Negroes in America and the social barriers [that exist for us] are disappearing. The Negro's consciousness and feeling of community has been powerfully strengthened, and they see with satisfaction that their cultural, scientific and artistic achievements are being recognized by the predominant majority of ready white folks in America. The colored citizens of the United States are an important cultural element and the controlling factors of the white population follow with sympathy this upswing and this rapid and forward-looking [*zukunftverheitzende*] development of the colored people. All the more do I look forward to a return to my

Much like the Fisk Jubilee Singers, African American performers of spirituals sought out European high art spaces in which to perform, thus legitimizing spirituals as art music. The Hampton Choir performed at the Salzburg Cathedral (where Mozart had worked) in the 1930s, Robeson sang 'Water Boy' in Vienna's *Konzerthaus*, and the Utica Singers performed in the Beethoven Hall in Berlin. Because they booked the most revered and sacred concert spaces in Central Europe, they implicitly encouraged their audiences to hear their music as superior to other forms of Black music. Audiences arrived to the concert hall already expecting or assuming that they would be hearing cultivated, serious music. By the nature of their performance spaces alone, these musicians were able to differentiate themselves from jazz performers in cabaret clubs or Black entertainers in dance halls.

The African American press in the 1920s and 1930s overwhelmingly endorsed these kinds of performances abroad. Writing approvingly of the Utica Singers performance in Berlin in 1930, African American journalist Lewis McMillan remarked,

> I was impressed with them. They are not loud and wild, as most road troups [*sic*]. They are a fine, natural, respectable set of young people. They do not pose as artists, and neither do they act the part of monkeys. I was really pleasantly surprised to find absent so much of the effect at making the audience laugh. There was some of it present and any of it is too much. But as I have said, the Utica Singers are at least respectable, that means also on the stage.[33]

The *New York Amsterdam News* made similar remarks about the Hampton Choir who traveled to Central Europe that same year: 'They are a band of earnest young men and women, eager to show England and Europe that the Negro race must be taken seriously.'[34]

Being respectable on the stage was an essential element to their roles as interpreters of African American spirituals. Anderson became an iconic figure in Central Europe as the anti-Josephine Baker because of her beautiful

---

American home'. 'Die Negersängerin Marian Anderson in Wien', *Neue Freie Presse* (21 November 1935).

33   'Utica Singers Score in Berlin Concert,' *Afro-American* (22 February 1930).

34   *New York Amsterdam News* (21 May 1930).

yet pious appearance. Arriving on stage in elegant, expensive, yet modest-looking gowns, she exuded primness, sincerity and artistry. Her sartorial choices were never supposed to distract the audience from the serious purpose of her art. The Viennese press dubbed Robeson 'Africa in European evening attire' because he always appeared in a tuxedo for his concerts of African American spirituals.[35] All of the musicians who performed spirituals in interwar Europe participated in a transatlantic politics of respectability through their dress, speech and behavior on stage.

Different musicians' promotional materials also tell us that they positioned themselves as upper-class performers of art music. A September 1931 issue of the industry journal *Radio Wien* features several African American performers of spirituals in concert dress (see Figure 6.3).

Dressed in the latest fashion or artfully arranged as an SATB choir inside a cathedral, the African American performers in the four images present a polished and edifying portrayal of African American musicians and their music.

What also ensured that German and Austrian audiences heard spirituals as art music were the musical programming choices of different singers. Whether they were performing for German or Austrian radio or on stage, nearly all of these musicians and musical groups juxtaposed African American spirituals with Western art music. African American classical musicians, for example, usually sang a few spirituals at the end of their concert program. After the singers had proved themselves as authentic and refined interpreters of Western art music by performing lieder by Schubert, Brahms, Wolf and others, they then performed a few 'Negro folk songs' as the proverbial icing on the cake of a musical evening, and the German and Austrian press treated them as such. Other choirs presented a mixed repertoire of songs, even though African American spirituals were the highlight of their program. It was not unusual for the concert program of the Hampton Choir to feature a Bach chorale, Russian liturgical music, Appalachian mountain folk songs and spirituals from the United States

---

35   'Afrika Singt: Paul Robeson im Mittleren Konzerthaussaal', *Die Stunde* (11 April 1929), 7.

Figure 6.3. Hans Ewald Heller, 'Negermusik', *Radio Wien* (4 September 1931), 12.

and the Caribbean.[36] Although Robeson only sang folk songs on his tour, he juxtaposed different folk songs, including Hungarian 'gypsy' music, Czech folk songs, Slavonic music and African American spirituals. Their mixed musical repertoires suggest that these musicians were comfortable performing not only the African diaspora but a broader transnationalism as well.

The African American spirituals that many musicians sang in Central Europe had been altered or rearranged for European tastes since the time of the Fisk Jubilee Singers. Hayes' performance in Berlin in 1925 featured a chamber music ensemble of strings and harp for his rendition of African American spirituals, and Anderson worked with her Finnish accompanist Kosti Vehanen to present her own interpretation of beloved African American spirituals.[37] Many musicians sang arrangements by African American composers who had formally studied classical music, such as Dett, Hall Johnson and Harry Thacker Burleigh. European art music greatly influenced their own musical renditions of African American music even as they launched ethnomusicological quests throughout the South to collect and preserve this music.[38]

The most notable example of how African American musicians blended African American spirituals with European art musical practices was the musical output of Dett. He arranged the African American spirituals that his ensemble, the Hampton Choir, sang in Europe, and his education as a classical composer shone through his compositions. Many of his compositions were German in form and style, such as his motets, chorales and cantatas. For example, the beginning of his most famous piece, 'Listen to the Lambs' – the opening number in Vienna – shares many musical

36   Schenbeck, 'Representing America', 31.
37   *Berlin Börsen-Courier* (15 September 1925).
38   See Jon Cruz, *Culture on the Margins: The Black Spiritual and the Rise of American Cultural Interpretation* (Princeton, NJ: Princeton University Press, 1999); Jon Michael Spencer, 'R. Nathaniel Dett's Views on the Preservation of Black Music', *The Black Perspective in Music* 10/2 (1982), 132–48; and Brian Moon, 'Harry Burleigh as Ethnomusicologist? Transcription, Arranging and "The Old Songs Hymnal"', *Black Music Research Journal* 24/2 (2004), 287–307.

characteristics with several Brahms lieder, especially 'Verlorene Jugend' [Lost Youth] from his *Fünf Gesänge* (opus 104) [*Five Songs*] and 'Darthulas Grabgesang' [Dirge of Darthula] from *Drei Gesänge* (opus 42) [*Three Songs*]. The intention to sound Brahmsian in Dett's music was deliberate. In a 1918 article, Dett articulated his desire to blend African American music and European art music together:

> We have this wonderful folk music – the melodies of an enslaved people, who poured out their longings, their griefs and their aspirations in the one, great, universal language. But this store will be of no value unless we utilize it, unless we treat it in such manner that it can be presented in choral form, in lyric and operatic works, in concertos and suites and salon music – unless our musical architects take the rough timber of Negro themes and fashion from it music which will prove that we, too, have national feelings and characteristics, as have the European peoples whose forms we have zealously followed for so long.[39]

Other musicians, such as the Utica Singers, who traveled to Berlin, Breslau, Frankfurt/Main, Vienna, Cologne, Prague and Budapest, also preached the evolutionary nature of spirituals from the time of slavery until the present day.[40]

Singing Harry T. Burleigh's 'Deep River' to white Central European audiences in the 1920s and 1930s, African American performers shared their perspective on African American music, one based on decades of prior transatlantic travel. Steeped in moral purity, respectability politics and classical music training, their musical performances sought to divorce Black high art music from popular assumptions of Blackness, even if, one might argue, they affirmed such ways of thinking.

---

39   May Stanley, 'R. N. Dett, of Hampton Institute: Helping to Lay Foundation for Negro Music of Future', *Black Perspective of Music* 1/1 (1973), 66, quoted in Lawrence Schenbeck, 'Hampton Choir Tours Europe'. Schenbeck also writes that 'it is also helpful here to recall the degree to which "development" of the spirituals was bound up with the black elites' broader project of achieving parity with white America' (15).

40   J. Rosamand Johnson, ed., *The Utica Jubilee Singers Song Book* (Philadelphia: Oliver Ditson Company, 1930), xv.

Are They African or American? Coming to Terms with the Black Diaspora and African American Spirituals in Nineteenth-Century Central Europe

In spite of African American attempts to dictate to Germans how to listen to 'Negro music', audiences still relied heavily on their own discourses of Blackness and primitivism to make sense of these performances. Indeed, Central European reception of African American spirituals reveals audiences' great difficulties in coming to terms with the complexities of the Black Diaspora. African Americans did not comply with listeners' tight formulations of race, ethnicity, culture and nationality. The difficulties in parsing out the differences between being Black and being African were nearly insurmountable, given white European constructions of what these identities were thought to entail. Moreover, the growing distinction between African American high art music and African American popular music became a point of debate among academics and music critics over whether or not Black diasporic cultures had the potential to evolve and change.

Part of what was at stake in changing German formulations about the Black diaspora concerned the blurring of the dichotomy between *'Naturvölker'* [natural or primitive peoples, usually non-European] and *'Kulturvölker'* [civilized or cultured peoples, usually white European] that had been established in the nineteenth century. As Andrew Zimmerman, Pascal Grosse and others have argued, academics in the nineteenth century divorced non-European peoples from narratives of Western civilization and progress. 'Instead of studying European "cultural peoples" (*Kulturvölker*), societies defined by their history and civilization', Zimmerman writes, 'anthropologists studied the colonized "natural peoples" (*Naturvölker*), societies supposedly lacking history and culture.'[41] African American culture indicated a blurring or even a disintegration of these constructed categories, which frustrated Central European productions of clear, consistent and organized racial knowledge. Some listeners found it inconceivable

41   Zimmerman, *Anthropology and Anti-Humanism in Imperial Germany*, 3.

for African Americans to be considered *Kulturvölker* in a European sense. Yet the music of African American spirituals could be listened to in that key. Heard as both Western and non-Western, African American music both possessed *and* lacked an ethnic authenticity because of its ambiguous origins in the Middle Passage and because of its romanticized roots in plantation life in the deep South.

In the nineteenth century, music critics heard African American spirituals as a kind of European folk music; they were in the same category as the music of other European Others. Compared to the music of Hungarians, Roma and Sinti, Jews, French Huguenots, Greeks, Serbs, Poles and the Swiss, African American spirituals seemed to embody all that was different from German art music and belonged instead to a larger melting pot of other national and ethnic styles. For example, the *Leipziger Allgemeine Musikalische Zeitung* wrote that, 'like the Tyrolers or the Swedes, they, too, bring the songs of their people, songs of faith, of hope, of belief, and yet at other times, songs full of humor, songs which have been handed down by slaves who couldn't read a line of poetry and never learned how to write a note'.[42]

Later in 1905, popular German music journal *Die Musik* also confirmed that African American spirituals were in actuality folk music; this time, the critic heard them as Scottish and Irish folk songs: '[o]ne finds the same five-tone scales (without the quarter and leading tones) in the music of the Scots (behold Mendelssohn's Scottish Symphony), the same accent on the weak beat in Irish songs, the quick six-eight tempo in Irish jigs and the refrain in the English ballad (not to be mixed up with the German '*Ballade*')'.[43]

As musicologist Richard Taruskin explains, the nineteenth-century fascination with folk music entails

> a mere recycling of an ancient idea, that of 'primitivism', the belief that the qualities of technologically backward or chronologically early cultures are superior to those of contemporary civilization, or more generally, that it is those things that are least socialized, least civilized – children, peasants, 'savages', raw emotion, plain speech

42   *Leipziger Allgemeine Musikalische Zeitung* (20 March 1878), 190.
43   Martin Darkow, 'Die Musik der amerikanischen Neger', *Die Musik* (1905), 279.

– that are closest to truth ... No one had ever more effectively asserted the superiority of unspoiled 'nature' over decadent 'culture'.[44]

The formulation of 'nature' vs. 'culture' within nineteenth-century German music criticism of folksongs bears striking similarities to German anthropological discourse in the nineteenth century. This generally assumed dichotomy explains why German music critics' comparison of African American spirituals to European folk traditions was not a radical departure in perspective on the sonic qualities of African American music, even if critics claimed to hear spirituals in a European tone. Rather, these criticisms sought to reaffirm their conviction that African American spirituals were at an earlier stage of musical development than Western art music.

Because critics in the nineteenth century had chosen to locate African American spirituals within the evolutionary plane of European folk songs, what they emphasized was that, much like how primeval European folk music had developed over centuries (and with the aid of 'genius' composers such as Liszt or Brahms), African American music possessed the *potential* to become European art music. A journalist for the *National-Zeitung*, for example, argued in 1877 that the spirituals 'were simply the lingering reverberations of European music'.[45] The *Neue Berliner Musikzeitung* concluded after hearing the Fisk Jubilee Singers sing at the Berliner Dom,

> Hungarian music had to wait a few years before it could – through the efforts of Liszt, Brahms and others – be made accessible to German friends of the arts and then positively influence German production. Should Negro music find an apostle with the same energy and talent as those found in Hungarian music, who knows if the music won't achieve a similar position in our musical life?[46]

With the right musical genius, the critic believes, the music of African Americans could be improved upon to enter into the Western art music canon.

44   Richard Taruskin, 'The Discovery of the Folk', *Oxford History of Western Music* <http://www.oxfordwesternmusic.com/> accessed 20 May 2016.
45   *National-Zeitung* (9 November 1877), 3.
46   *Neue Berliner Musikzeitung* (15 November 1877), 362.

The singers themselves also demonstrated much potential to become practitioners of European culture. The *Volkszeitung* praised Fisk Jubilee Singer Frederick Loudin in such a manner. 'He is master of a very grand voice of great compass (over two octaves)', the critic raved, '[and] the wonderful subtle soft and sure falsetto and the clear intonation are all perfect; and if Mr Loudin understands how to sing European music, which we have no reason to doubt, he would be one of the finest singers in Europe'.[47] Lying in close proximity to European art music, Loudin's musicianship was deemed worthy of cultivation because it had the potential to transform into something considered more dignified than ethnic folk singing.

German music criticism, however, always placed a double bind on African American spirituals: whatever appeared in close proximity to German music performances was then later rendered imitative in order to locate the origins of culture in white Europe. Beginning in the 1890s, for example, ethnomusicologists and anthropologists also became invested in defining and describing African American spirituals in relation to European art music. Although they believed that African Americans had created the most sophisticated 'Negro music' within the Black diaspora, they concluded that it lacked authenticity because of its imitative European qualities. Their lamentations of Black music's decline align with scholars' observations that German thinkers sought a pure, uncorrupted primitive culture against which they could position themselves. 'From the beginning', Zimmerman writes, 'anthropologists complained that the people they encountered were corrupted by contact with Europeans and thus were poor examples of natural peoples'.[48] They feared, Anne Maria Busse Berger argues, a 'hybrid form of music (European-African)' that they denounced as inauthentic.[49]

---

47   *Volkszeitung* (7 November 1877), 3, repr. and trans. in *The Christian Recorder* (3 January 1878). German transcription from the newspaper archive at the Staatsbibliothek zu Berlin.

48   Zimmerman, *Anthropology and Anti-Humanism in Imperial Germany*, 7.

49   Anna Maria Busse Berger, 'Spreading the Gospel of *Singbewegung*: An Ethnomusicologist Missionary in Tanganyika of the 1930s', *Journal of the American Musicological Society* 66/2 (2013), 162.

Austrian comparative musicologist Richard Wallaschek, for example, dismissed the originality and authenticity of spirituals in his book, *Primitive Music*, in the 1890s. 'It is a remarkable fact', he writes, 'that one author has frequently copied his praise of Negro-songs from another, and determined from it the great capabilities of the Blacks, when a closer examination would have revealed the fact that they were not musical songs at all, but merely simple poems'.[50] He complained, 'I cannot think that these and the rest of the songs deserve the praise given by the editors, for they are unmistakably "arranged" – not to say ignorantly borrowed – from the national songs of all nations, from military signals, well-known marches, German student-songs, etc.; unless it is pure accident which has caused me to light upon traces of so many of them'.[51]

What might be uniquely African American, he offered instead, are their 'peculiar guttural sounds and rhythmical effects', which were as difficult to reproduce as 'the songs of birds or the tones of an Aeolian harp'.[52] Did whites influence African American spirituals or were spirituals simply an imitation of white music? He was not sure. He worried that African American spirituals were 'mere imitations of European compositions which the Negroes have picked up and served up again with slight variations', yet he nonetheless argued throughout his treatise that they were the only form of Black music making worth listening to.[53] But the music, he lamented, is 'no longer primitive, even in its wealth of borrowed melody'.[54]

Ethnomusicologist Erich von Hornbostel also lamented the civilized nature to African American spirituals in his famous treatise, *African Negro Music*. He noted,

50 Richard Wallaschek, *Primitive Music: An Inquiry into the Origin and Development of Music, Songs, Instruments, Dances and Pantomimes of Savage Races* (1893; repr. New York: Da Capo Press, 1970), 60.
51 Wallaschek, *Primitive Music*, 61.
52 Wallaschek, *Primitive Music*, 61.
53 Wallaschek, *Primitive Music*, 61.
54 Wallaschek, *Primitive Music*, 61.

The African Negroes are uncommonly gifted for music – probably, on an average, more so, than the white race. This is clear not only from the high development of African music, especially as regards polyphony and rhythm, but a very curious fact, unparalleled, perhaps, in history, makes it even more evident; namely, the fact that the Negro slaves in America and their descendants, abandoning their original musical style, have adapted themselves to that of their white masters and produced a new kind of folk music in that style. Presumably no other people would have accomplished this. (In fact the plantation songs and spirituals, and also the blues and rag-times which have launched or helped to launch our modern dance music, are the only remarkable kinds of music brought forth in America by immigrants.) At the same time this shows how readily the Negro abandons his own style of music for that of the European.[55]

Such criticism located the origins of African American spirituals in whiteness and in European musical traditions, at the expense of Black musical originality. Because *Kulturvölker* could only come from Europe, that which they identified musically as civilized (polyphonic, harmonic musical language) could only be European in origin.

Maintaining these strict cultural dichotomies and rhetorically tap-dancing their way through what they perceived to be profound cultural and racial paradoxes was exhausting, and music critics and anthropologists in the nineteenth century frequently wrote of African American spirituals in tones of exasperation. How could music so 'simple' nonetheless be so difficult for Europeans to fully grasp? How was it possible for the music to be both new and exciting while also ultimately derivative? Their dichotomies – Black vs. white, natural vs. civilized, pure vs. decadent, simple vs. sophisticated – frequently collapsed even as they continually tried to shore them up. The sonic ambiguities and musical complexities within African American spirituals were precisely that with which music criticism could not come to terms. None of the categories that critics or anthropologists urged listeners to use ultimately served the functions critics claimed they did (or hoped they would).

---

55   Erich Moritz von Hornbostel, *African Negro Music* (Oxford: Oxford University Press, 1928), 60.

Blackness and Art Music Revisited: Central European Reception of African American Spirituals in the Jazz Age

In the 1920s and 1930s, Central European audiences continued to applaud spirituals in the same key but with a slight variation: African American spirituals now offered an alternative to jazz and stood alone as the one particular kind of 'Negro music' that some listeners accorded respect. Their comments were an obvious response to the boom in popularity of jazz in the interwar era, yet they were also consistent with previous generations' evaluations of spirituals. The language of racial uplift and respectability and the aesthetics of folk music and art music continued to determine how Central Europeans understood African American spirituals in the interwar period. Critics again expressed pleasant surprise upon hearing spirituals in contrast to other forms of 'Black music'.

African American spirituals were 'unspoiled' and 'pure' in comparison to 'decadent', jazz-obsessed Europe. Steeped in romanticism and exoticism, critics' praise reflected their fascination with slavery, plantation life and the Mississippi. The *Berliner Tageblatt* marveled that the spirituals Hayes performed were 'sung like they were on the plantation'.[56] When Robeson sang 'Water Boy' in Vienna, one critic wrote that Robeson 'brought more of the nature of his people than a half dozen scientific publications and lectures [could teach us]'.[57] In other words, Taylor's formulation of non-European cultures being understood anthropologically applies quite easily to 1920s music criticism in Vienna: Robeson's performance, as many others, was an ethnomusicological lesson in Black American culture.

Much like in the nineteenth century, German critics again described African American spirituals as childlike, pure, simple and melancholic music, even despite the arrangements presented to them by Anderson, Hayes and different musical ensembles. After Anderson's famous debut in

56   *Berliner Tageblatt und Handels-Zeitung* (17 May 1924), 4.
57   *Die Stunde* (11 April 1929), 7.

Salzburg in 1935, a critic for the conservative daily newspaper *Salzburger Volksblatt* wrote that the African American spirituals she performed were sweet and lovely. They reflected what it was like for 'a child's mind to deal with God'.[58] Describing the thirty-eight-year-old singer as a 'little brown girl, sweet, polite and happy to receive the homage', the critic wrote that Anderson's performance reminded him of a child whose eyes look up to the heavens 'with a religious joy'.[59] Another critic described the spirituals Hayes performed in Vienna as a mix of 'soothing, bright child piety and dark ecstasy',[60] and when Robeson sang in Vienna in 1929, the Viennese press also emphasized his child-like qualities: after an interview with the singer, the press reported that he 'spoke like a happy child' about his success in Vienna.[61]

Most reports sensationalized these singers as African primitives who had transformed audiences' appreciation for 'Negro music'. 'The public', a journalist for the Viennese daily newspaper *Die Stunde* writes, 'foreshadowing a sensation, filled the hall like [we haven't seen] in a long time. One wanted to hear a Negro sing, one wanted to also see a Negro, how a Negro sings ....'.[62] Instead, the audience discovered, they had 'stumbled suddenly into the middle of an eminently artistic matter'.[63] Black musicians, in this critic's formulation, are not artists. But, he writes, Robeson challenged the audiences' expectations:

> The cheap public sensation failed to appear and another one was put in [its place]. This magnificent grown[-up] Negro in the smoking jacket with a luminously white front shirt – Africa in European evening attire – is a phenomenon of the voice, a wonder of inner expression, and one sits opposite, dumbfounded and hit over the head by the magic of such an achievement.[64]

58   *Salzburger Volksblatt* (29 August 1935).
59   *Salzburger Volksblatt* (29 August 1935).
60   *Deutsche Tageszeitung* (15 May 1924).
61   *Die Stunde* (11 April 1929), 7.
62   *Die Stunde* (11 April 1929), 7.
63   *Die Stunde* (11 April 1929), 7.
64   *Die Stunde* (11 April 1929), 7.

After hearing Robeson so artfully sing spirituals for him, the journalist now understood why Vienna had begun to 'beat the Negro drum'.[65] Because of Robeson's showmanship, his ability to possess the 'original elements of his race [in the art] of theatricality' and embody 'the tragedy of the colored people in a white society', he gave a convincing performance of African American spirituals.[66] As soon as Robeson began 'to sing one of the deepest melancholiest fulfilling Negro spirituals', the concert hall became 'eerily quiet'.

Following Robeson's last performance, the audience showered him with thunderous applause. 'One stomped and screamed. The savages were on the parquet, and above [on the stage] was a humble Negro'.[67] In this instance, the critic reverses the dichotomy of *Naturvölker* and *Kulturvölker* in a similar manner as Ivan Goll's essay 'The Negroes are Conquering Europe' or Alice Gerstel's 'Jazz Band': it was not African-descended peoples who were the real barbarians, but rather Europeans.[68] This compliment, however, was a backhanded one. Dating back to the time of the Fisk Jubilee Singers' tour in the 1870s, Central European critics routinely thanked Black Americans for coming to Europe to rescue Germans and Austrians from themselves. Europeans, destroyed by their own sophisticated culture, were now in need of a primeval simplicity (that Blacks supposedly possessed) that could serve as the foundation for their regeneration.

Much of what anchored Central European praise for African American performers of spirituals concerned genre: it was not jazz or Black popular music. No longer contrasted against European folk music, African

---

65   *Die Stunde* (11 April 1929), 7.
66   *Die Stunde* (11 April 1929), 7.
67   *Die Stunde* (11 April 1929), 7.
68   Of course, some audiences still insisted on the musical inferiority of African American spirituals. When Hayes visited Leipzig in 1926, his performance at the *Gewandhaus* went terribly. In addition to singing Bach in the *Bachstadt* [home of Bach] for his audience, he sang African American spirituals for them as well to tepid applause. Reviews in the Leipzig press later complained that the African American spirituals were their least favorite pieces on his program. The critic scathingly said that they did not even sound like music. See Helm MacKinley, *Angel Mo' and Her Son* (New York: Greenwood Press, 1969), 215.

American spirituals in the interwar era instead gained their admiration
from critics by virtue of their form of Black musical representation. Central
European audiences applauded these musicians and their music precisely
because what they performed was not Black popular music. Classically
trained baritone Pankey, critics wrote, deserved praise for singing both
Schubert and spirituals because he presented a musical alternative for listeners who loathed jazz music. As one critic stated, 'He is a boon for our period
where one is very easily inclined to see in all Negro musicians mere Jazzband
Clowns'.[69] Pankey also sang in Berlin, performing Schubert's 'Wanderer'
[Wanderer Fantasy] and 'Nacht und Träume' [Night and Dreams], and
he concluded with a series of African American spirituals, including 'The
Day is Done'.[70] Audiences thoroughly enjoyed Pankey's concert, especially his renditions of African American spirituals. The critic of the *Berlin
Börsen-Courier* wrote, '[o]n the same evening one heard as an Intermezzo
to *Carmen* a Negro baritone in the Bechstein auditorium. Aubrey Pankey
sang spirituals. They do not interest [me] anymore. But rarely have I heard
them carried out with so much taste, with such singing skill, with so much
inner force than I heard them from the reserved and debonair Pankey'.[71]
Singers such as Pankey had freed themselves from the commercial grip of
jazz and other forms of Black popular music through their perfection of
spirituals as a musical genre and had quite possibly become practitioners
of a Black high art.

Composers such as Ernst Krenek, who wrote the jazz opera *Jonny
spielt auf* [*Jonny Plays*], also suggested that spirituals were the superior form
of 'Negro music'. 'Whoever knows the unheard of power of expression
that lies in the spirituals and folk songs (*Heimatgesänge*) of the American
Negro', he stated, 'in which with an almost crushing intensity the entire
naïve and unbroken emotional strength of a strong and tragic people are
expressed in all possible shades of human feeling, will see jazz music as

---

69   Darryl Glenn Nettles, *African American Concert Singers Before 1950* (Jefferson, NC:
     McFarland, 2003), 126.

70   Nettles, *African American Concert Singers Before 1950*, 126.

71   'Armenischer Tenor und schwarzer Bariton', *Berliner Börsen-Courier* (13 May
     1932), 2.

more than a comic form of entertainment'.[72] For those who truly wished to
engage with meaningful Black musical expression, Krenek argued, African
American spirituals were the best place to start because they were simply
foundational. Inspired by African American poetry and spirituals during the
Harlem Renaissance, German and Austrian composers such as Alexander
Zemlinsky, Kurt Pahlen and Wilhelm Grosz sought to incorporate 'Negro
music' into their compositions as well.[73]

But in pitting the two genres – cultivated African American spirituals vs. Black popular entertainment music – against each other, German
listeners devalued both. Music critics' claims that spirituals were more or
less authentic than jazz encouraged audiences to assume that there was
only one legitimate way to perform 'Negro music'. Debates about 'Negro
music' in the interwar period reveal how Austro-German musical culture
both celebrated and marginalized Black musicality. Listeners' quests to
discover and champion an authentic genre of Black music illuminate their
own evolving constructs of Blackness and whiteness at work in one of the
most studied transatlantic eras. The ambiguous place of African American
spirituals in German musical culture – sophisticated but inauthentic, beautiful yet derivative, possessing moral qualities supposedly found lacking in
popular Black entertainment but nonetheless artistically naïve or simple
– formed the tenor of Central European listening practices in the early to
mid-twentieth century.

Conclusion: Postwar Reverberations

In a city still recuperating from the traumas of war, African American
soprano Ellabelle Davis arrived in 1948 to offer the Viennese a *Liederabend*
[lied recital]. One of the first singers of color to perform in Vienna's elite

---

72   Jonathan Wipplinger, 'Performing Race in *Jonny spielt auf*, in Naomi André, Karen
     M. Bryan and Eric Saylor, eds, *Blackness in Opera* (Urbana-Champaign: University
     of Illinois Press, 2012), 243.
73   See Cole, '"Afrika singt"'.

spaces again since before the war, she conjured memories of a recent prewar past in the minds of the Viennese. Her performances of spirituals especially, the critic wrote nostalgically, reminded everyone of Anderson and her interpretations of them.[74] Spirituals had returned to Central Europe.

Yet again they became a valuable marker of deviation away from Black popular music. In communist East Germany, for example, officials denounced jazz as a capitalist product of American imperialism yet applauded African American folk music and spirituals as the only true and authentic expression of African American culture.[75] The only music worthy of reverence and esteem, African American spirituals and their performers became part of a narrative in the German Democratic Republic that celebrated only a particular kind of Blackness that was the most useful for East German political purposes.[76]

African American spirituals – as a genre of music that became associated with high art music or serious concert music – became a marker of difference within the Black Diaspora. At the top of a Black musical pyramid, African American spirituals served an important function in the history of German hierarchization of Black peoples. Performers of African American spirituals resisted the notion that African American music (and hence, African American people) were primitive through their presentations of the music. German and Austrian listeners applauded spirituals if they sounded like European art music, but simultaneously dismissed them for their perceived European qualities that deemed them not truly Black. Central European reception of spirituals was always contingent upon

---

74   'Konzert Ellabelle Davis', *Wiener Tageszeitung* [later *Österreichische Neue Tageszeitung*] (4 April 1948), 5.

75   Martin Klimke, and Maria Höhn, *A Breath of Freedom: The Civil Rights Struggle, African American GIs and Germany* (New York: Palgrave MacMillan, 2010), 129. See also Uta Poiger, *Jazz, Rock and Rebels: Cold War Politics and American Culture in a Divided Germany* (Berkeley: University of California Press, 2000) and Danielle Fosler-Lussier, *Music in America's Cold War Diplomacy* (Berkeley: University of California Press, 2015).

76   Sara Lennox, 'Reading Transnationally: The GDR and Black American Writers', in Elaine Kelly and Amy Wlodarski, eds, *Art Outside the Lines: New Perspectives on GDR Art Culture* (New York: Rodopi, 2011), 111–30.

competing and conflicting notions of Blackness and where it was located, on unstable definitions of authenticity, on changing musical aesthetics and on the performers themselves. Loved and dismissed, applauded but negated, African American spirituals always represented the best of the Black Diaspora and its limitations in German musical culture.

Bibliography

Adeleke, Tunde, *UnAfrican Americans: Nineteenth-Century Black Nationalists and the Civilizing Mission* (Lexington: University of Kentucky Press, 1998).

Arnheim, Rudolf, *Stimme von der Galerie: 25 kleine Aufsätze zur Kultur der Zeit* (Berlin: Verlag Dr. Wilhelm Bernary, 1928).

Beck, Earl R., 'German Views of Negro Life in the United States, 1919–1933', *Journal of Negro History* 48 (1963), 31.

Berger, Anna Maria Busse, 'Spreading the Gospel of *Singbewegung*: An Ethnomusicologist Missionary in Tanganyika of the 1930s', *Journal of the American Musicological Society* 66/2 (2013), 475–522.

Ciarlo, David, *Advertising Empire: Race and Visual Culture in Imperial Germany* (Cambridge, MA: Harvard University Press, 2011).

Cole, Malcolm S., '"Afrika singt": Austro-German Echoes of the Harlem Renaissance', *Journal of the American Musicological Society* 30/1 (1977), 72–95.

Cruz, Jon, *Culture on the Margins: The Black Spiritual and the Rise of American Cultural Interpretation* (Princeton, NJ: Princeton University Press, 1999).

Darkow, Martin, 'Die Musik der amerikanischen Neger', *Die Musik* (1905).

Deaville, James, 'African-American Entertainers in *Jahrhundertwende* Vienna: Austrian Identity, Viennese Modernism and Black Success', *Nineteenth-Century Music Review* 3/1 (2006), 89–112.

Duberman, Martin, *Paul Robeson* (New York: Knopf, 1989).

Eze, Emmanuel Chukwudi, *Race and the Enlightenment: A Reader* (Hoboken, NJ: Wiley-Blackwell: 1997).

Fosler-Lussier, Danielle, *Music in America's Cold War Diplomacy* (Berkeley, CA: University of California Press, 2015).

Gaines, Kevin, *Uplifting the Race: Black Leadership, Politics and Culture in the Twentieth Century* (Chapel Hill: University of North Carolina Press, 1996).

Hagemann, Karen and Jean Quataert, eds, *Gendering German History: Rewriting Historiography* (New York: Berghahn, 2007).

Harer, Ingeborg, "'Dieses böse Etwas, der Jazz": Varianten der Jazz-Rezeption in Österreich von der Jahrhundertwende bis zu den 1920er Jahren', in Rudolf Flotzinger, ed., *Fremdheit in der Moderne* (Vienna: Passagen, 1999), 138–72.

Hayes, Roland, *My Favorite Spirituals: 30 Songs for Piano and Voice* (Mineola, NY: Dover Publications, 2001).

Heng, Geraldine, 'The Invention of Race in the European Middle Ages I: Race Studies, Modernity and the Middle Ages', *Literature Compass* 8/5 (2011), 258–74.

Hitchcock, H. Wiley, *Music in the United States: A Historical Introduction*, 4th edn (Upper Saddle River, NJ: Prentice Hall, 2000).

Johnson, J. Rosamand, ed., *The Utica Jubilee Singers Song Book* (Philadelphia: Oliver Ditson Company, 1930).

Lennox, Sara, 'Reading Transnationally: The GDR and Black American Writers', in Elaine Kelly and Amy Wlodarski, eds, *Art Outside the Lines: New Perspectives on GDR Art Culture* (New York: Rodopi, 2011), 111–30.

Klimke, Martin, and Maria Höhn, *A Breath of Freedom: The Civil Rights Struggle, African American GIs and Germany* (New York: Palgrave MacMillan, 2010).

Langbehn, Volker, ed., *German Colonialism, Visual Culture and Modern Memory* (New York: Routledge, 2010).

Lemke, Sieglinde, *Primitivist Modernism: Black Culture and the Origins of Transatlantic Modernism* (New York: Oxford University Press, 1998).

Lloyd, Jill, *German Expressionism: Primitivism and Modernity* (New Haven, CT: Yale University Press, 1991).

Locke, Ralph, 'On Exoticism, Western Art Music and the Words We Use', *Archiv für Musikwissenschaft* 69/4 (2012), 318–28.

McClintock, Anne, *Imperial Leather: Race, Gender and Sexuality in Colonial Conquest* (New York: Routledge, 1995).

MacKinley, Helm, *Angel Mo' and Her Son* (New York: Greenwood Press, 1969).

McMaster, Neil, *Racism in Europe, 1870–2000* (New York: Palgrave, 2001).

Moon, Brian, 'Harry Burleigh as Ethnomusicologist? Transcription, Arranging and "The Old Songs Hymnal"', *Black Music Research Journal* 24/2 (2004), 287–307.

Nenno, Nancy, 'Femininity, the Primitive and Modern Urban Space: Josephine Baker in Berlin', in Katharina von Ankum, ed., *Women in the Metropolis: Gender and Modernity in Weimar Culture* (Berkeley, CA: University of California Press, 1997), 141–67.

Nettles, Darryl Glenn, *African American Concert Singers Before 1950* (Jefferson, NC: McFarland, 2003).

Pieterse, Jan Nederveen, *White on Black: Images of Africa and Blacks in Western Popular Culture* (New Haven, CT: Yale University Press, 1992).

Poiger, Uta, *Jazz, Rock and Rebels: Cold War Politics and American Culture in a Divided Germany* (Berkeley, CA: University of California Press, 2000).

Radano, Ronald, *Lying Up a Nation: Race and Black Music* (Chicago: University of Chicago Press, 2003).

Ramey, Lynn, *Black Legacies: Race and the European Middle Ages* (Gainesville: University of Florida Press, 2014),

Retallack, James, ed., *Imperial Germany, 1871–1918* (Oxford: Oxford University Press, 2008).

Schenbeck, Lawrence, *Racial Uplift and American Music, 1878–1943* (Jackson: University of Mississippi Press, 2012).

——, 'Representing America, Instructing Europe: The Hampton Choir Tours Europe', *Black Music Research Journal* 25/1–2 (2005), 3–42.

Spencer, Jon Michael, 'R. Nathaniel Dett's Views on the Preservation of Black Music', *The Black Perspective in Music* 10/2 (1982), 132–48.

Stanley, Mary, 'R. N. Dett, of Hampton Institute: Helping to Lay Foundation for Negro Music of Future', *Black Perspective of Music* 1/1 (1973), 64–69.

Taruskin, Richard, 'The Discovery of the Folk', in *Oxford History of Western Music* <http://www.oxfordwesternmusic.com/> accessed 20 May 2016.

Taylor, Timothy, *Global Pop: World Music, World Markets* (New York: Routledge, 1997).

Thurman, Kira, 'Singing the Civilizing Mission in the Land of Bach, Beethoven and Brahms: The Fisk Jubilee Singers in 19th Century Germany', *Journal of World History* 27/3 (2016), 443–71.

von Hornbostel, Erich Moritz, *African Negro Music* (Oxford: Oxford University Press, 1928).

Wallaschek, Richard, *Primitive Music: An Inquiry into the Origin and Development of Music, Songs, Instruments, Dances and Pantomimes of Savage Races* (1893; repr. New York: Da Capo Press, 1970).

Wipplinger, Jonathan, *The Jazz Republic: Music, Race and American Culture in Weimar Germany* (Ann Arbor: University of Michigan Press, 2017).

——, 'Performing Race in *Jonny spielt auf*', in Naomi André, Karen M. Bryan and Eric Saylor, eds, *Blackness in Opera* (Urbana-Champaign: University of Illinois Press, 2012), 236–59.

——, 'The Racial Ruse: On Blackness and Blackface Comedy in "Fin-de-Siècle" Germany', *The German Quarterly* 84/4 (2011), 457–76.

Zimmerman, Andrew, *Anthropology and Anti-Humanism in Imperial Germany* (Chicago: University of Chicago Press, 2001).

VANESSA D. PLUMLY

7   Re-Fashioning Postwar German Masculinity Through Hip-Hop: The Man(l)y BlackWhite Identities of Samy Deluxe

ABSTRACT

Exploring the intersection of race, gender, the German nation and the African diaspora, this chapter situates the popular Black German hip-hop artist Samy Deluxe as performing postwar Afro-German masculinity in hip-hop. Through an analysis of his continually shifting musical styles and accompanying lyrics (from hardcore hip-hop to reggae and pop-like music) and the non-static modes of self-fashioning of his own Black male body on the covers of his albums, Samy Deluxe's oeuvre demonstrates that gender and race are performative acts produced both in and through discourse. The album covers stress that these categories of identity must be simultaneously viewed within the socio-historical and cultural contexts that have conditioned the very performances of them, as well as understood as consciously performed, malleable styles. In fact, Samy Deluxe illustrates how identity itself consists of multiple assumed self-positionings in addition to external placements (performed by others) in national, diasporic, gendered and racial paradigms.

Hip-hop is about embodiment, enacting a performance shaped by race, gender, sexuality, national identity, class and their intersections. Historically, the Black body has often served as a site of disembodiment, of fragmentation and of objectification, especially through the construction of race at the crossroads of capitalist exploitation and white supremacy. In the process, the Black subject was almost always rendered nonhuman, revoking the subject's (corpo)reality through a partial to complete denial of Black humanness and its subsequent commodification.[1] Hip-hop, among others, is a musical genre that has made these specific intersections highly visible, resulting from its mass consumption and global dissemination as a popular cultural art form in the late twentieth and early twenty-first centuries. While one could argue that other musical genres like the blues and jazz also have had such an impact, hip-hop centers the performative element of the body in its self-styling and presentation. Hip-hop's essence is both in and of the body. Beyond the musical and vocal elements, hip-hop, as a holistic concept, is tied to the body's movement, its creative talent, its representation and its expression.[2] While initially evolving out of the Bronx among Communities of Color as a form of social critique in 1970s, male hip-hop artists have also branded the genre's performative acts in relation to gendered and sexualized discourses. Hardcore and toxic masculinity and masculine performance remain prevalent within contemporary global hip-hop music,[3] maintaining a reputation for misogyny, violence and homophobia. However, other modes of male self-representation can and have been enacted in hip-hop culture that call into question this essentialized form

*   I would like to thank Tiffany N. Florvil for her thorough edits of this and other work of mine and her always accurate feedback, as well as Kim Singletary, Tanja Nusser, Alex Hogue, Richard Hagen, Michelle Dietz and members of the Black Diaspora Studies Network at the GSA for initial feedback on this chapter. Special thanks go to Samy Deluxe and Gisela Sorge for the permission to reprint the album covers and to Laura Silvernail for helping scan them. This research was funded at various stages through financial support including: the DAAD German Studies Summer Research Grant, the University of Cincinnati's GSGA Diversity Fellowship, the University of Cincinnati's Research Council Grant, the University of Cincinnati's Taft Graduate Enhancement Award and its Taft Dissertation Completion Fellowship, as well as SUNY New Paltz's Individual Development Award.

1   Alexander Weheliye, 'Introduction', in *Habeas Viscus: Racializing Assemblages: Biopolitics, and Black Feminist Theories of the Human* (Durham, NC: Duke University Press, 2014), 1–16.
2   Rapping is just one of the four elements of hip-hop that also includes MCing, graffiti and breakdancing.
3   See Sascha Verlan and Hannes Loh, *20 Jahre HipHop in Deutschland* (Höfen: Hannibal Verlag, 2002), 258–61.

of hegemonic masculinity, although this does not absolve them of their role in continuing to perpetuate it.[4]

This chapter unpacks the styles that fashion postwar Black German masculinity in its diverse iterations in Samy Deluxe's hip-hop oeuvre. Of specific interest are the intersecting discourses of race, gender, sex and sexuality, revolving around (dis)embodiment and performativity. I assess how Samy Deluxe's range of identity performances on his album art covers can be interpreted within the frameworks of Michelle M. Wright's diasporic postwar epistemology and Alexander Weheliye's conceptualization of racializing assemblages.[5] The former offers a paradigm for locating and situating Blackness beyond the Black Atlantic and the Middle Passage. It presents a new perspective on Black embodiment and diasporic *spacetime* that questions and expands the prevailing dominant framework. Wright argues that the Middle Passage Epistemology of African diasporic identity homogenizes Blackness and fixes time.[6] She calls for alternative ways of thinking about the diaspora that do not occlude those Black identities existing beyond the *spacetime* of slavery. The latter framework provides a template through which to view the breadth and depth of competing discourses and the structures that support them and then produce meaning inscribed onto the Black (male) body and the skin/flesh or what Weheliye terms the 'habeas viscus'.[7] German masculinity and national identity still

---

4   Even early hip-hop seems to bear this stigma. Not until 1982 with Grandmaster Flash and the Furious Fives' 'The Message' did hip-hop take a turn from topics such as who gets with the most women and who has the best rhymes or parties, to the hard life and circumstances of the ghetto. Sascha Verlan, and Hannes Loh, *20 Jahre HipHop*, 41.

5   Weheliye, *Habeas Viscus* and Michelle M. Wright, 'Middle Passage Blackness and Its Diasporic Discontents: The Case for a Post-war Epistemology', in Eve Rosenhaft and Robbie Aitken, eds, *Africa in Europe: Studies in Transnational Practice in the Long Twentieth Century* (Liverpool: Liverpool University Press, 2013), 217–33.

6   Wright, 'Middle Passage Blackness', 218.

7   Weheliye adds an erased element to the politics of bare life and biopolitics – that of race, which has always already pre-classified humans into full humans, not-quite-humans and nonhumans. Weheliye, *Habeas Viscus*, 3–8. Moreover, Weheliye asserts that '[t]aking leave from considering racial categorization as a mere ideological

perceived as white in the postwar period also enter into this reading of Samy Deluxe's hip-hop persona/corpus. His positionality – what he coins as BlackWhite – destabilizes the false dichotomies established through white German postwar masculinity, in turn sending it into further crisis and also opening up new possibilities for being (German/manly).

Discerning Samy Deluxe's articulation of postwar Black German masculinity, I focus on the cover images from his albums *Verdammtnochma!* [*Damn it!*] (2004), *SchwarzWeiss* [*BlackWhite*] (2011) and *Männlich* [*Manly*] (2014).[8] These are his second, fourth and fifth albums,[9] respectively, and they represent changes in his self-performance and presentation that span the body in and of his work. The enunciative acts of self-articulation in the lyrics of select songs, including 'Warum' [Why], 'Hände hoch' [Hands up], 'Poesie Album' [Poetry Album] and 'Penis', on these albums serve as hermeneutic structural support that vocalize and elaborate upon what is visualized and conveyed on the covers. Both image and text merge in the creation of Samy Deluxe's BlackWhite artistic and masculine personas. I assert that the means through which Samy Deluxe establishes a postwar BlackWhite German masculinity and constructs his multiple identities through performance on the covers, concomitantly exposes the superficiality and façade of these acts and their essentialized interpretations. At the same time, the enunciative acts in the songs' lyrics remain ambivalently coded. The covers and lyrics support and call into question hegemonic constructions of masculinity and race. These contradictory yet ambiguous performances must be read through the historical lenses that shape them. The covers' performative acts expose a degree of shallowness in their

---

imposition of scientifically "wrong" phenomena, habeas viscus, as an idea, networks bodies, forces, velocities, intensities, institutions, interests, ideologies, and desires in racializing assemblages', *Habeas Viscus*, 12.

8   Samy Deluxe, *Verdammtnochma!* (Deluxe Records, 2004); Samy Deluxe, *SchwarzWeiss* (EMI Music, 2011) and Samy Deluxe, *Männlich* (Vertigo/Capitol, 2014). All translations of titles and quotes in this chapter are my own unless otherwise cited.

9   It can be debated whether this is his sixth album, since the 'v', standing in for the 'u', in Deluxe could be interpreted as the Roman Numeral V. In this case, the album released under Samy Deluxe's assumed alter ego, Herr Sorge, which technically would be the artist's fifth album, would not be counted among the albums ascribed to the artist Samy Deluxe.

'projection' of a tangible racial and gendered core – one that is often also tied to sexuality in the Black German context. While these performative acts of race, gender, sex and sexuality that are produced both through and in discourse have the potential to be subversive, as philosopher and gender theorist Judith Butler already demonstrated,[10] these constructs must simultaneously be viewed within the socio-historical frameworks that condition the very performance of identity.[11] They must be understood as consciously performed, malleable styles, which can shift in each identity act.

Before approaching Samy Deluxe's man(l)y identities, it is necessary to establish the environs from which Black German (masculine) identities not only are self-made but also continue to be forcibly positioned in both the past and present. Partially as a result of their vital role in the development of the Afro-German movement and of the transnational reach of their publications, Afro-German women's political work and cultural production has predominantly been at the center of analyses in the field of Black German Studies.[12] Many of these Afro-German women were self-proclaimed feminist lesbians and, consequently, their contributions in the cultural realm tend to be more inclusive with regard to gender, sex and sexual identity or orientation, as cultural theorist Fatima El-Tayeb has highlighted in her exploration of Afro-German identity in hip-hop.[13] The position of women at the epicenter of the movement and at the center of Black German Studies, nevertheless, has overshadowed to some extent the

---

10   While Butler was specifically theorizing the performance of gender, the paradigm can equally be applied to the performance of race. Judith Butler, *Gender Trouble: Feminism and the Subversion of Identity* (New York: Routledge, 1990).

11   Stuart Hall situates Blackness as needing to be interpreted from a historical context. Stuart Hall, 'Cultural Identity and Diaspora', in Jana Evans Braziel and Anita Mannur, eds, *Theorizing Diaspora* (Oxford: Wiley Blackwell, 2003), 237. Wright points to the need to determine its essence in the 'when' and 'where'. Michelle M. Wright, *Physics of Blackness* (Minneapolis: University of Minnesota Press, 2015), 3.

12   Priscilla Layne, 'Afro-German Fiction and the Politics of Publishing' unpublished paper given at the 38th Annual Conference of the German Studies Association, Kansas City, Missouri, 19–21 September 2014, 9,12. Cited with permission of the author.

13   Fatima El-Tayeb, '"If You Can't Pronounce My Name, You Can Just Call Me Pride": Afro-German Activism Gender, and Hip Hop', *Gender and History* 15/3 (2003), 464.

anti-racist activist work Black German men undertake, as Black German
artist, author and activist Philipp Khabo Koepsell has highlighted on multiple occasions.[14] These men, too, actively critique German society and its
normative modes of (re)production, albeit still oftentimes problematically
perpetuating those selfsame norms. This is frequently the case with some
male Black German hip-hoppers. The academic privileging of literature
also undoubtedly plays a role in the sidelining of other modes of cultural
production – here by Black German men. Next to autobiography, hip-hop
and spoken word poetry, which itself shares similarities with hip-hop as
a genre, have been the main outlets of expression for Black German men
to critique German society and politics. The creative and artistic works of
Black German men provide insight into their distinct perspectives and aid
in the uncovering of potential reasons for the previous neglect of their work.

Pre- and Postwar (Re)construction/s: Constructing Masculinity, Constructing Blackness

According to Michelle M. Wright, Blackness 'cannot be 1) limited to a particular national, cultural, and linguistic border, or 2) produced in isolation
from gender and sexuality', and 'one cannot divorce the Black Other and

14   *Orlanda Frauenverlag* was an important publication outlet for Black German women.
      Priscilla Layne points to the difficulties in relation to publishing companies and the
      requirement of publication fees in her recent research. In her interviews with Philipp
      Khabo Koepsell and Michael Götting, both addressed the issue of finding publish-
      ing options and, in Koepsell's case, affordable ones. Layne, 'Afro-German Fiction',
      1–12. Köpsell and I had a similar discussion in Berlin, where we discussed the lack of
      critical engagement with and visible reception of Black German male cultural pro-
      ductions. Philipp Khabo Koepsell, interview with Vanessa Plumly, Berlin, Germany,
      24 August 2012. Koepsell also articulates how literary scholars often separate Black
      German activist work from Blacks who lived, worked and published their writing
      in Germany. See also Koepsell and Asoka Esuroso, *Arriving in the Future: Stories of
      Home and Exile* (Berlin: epubli, 2014), 36–47.

Black subject that follows from the specific historical, cultural, and even philosophical discourses through which s/he is interpellated'.[15] Likewise, clinical psychologist Roy Jerome writes in *Conceptions of Postwar German Masculinity* that 'an analysis of masculine identity must include an investigation of specific socio-historical events that have conditioned that identity'.[16] These claims anticipate the need for understanding the 'when' and 'where' of Blackness[17] and masculinity, exposing the circumstances through which both are simultaneously (trans)nationally constituted via discursive, cultural and historical developments.

The Black male subject and his body, especially in the German context, are, and always have been, marked as deviant from the white norm. In Germany and in the Western world, Blackness and the production of racial Otherness are the result of centuries of white Germans' racial, colonial, philosophical and pseudoscientific treatises and discourses. These discourses have produced a constructed cultural divide between the civilized, moral and intellectual characteristics that whites attached to their own bodies and the uncivilized, immoral and unintellectual characteristics that they ascribed to Black bodies.[18]

When considered in terms of the visual colonization and the discourse of racialized Othering, colonialism has endured well beyond the historically defined period of German colonization (1884–1919, ending officially with the Treaty of Versailles). German colonial advertisements and historical postcards framed through the white European gaze visually represented Black men and Black bodies as the 'Other', as Silke Hackenesch's contribution to this volume makes clear.[19] Scholars, such as Sara Friedrichsmeyer,

---

15   Michelle M. Wright, *Becoming Black: Creating Identity in the African Diaspora* (Durham, NC: Duke University Press, 2004), 4–5 and 28.

16   Roy Jerome, *Conceptions of Postwar German Masculinity* (Albany, NY: SUNY Press, 2001), 4.

17   Wright, *Physics*, 3.

18   Michael Chaouli, 'Laocoön and the Hottentots', in Sara Eigen and Mark Larrimore, eds, *The German Invention of Race* (Albany, NY: SUNY Press, 2006), 23–34 and Wright, *Becoming Black*, 29–30.

19   Silke Hackenesch, '"*Hergestellt unter ausschließlicher Verwendung von Kakaobohnen deutscher Kolonien*" – On Representations of Chocolate Consumption as a Colonial

Sara Lennox, Susanne Zantop and David Ciarlo, have examined this era
in depth, describing the emergence of an 'imperialist imagination' and an
'advertising empire'.[20] The former functions in relation to the production
of difference and the construction of Blackness (among other forms of
'Othering') in the German imaginary, while the latter operates in relation
to its mediated consumption. Both of these racializing regimes continue
to influence the way that Germany conceives, marks and markets race
today. Oftentimes, they intersect at the level of the skin in an assemblage
of projections onto Black Germans' bodies.[21]

International and national media coverage and propaganda campaigns
during the post-World War I era portrayed Black French colonial troops in
the Rhineland as explicitly hypersexual and threatening. Indeed, Germany's
defeat and occupation in the interwar period informed post-World War I
conceptions of race that remained inextricably tied to narratives of racial
miscegenation adopted from Germany's former colonial policies. This
occurred despite the fact that German colonialism 'officially' ended with
the loss of the war. As a result, racialized perceptions of Blackness continued to influence men of Color within the German territory. The fear of
the invading (male) dark-skinned Other embodied in the French Algerian,
Madagascan, Senegalese, Moroccan and Tunisian occupation soldiers

---

Endeavor', in Tiffany N. Florvil and Vanessa D. Plumly, eds, *Rethinking Black
German Studies: Approaches, Interventions and Histories* (Oxford: Peter Lang, 2018),
Chapter 1.

20   David Ciarlo, *Advertising Empire: Race and Visual Culture in Imperial Germany*
(Cambridge, MA: Harvard University Press, 2011), and Sara Friedrichsmeyer, Sara
Lennox and Susanne Zantop, eds, *The Imperialist Imagination: German Colonialism
and Its Legacy* (Ann Arbor: University of Michigan Press, 1998). See also, Anne
McClintock, *Imperial Leather: Race, Gender and Sexuality in the Colonial Contest*
(New York: Routledge, 1995) in which she theorizes the interplay of power at the
intersection of the colonial imagination.

21   'Habeas viscus accents how race becomes pinioned to human physiology, exposing how the politicization of the biological always already represents a racializing
assemblage'. Weheliye, *Habeas Viscus*, 12.

following World War I reduced their bodies to a racially deviant sexuality.[22] The national and international campaign of the '*Schwarze Schmach am Rhein*' [Black Horror on the Rhine] presented these men as sexually violent invaders who were destroying German women and by extension the white German race.[23] This framing also represented an extension of the soldier's Blackness to his male genitalia, an appendage that produced a racialized assemblage of oversignification and reduced him to his sexuality by visually representing his penis as his most dangerous weapon, even more so than military arms. The penis stands in for the activation of a new form of weapon – a racialized appendage demonstrative of virility during the disarmament/military 'castration' period of post-World War I Germany. This hypersexual imagery is most clearly displayed in German propaganda images and minted coins that depicted Black French troops' occupation of the Rhineland.[24] White German discourses and representations portrayed these men as sexually aggressive Black brutes who, in a King-Kong-like fashion, arrived to rape innocent, respectable white German women whose bodies symbolically stood in for the German nation's 'purity'.[25] In

22   Tina Campt, *Other Germans: Black Germans and the Politics of Race, Gender, and Memory in the Third Reich* (Ann Arbor: University of Michigan Press, 2004), 35–36.

23   See Campt, *Other Germans*, 36–37, and Julia Roos, 'Women's Rights, Nationalist Anxiety, and the "Moral" Agenda in the Early Weimar Republic: Revisiting the "Black Horror" Campaign against France's African Occupation Troops', *Central European History* 42/3 (2009), 473–508.

24   Heide Fehrenbach, *Race after Hitler: Black Occupation Children in Postwar Germany and America* (Princeton, NJ: Princeton University Press, 2005), 53–54. On one side of the coin was a racially charged image of a French African soldier's head in a helmet and on the other side was a white German woman strapped to what appears to be a tree but, upon closer examination, is a penis.

25   *King Kong*, a giant ape figure, is presented in the 1933 Hollywood feature film *King Kong* and in the lost Japanese short *Wasei King Kong* (also 1933), but he is not only this. The image and conception of King Kong has earlier origins that have traveled transnationally and served various discourses. See Cynthia Marie Erb, *Tracking King Kong: A Hollywood Icon in World Culture* (Detroit, MI: Wayne State University Press, 2009), 3. The French artist Emmanuel Frémiet's 1859 sculpture 'Gorille enlevant une *négresse*' depicts an ape carrying a black woman off with the intent to rape her. Ted Gott, 'Stowed Away: Emmanuel Frémiet's Gorilla Carrying off a Woman',

doing so, they cast white German masculinity and heterosexuality as the controlled and contained norm and contrasted it to a destructively violent Black masculinity and hypersexuality.

In her reading of Blackness in relation to Black men, bell hooks asserts: '[s]een as animals, brutes, natural born rapists, and murderers, black men have had no real dramatic say when it comes to the way they are represented. [...] Negative stereotypes about the nature of black masculinity continue to overdetermine the identities black males are allowed to fashion for themselves'.[26] Although her reading of Black masculinity is located within the context of the United States, the construction of Black masculinity in Germany in the post-World War I period signifies precisely the same modes of embodiment and inscription that shaped the racializing assemblage of Black male bodies throughout the Western world.

Implementing policies, Nazi Germany attempted to suppress and contain the sexual desire and expression of sexuality in those it deemed non-human or deviant subjects, including Black Germans, Jews, homosexuals, Roma and Sinti, the disabled and others classified as 'asocials'. The Third Reich sought to eliminate the reproductive capabilities of these individuals in some cases through the forced sterilization of these subjects.[27] As

---

Art Journal of Victoria 45 (2005) <http://www.ngv.vic.gov.au/essay/stowed-away-emmanuel-fremiets-gorilla-carrying-off-a-woman-2-2/> accessed 20 March 2017. Ironically, Germans would use this image to depict African soldiers occupying the Rhine as barbaric apes coming to rape white German women, and it was also the image that American anti-German war posters employed during World War I to depict German barbarism. I use the term King-Kong-like to refer to the images of the Rhineland occupation since the King Kong filmic narrative has been interpreted as an encounter of the Western world with the exoticized Other as portrayed by white film directors and since the image evokes multiple discourses.

26   bell hooks, *We Real Cool: Black Men and Masculinity* (New York: Routledge, 2004), xii.

27   This policy was not consistent and not all Black Germans were ultimately sterilized. See Reiner Pommerin, *Sterilisierung der Rheinlandbastarde: Das Schicksal der farbigen deutschen Minderheit 1918–1937* (Düsseldorf: Droste, 1979), Hans Massaquoi *Neger, Neger, Schornsteinfeger: Meine Kindheit in Deutschland* (Bern: S. Fischer Verlag, 1999), in particular, the section titled 'Gretchen', 166–74, Gert Schramm's autobiography *Wer hat Angst vorm schwarzen Mann* (Berlin: Aufbau, 2011), 27.

Hans Massaquoi articulated in his autobiography, *Destined to Witness: Growing Up Black in Nazi Germany*, his sexuality, perceived as threatening, was something that he had to suppress. Black German Gert Schramm also confirms this in his autobiography, detailing his experience during the Third Reich and his internment in Buchenwald.[28] Black masculinity and sexuality in Germany in the first half of the twentieth century was therefore discursively produced as something simultaneously beyond control and something to be controlled biopolitically at all costs. It was contradictorily constructed as existing both external to the nation, while also threatening it from within. Consequently, white German masculinity perceived Black German masculinity as a disruptive menace that jeopardized the hegemonic function of the former's contrived stability prior to, during and after World War II.

Again, according to Massaquoi, the postwar period exhibited Blackness and its affiliation with an African American identity as something that transformed into an attractive, desirable and sexually consumable object. Yet Germans associated a modern and hip American Blackness with American GIs not with Black Germanness or Black Germans, unless they managed to pass as African American. The two different, yet similar, national contexts for Blackness – African American and Black German – could be and often were exchanged for one another on the surface. Massaquoi demonstrates this in his own deployment of American Blackness to woo German women until a friend exposes his 'American-Number' performances as precisely

---

Tina Campt explains that of the 600–800 children of the Black German diaspora resulting from the Rhineland occupation, around 385 were sterilized. Campt, *Other Germans*, 63–80 and 91–135.

28 Massaquoi, *N-, N-, Schornsteinfeger*, 194–203. In his autobiography, Gert Schramm cites a report that he and his mother received in 1941 warning of his coming of age and entrance into manhood. Particularly the fact that he would be around young women, the document states that discretion is warranted: '*Gert Schramm befindet sich in einer gemischten Klasse, also auch mit Mädchen zusammen. Bei dem Eintritt geschlechtlicher Reife ist größte Vorsicht geboten*'. [*Gert Schramm is in a mixed class, meaning also together with girls. With entry into sexual maturity, great precaution is advised*]. Schramm, *Wer hat Angst*, 27.

that – an act.[29] During this time, images of African American soldiers in uniform proliferated, deeming these men as acceptable and cultured; they exuded palatable, modern Blackness. While white Germans' racist gaze became detached from formally implemented Nazi race laws and images of African American occupation troops presented them as friendly, white Germans still viewed them as problematic, especially when in liaisons with white German women. For this meant that once again Black men threatened the homogenously conceived postwar white German nation, its racially white *Volk* and the normative construction of white German heterosexual masculinity.[30]

Germany's military defeat in World War II resulted in 'unleashing a crisis of German masculinity'.[31] This crisis was undeniably that of a specifically *white* German postwar masculinity. In many ways, the war produced an emasculation of the white German nation with its large loss of men and with its failure to emerge as a victor. Those remaining in the aftermath experienced a loss of their status as what Heide Fehrenbach terms, 'protectors,' 'providers' and 'procreators'.[32] Indeed, these were characteristics that Black (German) men had never embodied since white Germans had always viewed them as threatening, evil and licentious – most recently during the Third Reich.

29   Fehrenbach, *Race after Hitler*, 29, 33. In this passage, he refers to this as his 'Ami-Nummer' [American number]; it is an act in which he details his own performativity of American Blackness so that German police treat him differently and in order to impress a young white German woman he encounters. Massaquoi, *N-, N-, Schornsteinfeger*, 347–49. In the prologue to the English version, he also writes about not having a 'legal social outlet' when he 'reached puberty', referencing an 'absence of black females', since white German women were off limits. Hans Massaquoi, *Destined to Witness: Growing Up Black in Nazi Germany* (New York: Harper Collins, 1999) xii.
30   Black men did not pose the only postwar racial threat to Germany's imagined whiteness. Robert Stemmle's 1952 postwar film, *Toxi*, demonstrates that the white German national imaginary would prefer to rid Germany of all visible traces of racial miscegeny, including young Afro-German girls. *Toxi*, Robert Stemmle, dir. (Fono Film, 1952).
31   Fehrenbach, *Race after Hitler*, 12.
32   Fehrenbach, *Race after Hitler*, 49.

In contrast to this crisis of white German masculinity, then, young Black German men, like Massaquoi, saw the collapse of the Nazi regime as enabling them to practice a sexuality that partially freed them from the prior constraints of the government and society. This opened up opportunities for reasserting heteronormative masculinity that white Germans had previously denied them, even if Black German men's affirmation of their sexuality remained mired in its pre-conceived, historically constructed deviancy. Such insight further points to the different experiences that the postwar masculinity 'crisis' produced between Black and white German men. The perception of Black German men and the constructions of their heteronormative masculinity in this period were positioned somewhere ambivalently at the interstices of multiple shifting contexts. These included the crisis of white German masculinity, Black German men's own crisis of masculinity under the Third Reich and the acceptance and desire of a modern and foreign or Black American masculinity that, in some cases, Black Germans adapted, adopted and benefitted from, even if fleetingly so.

This depiction of pre- and postwar Germany has offered a brief historical foray into the evolution, construction and strategic deployment of race and gender from colonialism to the postwar period of the German nation's (re)construction. Certainly, racial and gendered paradigms do not end at the *Stunde Null*. Their transference from the pre-war era into new, albeit familiar constellations, still inhabit the particular *spacetime* of racialized masculinity as it developed and evolved in West Germany in the postwar period and in reunified Germany in the post-*Wende* era. This is what Wright refers to as '[e]piphenomenal time', which 'comprises only the "now" – but a "now" that encompasses what is typically labeled the past and the future'.[33] Evolving over time in multiple and often contradictory or competing contexts and evincing both continuity and rupture, the complicated intersection of these hegemonic discourses must be continually (re)considered in the interpretation of Samy Deluxe's hip-hop oeuvre below. How, then, can we understand Black German men's own active articulations of heteronormative masculinity in the twenty-first century

33   Wright, *Physics*, 41.

with this historical postwar backdrop? More specifically, what role might hip-hop play in rendering a postwar Black German masculinity articulable?

Hip-Hop in Germany

In the 1970s, hip-hop began to emerge in the United States. By the 1980s, American military bases still located across West Germany offered sites through which small enclaves developed for migrant communities to engage in the increasingly transnational culture of hip-hop.[34] The transfer of American culture through material imports and the transnational flow of music with groups such as The Sugarhill Gang and Grandmaster Flash and films such as *Wild Style* and *Beat Street* paved the way for the emergence of hip-hop in Germany and Europe as a whole.[35] In the German context, hip-hop artists and the mediated reception of them often interpret the genre as evolving within a predominantly male culture, though female rappers do exist.[36] With the group *Die Fantastischen Vier* (Fanta 4) dictating the origin narrative, hip-hop in Germany is seen as an initially white art form.[37] The fact that many first-generation German hip-hoppers, particularly those with migrant backgrounds, deliberately rapped in English, Turkish and other non-German languages, meant that their simultaneously evolving and even previously budding hip-hop cultures were lost.[38] This naturally poses the questions: what constitutes German hip-hop, the *language* of its production – here, I am referring specifically to rap music, which is just

---

34   Verlan and Loh, *20 Jahre HipHop*, 101.
35   Verlan and Loh, *20 Jahre HipHop*, 33, 45, 88–89, and 93.
36   Verlan and Loh, *20 Jahre HipHop*, 258–61.
37   Verlan and Loh, *20 Jahre HipHop*, 44–46.
38   Ade Odukoya, '"Fill the Gap": Adegoke Odukoya über Deutschrap, Ausgrenzung und verpasste Chancen', in Sascha Verlan and Hannes Loh, eds, *20 Jahre HipHop in Deutschland* (Höffen: Hannibal, 2002), 144.

one element of hip-hop culture – or the cultural *space* and *content* of its production? Is it not, perhaps, *both*?

Samy Deluxe is a German hip-hopper with a remarkable flow in the German language. While his Germanness is seemingly a stable identity via language, his performance of a postwar BlackWhite German masculinity is anything but unchanging. In fact, a quick glance at his released album covers demonstrates his evolving performative self and a multiplicity of manly identities. Samy Deluxe performs his Blackness and masculinity each time anew in relation to both the German nation and the transnational hip-hop nation. However, this is not to claim that his identity performances follow a linear trajectory. Indeed, his identity only allows us to define him in the epiphenomenal 'now' of its enunciation. It is in this way that both gender and race can be understood as what Judith Butler refers to as a performative construct, 'an identity tenuously constituted in time ... through a *stylized repetition of acts*' and that reveals 'the temporal and contingent groundlessness' of these identities.[39] Nevertheless, these identities are still shaped by the 'when' and 'where' or the space and time of their phenomenological occurrence,[40] which is equally articulated in the how or manner of their performance.

Identifying Samy Deluxe

Born in Hamburg in 1977 to a Sudanese father, who did not play a role in his life, and a white German mother, Samy Sorge – alias Dynamite Deluxe, Sam Semilia, Big Baus of the Nauf, Wickeda MC and Herr Sorge – is best known as Samy Deluxe and has been a mainstream musician since his 2001

---

39 Butler, *Gender Trouble*, 140–41.
40 According to Wright, 'Blackness, then, is largely a matter of perception ... made up of moments of performance in which performers understand their bodies as Black'. Wright, *Physics of Blackness*, 3.

debut bearing his stage name *Samy Deluxe*.[41] Already gaining credibility in the 1990s through his presence at Germany-wide jams, he is likely the German hip-hopper with the most accolades to date. In an issue of the American magazine *Billboard*, dated from December 2002, before some of his chart-topping albums had yet to be released, the article noted that: 'Samy Deluxe is undoubtedly one of Germany's most successful hip-hop acts and one of the few boasting a gold album (150,000 units)'.[42] Additionally, he has been the recipient of the MTV Europe Music Award, the Echo Award, the Bravo Otto and the Comet Award, to name but a few.[43]

Over the course of his life's work, Samy Deluxe has explored different musical styles from more hardcore rap to reggae-infused beats and pop melodies. Despite such variance, he has met with great success in Germany. Not only can no single musical genre easily be affixed to his work, but also his self-performance exceeds the confines of his album covers' own frames. His most successful album from 2011, *SchwarzWeiss* [*BlackWhite*], reached number one on the German charts. He released his 2012 album, *Verschwörungstheorien mit schönen Melodien* [*Conspiracy Theories with Beautiful Melodies*] under his assumed alter ego Herr Sorge [Mr Sorge/Mr Worry], and it hit the top 50.[44] This album represented a major transition from his past, hardcore hip-hop music to pop-like music expressing a sort of pessimistic apocalyptic mood with songs such as 'Die Zukunft vorbye' [The Future Over]. Furthermore, on the cover and in the music videos to the album's songs, he became a figure that resembled a hybrid homage to such whimsical characters as Willy Wonka and the Mad Hatter (see Figure 7.1).

41   The stage name Samy Deluxe is taken from an album from Felix de Luxe that Samy Deluxe came across at a party in Hamburg. Samy, from Arabic, is his real first name (Samy Sorge). Samy Deluxe, *Dis wo ich Herkomm: Deutschland Deluxe* (2nd edn, Hamburg: Rowohlt Taschenbuch, 2010), 14–15.

42   Olaf Furniss, 'Rap/Hip-Hop: World Rap-Up Shows How Hip-Hop Travels. Samy Deluxe', *Billboard Magazine* 114/49 (7 December 2002), 50.

43   Samy Sorge, [Samy Deluxe], 'Mensch und Marke-Differenzierung aus Sicht eines Künstlers', in Ulrich Görg, ed., *Erfolgreiche Markendifferenzierung: Strategie und Praxis professioneller Markenprofilierung* (Wiesbaden: Fachverlage, 2010), 399.

44   Herr Sorge, *Verschwörungstheorien mit schönen Melodien* (Universal Music Domestic Rock/Urban, 2012).

Figure 7.1. Cover image of *Verschwörungstheorien mit schönen Melodien.* Permission to
reprint the cover image obtained from Gisela Sorge and Management Samy Deluxe.

In the cover image, Herr Sorge dons a top hat that covers his long hair and
is framed by a colorful and imaginative palette; he also presents a more
rugged and ragged style as a dilapidated dandy, given the tattered clothes
he wears in some of the music videos for the album. This shift in his performative image and musical style is likely one reason for the limited market
success that this album received.

Moreover, his alter ego presented in conjunction with this album may
also serve as an aberration and temporary digression from his persona as
Samy Deluxe. Many consider the Herr Sorge album not to be a part of the

Samy Deluxe oeuvre, thus, making it an outlier in his repertoire. Another of
Samy Deluxe's albums debuted in 2014 under the title *Männlich* [*Manly*]
and reached the top five on the charts. This cover's dual image – one which
was released for the regular album and another for the Deluxe edition –
presents a further change in Samy Deluxe's hip-hop identity. It signals a
return to a harder image of his performed gender identity, particularly in
comparison to his prior alternate persona as Herr Sorge. Nevertheless, it
questions precisely the projection of hardness seen on the cover through
the lyrics of the songs on the album, as I will extrapolate later.

In 2016, Samy Deluxe released what is seemingly his final album bearing the title *Berühmte letzte Worte* [*Famous Last Words*].[45] On this cover,
he pays respect to African American leaders from Malcolm X and Martin
Luther King Jr. to the former United States President Barack Obama in his
presentation of himself wearing glasses and standing behind a podium. The
lectern is constructed as a stereo sound system, and Samy Deluxe points
from behind it with his hand and finger. Not only are gestures in hip-hop
significant, but this specific act is also undeniably a nod to the aforementioned leaders, who themselves engaged in performative acts during their
powerful speeches revolving around racism, civil rights and hope for the
future. Moreover, overt references to the political campaign artwork of
President Barack Obama are visible in the text and in the colors of the
album cover that are almost, but not quite red, white and blue (green on
the album's cover). Similarly, the three stars in the 'S.' are a symbolic nod
to the U.S. flag and complete these references (see Figure 7.2).

Samy Deluxe's desire to constantly reimagine himself – a fugitive
aspect of his performative identity – is why his work merits closer attention.

A quick glance at the covers of each of the aforementioned albums
shows Samy Deluxes's re-fashionings of his performative body at the center
of all of them, marking his identity as constantly in flux.[46] Conveying the
'hip-hop body' as 'an index of hipness,' cultural theorist Miles White states,
'the hip-hop body is anything but static; it is dynamic and fluid, signifying

---

45   Samy Deluxe, *Berühmte letzte Worte* (Vertigo/Capitol, 2016).
46   One exception to his album covers might be the cover for the album *Samy Deluxe*.
      Although the cover does not present the physical representation of Samy Deluxe's
      performative body, the symbolic substitution of the dollar sign stands in for Samy
      Deluxe and can be problematized in relation to commodity fetishism.

Figure 7.2. Cover Image of *Berühmte letzte Worte*. Permission to reprint the cover image obtained from Gisela Sorge and Management Samy Deluxe.

meaning that functions within a broader socio-cultural context.'[47] In his own self-conception of his hip-hop identity and cultural/political representation, Samy Deluxe maintains:

---

47   Miles White, *From Jim Crow to Jay Z: Race, Rap, and the Performance of Masculinity* (Chicago: University of Illinois Press, 2011), 22.

Seit dem Moment, in dem ich Hip Hop für mich entdeckt habe und Rapper werden
wollte, wusste ich genau, wofür ich stehen wollte, auch wenn es sich über die Jahre
hinweg konstant verändert hat, manchmal leicht, manchmal radikal.[48]

[Since the moment that I discovered hip-hop and wanted to become a rapper, I
knew exactly what I wanted to stand for, even if it constantly changed over the years
– sometimes slightly and other times radically].

In following this claim, what cultural analysis can be drawn from the hip-
hop, self-styled body presented on Samy Deluxe's album covers, and what
meaning/s do they ultimately signify when read in conjunction with some
of the album's song lyrics?

Gazing at the Surface

Samy Deluxe's second album, *Verdammtnochma!* [*Damn it!*] from 2004
warrants a close analysis because of his homage to African American hip-
hop iconography. This album cover pictures him wearing a baggy leather
sports jacket, a Boston Celtics cap and a silver and a gold chain – the latter
bearing the initials (SD) of his hip-hop persona.[49] The green vest he dons
over the jacket is held in a firm grasp with his hands in fists with a gold ring
on his left hand. The shadow of the ball cap casts darkness over his eyes,
refusing the viewer access to Samy Deluxe's gaze. Thus, the top part of his
face remains anonymous and hidden. His mouth is pursed in an almost
aggressive fashion that demonstrates his performance of hardcore manliness,
intensifying the image. Beyond this presentation of masculine hardness, on
the left-hand side of the cover album is its title. On the right-hand side is a
symbol that resembles the American dollar sign with sharp edges, which is
a reference to the cover of his first album *Samy Deluxe*. The logo that the

48   Sorge [Samy Deluxe], 'Mensch und Marke', 387–88.
49   This symbol is also that of the San Diego Padres team that has been re-appropriated.

dollar sign on the cover forms also bears three of Samy Deluxe's hip-hop personas, Sam Semilia, Samy Deluxe and Wickeda MC (see Figure 7.3).

Figure 7.3. Cover image of *Verdammtnochma!* Permission to reprint the cover image obtained from Gisela Sorge and Management Samy Deluxe.

Thus, this move already indicates Samy Deluxe's non-static hip-hop identity and contradicting personas. Moreover, the dollar sign appears to be constructed of emeralds, injecting the image with non-traditional bling.

Hip-hop in the U.S. framework is often affiliated with gold and bling, money – a symbol of value and worth – and hypersexualized women that African American male hip-hoppers brought into visual and material focus.

Drawing on cultural capital from abroad, Samy Deluxe inscribes himself
into multiple, even competing discourses. The dollar sign has three bars
through it, hinting at the criminalization of Black men and the deviance
associated with them as rappers. Miles White articulates: '[t]he black body
and representations of black masculinity in hardcore styles of hip-hop performance are socially constructed kinds of gender and racial performance
that are historically marked by notions around criminality, deviance, and
pathology'.[50] Samy Deluxe draws on the African American hip-hop tradition because it has a past, whereas Germany does not have this particular
reference point. But it is within these ambivalent structures that he embeds
his self-performance.

   In his younger years, Samy Deluxe always wanted to identify as African
American, believing the United States would be a place where he would
finally belong.[51] He pays homage to the established culture of African
American hip-hop, looking to this cultural paradigm for Black male role
models. As a Black youth in Germany, Samy Deluxe found positive points of
identification in Black American actors, basketball players and musicians.[52]
He explains his initial fascination with the United States in his autobiography, *Dis wo ich herkomm: Deutschland Deluxe* [*Dis where I'm from:
Germany Deluxe*], published in 2010 under his pseudonym. Described as
a desire carved out of projections vis-à-vis his imagination that life would
be better in the U.S. for him without having ever actually been there, Samy
Deluxe later changed his mind after he visited. Still, he cites the import of
African American culture to Germany as making Blackness cool, and his
being mistaken for an American as one particular advantage of this, particularly within the hip-hop scene.[53] This is of course reminiscent of Hans
Massaquoi's description of his experience after World War II.

   Samy Deluxe's cover image evokes similar representations of African
American hip-hoppers at the time whose self-styling was considered a

50   White, *From Jim Crow to Jay-Z*, 23.
51   Deluxe, *Dis wo ich herkomm*, 26.
52   Deluxe, *Dis wo ich herkomm*, 26.
53   Deluxe, *Dis wo ich herkomm*, 26.

visible marker of hip-hop culture in the late 1990s and 2000s.[54] As White asserts about American hip-hop: '[t]he wearing of ostentatious jewelry, including expensive chains, earrings, and 'grillz' [...], tattoos, stylized athletic apparel or brand-name urban street wear, [...] are ways that visually display masculine power and sexuality by privileging the objectified and spectacularized body'.[55] Not only is the image of Samy Deluxe on the cover of the album one of this objectified and reified masculine body meant to be consumed and also meant to consume (other objectified female bodies) as a hypermasculine heteronormative male, but it also evokes racial narratives of the consumption of the Other. bell hooks theorized this notion that race is 'commodified for [...] pleasure'.[56] Samy Deluxe sells himself in similar attire to hip-hop performers in the U.S. and becomes a part of this chain of objectified signification.

Hip-hop is consumed and produced worldwide, even if it is a musical form most often associated with the U.S. The most forceful reading of hip-hop places it as an American product, oddly genuine in its replication of specific signs and symbols and the employment of codes that register an 'authentic' but also essentialized image of hip-hop that reduces it to easily recognizable tropes.[57] In accordance with constructions of Blackness in the hip-hop narrative, the donning of basketball gear for Samy Deluxe's *Verdammtnochma!* cover image reminds the viewer that, in Germany and the United States, Blackness and Black masculinity is often equated with American basketball in popular culture. In a similar way to the diasporic haunting Kimberly Alecia Singletary discusses in her chapter in this volume,

---

54   It is also hardly ironic that a google search of hip-hop garb produces an image of the rapper Nelly positioned in the exact same way as Samy Deluxe and modeling his line of clothes, under the brand name Vokal. One can all but assume that this image was a point of reference for Samy Deluxe, as Nelly's brand became popular in the late 1990s and early 2000s and lost its desirability right around the time following the release of Samy Deluxe's album *Verdammtnochma!*

55   White, *From Jim Crow to Jay-Z*, 25.

56   bell hooks, 'Eating the Other: Desire and Resistance', in *Black Looks: Race and Representation* (Boston, MA: South End Press, 1992), 21–39.

57   White, *From Jim Crow to Jay-Z*, 24.

American Blackness erases the possibility of Black Germanness.[58] Yet, in this instance, invisibility is created both through the white audience's imaginary and Samy Deluxe's own self-identification with the African American cultural contexts in which Blackness is performed via hip-hop and basketball. Here, the Black subject is presented in its non-threatening form within the German nation as foreign, and he is also visually produced as outside of the nation, to be sold to Germany for the purpose of consumption. As a sport, basketball is, according to hip-hop scholar Todd Boyd, 'one of the few cultural arenas [...] dominated by Black male participants'.[59] He continues arguing that basketball is 'a sport where race has been normalized through performance, and class starts to assume a prominent position in articulating Black masculinity'.[60] The same of course is true for the cultural arena of hip-hop as it evolved in the U.S. and was adapted to other cultural contexts. Although he grew up in a single-family household, class does not play as central of a role in Samy Deluxe's performance of masculinity, at least not to the extent that it has in hip-hop in the U.S.[61] Yet, it factors in with his effort to attain a higher social status and to accumulate capital in Germany.

Still, the intersection of racial constructions in the U.S. and in Germany through the cultural arenas of hip-hop and basketball demonstrates the overlap in the commodification of Black male bodies and their 'personas' in these spaces.[62] The image of Samy Deluxe on this album cover speaks to

---

58   Kimberly Alecia Singletary, 'Everyday Matters: Haunting and the Black Diasporic Experience', in Tiffany N. Florvil and Vanessa D. Plumly, eds, *Rethinking Black German Studies: Approaches, Interventions and Histories* (Oxford: Peter Lang, 2018), this volume, Chapter 4.

59   Todd Boyd, *Am I Black Enough for You? Popular Culture from the 'Hood and Beyond* (Bloomington: University of Indiana Press, 1997), 106.

60   Boyd, *Black Enough*, 106.

61   Class is neither at the center of his societal critique, nor is it something he often thematizes. 'Ich bin zwar in keinem Ghetto aufgewachsen, habe mich aber aufgrund meiner Hautfarbe oft wie in einem gefühlt'. [I was of course not raised in a ghetto, but as a result of my skin color I often felt as if I were inhabiting one'.] Sorge [Samy Deluxe], 'Mensch und Marke', 387.

62   Boyd, *Black Enough*, 117.

a uniformity of the contemporary capitalist, heteronormative masculine identity that with such a performance, literally markets itself in the realms of both hip-hop and sports. Thus, the performance is a partial exploitation of the self, compounded through the powerful gaze of white consumers. Employing visual forms of colonizing regimes in relation to the spectacle, the Black body becomes framed as commodity and fetish. These trans-cultural references that situate the Black German body within an African American cultural framework also point to the influence of the United States as an occupying force in the postwar construction of (Black) German identity and, in particular, a Black German masculinity. The images of the Black body as an African American, a basketball player and a hip-hopper permeate the German racial imaginary, forming an essentialized assemblage of hardcore gangsta rapper Blackness.

Moreover, Miles White explains:

> [w]hites and other racial and ethnic groups who may have had little contact with black males except through such representations may find it difficult to see beyond the persona of the hardcore gangsta as performance, or in any case, as one kind of performance of black maleness that may be part real and part artifice.[63]

White further asserts that 'in hardcore styles of hip-hop, facial expressions are used to telegraph hypermasculinity and ideals of physical and psychic hardness that are critical in the construction of performers' persona'. Smiling, though, is understood as its opposite, a presentation of 'weakness, feminization'.[64] As Samy Deluxe writes in his autobiography, 'Doch besonders für Rapper – überall auf der Welt und immer mehr auch in Deutschland – ist Härte vor allem ein Synonym für Männlichkeit' [especially for rappers – everywhere in the world and ever more so in Germany, being hard is above everything a synonym for masculinity].[65]

Masculine hardness permeates Samy Deluxe's album *Verdammtnochma!*, especially with the song 'Warum' [Why]. In it, he objectifies women, rapping, 'schau'n wir uns eure Körper an, da musst ihr wohl mit leben!/ Ein

---

63 White, *From Jim Crow to Jay-Z*, 23.
64 White, *From Jim Crow to Jay-Z*, 26.
65 Deluxe, *Dis wo ich herkomm*, 136.

Blick ist wie ein Kompliment' [we look at your bodies, you'll have to live with that; a gaze is like a compliment] and 'jeder hat 'ne Schwäche/ meine is' das weibliche Geschlecht' [everyone has a weakness!/ mine is the female gender/sex!].[66] In these lines, he positions his masculinity through his hegemonic and compulsory heterosexuality. Moreover, Samy Deluxe not only establishes his masculinity in opposition to women and their feminine appearance and sexual attributes, but also exposes the fact that his construction and enactment of heterosexual masculinity is equally dependent upon them. Such a performance – claiming weakness as something inherent to everyone and as a part of himself – destabilizes the gendered power dynamic that typically asserts weakness as an explicitly feminine trait and hardcore masculinity as solid and unyielding as cited in White above. In portraying women as the ones lording power over men, given their influence on him and his resulting heterosexual desire/arousal (physical hardening/ erection), his articulation of his *own* weakness undermines the façade of hardcore masculinity on the cover. At the same time, his self-perceived weakness is contradictory in that it re-inscribes his cis-gendered heterosexual masculinity. Thus, while this album performs man(l)y identities on the cover, including hardcore masculinity, it, to some extent, challenges traditionally ascribed gender paradigms through the lyrics in the album, and rather than undoing them, Samy Deluxe's subversive act of uncovering actually perpetuates them. Nevertheless, his assertion of his Black German heterosexuality is rebellious when read in the postwar German context.

The second cover, for the album *SchwarzWeiss [BlackWhite]*, unites what has been produced through discourse, particularly pseudoscientific and philosophical ones, as two binary oppositions, black and white, in the racial imagination and in the racially structured German empires of the past. Even today, many white Germans still consider the existence of Black Germans to be contradictory, despite historical documentation of Blacks and Afro-Germans in Germany dating back to the Middle Ages and the changing of the blood-based citizenship that falsely assumed a homogenously white German corpus in the national imaginary. The title

66   Samy Deluxe, 'Why', *Verdammtnochma!* (Deluxe Records, 2004), Verse 1 lines 16–17 and Verse 2 lines 11–12.

of this album, while keeping the two supposedly incompatible and contradictory colors black and white separate, also combines them in order to create a compound word, as is German linguistic practice. It has value in its unifying power that evokes a Du Boisian sense of double-consciousness.[67] Furthermore, it references Afro-German poet May Ayim's first poetry compilation *blues in schwarz-weiss [Blues in Black-White]* and the poem from which the title of her volume is taken.[68] Samy Deluxe and May Ayim's cultural productions establish the missing connection (in Ayim's poem, 'blues in schwarz-weiss', it is the hyphen suturing black to white) that joins the two dichotomous constructs of race and the seemingly incompatible African and European identities they are said to represent (see Figure 7.4).

Both Ayim and Samy Deluxe achieve this through their corresponding maternal and paternal filial bonds. This combination of *SchwarzWeiss* is capable of de-constructing a supposed singular and static origin, through the subversive practice of conveying race as ambivalent, albeit still intertwined within dominant power structures. It also follows Butler's reading of norms in *Undoing Gender*, wherein she states that '[t]he question of what it is to be outside the norm poses a paradox for thinking, for if the norm renders the social field intelligible and normalizes that field for us, then being outside the norm is in some sense being defined still in relation to it'.[69] So how does the album title connect to the cover image?

Samy Deluxe's album cover art offers a visible representation of his hybridity as a BlackWhite German and the compatibility of black with white. Created by graphic designer Wes21 (Remo Lienhard), Samy Deluxe's portrait is situated at the center of the album cover. It is presented as a graffiti-like image produced with partially dripping and running paint

---

67   The concept of double-consciousness for Du Bois is the idea that one feels one's Blackness and nationality and sees one's self as two competing entities in the eyes of the self and other. W. E. B. Du Bois, *The Souls of Black Folk* (New York: Simon and Schuster 2009), 7.

68   May Ayim, 'Blues in SchwarzWeiss', in *Blues in Schwarz Weiss* (Berlin: Orlanda Frauenverlag, 1995), 82–83.

69   Butler, *Undoing Gender*, 42.

Figure 7.4. Cover image of *SchwarzWeiss*. Permission to reprint the cover image
obtained from Gisela Sorge and Management Samy Deluxe.

from a spray can. In addition to the paint, brush strokes and marker lines
appear, adding to this artistic style. The black and white on the page are
meant to contrast one another but end up converging and mixing in his
face and hair. This is worthy of further consideration, given the value placed
on hair in racial contexts. In South Africa, hair was a policy of Apartheid
and determined racial status. For instance, if a pencil stuck in your hair,
then you were considered 'colored'. If it somewhat stuck, then you would
be considered mixed race. Colonial conquest in South Africa's neighboring
Namibia, formerly 'German South-West Africa', undeniably shaped this

racist system of oppression.[70] In a *Deutsche Welle* (DW) interview with Samy Deluxe, he stated that as a young boy his friends would call him the N-word, only later to revoke this comment by claiming that his hair was straight. In the same interview, he referenced the signifier Afro-German as a term that does not refer to himself. An Afro, he rightly claims (in one of its denotative contexts), is a hairstyle, and his hair is straight. Instead, he articulated that he refers to himself as being BlackWhite.[71]

Coinciding with this racial classification system, other norming structures are present in the cover's image. They establish yet another convergence, that of race and gender in the imperialist imaginary. The cover image undeniably evokes the profiles used in nineteenth-century studies, including Josiah Nott and George Gliddon's *Types of Mankind, Or Ethnological Researches*, often used to delineate racial categories,[72] racial difference and a racial hierarchy of the 'family of man'. The visual parallels are clear in the use of the profile, yet Samy Deluxe's profile faces to the right, looking to the future, whereas the profiles from Nott and Gliddon's work face to the left, looking to the past. One can of course also argue that the profile holds a significant place in African art. A contemporary example is Black German artist Patricia Vester's metal sculpture designed for the May-Ayim Award, which presents the profile of Ayim surrounded by Ghanaian Adinkra symbols.[73]

70   Ariefdien Shaheen, and Rico Chapman, 'Hip Hop, Youth Activism, and the Dilemma of Colored Identity in South Africa', in Msia Kibona Clark and Mickie Mwanzia Koster, eds, *Hip Hop and Social Change in Africa: Ni Wakati* (London: Lexington Books, 2014), 96.

71   In an interview, Samy Deluxe expressed his belief that he represents art and culture in contemporary society, and it resonates with an audience. *Deutsche Welle*, 'Unser Gast: Samy Deluxe, Rapper-Typisch Deutsch', *DW Deutsch* (16 February 2010) <https://www.youtube.com/watch?v=PtYj_cZvm5k> accessed 12 January 2017.

72   J. C. Nott and George Gliddon, *Types of Mankind, Or Ethnological Researches Based Upon the Ancient Monuments, Paintings, Sculptures, and Crania of Races, and Upon Their Natural, Geographical, Philological and Biblical History* (9 edn, Philadelphia: Trübner & Co. 1868), 458.

73   Patricia Vester, 'Eine Skulptur mit Bedeutung: eine Betrachtung', in Natasha Kelly ed., *Sisters and Souls: Inspirationen von May Ayim* (Berlin: Orlanda Frauenverlag, 2015), 105–9.

These competing discourses embody the duality that the BlackWhite image of the album cover signifies. Elements that subvert a hegemonic reading from the ethnological perspective are equally visible. One could read the running white paint as a money/cum shot, tied to capitalist objectification, but also tied to sexuality. Such a reading situates Samy Deluxe's mixed-race body as a site of miscegenation, with the black dripping paint destabilizing the German idea of a blood-based white German nationality. It further indicates his belonging to a category all to its own on the racial hierarchy. While BlackWhite is a category that is non-existent, it is fashioned as fluid and capable of taking on multiple identities as a result of the blurred boundaries the dripping paint yields. This act deconstructs the performed identity of race that it parodies, but also points to the invisibility of Black Germans in the racial narratives of the German nation, given that one could only be either African or European in this pseudoscientific framework.

Other dimensions generally tied to the racial binary are the 'racist constructions of blackness [that] associate it with denigration, impurity, and nature [...]; the devaluation of performance in Western intellectual traditions simultaneously coincides with the devaluation of black people as subjects of inquiry in the academy and in society'.[74] To counter the aesthetic hegemony of whiteness, Samy Deluxe develops his own BlackWhite aesthetic (an aesthetic of contradictions) that is neither/nor, but rather both/ and. He positions himself as a Black German performer in a white European tradition, battling for his place among other great white German men as a purveyor of German culture, albeit fully aware that his Blackness occludes his inclusion in this canon. This struggle, however, is not his alone. It is one that May Ayim and other women *and* men of color in Germany continue to face today. The lyrics to the songs 'Hände Hoch' [Hands Up] and 'Poesie Album' [Poetry Album] confirm this reading. He raps in 'Hände Hoch',

> Dies is' 'ne Kultur dies is [*sic*] mehr als Unterhaltung / ... / Mehr als deutscher Rap dies is' allgemeine Bildung *(hebt die Hände hoch)* / Kaum aufgenommen, schon 'n Klassiker

74   White, *From Jim Crow to Jay-Z*, 27.

/ ... / Dies is' keine Promotour, dies is' deutsche Hochkultur / ... / Hör wie elegant ich diese Sprache hier spreche / Als ob ich diese dunkle Hautfarbe nicht hätte.[75]

[This is culture, this is more than entertainment / ... / more than German rap this is general education (raise the hands high) / hardly just recorded already a classic /... / this is no promo tour, this is German high culture / ... / hear how elegant I speak this language / as if I didn't have this dark skin color].

Similarly, in 'Poesie Album', Samy Deluxe raps, 'ich bin so Schiller, so Goethe, so bitter so böse, aber noch immer der größte Poet, der hier lebt' [I'm so Schiller, so Goethe, so bitter so evil, still the greatest poet that lives here].[76] These lexical performances that claim his superior status in high art and employ Goethe and Schiller as adjectives to describe himself, place Samy Deluxe in the realm of elite, white, male-dominated classical and canonical literature in a battle for cultural representation. Boyd argues that '[a]s a consequence of the limited opportunities for African Americans to participate in the "legitimate" art world in the past, we have often seen a renegotiation of those arenas that were available. This is best represented in music'.[77] The same context applies for Black Germans, particularly Black German men, in the realm of hip-hop. Samy Deluxe articulates this in the cover and the lyrics to his album *SchwarzWeiss*; for him, hip-hop is a new form of cultural expression; he is producing and critiquing German culture in contemporary times, as Goethe and Schiller did in their era.

Analyzing the album cover of *Männlich* [*Manly*] from 2014 signals the coinciding historical and discursive elements of race and gender for Black German men. A skeletal image, presented in gold, of Samy Deluxe's skull from what seems to be an x-ray appears on the cover image to this album (see Figure 7.5).

---

75   Samy Deluxe, 'Hände Hoch', *Verdammtnochma!* (Deluxe Records, 2004), Verse 2 Lines 1, 4–5 and 11, Verse 3 Lines 10–11.
76   Samy Deluxe, 'Poesie Album', *SchwarzWeiss* (EMI Music, 2011), Verse 2 Lines 1–2.
77   Boyd, *Black Enough*, 113.

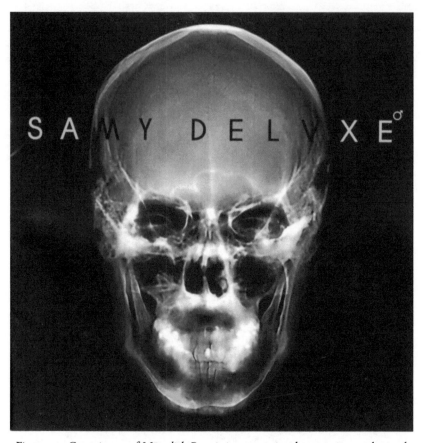

Figure 7.5. Cover image of *Männlich*. Permission to reprint the cover image obtained
from Gisela Sorge and Management Samy Deluxe.

In contrast, on the Deluxe Limited edition, the skull represents only one
half of the image and his face the other half.[78] I believe these two covers must
be read in conjunction with one another. Once again, the covers depict
a hardcore image of masculinity with his chosen stern facial expression,
his inward slanting eyebrows and bowed head, as well as his tight, straight

---

78   Unfortunately, I was unable to obtain a copy of this album and its cover image.
      However, the image is readily available online, if searched.

mouth in the Deluxe Limited edition. On the regular album cover his eyes penetrate the x-ray image, gazing at the viewer. The Deluxe Limited edition image returns us to the first cover examined in this chapter, given its seemingly hardcore presentation of masculinity on the right half of the image. But this cover, I would argue, asks the consumer to look beyond the surface to un*cover* what is to be found behind this masculine performance. It calls for scrutinization of the self, particularly of those who inhabit the white gaze; moreover, it achieves this via the x-ray-like image that sees under the skin. This is not normally visible to the human eye since it inhabits the body under the skin and its assemblages. As such, its alternatively conceptualized double-consciousness points to the surface of the racialized assemblage of the Black male body or the habeas viscus as Weheliye understands it. But it also hints at the discourse of posthumanism in its use of the cyberpunk aesthetic on the gold skeletal half. In its nod to the posthumanist high-tech future, the image may be articulating that this idea itself is but a cover, especially given that 'sociopolitical relations that discipline humanity into full humans, not-quite-humans, and nonhumans' persist.[79] White Europeans employed biotechnology and biopower to lend validity to this hierarchy and control and police Black masculinity and sexuality. These discourses jointly structure and support the reading of aggressive and threatening Black masculinity on the other half of the image. Similarly, the cover references what sociologist and feminist hip-hop scholar Antonia Randolph has identified as the absent 'luxury of not having their bodies examined' that is a privilege only awarded to the white body.[80] The double bind of an amalgamation of meaning located at

---

79   Weheliye, *Habeas Viscus*, 3.
80   Antonia Randolph, '"Don't Hate Me Because I'm Beautiful": Black Masculinity and Alternative Embodiment in Rap Music', *Race, Gender & Class* 13.3/4 (2006), 201. This resonates strongly in German historical contexts, given the collection, transportation, storage, examination and study of Nama and Herero skulls – to further white supremacist theories of craniology – acquired during German colonialism in Namibia. The Berlin Charité Hospital maintained possession of them in their medical history museum; only recently, the German government began their repatriation. Marc Röhlig, 'Koloniales Erbe in Namibia: Charité gibt Herero-Gebeine zurück', *Der Tagesspiegel* (5 March 2014) <http://www.tagesspiegel.de/

both the site and the sight of the Black male body as well as the medical
and technological dissection and gaze upon the Black male body/skull
constitute Samy Deluxe's dis/embodiment and split persona visualized in
the *Männlich* Deluxe Limited album cover image. In both cases, the self is
seen through the eyes of the white other, which brings the audience back
to the previous album cover in its approach to double-consciousness and
to the first album cover's image of hardcore masculinity. Samy Deluxe's
own representation of self lies somewhere outside of this cover's frame.

Returning to White, he asserts that 'the performance of hardcore masculinity rejects the softening of one's facial features in favor of the cold, hard
stare intended to project strength and inspire fear if not respect.'[81] Indeed,
this is the stare we encounter on the cover of the two *Männlich* albums;
however, it does not explain Samy Deluxe's employment of such a hardcore
representation of masculinity, one that is aggressively depicted and returns
us to the white German racial conceptualizations of the Black male brute
following World War I and during the Third Reich. Why, then, make this
the cover of an album entitled *Männlich*? I posit that this move is meant
to interrogate precisely the long-held image of hip-hop masculinity on the
one hand and, on the other hand, to probe the construct of Black masculinity more broadly speaking. This is clearly demonstrated in the song titled
'Penis' in German and its English translation. The song is a collaboration
on the album that features the white German rapper and soul singer Flo
Mega. Read within the context of hip-hop and the album's cover image and
when placed within the socio-historical conditioning of the Black German
male, it immediately evokes those images of the 'Black Horror on the Rhine'
addressed earlier in this chapter and the hardcore (hetero)sexuality of male
hip-hoppers. Yet what the song conveys is something entirely different.
The song's lyrics instead probe, 'Warum sieht das Herz nicht weiter als das
Auge / Kein Schwanz der Welt ist härter als Liebe und Vertrauen' [why
the heart doesn't see further than the eye' and affirms that 'no penis in the

---

wissen/koloniales-erbe-in-namibia-charite-gibt-herero-gebeine-zurueck/9575300.
html> accessed 3 January 2015.

81   White, *From Jim Crow to Jay-Z*, 24.

world is harder than love and trust].[82] This establishes the main organ of importance as the heart and not the phallus. Samy Deluxe critiques the strong and hard man: 'scheint die Männheit ist seit zwanzig Jahren kein' Schritt voran gekommen' [it appears as if mankind hasn't moved a step further since the past twenty years].[83] Such a comment poses the question of progress in science (in its reference to space exploration and the moon landing) and society, but also asks who or what is the object of critique? Is it men, men's behavior and false sense of progress, or men's performance of hardness/hardcore masculinity? Here, Samy Deluxe uses the German neologism *Männheit* intentionally to refer to men specifically. The word for humanity in German is *Menschheit*. With this, he exposes the conflation of humanity with men over the course of history and also criticizes men's complacency with normalized masculine gender roles.

Although Samy Deluxe critiques society and constructions of manliness and 'men', he does not necessarily see his position as one that can promote change. Instead, he uses the fact that he is a man to defend his actions; speaking from the position of someone questioning him, he inquires, 'Warum bringst du ihnen nichts bei?' [why don't you teach them [young men] anything?] to which he responds, 'äh, keine Ahnung, schätze weil ich / selber ein Kerl bin' [uh, no idea, probably because I too am a guy].[84] His shifting of the blame to the older generations and the cop out that he also is a man seem to be an attempt to remove himself from any culpability in perpetuating masculine constructs of hardness in the here and now.[85] Yet, who better to challenge and change these outdated gender roles than men themselves?

The lyrics do, nevertheless, force the viewer to question, whether it is a cold, hard stare Samy Deluxe casts on the cover, or if he is hinting at something else altogether. Is it not more likely the frustration and anger or rage that is tied to the socio-historical paradigms of race, gender, sexuality and their intersections in the construction of Black German postwar

---

82   Samy Deluxe, 'Penis', Männlich (Vertigo/Capitol, 2014), Verse 2 Lines 1–2.
83   Deluxe, 'Penis', Verse 2 Line 4.
84   Deluxe, 'Penis', Verse 3 Lines 17–19.
85   Deluxe, 'Penis', Verse 3 Lines 9–12.

masculinity? The cover image on the album *Männlich* represents a return of the gaze – a form of looking back that is oppositional and read as what bell hooks refers to as an act of resistance.[86] Interpreting the cover from this viewpoint would mean rejecting a reading of the Black male body through racial, heterosexual, gendered and sexed hegemonic structures that interpret the image as an adaptation of the brutish performance of hardcore hypersexual Black masculinity. Samy Deluxe interrogates the viewer's perceptions and inscriptions of the Black male body. In doing so, he calls the performance of race and gender into question.

Likewise, hardcore masculinity, which is said to demand respect, is something that Samy Deluxe actively critiques and questions in his autobiography, written four years prior to the release of *Männlich*. In it, he asserts:

> Dieser Weg [der männlichen Härte] führt unwiderruflich zu einem unnatürlichen, wahrscheinlich gewaltsamen Ende. Wer das für erstrebenswert hält muss vor allem hart an der Grenze zum Schwachsinn sein. Man sollte sich fragen: Ist ein Rapper, der in seinen Texten vom 'Abstechen' spricht, weil er zu viel unkontrollierte Wut in sich hat und mit seinen Aggressionen nicht vernünftig umgehen kann, härter als einer, der seiner Familie ernährt und ein Business am Start hat? Ist es wirklich härter, sich hart zu geben, als mit dem Leben in all seiner Härte klarzukommen?[87]

> [This path [that of hardcore masculinity] leads irrevocably to an unnatural, and most likely violent end. Whoever considers this worth striving for, must above all be firmly on the border to feeblemindedness. One should ask oneself: is a rapper, who speaks in his texts of stabbing because he has too much uncontrolled rage in him and cannot reasonably deal with his aggression any harder than one who nourishes his family and has the beginnings of a business? Is it really harder to portray yourself as hard, than to be able to deal with life in all of its hardness?]

Here, Samy Deluxe exposes a performed strength as the weakness it is. Later in this section, he interprets hardness as power, explaining that possession of power used positively can lead to respect, but misuse of power

---

86   bell hooks, 'The Oppositional Gaze', in *Black Looks: Race and Representation* (Boston, MA: South End Press, 1992), 115–31, especially 116.
87   Deluxe, *Dis wo ich herkomm*, 136–37.

only leads to fear.[88] With this awareness, Samy Deluxe criticizes to some extent his own self-performance, even if he is not directly articulating this or always following his own advice. Not only does he expose one form of performed hardness as something weaker than what he sees as an actual true hardness – not avoiding or displacing the challenges of life, but he also addresses the power dynamics within which such hardness operates at the expense of others through violent means. The album cover functions as an intervention in this sense; it calls into question the need for a hard, outer performance, if hardness is something that any individual might attain through life experiences, albeit different ones. It demands respect rather than evokes fear, and it does so by calling implicit ways of thinking into question. The cover presents the dominant conditions and projections through which the white gaze has historically interpellated and erased Black male bodies and the conditions through which rappers often inscribe themselves with a hardcore, external performance. Similarly, it undoes the intersecting performance of race and masculinity that supposedly signifies some tangible internal reality – one that does not exist or is in a perpetual state of becoming and must therefore always be reassembled. Through acts of performance, Black masculinity is projected onto the surface, but still articulates nothing or almost nothing about what might actually lie beneath it.

Conclusion: Under the Covers, Beneath the Surface

Samy Deluxe's fashioning of a postwar BlackWhite German masculinity in hip-hop is just one among many. His masculine and racialized self-performances reveal that it is always possible to change the way in which one performs and others perceive the performative self. However, these changes can also be regressive in nature or reassert cultural and societal

88   Deluxe, *Dis wo ich herkomm*, 145.

norms, while attempting to expose them for the façades that they are. The performances can also return – oftentimes purposefully so – to one's own previously discarded notions of masculinity. Or they can even evoke them with or without the intent to change perception or bear the burden of responsibility. As the identities of Samy Deluxe have evinced, the person performing can actively disassemble constructions of gender and race. Yet they are also subjected to the normative powers that discursively produce and constantly seek to reinforce and sustain them, as well as to the audience's own acknowledgment of the performativity of any identity.

In deconstructing race, both gender and sexuality must also be scrutinized, as they are inextricable in history, especially in the German context. One cannot be undone without the undoing of the others. In the process of this undoing, the self is continually constituted anew. Thus, in answer to his own questioning of who he is, Samy Deluxe writes in his autobiography: '[e]s gibt keine, zumindest keine endgültige. Was bringt es mir, bis ins kleinste Detail zu definieren, wer ich bin, wenn ich mich ständig verändere?' [there is no answer, at least not a final one. What good does it do to try to define who I am in every little detail, if I am constantly changing?].[89] This statement is strikingly similar to Michelle M. Wright's understanding of *Becoming Black*. Returning to her theorization, she states that the conceptualization 'asks us to understand any and all negotiations of the subject – white, Black, or otherwise – as negotiations always already in the making, and not the final word'.[90] Although, according to bell hooks 'Black males who refuse categorization are rare',[91] as this analysis of Samy Deluxe's BlackWhite postwar masculinity has shown, he is among the few who have sought to intervene and disrupt, though not wholly defy categorization. His performances expose the fact that gender and race are just identity 'covers' under which any *true* self – a self that is undergoing constant change – might seemingly *lie*.

89   Deluxe, *Dis wo ich herkomm*, 18.
90   Wright, *Becoming Black*, 26.
91   hooks, *We Real Cool*, xii.

Bibliography

Ariefdien, Shaheen, and Rico Chapman, 'Hip Hop, Youth Activism, and the Dilemma of Colored Identity in South Africa', in Msia Kibona Clark and Mickie Mwanzia Koster, eds, *Hip Hop and Social Change in Africa: Ni Wakati* (London: Lexington Books, 2014).

Ayim, May, *Blues in Schwarz Weiß* (Berlin: Orlanda Frauenverlag, 1995).

Boyd, Todd, *Am I Black Enough for You? Popular Culture from the 'Hood and Beyond* (Bloomington: University of Indiana Press, 1997).

Butler, Judith, *Gender Trouble: Feminism and the Subversion of Identity* (New York: Routledge, 1990).

——, *Undoing Gender* (New York: Routledge, 2004).

Campt, Tina, *Other Germans: Black Germans and the Politics of Race, Gender, and Memory in the Third Reich* (Ann Arbor: University of Michigan Press, 2004).

Chaouli, Michel, 'Laocoön and the Hottentots', in Sara Eigen and Mark Larrimore, eds, *The German Invention of Race* (Albany, NY: SUNY Press, 2006), 23–34.

Ciarlo, David, *Advertising Empire: Race and Visual Culture in Imperial Germany* (Cambridge, MA: Harvard University Press, 2011).

Deluxe, Samy, *Berühmte letzte Worte* (Vertigo/Capitol, 2016).

——, *Dis wo ich herkomm: Deutschland Deluxe* [*This Where I'm From: Germany Deluxe*] (2nd edn, Hamburg: Rowohlt Taschenbuch Verlag, 2010).

——, *Männlich* (Vertigo/Capitol, 2014).

——, 'Penis', on *Männlich* (Vertigo/Capitol, 2014).

——, 'Poesie Album', on *SchwarzWeiss* (EMI Music, 2011).

——, *SchwarzWeiss* (EMI Music, 2012).

——, *Verdammtnochma!* (Deluxe Records, 2004).

——, 'Warum', on *Verdammtnochma!* (Deluxe Records, 2004).

Deutsche Welle. 'Unser Gast: Samy Deluxe, Rapper-Typisch Deutsch', *DW Deutsch* (published online 16 February 2010) <https://www.youtube.com/watch?v=PtYj_cZvm5k> accessed 12 January 2017.

Du Bois, W. E. B, *The Souls of Black Folk* (New York: Simon and Schuster, 2009 [1903]).

El-Tayeb, Fatima, '"If You Can't Pronounce My Name, You Can Just Call Me Pride": Afro-German Activism Gender, and Hip Hop', *Gender and History* 15/3 (2003), 460–86.

Erb, Cynthia Marie, *Tracking King Kong: A Hollywood Icon in World Culture* (Detroit, MI: Wayne State University Press, 2009).

Fehrenbach, Heide, *Race after Hitler: Black Occupation Children in Postwar Germany* (Princeton, NJ: Princeton University Press, 2005).

Friedrichsmeyer, Sara, Sara Lennox and Susanne Zantop, eds, *The Imperialist Imagination: German Colonialism and Its Legacy*, 4th ser. (Ann Arbor: University of Michigan Press, 1998).

Furniss, Olaf, 'Rap/Hip-Hop: World Rap-Up Shows How Hip-Hop Travels. Samy Deluxe', *Billboard Magazine* 114/49 (7 December 2002), 50.

Gott, Ted, 'Stowed Away: Emmanuel Frémiet's Gorilla Carrying off a Woman', *Art Journal of Victoria* 45 (2005) <http://www.ngv.vic.gov.au/essay/stowed-away-emmanuel-fremiets-gorilla-carrying-off-a-woman-2-2/> accessed 20 March 2017.

Hackenesch, Silke, "'*Hergestellt unter ausschließlicher Verwendung von Kakaobohnen deutscher Kolonien*" – On Representations of Chocolate Consumption as a Colonial Endeavor', in Tiffany N. Florvil and Vanessa D. Plumly, eds, *Rethinking Black German Studies: Approaches, Interventions and Histories* (Oxford: Peter Lang, 2018), this volume, Chapter 1.

Hall, Stuart, 'Cultural Identity and Diaspora', in Jana Evans Braziel, and Anita Mannur, eds, *Theorizing Diaspora* (Oxford: Wiley-Blackwell, 2003), 233–46.

'Hände Hoch', Samy Deluxe, *SchwarzWeiss* (EMI Music, 2012).

Herr Sorge, *Verschwörungstheorien mit schönen Melodien* (Universal Music Domestic Rock/Urban, 2012).

Höhn, Maria, *GIs and Fräuleins: The German-American Encounter in 1950s West Germany* (Chapel Hill: University of North Carolina Press, 2002).

hooks, bell, *Black Looks: Race and Representation* (Boston, MA: South End Press, 1992).

——, *Talking Back: Thinking Feminist, Thinking Black* (Boston, MA: South End Press, 1999).

——, *We Real Cool: Black Men and Masculinity* (New York: Routledge, 2004).

Jerome, Roy, ed., *Conceptions of Postwar German Masculinity* (Albany, NY: SUNY Press, 2001).

Koepsell, Philipp Khabo, Personal Interview 24 August 2012.

Layne, Priscilla, 'Afro-German Fiction and the Politics of Publishing' paper given at the 38th Annual Conference of the German Studies Association, Kansas City, Missouri, 19–21 September 2014.

McClintock, Anne, *Imperial Leather. Race Gender and Sexuality in the Colonial Contest* (New York: Routledge, 1995).

Massaquoi, Hans, *Destined to Witness: Growing Up Black in Nazi Germany* (New York: Harper Collins, 1999).

——, *Neger, Neger, Schornsteinfeger: Meine Kindheit in Deutschland* (Bern: S. Fischer Verlag, 1999).

Nott, J. C., and George Gliddon, *Types of Mankind, Or Ethnological Researches Based Upon the Ancient Monuments, Paintings, Sculptures, and Crania of Races, and Upon Their Natural, Geographical, Philological and Biblical History* (9 edn, Philadelphia: Trübner & Co. 1868).

Odukoya, Ade, '"Fill the Gap": Adegoke Odukoya über Deutschrap, Ausgrenzung und verpasste Chancen', in Sascha Verlan and Hannes Loh, eds, *20 Jahre HipHop in Deutschland* (Höffen: Hannibal, 2002), 140–44.

Pommerin, Reiner, *Sterilisierung der Rheinlandbastarde: Das Schicksal der farbigen deutschen Minderheit 1918–1937* (Düsseldorf: Droste, 1979).

Randolph, Antonia, '"Don't Hate Me Because I'm Beautiful": Black Masculinity and Alternative Embodiment in Rap Music', *Race, Gender & Class* 13.3/4 (2006), 200–17.

Röhlig, Marc, 'Koloniales Erbe in Namibia: Charité gibt Herero-Gebeine zurück', *Der Tagesspiegel* (5 March 2014) <http://www.tagesspiegel.de/wissen/koloniales-erbe-in-namibia-charite-gibt-herero-gebeine-zurueck/9575300.html> accessed 3 January 2015.

Roos, Julia, 'Women's Rights, Nationalist Anxiety, and the "Moral" Agenda in the Early Weimar Republic: Revisiting the "Black Horror" Campaign against France's African Occupation Troops', *Central European History* 42/3 (2009), 473–508.

Singletary, Kimberly Alecia, 'Everyday Matters: Haunting and the Black Diasporic Experience', in Tiffany N. Florvil and Vanessa D. Plumly, eds, *Rethinking Black German Studies: Approaches, Interventions and Histories* (Oxford: Peter Lang, 2018), this volume, Chapter 4.

Sorge, Samy [Samy Deluxe], 'Mensch und Marke-Differenzierung aus Sicht eines Künstlers', in Ulrich Görg, ed., *Erfolgreiche Markendifferenzierung: Strategie und Praxis professioneller Markenprofilierung* (Wiesbaden: Fachverlage, 2010), 387–99.

Toxi, Robert Stemmle, dir., (Fono Film, 1952).

Verlan, Sascha, and Hannes Loh, eds, *25 Jahre HipHop in Deutschland: 1980–2005* (Höfen: Hanibal Verlag, 2006).

Vester, Patricia, 'Eine Skulptur mit Bedeutung: eine Betrachtung', in Natasha Kelly, ed., *Sisters and Souls: Inspirationen von May Ayim* (Berlin: Orlanda Frauenverlag, 2015), 105–9.

Weheliye, Alexander, *Habeas Viscus: Racializing Assemblages: Biopolitics, and Black Feminist Theories of the Human* (Durham, NC: Duke University Press, 2014).

White, Miles, *From Jim Crow to Jay Z: Race, Rap, and the Performance of Masculinity* (Chicago: University of Illinois Press, 2011).

Wright, Michelle M., *Becoming Black: Creating Identity in the African Diaspora* (Durham, NC: Duke University Press, 2004).

——. 'Middle Passage Blackness and Its Diasporic Discontents: The Case for a Postwar Epistemology', in Eve Rosenhaft, and Robbie Aitken, eds, *Africa in Europe: Studies in Transnational Practice in the Long Twentieth Century* (Liverpool: Liverpool University Press, 2013), 217–33.

——. *Physics of Blackness: Beyond the Middle Passage Epistemology* (Minneapolis: University of Minnesota, 2015).

JAMELE WATKINS

8 Performing Oppression and Empowerment in *real life: Deutschland*

ABSTRACT

real life: Deutschland (2008) was a three-year theater project that focused on Black youth empowerment and brought Afro-German teenagers together for workshops. As participants in the YoungStars (the youth group affiliated with the project), the teenagers re-enacted their experiences with racism and attempted to navigate their way through them. This chapter examines the ways *real life: Deutschland* combined theories from Augusto Boal's 'Theater of the Oppressed' and Paulo Freire's critical pedagogy with Afro-diasporic practices as a way to advance its goals of improvisation, collaboration and empowerment – goals that were essential to helping participants process and counteract their experiences of racism. Drawing on oral interviews with the project's organizers, as well as the project's *Dokubroschüre*, this chapter explores the YoungStars' contributions to anti-racist activism in contemporary Germany. I contend that the YoungStars created a safe space where participants were validated and recognized in their expression of anger about racism in Germany.

Bringing *real life* to the Stage: From Performance and Process to Empowerment

The Black youth empowerment theater project *real life: Deutschland* took place between 2006 to 2009. Arranged as a series of vignettes focused on intersectional racist experiences, the project was based on improvisation, which it employed as a way for youth to devise new ideas through which to think about oppression. Sebastian Fleary designed this as his final project for a certificate in theater pedagogy at the University of Bielefeld. Given that he had to work with youth as part of the certificate requirement, Fleary knew that he wanted to engage Black German adolescents across Germany.[1] At a 2005 *Initiative Schwarze Menschen in Deutschland* [Initiative of Black People in Germany, or ISD] annual *Bundestreffen* [national meeting] in Bavaria, he gauged interest in pursuing such a theater project among teenagers who were present.[2] After Fleary gathered interested teens at the *Bundestreffen*, he organized educational workshops on oppression and improvisation for youth (aged 16–21 years of age) over the course of several subsequent weekends.[3] Included in these workshops were teaching back extemporizations that dealt with oppression. Together, Fleary and the teens decided to perform memorable, improvised scenes for a public event in Bielefeld and then met consecutively for two weeks prior to the premiere in October 2008. For many of these youth, the weekends provided a safe space for them to socialize without having to endure the pressure and microaggressions present in the white German majority culture.[4] This

1   Sebastian Fleary, interview with Jamele Watkins, digital recording, Berlin, Germany, 9 July 2014.

2   ISD's *Bundestreffen* takes place annually over a weekend in early August and serves as a safe space for Black Germans and African descended people in Germany to meet. The three-day event often includes lectures, discussions, information booths, workshops and children's programs. Because Fleary's project began at the *Bundestreffen*, only certain Afro-/Black German youth were involved. It is a Black space and not every child has an African descended parent or guardian. The physical site of the collective meeting affected who had access to the project. The teens' engagement with ISD can be seen as a demonstration of both their own and their parents' political and cultural interest in Black people in Germany.

3   Within the confines of the paper, I refer to the 16- to 21-year-olds as youth, teenagers, adolescents and children because they evoke childhood experiences in their project as well as the larger issue of Black children being perceived as adults as evidenced by Tamir Rice, Michael Brown, and many others in the United States.

4   Dr. Derald Wing Sue describes microaggressions as 'the everyday verbal, nonverbal, and environmental slights, snubs, or insults, whether intentional or unintentional, which

forum also allowed the adolescents to be in community with each other on a regular basis, and they were eager to participate in the project. The teens involved in the project explained: 'Mit der Projektarbeit und unserem Stück wollten wir Rassismus in Deutschland zur Sprache bringen; ihn mit der anschließenden Tour für die Zuschauenden sichtbar machen und seine Existenz und Auswirkung auf das Leben festhalten' [With this project and our work, we wanted to bring up the issue of racism in Germany. The project and the closing tour were intended to make racism apparent to the audience and to record its existence and impact on life].[5] The project as a whole gave them a forum to experiment, to play and to develop their own models for liberation and resistance, without having to censor themselves. Indeed, this project served as a significant example of Black German drama due to its duration and format, allowing Black German youth to participate in a groundbreaking and personally meaningful, enriching performance.

About a dozen Black German youth participated in the project. A few others joined and left the group throughout the process, but many knew each other before the project's genesis. These established relationships enabled them to cultivate strong bonds to improvise and experiment and to establish trust.[6] Naming themselves the YoungStars, the teenagers were in charge of organizing a central part of the project, for which they produced a play to be performed in their respective hometowns. As a result, Black German youth gained agency through their involvement in

---

communicate hostile, derogatory, or negative messages to target persons based solely upon their marginalized group membership'. Derald Wing Sue, 'Microaggressions: More than Just Race', *Psychology Today* (17 November 2010) <https://www.psychologytoday.com/blog/microaggressions-in-everyday-life/201011/microaggressions-more-just-race/> accessed 28 April 2018.

5   YoungStars, 'Dokubroschüre: Dokumentation des YoungStar Theater Projektes' [Brochure: Documentation of the YoungStar Theater Project] (unpublished manuscript, 2008), 6. All English translations of the YoungStars' brochure are my own.

6   Fleary, interview with Jamele Watkins, digital recording, Berlin, Germany, 24 July 2014.

the play's production process as well as took on leadership roles by organizing the performances. The youth approached topics that reflected their age and specific experiences of their childhood – for instance encounters on the playground and/or at school; their engagement with these topics represented their previous racialized experiences as young adults. Thus, as a project and improvised play conceptualized by Black German adolescents, *real life: Deutschland* presents a particular consideration: that these youth were autodidactic actors who approached their identity in a more nuanced way than professional adult actors.

Additionally, the improvisational nature of this theater project remained a crucial component. The project went through different metamorphoses as time went on. On the one hand, the absence of a fixed direction of the project could be taken as a criticism, while on the other, logistical financial concerns certainly played a role. This organically evolving process illustrates that the lack of a particular end goal led to a more process-oriented, rather than performance-oriented, experience. For instance, through my interviews, I found that the improvisation process yielded a different type of empowerment for the youth than the actual performance. That aspect required the performers to actively participate and generate knowledge; they did so by performing their own positionalities and seeking ways out of oppression through crowdsourcing ideas. In contrast to traditional notions of theater, improvisation does not demand an audience per se, but instead can entail a group of actors collaborating and experimenting with each other in order to create something new. It targets the actors themselves, and, in doing so, the adolescents shift traditional dynamics in theater from the audience to the individual performer. Memorable scenes from their weekend improvisation workshops were carried over into the stage performance that drew connections to music, literature and theory from across the African diaspora.

The unconventional dimensions of this theater project extended to the choice to perform in cultural centers throughout Germany. Such sites do not always attract the same audiences as a commercial theater, but there were benefits to choosing this type of venue. Cultural centers offered the youth a place to perform without providing input on or taking creative control of the play. Thus, the actors and creators in *real life: Deutschland* had ownership over the process, the subject matter and the length of the production. The patchwork play lasted approximately one hour, not including intermission, and was performed on stage at several cultural centers across Germany, including: *IBZ* Bielefeld, *Westwerk* in Hamburg, *Werkstatt der Kulturen* in Berlin, *GeyserHaus* in Leipzig, *Kulturzentrum Merlin* in Stuttgart and the *Jugendhaus Heideplatz* in Frankfurt am Main. Each city was one of the performers' hometowns with the exception of Leipzig and Frankfurt. The YoungStars chose the last two cities because they knew there were significant Black populations there.[7]

Like all of the work Black Germans produce, this play is intersectional. The plot of the performance collaboration was also utilized as part of the plot of the play as it represented childhood experiences of racism and exclusion. Along with leaders Sebastian Fleary, Patricia Göthe and Sharon Otoo, the youth devised a performance of eleven short scenes. The play begins with the youth dancing under a curtain as other youth on stage 'oohhhh' and 'ahhhh' at them. The next scene features a reading of a May Ayim poem, 'Blues in black and white', over the loud speakers. Subsequent scenes focus on childhood experiences: playing cards, playing on the playground, singing the song 'Wer hat Angst vorm schwarzen Mann?' [Who is afraid of the Black man?], as well as hearing words like 'dirty' or the 'N-word' thrown at them and then not finding other children to play with. Later scenes depict more adolescent experiences, such as dealing with a racist white German teacher, being aggressively approached in a nightclub by an older white German man, dancing to a song and imagining what Sojourner Truth would say about racial and gendered oppression in contemporary society. Engaging with these experiences of everyday racism and drawing on them to learn how to cope and turn these moments around, the youth saw the play as an opportunity for them to stand in acknowledgment of the truth about their daily lives and to be empowered as Black people in Germany.

7   Fleary, interview, 9 July 2014.

While the project no longer exists today, its positive effects can be
seen through the lives of those involved, and its influence on the emerging genre of Black German theater that continues to combine the educational roles that theater performance and activism can and do play. In
addition to the performances and process of creating them, youth were
also empowered through telling their intentions and inspirations in their
Dokubroschüre [Docu-Brochure]. The brochure, entitled *Dokumentation
des YoungStar Theater Projektes* [Documentation of the YoungStar Theater
Project], is a fifty-two-page unpublished document written collaboratively by members of the group and sold at the performances.[8] It outlines
the weekend workshops, methods and inspiration behind the project.
According to the self-produced brochure and supported by my interviews with Fleary and other participants, the YoungStars project and
their play, *real life: Deutschland*, drew inspiration from Brazilian radical
theater theorist Augusto Boal and Brazilian critical pedagogy theorist
Paulo Freire.

    In the analysis that follows, I turn to the work of these theorists and
other African diasporic cultural icons and iconic texts that the teens evoked
in their play, as well as the cultural significance behind them. In doing so,
I demonstrate how the theater project makes use of the aforementioned
'diasporic resources' to advance the project's aims of empowerment through
improvisation and performance.[9] The combination of different diasporic
threads aided the teenagers in creating their own identity. Cultural theorist
Fatima El-Tayeb explains that Black Germans have to create an identity
simultaneously within the German nation state and as a transnational

8   Authors included adult leaders Fleary, Patricia Göthe and Sharon Otoo. The youth
     listed as co-authors included Joshua Aikins, Siraad Wiedenroth, Amina Eisner and
     Jonathan Aikins. Secondary authors outside the project included: Toan Nguyen,
     ManuEla Ritz, Nicola Laure al-Samari and Arun Singal.
9   Jacqueline Nassy Brown, 'Black Liverpool, Black America, and the Gendering of
     Diasporic Space', in *Dropping Anchor, Setting Sail: Geographies of Race in Black
     Liverpool* (Princeton, NJ: Princeton University Press, 2005), 53.

entity.[10] Integrating these different pieces and perspectives of the diaspora helped the YoungStars negotiate their own identities. More importantly, these pieces empowered the teens. The teens (as performers) are able to look within and focus on themselves and to include the audience in the journey in refashioning their identity. As performers, the inward turn is integral; it supports my claim that this project was primarily beneficial for the teens themselves instead of something implemented with an audience in mind. Additionally, I draw upon video footage of the *real life: Deutschland* performance in Cologne in December 2008 and interviews that I conducted with the actors and director in the summer of 2014 in Berlin.

Improvisation and Theoretical Tools

real life: Deutschland had its origins in ten weekend collaborative empowerment workshops near Bielefeld. The initial improvisation during the weekend workshops fell under the following two categories: 'Diskriminierung/ Status und emotionales Theater' [Discrimination Status and Emotional Theater] and 'Beobachtung, Bewegung mimen, Bewegung werden/Schwarz sein' [Observation, Mimicking Movements, Becoming Movements/Being Black].[11] During these weekends, a teacher led a workshop on global oppression with different foci at each meeting. The varied topics included: self-reflection on racism, acquisition of historical knowledge of oppression in the world, dance theater through the 2004 film *Rhythm is it!* and engagement with the work of pioneers of improvisational theater, including prominent British-Canadian Keith Johnstone and Brazilian Augusto

10 Fatima El-Tayeb, 'Dimensions of Diaspora: Women of Color Feminism, Black Europe, and Queer Memory Discourses', in *European Others: Queering Ethnicity in Postnational Europe* (Minneapolis: University of Minnesota Press, 2011), 65.

11 YoungStars, 21.

Boal.[12] Other inspiration for their empowerment work further included: Tanja Bidlo, Maisha Eggers (now known as Maisha Auma), Kien Nghi Ha, Norbert Herriger, David Hoppe, Thomas Köller, Cornelia Rössler, Eleonore Wiedenroth-Coulibaly, Halil Can and Nuran Yiğit.[13] At these workshops, Black German adolescents improvised scenes based on what they learned about oppression in the educational workshops and taught the information back to everyone, becoming co-producers of knowledge. In this way, learning was not unidirectional, but dialogic in nature.

Such a collaborative learning style proved imperative to Brazilian critical pedagogical theorist Paulo Freire, whom the YoungStars reference as a source of inspiration in their *Dokubroschüre*.[14] Freire's theory of communal learning was an integral part of the YoungStars' project. While Fleary was in charge of the funding sources, grant writing and weekend organizing, the teenagers had artistic independence and could steer the project's direction.[15] Everything from terminology (i.e. the term 'Afro-German' found in the brochure), to the decisions to perform, where to perform and what to perform were decided collectively and intentionally. This collaboration and decision-making did not come solely from the instructor, but equally from the students and embodies the co-production of knowledge that Freire promoted. Freire believed that teaching one another, drawing connections that may have been otherwise unseen, engaging teens in these processes early enough as to not give the teacher more power, ideally questioning and jointly and actively producing and critiquing knowledge in the present and the future was integral to their growth. In many ways, there was a multidirectional exchange that benefited both the students and the instructor in his pedagogy and that was put into action in *real life: Deutschland*.

The YoungStars equally drew upon the improvisational theories of Augusto Boal from the 1970s and 1980s.[16] Boal was a Brazilian theorist who

12   YoungStars, 24–27.
13   YoungStars, 50.
14   YoungStars, 18.
15   Fleary, interview, 24 July 2014.
16   YoungStars, 18.

worked on Improvisation Theater for the lower classes in order to challenge the upper classes, and his ideas confronted the realities of oppressed people in an effort to workshop ways to tackle unbearable situations the next time they occur. Performance Studies scholar Marvin Carlson said of Boal: '[p]robably no contemporary theorist has explored the political implications of the performance-audience relationship in so searching and original a manner'.[17] Similar to his friend Freire, Boal's theories were about attaining empowerment from oppression and entailed the oppressed classes liberating themselves. Boal's theories remain equally useful in an understanding of the YoungStars's performance. Using their improvised educational skits and choosing the most memorable scenes from the workshops, the teens decided to create the full-length play. Under the guidance of Fleary, they constantly kept the audience and the purpose behind the project in mind, making the process even more collaborative, thoughtful, reflective and intentional.

In particular, Augusto Boal's *Theater of the Oppressed* (1973) was effective in thinking about empowerment and the dismantling of injustice for the youth. Boal has shown that improvisation serves to imagine an alternative to oppression and helps one react differently when discrimination occurs. For him, theater was liberating:

> In this book [*Theater of the Oppressed*] I also offer some proof that the theater is a weapon. A very efficient weapon. For this reason one must fight for it. For this reason the ruling classes strive to take permanent hold of the theater and utilize it as a tool for domination ... But the theater can also be a weapon for liberation.[18]

Thus, according to Boal, theater is one tool to utilize in the fight against oppression. During the military junta and political instability of Brazil in the 1960s and into the 1980s, Boal employed theater to provide a space to imagine possibilities for the lower classes to combat their oppressors and taught adults and youth alike how to improvise in order to break free from

---

17 Marvin Carlson, *Theories of the Theater* (Ithaca, NY: Cornell University Press, 1993), 475.

18 Augusto Boal, *Theater of the Oppressed* (New York: Theater Communications Group, 1985), ix.

them. While living in exile, he adapted his theater techniques for new spaces and countries.[19] Boal, with his efforts, intended to bring about social and political change not only in Brazil but worldwide.

Using this form of theater was inherently radical, as it added fluidity to traditional roles. As Boal explained, '[i]n forum [theater], roles are not fixed – not only character [roles] but the roles of [the] "actor", "playwright", and "director". So forum is radical in relation to dramaturgy'.[20] This type of theater alters the standard roles of individuals (actor, playwright, director), allowing for more fluidity and collaboration. By breaking the rigid roles of actor and spectator, it is revolutionary and unlike theater traditions that came before. This lack of defined roles allows for the possibility for something brand new to develop. Instead of watching passively, then, the teens in *real life: Deutschland* were what Boal called 'spect-actors' participating in the play. Essentially, he envisioned the possibility to overcome alienation of the audience member through the agency of the spect-actor, as opposed to the passive spectator.[21] Boal, who saw himself differing from the German playwright and theater director Bertolt Brecht,[22] believed that the typical spectator does nothing but consume, and, thus, he urges the spectator to become involved in the action of the play as a spect-actor. For Boal, the process of engaging an audience member as an actor is more important than hoping for the viewer to draw an analogy or learn from the main character. He encouraged participation and collaboration working toward multiple solutions more than drawing simplistic analogies. Rather, the audience

19   Boal lived in Argentina, Peru and was in exile in Europe. Mady Schutzman and Jan Cohen-Cruz, eds, 'Introduction', *A Boal Companion* (Taylor and Francis: New York, 2006), 3.

20   Augusto Boal, Michael Taussig, and Richard Schechner, 'Boal in Brazil, France, the USA: Interview', *TDR* 34/3 (1990), 58.

21   Boal, *Theater of the Oppressed*, 122.

22   Boal criticizes Brecht for having a dominating main character. Boal's actor, character, and audience member are the same. He says, 'Brecht proposes a poetics in which the spectator delegates power to the character who thus acts in his place but the spectator reserves the right to think of himself, often in opposition to the character', *Theater of the Oppressed*, 122.

engages as a subject instead of an object because s/he contributes to the action of the performance.[23]

Boalian theater also allowed people to spontaneously imagine alternatives, thereby creating a site for experimentation. While contemporary theater worked in the indicative 'I do', Boal thought that actors should pose the question, 'What if I had done this?' and in the future, 'What if I were to do this?'[24] For Boal, the theater was the subjunctive.[25] He illustrates:

> [The subjunctive mood] is the comparison, discovery and counter position of possibilities, not of a single certainty set against another, which we have in reserve. It is the construction of diverse models of future action for a particular given situation, enabling their evaluation and study.[26]

Through the notion of 'improvising into being', theater relies on the oppressed classes coming together to imagine new and different possibilities for their world. Indeed, this type of theater was liberating: '[t]he spectator no longer delegates power to the characters either to think or to act in his place. The spectator frees himself; he thinks and acts for himself!'[27] Contemporary stage theater was spectacle, and Boal argued: the oppressed classes 'do not know yet what their world will look like; consequently their theater will be the rehearsal, not the finished spectacle'.[28] In his *Theater of the Oppressed*, the spectators are free to act, and the end remains unknown as they use their agency to be protagonists.[29]

Within the context of Boal's experimental theater, one spect-actor recalls a moment of oppression and acts it out. Then s/he reenacts the moment(s) with alternative responses to oppression. For Boal, acting out

---

23 Boal, *Theater of the Oppressed*, 132.
24 Augusto Boal, *An Aesthetics of the Oppressed*, tr. Adrian Jackson (New York City: Routledge, 2006), 40.
25 Boal, *An Aesthetics of the Oppressed*, 37.
26 Boal, *An Aesthetics of the Oppressed*, 40.
27 Boal, 'Theater as Discourse', in Michael Huxley, and Noel Witts, eds, *The Twentieth Century Performance Reader* (New York: Routledge, 2014), 98–99.
28 Boal, *Theater of the Oppressed*, 142.
29 Boal, 'Theater as Discourse', 88.

options gives the spectators/actors the ability to see the actions they could take in order for change to occur: '[t]his game of images offers many other possibilities. The important thing is always to analyze the feasibility of the change'.[30] The actors actualize the steps necessary to see the ideal image come to fruition.[31] This is not intended to be cathartic; instead, rehearsing various outcomes will give the participant practice for dealing with oppression in the future.[32]

Boal's theories are particularly applicable to a youth group like the YoungStars. In his own work with youth, Boal stressed the lack of available language and concepts. Boal identified the reasons that youth engage in theater, '[b]ecause the children, even if they learn a lot, they have a very limited vocabulary. And sometimes they don't articulate their thoughts well ... But if you ask them in image, they are going to build their own vocabulary'.[33] The children Boal worked with were better at expressing themselves through their bodies, which was exactly what this type of theater demands. Theater can therefore be used as a language if youth do not have the words to communicate how they are feeling. For example, Boal revealed, '[w]hen we work with young people, sometimes we don't even use the word oppression. Many times, they don't know what oppression is'.[34] Analyzing the terminology together will open their eyes to the oppression around them and to the ways in which they can begin to liberate themselves from that oppression. To show them that they are oppressed as a child – before they may realize it on their own – changes the dynamic of power from weakness and dependency to strength and empowerment. As such, Boal's beliefs demonstrate the need for understanding linguistic expression in relation to lived experience in order to politically articulate oppression.[35]

---

30   Boal, *Theater of the Oppressed*, 139.
31   Boal, *Theater of the Oppressed*, 138.
32   Boal, 'Theater as Discourse', 94.
33   Peter Duffy, 'The Human Art: An Interview on Theater of the Oppressed and Youth with Augusto Boal', in Peter Duffy, and Elinor Vettraino, eds, *Youth and Theater of the Oppressed* (New York: Palgrave, 2010), 252.
34   Duffy, 'The Human Art', 258.
35   Another example of this is the coining of the terms Afro-German and Black German set against the oppressive and derogatory names as noted by Katharina Oguntoye

Through Boal's work with youth, who did not have the vocabulary to articulate their experiences, he determined that they needed to act out their oppression in order to fully comprehend it.

In the case of the YoungStars, they dealt with terminology in the weekend workshops. Their longstanding engagement with ISD also put them in a different position than the youth Boal himself mentioned, given that this political and cultural organization promotes discourses on race and Blackness in Germany. Nevertheless, in the theoretical and practical work of Boal, the YoungStars found someone whose ideas were useful and who resided outside of the predominantly white German theater canon. The YoungStars thus gave precedence to a non-European theorist in their process-based project.

Process(ing) as the Goal

The process-oriented nature of the project further revealed the dynamics of the performance since *real life: Deutschland* was not originally intended to be performed for a paying audience. Instead, it was improvised for the teens themselves. It was their improvisation and their time as spect-actors that was the most fruitful aspect of the project and not the actual performance itself. Performing the play primarily for themselves afforded the YoungStars the opportunity to engender a space in which they found strength and independence in a white majority society through self-portrayal, self-reflection, negotiation and self-awareness. Thematically, their plays referenced their experiences in childhood. Recalling tensions within diverse power relationships, the youth offer opportunities to intervene and change those dynamics. In one sketch, for example, the performers act out a scene from a classroom, in which a teacher uses inappropriate language

and May Ayim in the 'Editor's Introduction', in May Ayim, Katharina Oguntoye and Dagmar Schultz, eds, *Showing Our Colors: Afro-German Women Speak Out* (Amherst: University of Massachusetts Amherst Press, 1991), 12.

to describe Black people in a lesson. The students gently suggest different terminology, showing the audience that, in spite of the teacher/pupil power dynamic – especially considering the teachers' control over one's future in the German school system – it is possible to confront those in power on the problematic usages of offensive language in the classroom and on microaggressions. In another instance, an actor playing a child on the playground is called the N-word, and she asks her father, played by another teen, what the word means. This scene performs the process involved for youth on the receiving end of the term. In this scene, the child does not understand the definition but understands that the word's connotation is negative. The parent explains that people still use the N-word regardless of socio-cultural changes over time. This scene represents a common microaggression that Black people across the Diaspora experience and thus elicits emotions from Black audience members. It also prompts a degree of awareness for white audience members who may not know that their family members and friends are still called such hurtful words, or that such a word is actually violent.

In her monograph *Excitable Speech*, Judith Butler explains the violence in the regurgitation of vitriol as it evokes previous uses of hateful speech. Butler illustrates the performative nature of violent speech: 'that action echoes prior actions and *accumulates the force of authority through the repetition or citation of a prior and authoritative set of practices*. It is not simply that the speech act takes place *within* a practice, but that the act itself is a ritualized practice'.[36] The impact of hateful speech elicits previous iterations of the same actions and connects the speaker to other hateful people. Butler continues: '[w]hen the injurious term injures (and let me make clear that I think it does), it works its injury precisely through the accumulation and dissimulation of its force. The speaker who utters the racial slur is thus citing that slur [and] making a linguistic community with a history of speakers'.[37] In the same way, hearing the hateful term bonds you, as a listener, to the other listeners historically speaking. These scenes,

---

36   Judith Butler, *Excitable Speech* (New York: Routledge, 1997), 51. Italics are Butler's emphasis.
37   Butler, *Excitable Speech*, 52.

cathartic for some, enraging for others, validate the experiences of Black people in Germany.

Often validation within the theater world comes in the form of staging and receiving payment for one's performance. It was not until 2008 that the group decided to perform for the general public and charged admission for their shows.[38] This alone leads me to believe that the performance was not the end goal that the performers and organizers had in mind. In an interview, Fleary reinforced this idea that monetary profit was not the intention of the performances.[39] As a result, even the public performances of the play were still meant for the youth in the end. Moreover, in choosing to perform for audiences in their hometowns, they were not in front of strangers but, rather, in front of friends, relatives and classmates.[40] Rendering their work visible to others was a part of their process. Thus, they were able to transmit their performance to other youth. The staging also made further performances by Black youth possible.

The improvisational techniques that the YoungStars used benefited the actors and gave them a safe space to imagine alternatives to their daily life in Germany, including, as already stated above, how to challenge a teacher about using problematic language in a respectful way and how to approach parents in talking about the racism they faced on the playground. For the group, improvisation led to the creation of something new, especially as the YoungStars wrote in the *Dokubroschüre*: '[e]s geht dabei darum, [gemeinsam in Bewegung zu kommen] ... gemeinsam etwas noch nie Dagewesenes zu kreieren. Auf der Bühne sollen solche Geschehnisse entwickeln können, die wir im Leben nie zulassen würden' [It is about coming together in movement [...] to create something together that never existed before. On the stage such occurrences are supposed to develop, that we wouldn't otherwise tolerate].[41] The process of collectively creating together, then, served as the primary focus – something they had not been privy to in their

---

38   YoungStars, 27.
39   Fleary, interview, 9 July 2014.
40   The exact number of attendees is not clear, but each performance was full to capacity. Fleary, interview, 24 July 2014.
41   YoungStars, 17.

daily lives. The improvisation and process of production enabled them to be empowered as agents of change on their own terms. Black British and Berlin-based activist and writer Sharon Otoo acted in the performances and felt the impact of the project. In her time with the YoungStars, she, too, learned that 'the process was more important' than the outcome.[42] In this way, the performance was not vital to the project's impact. It was the working through topics, impromptu performances and the time negotiating and trying things out that was significant. The collaboration was an ongoing process, without tying the height of achievement to a performance but, rather, centering it on ongoing learning.

Moreover, their emphasis on process relates directly back to Boal's ideas of improvisation. Though Boal focused specifically on the oppression of the lower classes, his ideas nevertheless were and remain applicable to the racial oppression the YoungStars faced as teens. Working through their feelings of belonging and community allowed the youth to support each other, and improvisation and co-education contributed to their empowerment. This is what Boal and Freire also promoted and accomplished. As evidenced in the *Dokubroschüre*, printed in conjunction with the performances, empowerment was a necessary focal point of the project. The YoungStars explained the situation for People of Color in Germany as follows:

> PoC stehen unter einem permanenten, ihre Identität betreffenden Legitimationszwang, der von der weißen Mehrheitsgesellschaft ausgeübt wird. Die Allgegenwärtigkeit von Rassismus und die ihm innewohnende Gewalt haben direkte Auswirkungen auf Selbstwertgefühl und die Persönlichkeitsentwicklung Schwarzer Menschen.

> [PoCs are under a permanent identity-related legitimization pressure that is executed by the white majority society. The ubiquity of racism and the inherent violence has a direct impact on the self-esteem and the personal development of Black people].[43]

The goal of the project was not to generate sympathy in the audience or to act out the experiences of Black Germans but instead to give the audience a chance to reflect and think about the skits. The audience, too, witnessed

---

42   Sharon Otoo, interview with Jamele Watkins, digital recording, Berlin, 9 July 2014.
43   YoungStars, 8.

consciousness-raising moments that these Black German youth experienced. Thus, empowerment was key to the project:

> Empowerment-Strategien wirken darauf hin, weiße, dominante Deutungshoheit zu schwächen bzw. zu brechen und alternative Deutungsräume und Lebensbezüge anzuregen. Diese sollen PoC befähigen, ihre Forderungen an die Dominanzgesellschaft nicht aus einer Position der Abhängigkeit heraus, sondern der Unabhängigkeit und Stärke, zu formulieren.

> [Empowerment strategies work in order to weaken and break the white dominant authority and to stimulate alternative ways of thinking and ways of living. These [strategies] are supposed to empower PoCs to combat the dominant society not from a position of dependence, but instead from a position of independence and strength].[44]

By the end of the project, the youth had a better idea of what an empowerment project entailed and they 'came out as different people'.[45] They created a space to share their practices with others who had common experiences, which made them and their narratives visible through theater performance.

What the YoungStars' performances suggest is that the space of improvisation is key to recovering Black German identity,[46] because other examples of breaking out of oppression do not exist for the teens. The play's use of improvisation allows the youth to liberate themselves from discrimination when they otherwise have so few spaces in which to do so. As bell hooks explains, '[w]e are called upon to constantly create our models'.[47] In her chapter 'Choosing the Margin as a Space of Radical Openness' from her 1990 book of essays entitled *Yearning*, bell hooks describes that resistance and survival is based on improvisation:

---

44   YoungStars, 9.

45   Otoo, interview, 9 July 2014.

46   Quotation by Tiffany N. Florvil: 'Identity is not just who other people say you are, but also who you say you are', 'Black German Studies Then and Now' Seminar, German Studies Association Conference, 21 September 2014, Kansas City, Missouri.

47   bell hooks, *Black Looks: Race and Representation* (Boston, MA: South End Press, 1992), 2.

> Those of us who live, who 'make it,' passionately holding on to aspects of that 'down-home' life we do not intend to lose while simultaneously seeking new knowledge and experience, invent spaces of radical openness. Without such spaces we would not survive. Our living depends on our ability to conceptualize alternatives, often improvised.[48]

Here, hooks refers to daily performance and not theater performance. However, it is possible to draw the same conclusions for the YoungStars' stage as such a space. The improvisation and process of production provided a space for openness. For the YoungStars, the stage is an aesthetic and a transformative site, which the youth have reclaimed through their creative expression. In their improvisations, they reflect on moments of discrimination, and, more importantly, these performances afforded the YoungStars an opportunity to make sense of themselves in the world. Specifically, they address injustices that are often overlooked in German society. The YoungStars' staging of *real life: Deutschland* helped to shed light on the inequalities that women and People of Color (PoC), particularly, experience on a daily basis.

Furthermore, by drawing on bell hooks's critical work, the YoungStars used *real life: Deutschland* to tackle what it means to be not only a racialized person, but also a gendered individual who experiences oppression in German society. With their staging, the YoungStars performed Black female identities that helped them attend to the intersectional experiences of Black women. In contemplating oppression and racial and gendered power, the YoungStars find inspiration from hooks's *Yearning*.[49] The book examines the complexities of race and gender in everyday society. Building from *Yearning*, hooks further engages these intersectional themes in her book *Black Looks* (1992). hooks's theory of 'eating the other' as developed in this work describes the way in which People of Color are appropriated in white mainstream society. Here, she explains white society's consumption of Black culture:

48   hooks, 'Choosing the Margin as a Space of Radical Openness', in *Yearning: Race, Gender and Cultural Politics* (Boston, MA: South End Press, 1990), 149.
49   YoungStars, 50.

> [w]hen race and ethnicity become commodified as resources for pleasure, the culture of specific groups, as well as the bodies of individuals, can be seen as constituting an alternative playground where members of dominating races, genders, sexual practices affirm their power-over in intimate relations with the Other.[50]

In this case, the body and nation are intertwined in terms of expected access, and this proves significant, specifically in the German colonial imagination, in which access to Black women's bodies equaled access to land. In *real life: Deutschland*, the youth engage, then, not only with the issues of pervasive racism and the intersections of race and gender, but also with the concepts of power and *Heimat*, or home, in Germany. In the process of their exploration, the improvised staging acts serve as a critical framing principle used in order to highlight both the emotional and sociological impacts of institutionalized oppression.

Black Internationalism and Empowerment

Not only did the YoungStars implement Boal's theory regarding improvisation, but they also further supplemented it with Black theorists and artists from around the globe. By doing so, they made their realities visible to German audiences and practiced 'connected differences' to other oppressed groups worldwide.[51] Among these theorists, the work of Black women was emphasized, such as that of African American feminist and theorist bell hooks, as previously highlighted, and others such as Afro-Portuguese, Berlin-based writer, professor and artist, Grada Kilomba. The youth group integrated additional cultural texts of the African diaspora in the production, including the following: African American feminist and abolitionist Sojourner Truth's 'Ain't I a Woman?' speech; the African American

---

50   hooks, *Black Looks*, 23.
51   Audre Lorde, 'Forward to English Language Edition', in May Ayim, Katharina Oguntoye and Dagmar Schultz, eds, *Showing Our Colors: Afro-German Women Speak Out* (Amherst: University of Massachusetts Press, 1992), vii.

abolitionist Frederick Douglass's writings; Afro-German author May Ayim's
poems 'afro-deutsch I & II'; Afro-German singer Ayo's song 'Life is Real'
and 1990s African American R&B group En Vogue's song 'Hold On'. The
collage of these works demonstrates a variety of art forms (music, speech,
theory) and time periods (nineteenth, twentieth, and twenty-first centuries) in which Black people were critically engaging their identities. These
figures embody Black radicalism, empowerment and agency.

Prominent Afro-German artist and activist May Ayim empowered
others through her work and spoke honestly about racism in Germany. At
the beginning of the YoungStars' performance, the cast read Ayim's poems
'afro-deutsch I' and 'afro-deutsch II' ['afro-german I' and 'afro-german
II'] from her 1995 collection (the poems were originally written in 1984)
Blues in schwarz weiß [*Blues in Black and White*]. These well-known poems
deal with Black German identity in society and the difficulties of obtain-
ing social recognition. Ayim is celebrated as one of the trailblazers of the
Afro-German literary and political movement. In *real life: Deutschland*,
the performers read the poem intertwined with a similar dialogue on
stage that also thematized belonging. In doing so, they contribute to an
emerging literary corpus written by Black Germans and illustrate how
opinions towards Afro-Germans have stayed more or less the same since
the 1980s.

The YoungStars continued their political intervention in the performance of Ayim's poem 'afro-deutsch I'. The inclusion of Ayim's poetry highlights and honors the work of Black Germans who preceded them. The teens
insisted on staying in conversation with people who were no longer with
them; they remembered the work of people not present, thereby recalling
a longer history of Black Germans within the nation. They continued to
make political choices in the performance of the poem. The YoungStars
made space for an actor who could not attend the performance. The teenager who was cast to read Ayim's poem could not make her appearance in
person. Because the YoungStars played her recording, the teen was still
able to be part of the project without physically being there. Their inclusion of the actor living abroad shows their commitment to maintaining
diasporic connections with their Black German compatriot, transgressing
national boundaries.

Utilizing oppression existing in other global contexts, in this case in Australia, the teens unsettled normative ideas about beauty, community and kinship within Germany. During one of the workshops about global oppression, the teens watched Phillip Noyce's film *Rabbit Proof Fence* (2002). Based on a true story, the film depicted the attempt to whiten Aborigines – in other words committing cultural genocide – by kidnapping aboriginal children from their families and encouraging them to intermarry in order to destroy both them and their culture in Australia. After they learned about the injustices in Australia against Aborigines, it was the teens' turn to teach the information to the others. To do this, they broke up into smaller groups and brainstormed. After a certain amount of time, they were called back together to present their skits. In lieu of whitening Australia, one group proposed to Blacken Europe in order to rid them of the plague of their sun sensitivities and pale unattractiveness. In this scene on stage, the youth replicated pseudoscientific research about the inability of Black people to get sunburns and, at the same time, they reversed prevalent beauty aesthetics by preferring Black skin to white skin. Their examination of pseudoscience enacted and presented in the production was likely a jab at the pseudoscience depicted within the film. For example, the goals of the 'scientists' within the film were literally to whiten aboriginal people. By advocating for darker skin tones, the standard for beauty becomes Blackness. In this segment of the play, the youth envisioned a completely reversed power dynamic in an effort to critique oppression and parody racial constructs, demonstrating their irrationality and illogical base. This scene reveals their commitment to internationalism and their desire to understand how oppression and injustice work across the globe. In doing so, the YoungStars made this event in Australia more relevant to oppressed people in Europe, highlighting points of intersection transnationally.

Another example of diasporic connections is presented at the moment when the performers are calling each other scientists (in the play, referred to as 'wissenschaftliche Mitarbeiter'); the actors took questions from the audience, during which they could not break character and had to improvise. During the Cologne performance, some audience members asked, '[w]hat if the white people don't want to participate [and marry Black people]?'

As an answer, the actors laughed, responding, '[t]hat is ridiculous; why wouldn't they want to participate? We are helping them!'[52] Many white German audience members called this 'too extreme' and 'exaggerated'.[53] Audience members' reactions exposed the unwillingness to be confronted with an uncomfortable truth about racial cleansing. In their performance of this scene about oppression of Aborigines in Australia, the teens reminded audiences that ethnic cleansing is still prevalent by citing this example from more recent history. Evaluating these responses, the performers concluded that the skit made white audience members uncomfortable by suggesting an ideal that is not white. The scene further alarms white audience members because the actors unsettle what the norm is and who has power.

Some white audience members laughed during this particular scene. Analyzing the audience's reaction reveals the underlying engagement and awkwardness around watching race performed on stage. Kimberly Singletary described the laughter of white audience members as follows: '[i]nside the play you realize your complicity or the silence that you've allowed to happen'.[54] Otoo further clarified the problem with laughter and self-realization as: 'a realization that I should not be laughing'.[55] This response of laughter displays the absurdity of the actions on stage and that these actions are unacceptable. This scene reveals the farcicality as well as the actual threat of white supremacy; it exposes white supremacy as part of the social fabric and critiques the racialized science used against non-white people across the globe.

Indeed, this performance challenges whiteness and asks the audience to engage in self-reflection; underscoring Ayim's influence and refusing to center white identity and the white gaze, the performers actively decenter these power structures. The play further moves to empower Black female

---

52   *real life: Deutschland*, Sebastian Fleary, dir., performed by YoungStars (Cologne, 5 December 2008).

53   Fleary, interview, 24 July 2014.

54   Kimberly Alecia Singletary, 'Black German Studies Then and Now' Seminar, German Studies Association Conference, 21 September 2014, Kansas City, Missouri.

55   Sharon Otoo, 'Black German Studies Then and Now' Seminar, German Studies Association Conference, 21 September 2014, Kansas City, Missouri.

subjectivity and reclaim the Black female body. In two short skits, girls dance, covered with a white sheet, as the other characters 'ohhh' and 'ahhh', imitating the voyeurism of a white German audience. Voyeurism and the Black body on stage play an interesting role in Germany because Women of Color are sexualized and fetishized. Tina Campt, a prominent scholar of Black European Studies, describes the exoticism that Women of Color experience, remarking: '[i]n contemporary Germany, this Eurocentric notion of beauty rejects Women of Color as "other", while paradoxically giving positive value to "otherness" as "exotic", and thus exterior to this ideal'.[56] This exterior skin is shed in the process of the performance. In the play, the youth break free and release themselves from the thoughts, opinions, projections and desires of the white German public by literally shaking off the sheet that covers them to reclaim their bodies for themselves.[57] The dancing presents a dialogue on stage; they do not dance to be ogled. The dancing rejects the voyeurism and consumption that they know happens to them on the dance floor.

In yet another scene about voyeurism, young Black German teens reclaim their bodies in further ways throughout the play. Initially, two girls dance slowly to the first 1:05 seconds of En Vogue's song 'Hold On', which was released in 1990 on the album *Born to Sing*. The lyrics reveal that the song is about regret, love and desire. This scene takes a strong stance against the exoticism and eroticism that Black women endure in German culture. During the song, two female teens improvise a dance in darkness on a podium with a light only at their ankles and feet. This takes away the possible chances for voyeurism and consumption of the Black female body on stage for audiences because only part of the dance is visible. At the end of the dance the teens scream, 'Nein! Nein! Nein! Wir sind kein Produkt eurer pauschalisierenden Vorstellungen – wir sind INDIVIDUELL. Das sind eure Bilder – sie haben nichts mit uns zu tun' [No! No! No! We are not a product of your over-simplified imagination. We are individual! Those

56   Tina Campt, 'Afro-German Cultural Identity', *New German Critique* 58 (Winter 1993), 120.
57   Otoo, interview, 9 July 2014.

are your images and don't have anything to do with us].⁵⁸ Audiences are not able to see the teens dancing and are literally left in the dark. It feels like a subversive move on the part of the youth, as they force the audience to gaze into nothingness. Instead, the youth dance for themselves and thwart audience expectations of their ability to watch all events on stage. By dancing in the darkness, the teens lay claim to the stage and movement; they have the freedom to enjoy the song and dance as they choose, denying the white male gaze involved in spectatorship.

Taking an intersectional approach, *real life: Deutschland* rejects commodification. The youth performers highlight experiences Black teenagers and women experience. The young women occupy a particularly tough position because as teenaged girls (16+), they are allowed to go to the *Diskothek* [nightclub]. However, they deal with gendered and age-based oppression and unwanted sexual advances, as they are often much younger than the men at the club. In this scene, audiences are made aware of the potential gendered violence female youth of Color can experience. Performing this encounter and refusing their commodification as both racialized and sexualized bodies empowers the YoungStars.

The YoungStars deal with the complexity of age and race in the next scene. In it, a drunken white German man, Gregor, approaches, talks to and begins dancing with an Afro-German teen. The teens hoped not only to show the reality of sexualized racialization Black German women experience, but they also wanted the audience to think critically about the power dynamics involved in the scene.⁵⁹ There were heated debates regarding this particular scene in the planning. Otoo explains, '[b]ecause it was so extremely funny, it focused too much on Jonathan [who played Gregor] and not the experience of the girls'.⁶⁰ To include the audience, the actors stop the performance and another actor dressed in black comes on stage and asks the audience what they think will happen next (Was könnte passieren?) in a breaking of the fourth wall. Then she waits for the audience to actually come up with answers for a few minutes, and after the

58   YoungStars, 33.
59   Otoo, interview, 9 July 2014.
60   Otoo, interview, 9 July 2014.

audience shouts out three or four answers, she continues, 'Sehen wir mal wie es weitergeht' [let's see what happens next]. Otoo describes this scene as empowering, as 'it brings forth the perspective of the behavior of white men. When they are in that position, they are in a position of power. I think that scene was successful for turning around the power dynamic'.[61] This nightclub scene helps to foreground the Black girl's experience rather than the white German man's experience. The girl is at the club with her friend, but her friend goes to the bathroom. Alone, an adult male approaches her; he appears drunk, as he falls and tries to talk to her. The performance does not try to excuse his behavior as a harmless drunk or a guy who just wants to talk. The girl is visibly nervous and engages with him as much as she must. Further, there is no attempt to place blame on the girl for how she engages with him. Read in conjunction with the previous scene (dancing on the pedestal) that also centered on the Black teen's dancing for themselves rather than dancing for an audience, both of these scenes reclaim the Black female body.[62] The Black youth are protected, and their safety and feelings are prioritized above anything else. In this nightclub scene, a friend helps the Black teen escape a potentially dangerous situation, and then the two teens dance together. The pedestal scene and nightclub scene achieve different goals; dancing on stools reclaims the body and refuses objectification, and the nightclub scene offers instruction to other Black girls in the audience. This scene also points to the power of community in caring for each other in a society that does not give a damn about Black girls.

Showcasing strong women of the African diaspora, the teens also reclaim their body through the encouragement of an actress who plays Sojourner Truth. In the play, the abolitionist visits the girl from the nightclub saying, '[d]u hast selbst gelitten' [you have suffered yourself].[63] Sojourner Truth acknowledges the trauma of teens today, without comparing their experiences to her own. Sojourner Truth's 'Ain't I a Woman?' speech was the inspiration behind this scene according to the YoungStars'

---

61   Otoo, interview, 9 July 2014.
62   Otoo, interview, 9 July 2014.
63   *real life: Deutschland*, directed by Sebastian Fleary, Personal recording. DVD.

brochure. In the speech, Truth spoke about her multilayered identity as a Black woman in the nineteenth century.[64] Given the historically exclusionary nature of white women's movements, Sojourner Truth's speech is relevant here because it highlights the intersecting identities of being a Black woman in a majority white patriarchal society. Instead of just reading Truth's 'Ain't I a Woman?' speech, the teens opt to have Sojourner Truth transcend time and space to visit this teen and offer her words of encouragement. In her diasporic haunting (and in their imagination),[65] she reassures the girl of the truth: '[d]u bist stark, Schwarz, und schön' [You are strong, Black, and beautiful].[66] The idea that a Black woman in Germany is Black, strong and beautiful is revolutionary. Dr. Maisha Auma explains the dynamic of power and beauty in Nzitu Mawakha's photo collection *Daima*. The collection celebrates Black womanhood and empowers the contributors by allowing them to use their own words and in giving them an unrestrained subject matter. This knowledge project documents empowering images of Black female identity in Germany and the ways in which Black German stories are multifaceted. Auma explains, '[a]s a dark skinned Black Woman I am very visible in a world that reinforces whiteness as an aesthetic, or an economic, or a political norm. But at the same time I am also, quite apparently, invisible.'[67] Being strong, Black and beautiful means rejecting this whiteness and invisibility. With this line reinforcing their self-worth, the teens therefore celebrate themselves in a culture and society that denies their existence, let alone their beauty. As bell hooks also demonstrates, '[l]oving blackness as political resistance transforms our ways of looking and being, and thus creates the conditions necessary for us to move against

64   Patricia Hill Collins, and Sirma Bilge, 'Getting the History of Intersectionality Straight?' *Intersectionality* (Malden, MA: Polity, 2016), 67.
65   For more on haunting, see Kimberly Alecia Singletary, 'Everyday Matters: Haunting and the Black Diasporic Experience', in Tiffany N. Florvil and Vanessa D. Plumly, eds, *Rethinking Black German Studies: Approaches, Interventions, and Histories* (Oxford: Peter Lang, 2018), this volume Chapter 4.
66   *real life: Deutschland*, DVD.
67   Nzitu Mawakha, 'Maisha Eggers', in *Daima: Images of Women of Colour in Germany* (Münster: Edition Assemblage, 2013), 77.

the forces of domination and death and reclaim black life'.[68] As such, the teens transformed themselves on stage through self-love.

In one of the final scenes of the play, the youth reconcile their identities as Black Germans to embody both concepts instead of seeing these parts of their identity as oppositional. Tina Campt explains the tension for Black Germans surrounding national identity: 'the choice imposed upon Afro-Germans is less between "black" and "white" than between "Black" and "German" – a choice between claiming either their Black ethnicity or their German national and cultural heritage, each exclusive of one another'.[69] The teens challenge this expectation and instead define their identities as *both* Black *and* German, and they acknowledge the entanglement that this identity brings: '[i]ch bin Deutsche. Ich liebe klassische Musik. Ich liebe Milchreis mit ganz viel Zucker. Ich liebe Mathematik. Ich bin Deutsche. Ich bin stark, Schwarz und schön. Ich habe eine Verantwortung den nachfolgenden Generationen gegenüber, deswegen werde ich Lehrer' [I am German. I love classical music. I love milk rice with a lot of sugar. I love math. I am German. I am strong, Black, and beautiful. I have a responsibility to future generations, therefore I become a teacher (to them)].[70] Not only do the teens proclaim their pride in their Afro-German identities, but they also realize their role in helping future generations of Afro-German youth who are going to turn to them for understanding their identity against and in spite of a majority white German society.

The play ends with an empowering song that continues to signify a connection to the African diaspora and privileges diasporic cultural forms. After a hip-hop scene featuring three youths breakdancing, the play ends with Aretha Franklin's 1967 empowerment anthem 'Respect'. This song is a compelling choice in urging audience members to give respect across the intersections of identity and to make an effort to combat the forces of overlapping oppressions.

The credits roll with each youth's name along with her/his character's name. Below each of the credits, a caption adds a sentence about her/his

68   hooks, *Black Looks*, 20.
69   Campt, 'Afro-German Cultural Identity', 113.
70   *real life: Deutschland*, DVD.

character's future. There is also a caption about Gregor (in the scene from the nightclub): 'Gregor (der Typ aus der Disko) liegt mit gebrochener Nase im Krankenhaus. Eine Frau hatte ihm gegenüber diesmal eine klare Grenze gesetzt' [Gregor – the guy from the club – lays in the hospital with a broken nose. A woman made appropriate boundaries very clear to him].[71] A woman hit him, presumably in self-defense. This shows that although the Black teen did not do anything to Gregor, they can rest assured that he was punished for his actions, albeit in a comedic way. While comedic on the one hand, on the other, his violence is a scary reminder of the dangerous and predatory experiences women confront at clubs and bars and the need for self-defense. Way before the current moment of #metoo, this performance addressed the constant harassment women (and girls) experience, as well as the complexities of harassment that Women of Color face. The teens created an imaginary narrative that allows Gregor to finally get what is coming to him. The truth is, the teens lack this clear-cut agency; they cannot necessarily fight back in some instances. For centuries, Black female survival has meant the ability to quietly escape and navigate potentially dangerous situations. In some cases, they escape or find refuge with friends. For the YoungStars, it is no different.

Conclusion

The selected scenes analyzed from the performance *real life: Deutschland* attest to how the YoungStars used their marginalized position as Black youth to make space for non-European theorists, artists and authors on a German stage. By highlighting Black identity, they gave others ideas on how to have constructive discussions around race in the classroom or with a parent, how to respond in a situation in which they face racism and how to empower themselves. At the same time, the group does not attempt to answer all the

71   *real life: Deutschland*, Sebastian Fleary, dir.

questions. For example, they offer no solution for the problem Black girls face in nightclubs. Instead, they suggest that one day Gregor will get his comeuppance. As youth, gender and sexual harassment is something they will have to deal with now and in the course of their entire lives. Perhaps the answer is that it is our responsibility as an audience to resolve this issue. Boal, too, articulates that it is up to the audience (or spect-actors) to come up with alternative responses to the situations they see performed.

In addition to the many empowering aspects of the play itself, the reception of *real life: Deutschland* also furthered the YoungStars objective of empowering Black youth. Fleary shared, '[a]fter each performance, mostly Black and PoC came to me and gave their thanks [...] This [project] had a meaning for them'.[72] Sharon Otoo recalled that the play was 'cathartic' for Afro-German audiences. White Germans in the audience, on the other hand, criticized certain scenes of *real life: Deutschland* – many called it too extreme.[73] According to interviews with Fleary and Otoo, the race of the audience members impacted the reception of the play. The Leipzig performance was particularly difficult, and the discussion period afterward was not productive because some white audience members often centered themselves, instead of grasping the racial dynamics and centering the youth involved in the performance.[74]

While the *real life: Deutschland* project ended in 2008, its impact can still be seen, especially in the evolution of Black German theater. For instance, Amina Eisner, one of the teenagers involved, eventually studied as an undergraduate in Liverpool and wrote her thesis on theater after the YoungStars project ended. She recently co-wrote and has staged her play, *Jung, Schwarz, und Giftig* [*Young, Black, and Poisonous*] – a twist on Nina Simone's song 'To be Young, Gifted, and Black' and Lorraine Hansberry's play of the same title – since May 2015 at the widely known post-migrant theater venue Ballhaus Naunynstrasse. Reflecting on the YoungStars project, Eisner explains that she enjoyed the time it took to create the piece. There was no deadline in creating the performance; the teens were really able to

---

72 Fleary, interview, 24 July 2014.
73 Fleary, interview, 24 July 2014.
74 Otoo, interview, 9 July 2014.

develop scenes and experiment with them over a number of years. Both the project leader Sebastian Fleary and one of the performers, Jonathan Aikins were involved with the Black German theater group LiberatioNoir, now known as Label Noir. Label Noir is a Black German theater ensemble that performs throughout Germany. They have performed their own play about microaggressions and belonging, *Heimat, bittersüße Heimat* [*Home, bittersweet Home*] and will be performing other pieces in the next year. Through this project, Fleary learned that he wanted to turn empowering youth into a life-long career.[75]

The beginnings of Black German performance groups and projects inform practitioners and scholars alike as to how Black German theater has evolved and serves as a form of activism. Specifically, the project *real life: Deutschland* explored improvisation, promoted empowerment and encouraged collaboration. It served as the catalyst for the development of Black/Afro-German theater in Germany, offering a new form of artistic expression and establishing the stage as a space for performing microaggressions and imagining change. Indeed, calling yourself 'Schwarz, stark, und schön' [Black, strong, and beautiful] on stage in contemporary Germany was and still is a revolutionary act. The youth in the YoungStars took a proactive and informed approach to their theater in order to perform an improvised play with an activist viewpoint. They remained process-oriented instead of performance-oriented, resulting in ongoing learning and contemplation. Moreover, the YoungStars point to the productive potential of incorporating African American and Latin American theorists into theater's production and performance. With these 'diasporic resources',[76] the YoungStars searched outside and inside of Germany for ideas, models and theorists. Additionally, the teens referenced multiple Black women who refused tokenism and objectification in their own works on stage and in the production process. While the YoungStars did not overthrow any regime or start a revolution, as Boal imagined for his improvisation theater, their project was nevertheless revolutionary for themselves and Black German communities. The youth rejected the exclusive whiteness of German

---

75   Otoo, interview, 9 July 2014.
76   Brown, 'Black Liverpool, Black America, and the Gendering of Diasporic Space', 53.

cultural identity and German culture as well as the exoticism of the white gaze. Actors from this play are still involved in activism, perform in other theater groups and work with Black German youth today. Through the YoungStars, audiences witnessed racial and gendered issues addressed on stage. With their work laying the foundation, later Black German theater productions evinced a continuation of empowering artistic expression led and directed by Black Germans.

Bibliography

Auslander, Phillip, 'Boal, Blau, Brecht: The Body', in *From Acting to Performance: Essays in Modernism and Postmodernism* (New York: Routledge, 1997), 98–107.

Boal, Augusto, *An Aesthetics of the Oppressed*, tr. Adrian Jackson (New York City: Routledge, 2006).

Boal, Augusto, Michael Taussig and Richard Schechner, 'Boal in Brazil, France, the USA: Interview', *TDR* 34/3 (1990) 50–65.

Boal, Augusto, 'Theater as Discourse', in Michael Huxley, and Noel Witts, eds, *The Twentieth Century Performance Reader* (New York: Routledge, 2014), 88–100.

Boal, Augusto, *Theater of the Oppressed*, tr. Charles and Maria-Odilia Leal McBride (New York: Theater Communications Group, 1985).

Brown, Jacqueline Nassy, 'Black Liverpool, Black America, and the Gendering of Diasporic Space', in *Dropping Anchor, Setting Sail: Geographies of Race in Black Liverpool* (Princeton, NJ: Princeton University Press, 2005), 45–69.

Butler, Judith, *Excitable Speech* (New York: Routledge, 1996).

Campt, Tina, 'Afro-German Cultural Identity', *New German Critique* 58 (Winter 1993) 109–26.

——, 'The Crowded Space of Diaspora: Intercultural Address and the Tensions of Diasporic Relation', *Radical History Review* 83 (2002) 94–111.

Carlson, Marvin, *Theories of the Theater* (Ithaca, NY: Cornell University Press, 1993).

Collins, Patricia Hill, and Sirma Bilge, 'Getting the History of Intersectionality Straight?' *Intersectionality* (Malden, MA: Polity, 2016), 63–87.

Duffy, Peter, 'The Human Art: An Interview on Theater of the Oppressed and Youth with Augusto Boal', in Peter Duffy, and Elinor Vettraino, eds, *Youth and Theater of the Oppressed* (New York: Palgrave, 2010), 251–62.

Eisner, Amina, and Thandi Sebe, *Jung, giftig und schwarz* (Berlin, Germany, 23 May 2015).

El-Tayeb, Fatima, 'Dimensions of Diaspora: Women of Color Feminism, Black Europe, and Queer Memory Discourses', in *European Others: Queering Ethnicity in Postnational Europe* (Minneapolis: University of Minnesota Press, 2011), 43–80.

En Vogue, 'Hold On', *Born to Sing* (Atlantic, 1990) [digital].

Fleary, Sebastian, interview with Jamele Watkins, digital recording, Berlin, Germany, 9 July 2014.

——, interview with Jamele Watkins, digital recording, Berlin, Germany, 24 July 2014.

Franklin, Aretha, 'Respect', *I Never Loved a Man the Way I Love You* (Atlantic 1997) [digital].

Freire, Paulo, *The Pedagogy of the Oppressed*, tr. Myra B. Ramos (New York: Continuum International, 2003).

Heimat, bittersüße Heimat, Lara-Sophie Milagro and Dela Dabulamanzi, dirs (Nuremberg, Germany, 13 February 2013).

hooks, bell, *Black Looks: Race and Representation* (Boston, MA: South End Press, 1992).

——, *Yearning: Race, Gender and Cultural Politics* (Boston, MA: South End Press, 1990).

Lorde, Audre, 'Forward to the English Language Edition', in May Ayim, Katharina Oguntoye and Dagmar Schultz, eds, *Showing Our Colors: Afro-German Women Speak Out* (Amherst: University of Massachusetts Press, 1992), vii–xiv.

Mawakha, Nzitu, 'Maisha Eggers', in *Daima: Images of Women of Colour in Germany* (Münster: Edition Assemblage, 2013).

Otoo, Sharon, 'Black German Studies Then and Now' Seminar, German Studies Association Conference, 21 September 2014, Kansas City, Missouri.

——, interview with Jamele Watkins, digital recording, Berlin, Germany, 23 July 2014.

Rabbit Proof Fence, Phillip Noyce, dir. (Australia, Miramax and HanWay Films, 2002).

real life: Deutschland, Sebastian Fleary, dir. (Cologne, Germany, 5 December 2008).

real life: Deutschland, Sebastian Fleary, dir. Personal recording. DVD.

Schutzman, Mady, and Jan Cohen-Cruz, eds, 'Introduction', in *A Boal Companion* (Taylor and Francis: New York, 2006), 1–9.

Simone, Nina, 'To Be Young Gifted And Black', *Black Gold* (RCA 1970) [digital].

Singletary, Kimberly Alecia, 'Black German Studies Then and Now' Seminar, German Studies Association Conference, 21 September 2014, Kansas City, Missouri.

——, 'Everyday Matters: Haunting and the Black Diasporic Experience', in Tiffany N. Florvil and Vanessa D. Plumly, eds, *Rethinking Black German Studies: Approaches, Interventions and Histories* (Oxford: Peter Lang, 2018), Chapter 4.

Sue, Derald Wing, 'Microaggressions: More than Just Race', *Psychology Today* (17 November 2010), <https://www.psychologytoday.com/blog/microaggressions-in-everyday-life/201011/microaggressions-more-just-race/> accessed 28 April 2018.

YoungStars, *Dokubröschure: Dokumentation des YoungStar Theater Projektes* (unpublished manuscript, 2009).

MICHELLE M. WRIGHT

Afterword

Just over a decade ago, Tina Campt and I edited a special issue of the journal *Callaloo*, 'The Black German Experience', which was primarily geared towards introducing a new generation of U.S. Black studies scholars to a broad variety of twenty-first-century Black German creative and scholarly work. In many ways, the volume felt quite late in coming: after all, it was nearly a decade before that, in 1986, that the landmark anthology edited by May Ayim, Katharina Oguntoye and Dagmar Schultz, *Farbe bekennen: Afro-deutsche Frauen auf den Spüren ihrer Geschichte* [*Showing Our Colors: Black German Women Speak Out* (1991)], had been published to such richly deserved acclaim.

One might say that this volume, *Rethinking Black German Studies: Approaches, Interventions and Histories* is also greatly overdue; after all, *Farbe bekennen* not only created a foundation for Black German Studies, it laid claim to a broad range of histories, disciplines, philosophies, sociopolitical movements, cultures, and politics. It is rarely the case, I think, that the introduction to a new area of study is so apt in its engagement, wise in its reflections and enduring in its impact; with its mixture of historiographies, autobiographies, group and individual interviews not to mention poetry, *Farbe bekennen* imparts the intense polyvalent complexity of the Black German experience in virtuoso form. *Farbe bekennen* not only educated a population of fellow citizens, it inspired and motivated my generation of scholars to take up the challenge of working to understand the ways in which Blackness, Diasporas, and European identity itself needed to be rethought and re-theorized in the wake of this dazzling collection. As we can see in *Rethinking Black German Studies*, it has also spurred this latest generation to further enrich the reach and legacy of the Germanophone Black Diaspora.

This is no easy task: the politics of time and memory is a fraught one for all minorities, and in the politics of representation and acknowledgement, Blacks in the Germanophone world often seem more beset than most others because their histories are constantly abrogated, abridged, erased, revised and even denied. Not unlike the implied critique in the title of Joel Williamson's book *New People*, which looks at the long yet amnesia-ridden history of 'mulattos' in the United States, Black Germans are often misread as 'new people' – that is, continually 'rediscovered' by students and scholars in the United States, Canada (and likely elsewhere). The name itself, 'Black German' strikes so many as a contradiction in terms – and, unfortunately, this is perhaps most true among white Germans who at best are baffled at worst resentful and resistant to the idea that citizenship need not be determined by one's racial or ethnic identities. Yet, perhaps ironically (and like most Black Europeans), Black Germans existed before there was such a thing as a German state and as such 'predate' many other Black communities (such as U.S. Blacks), making their erasure and marginalization in Black Diaspora studies all the more frustrating.

In spite of this negligence, as Tiffany N. Florvil and Vanessa D. Plumly compellingly show here, Black German Studies also boasts over two decades of enriching scholarship and achievement that this anthology both celebrates and builds on. The new generation of scholars featured here bode well for the continued excellence of research in the field.

As the essays in this current volume demonstrate, the awesome complexity of Black German identities (not to mention Black European identities as a whole) has been both a boon and a curse. A boon because Black Germans boast a multitude of origins and histories, cultures and outlooks. A curse because this complexity belies the simplistic tool of a timeline to tell the story. Where do Black Germans begin to tell their story? Do they begin with Anton Wilhelm Amo, the eighteenth-century Ghanaian German scholar, or perhaps the Black Roman troops that fought with, conquered, and then settled into parts of what is now present-day Germany? Black

German collective identity might begin with the offspring of white German women and the occupying *tirailleurs senegalais*, or perhaps with the U.S. occupation of Germany after World War II when Black G.I.s could offer social and economic privileges to white German women – before they themselves were shipped back home to the land of Jim Crow. Today, Black Germans comprise all of these origins and more, including contemporary immigration from West and East Africa.

In short, there is no easy trajectory to trace, much less one overriding theme that can be placed comfortably on the entire history because Black Germans have arrived by both conquering and being conquered; in World War II alone one finds them as starving citizens denied ration cards and work; exterminated in death camps; a tiny but meaningful few fighting in Hitler's armies, and some staying alive (albeit briefly in many cases), by playing African savages in pro-colonial films for the Third Reich.

This new volume, *Rethinking Black German Studies*, could not have come too soon. Here one will find Black Germany and the Black Germanophone world placed front and center as a locus for intersection rather than a subsidiary of someone else's story. We move from Silke Hackenesch's magisterial and sweeping, yet nonetheless carefully detailed and nuanced analysis of the economic and cultural politics of Blackness, chocolate, and the West to Nancy P. Nenno's poignant analysis of the central role Black Austrians play in the Germanophone diaspora – and the equally insightful reasons as to why they have been marginalized and erased for so long. This volume boasts some of the best of this new generation of scholars and their impressively ambidextrous interpellation of the Black German world through such multifaceted phenomena as hip-hop, haunting, police violence and GDR Namibians.

Rethinking Black German Studies thus not only engages with Black Germanophone identities within their own specific contexts and details, it shows us how easily they intersect with broadly diasporic practices, traditions and experiences. This is essential work that needs to be done in Black and African Diaspora Studies, Black European Studies and African American Studies, not the least because it is increasingly untenable to deny or ignore all the different ways in which people can be and are Black. Rather than being a prohibitive identity, as some would claim or attempt to make true, being Black further layers and enriches our concepts of identity and belonging, not to mention what we think we know about history, culture and politics. This admirable challenge was first taken on by the previous generation, such as Tina Campt's interview and analysis of Hans Hauck in *Other Germans*. Campt compellingly argues that Hauck, a Black man who fought in Hitler's army, cannot be easily dismissed, praised, nor condemned: what is needed instead is deep thought and reflection on how tightly bound Blackness is to the myriad of human experiences rather than utterly estranged from it. As May Ayim demonstrates in her brilliant essay on the fall of the Berlin wall, 'Das Jahr 1990: Heimat und Einheit aus afrodeutscher Perspektive' [1990: Home/land and Unity from an Afro-German Perspective], to be Black in a majority white nation now celebrating its reunification forces us to reflect on the disturbing myths that have propped up the notion of white liberalism and the Western democratic nation-state.

In a white Western world in which whiteness, whether on the far left or far right, is increasingly convinced of its own moral superiority and rectitude, especially with regard to racial, gender and sexual politics, we need the scholars of *Rethinking Black German Studies* to re-center us, so to speak, to question our own norms and assumed timelines and trajectories, to step back from what we believe is 'authentically Black' or not authentically so. There may well be no better engagement than Black German Studies to bring the necessity of new, polyvalent analyses into relief.

Michelle M. Wright
Longstreet Professor of English
Emory University
Atlanta, GA, USA
4 August 2017

Notes on Contributors

TIFFANY N. FLORVIL is Assistant Professor of Twentieth-Century European Women's and Gender History at the University of New Mexico. She received her PhD from the University of South Carolina in Modern European History in 2013 and her MA from the University of Wisconsin-Madison in European Women's and Gender History in 2007. She is Co-Chair of the Black Diaspora Studies Network at the German Studies Association; the Network Editor for H-Emotions and an Advisory Board Member and a Network Editor for H-Black Europe. She has received fellowships from the American Council on Germany, German Academic Exchange Service (DAAD) and the Feminist Research Institute at the University of New Mexico. She has published in the *Journal of Civil and Human Rights* and *The German Quarterly*, as well as chapters in *Audre Lorde's Transnational Legacies, Gendering Post-1945 German History* and *Gendering Knowledge in Africa and the African Diaspora*.

SILKE HACKENESCH is Assistant Professor in the Department of North American History at the University of Cologne in Germany. A selection of her publications include *Chocolate and Blackness: A Cultural History* (Campus, 2017); "'These Black Americans Appear to Be the Color of Chocolate or Walnut or Caramel'. Zu Schokolade als *racial signifier* und Konstruktionen von Schwarzsein in den USA des 20. Jahrhunderts' in *Historische Anthropologie*, Vol. 25, No. 1, 2017 and "'I identify primarily as a Black German in America": Race, Bürgerrechte und Adoptionen in den USA der 1950er Jahre', in *Kinder des Zweiten Weltkrieges – Stigmatisierung, Ausgrenzung und Bewältigungsstrategien* (Campus, 2016). Currently, she is working on a manuscript exploring the contested terrain of transnational adoptions into the United States after World War II. Her work has been supported by numerous fellowships, including the German Academic Exchange Service (DAAD), the Thyssen Foundation, the German Research Foundation (DFG) and the German Historical Institute in Washington, DC.

KEVINA KING is a PhD student in German and Scandinavian Studies at the University of Massachusetts, Amherst, where she completed her MA on Black German history, narratives and music. She also completed a Graduate Certificate in African Diaspora Studies through the W. E. B. Du Bois Department of Afro-American Studies. Currently, she examines the Black German experience and its conceptualizations using Critical Whiteness Studies and notions of Germanness. Her other research interests include racial profiling, Black radical thought and critical race theory.

NANCY P. NENNO is Professor of German at the College of Charleston. She has published on a range of texts and films from the interwar period, including on Thomas Mann's *The Magic Mountain*, Anna Elisabet Weirauch's *Der Skorpion*, heritage tourism in the *Bergfilme* and Leni Riefenstahl. Her interest in representations of African Americans in German culture led to articles on Josephine Baker in Berlin, as well as on the film *Niemandsland* (Victor Trivas, 1931). She is currently engaged in research on the emerging field of Black Austrian Studies.

MEGHAN O'DEA received her PhD at Georgetown University from the Department of German in 2016. She has published an article on German-Polish relations in Robert Thalheim's 2007 film *Am Ende kommen Touristen* and is currently revising her dissertation on the topic of nostalgia and return journeys in literature by German expellees from today's Kaliningrad Oblast and northern Poland.

VANESSA D. PLUMLY received her PhD in German Studies in 2015 at the University of Cincinnati, where she also completed a certificate in Women's, Gender and Sexuality Studies. She is a lecturer and the program co-ordinator in German in the Department of Languages, Literatures & Cultures at SUNY New Paltz. She has published in the *German Studies Review*, *Women in German Yearbook* and co-published an article in *Die Unterrichtspraxis*. She serves as review editor for H-Black-Europe and is co-chair of the Black Diaspora Studies Network in the German Studies Association.

KIMBERLY ALECIA SINGLETARY is an independent researcher living in Chicago. She received her PhD in Rhetoric and Public Culture at Northwestern University in 2013. She was awarded the Gerald R. Miller Outstanding Doctoral Dissertation Award from the National Communication Association in 2014. She has received DAAD and Fulbright fellowships to Germany and Austria, respectively. Her work on Blackness in the global public sphere has been published and featured in various journals and online forums.

KIRA THURMAN is Assistant Professor of German Studies and History at the University of Michigan. She earned her PhD in 2013 at the University of Rochester under the direction of Celia Applegate. In addition to her major field in German history, she also completed a minor field in musicology at the Eastman School of Music. Her research, which has appeared in *German Studies Review,* the *Journal of the American Musicological Society,* the *Journal of World History* and *Opera Quarterly,* concerns the relationship between race, music and national identity across the Black Atlantic in the nineteenth and twentieth centuries. Her article 'Black Venus, White Bayreuth: Race, Sexuality and the Depoliticization of Wagner in Postwar West Germany' won the 2014 German Studies Association's prize for best article on German history.

JAMELE WATKINS is a Post-doctoral Fellow in German Studies at Stanford University, where she researches and teaches issues of race and gender. She is currently working on a book project that focuses on Black performance in Germany in relation to the African diaspora. Her article, 'Rearticulating Black Feminist Thought in *Heimat, bittersüße Heimat*', was published in the *Women in German Yearbook.* She completed her doctoral studies at University of Massachusetts Amherst with the completion of her dissertation, 'The Drama of Race'. Watkins has also studied at the University of Nevada, Las Vegas, Eberhard-Karls-Universität Tübingen and Albert-Ludwigs-Universität Freiburg.

MICHELLE M. WRIGHT is the Augustus Baldwin Longstreet Professor of English at Emory University. Her research focuses on literary, cultural, philosophical and political discourses on Blackness and Black identity in the Anglophone, Francophone and Germanophone African Diaspora from the eighteenth to the twenty-first centuries. Wright has published *Becoming Black: Creating an Identity in the African Diaspora* (Duke, 2004) and

Physics of Blackness: Beyond the Middle Passage Epistemology (Minnesota, 2015). She has also published in countless volumes including *From Black to Schwarz* and *Black Europe and the African Diaspora*, as well as journals such as *Callaloo, Frontiers* and *African and Black Diaspora: An International Journal*. She serves on the editorial boards of *The Black Scholar* and *The James Baldwin Review*. Her new project is *Feeling Europe: Black and African Diasporas in the Heart of Empire*.

Index

Studies in Modern German and Austrian Literature

Series Editors
Professor Robert Vilain, University of Bristol
Dr Benedict Schofield, King's College London
Dr Alexandra Lloyd, University of Oxford

Studies in Modern German and Austrian Literature is a broadly conceived series that aims to publish significant research and scholarship devoted to German and Austrian literature of all forms and genres from the eighteenth century to the present day. The series promotes the analysis of intersections of literature with thought, society and other art forms, such as film, theatre, autobiography, music, painting, sculpture and performance art. It includes monographs on single authors or works, focused historical periods, and studies of experimentation with form and genre. Wider ranging explorations of literary, cultural or socio-political phenomena in the German-speaking lands or among writers in exile and analyses of national, ethnic and cultural identities in literature are also welcome topics.

Proposals are invited for monographs, high-quality doctoral dissertations revised for book publication, focused collections of essays (including selectively edited conference proceedings), annotated editions and bibliographies. Senior figures in the academic profession as well as early career or independent scholars are encouraged to submit proposals. All proposals and manuscripts will be peer reviewed. We publish in both German and English. This series is a successor to *Studies in Modern German Literature*, edited by Peter D.G. Brown.

Volume 3   Dirk Göttsche (ed.)
Critical Time in Modern German Literature and Culture.
2016. ISBN 978-3-0343-1942-3

Volume 4   Emily Oliver
Shakespeare and German Reunification: The Interface of Politics and
Performance.
2017. ISBN 978-1-78707-070-7

Volume 5   Katya Krylova (ed.)
New Perspectives on Contemporary Austrian Literature and Culture.
2018. ISBN 978-3-0343-1984-3

Volume 6   Stephan Ehrig, Marcel Thomas and David Zell (eds)
The GDR Today: New Interdisciplinary Approaches to East German History,
Memory and Culture.
2018. ISBN 978-1-78707-072-1

Volume 7   Tiffany N. Florvil and Vanessa D. Plumly (eds)
Rethinking Black German Studies: Approaches, Interventions and Histories.
2018. ISBN 978-3-0343-2225-6

Volume 8   Liangliang Zhu
China im Bild der deutschsprachigen Literatur seit 1989.
2018. ISBN 978-1-78707-520-7